SENSORY MARKETING
RESEARCH ON THE SENSUALITY OF PRODUCTS

SENSORY MARKETING

RESEARCH ON THE SENSUALITY OF PRODUCTS

edited by
Aradhna Krishna

University of Michigan
Ann Arbor, Michigan

Routledge
Taylor & Francis Group
New York   London

Routledge   Routledge
Taylor & Francis Group   Taylor & Francis Group
270 Madison Avenue   27 Church Road
New York, NY 10016   Hove, East Sussex BN3 2FA

© 2010 by Taylor and Francis Group, LLC
Routledge is an imprint of Taylor & Francis Group, an Informa business

Printed in the United States of America on acid-free paper
10 9 8 7 6 5 4 3 2

International Standard Book Number: 978-1-84169-753-6 (Hardback) 978-1-84169-889-2 (Paperback)

Library of Congress Cataloging-in-Publication Data
Sensory marketing : research on the sensuality of products / editor, Aradhna Krishna.
p. cm.
Includes bibliographical references and index.
ISBN 978-1-84169-753-6 (hbk. : alk. paper) -- ISBN 978-1-84169-889-2 (pbk. : alk. paper)
1. Marketing--Psychological aspects. 2. New products--Psychological aspects. 3. Sensuality. 4. Senses and sensation. 5. Consumer behavior. I. Krishna, Aradhna.
HF5415.S3696 2010
658.8001'9--dc22   2009039303

Visit the Taylor & Francis Web site at
http://www.taylorandfrancis.com

and the Psychology Press Web site at
http://www.psypress.com

For Sidd and Kamya,
my extreme sensory stimulants.

Contents

SECTION VI   The Future

Preface and Acknowledgments

There was a minirebellion among the faculty at the Ross School of Business in 1990 when the library ran out of space and we were told that all the old journals would be scanned and we could only get electronic files for them. When asked precisely why we were so keen to keep the physical journals, we were all perplexed in coming up with what would seem like a "reasonable" argument. The urge to keep them was strong, but the reasons ran along the following lines: "I like to feel the paper," "I like to turn the pages," "I love the smell of libraries," "It's just not the same thing!" We realized that these reasons would not be considered sufficient for a prolonged physical library presence, so we tried to link these same responses with ones that sounded more rational and reasonable: "I think better in that atmosphere," "Lingering physically in the library makes me browse more than I would do electronically and come across more articles of interest."

There is a need to justify most sensorial longings. We buy perfume obviously for its smell, but we feel awkward telling someone that we are buying a specific car or cell phone or laptop because of its color. Similar hesitation also used to exist in research. When studying sensory perception, it had to be couched within a more mainstream area of interest. Thus, smell used to be studied within the context of affecting mood, taste too was studied as a mood manipulation, but there were few studies where the explicitly stated aspect of interest was the sense (smell or taste) itself. Research on the senses had negative connotations of being "touchy-feely" work, thus implying less science and rigor.

However, while consumer behavior researchers, who are typically in marketing departments of business schools, were couching their sensory work within broader areas, research in neuroscience and neuropsychology was making rapid advances on the senses. In fact, "Sensation and Perception" was fast becoming one of the most popular undergraduate courses, and neuroscience one of the most desirable undergraduate majors. This parallel development, with consumer behavior researchers avoiding focus on the senses but psychology and neurology researchers emphasizing it in a very concerted fashion, was puzzling. I felt that a natural domain to connect the two was "sensory marketing" research.

To make sensory marketing more mainstream within marketing academia, the close link between the senses and psychology, neuroscience, and neuropsychology needed to be made more salient. As such, in June 2008, I organized a conference on sensory marketing to do precisely that. This book is a result of the first sensory marketing conference that was held at the Ross School of Business, Ann Arbor, Michigan, on June 19–21, 2008. The specified objective for the conference was to get a core group of researchers together to pioneer a new field within marketing, that of sensory marketing. Although the term "sensory marketing" showed up in a Google search, it was not used to describe research on the various senses, even when it focused on highly sensory inputs and their impact on the consumer (e.g., product color, advertiser's speech characteristics, phonetic appeal of a brand name, haptic qualities of products, ambient odor, or product taste). The conference engaged marketing researchers, experts from psychology on specific senses (some of whom were neuropsychologists), and a few practitioners to share their knowledge and expand the field.

The conference was sponsored by the Ross School of Business, Marketing Science Institute, and the Yaffe Center for Persuasive Communication. Three keynote speakers at the conference were Roberta Klatzky (professor of psychology at CMU, an expert on haptics), Paul Rozin (Edmund J. and Louise W. Kahn, professor of psychology at University of Pennsylvania; an expert on nutrition, sensation, and perception), and Rachel Herz (visiting professor at the Brown University Medical School and an expert on smell). Key people who facilitated the conference were Joan Meyers-Levy, Maureen Morrin, Joann Peck, Laura Peracchio, and Priya Raghubir. The conference Web site is located at: http://www.bus.umich.edu/sensorymktg2008/default.htm and lists all the conference attendees. I thank all the conference participants for making the conference and the book possible.

I did not put together the conference or the book alone. I am highly indebted to Joan Meyers-Levy, Maureen Morrin, Joann Peck, Laura Peracchio, and Priya Raghubir for their continuous intellectual input in shaping the conference and the book and as coordinators for the different senses at the conference, a role they carried on for the book. Ryan S. Elder, my doctoral student, designed the conference logo, T-shirt, and bag and shepherded guests to the right venues along with my other two students at the conference, Nilufer Aydinoglu and Cindy Caldara. The conference would not have been possible without all the logistical arrangements done by Pam Russell, who was later helped by Karen Weber. Finally, in editing this book, Wendy Yang's services were invaluable. Andy is responsible for the sibling rivalry that spurs me to develop my ideas. A big thanks goes to Kamya, Sidd, and Jag for putting up with my rather odd dinner conversations; Ma, Papa, Vidya, Aditi, and Abhay for providing additional texture to my life; Marjorie, Poonam, Ditto, Sunita, Priya, Manish, Namita, Swati, Sangeeta, Seema, Yan, Kusum, Anne, Mimi, Sue, Ruma, Rohini, Eric, Prajit, Felicia, Aneel, Jaideep, Sendil, Angela, Harish, and Meera for conversation and succor; and my best friend for being there.

Aradhna Krishna
Dwight F. Benton Professor of Marketing
Ross School of Business
University of Michigan

About the Editor

Aradhna Krishna is the Dwight F. Benton Professor of Marketing at the Ross School of Business, University of Michigan, and a pioneer of the field of sensory marketing. She received her Ph.D. from New York University in 1989, and her MBA from the Indian Institute of Management, Ahmedabad in 1984. Before joining the University of Michigan, she spent time at Columbia University, New York University, the National University of Singapore, and also worked as a brand manager and a freelance journalist. Aradhna investigates how consumer perceptions and responses change as a function of the type of pricing, promotion, packaging and branding efforts undertaken by managers. Her research focuses on many forms of sensory perception—visual, haptic, olfactory, taste and combinations. Her research methodology combines experimental techniques with quantitative modeling approaches. She serves on the editorial boards of several journals, has published more than sixty articles in leading journals, and is considered among the top fifty most prolific marketing researchers. Aradhna is a sensuist who enjoys drinking second flush Darjeeling tea in porcelain cups, collecting figurative art prints, listening to atonal jazz, cooking foods with strong aromas, and gardening without gloves. She divides her time between Ann Arbor and Chicago.

Contributors

Nilufer Z. Aydinoglu is assistant professor of marketing at Koc University in Turkey. She received her Ph.D. in marketing from the University of Michigan in 2007. Her current work focuses on two major streams of research. One attempts to understand how perceptual processes and consumers' self-perception affect their responses to marketing communications. The other focuses on consumer preference between global and local brands.

Victor Barger is a doctoral student in marketing at the Wisconsin School of Business at the University of Wisconsin–Madison. Victor earned his M.B.A. at the University of Wisconsin–Madison and holds a bachelor's degree in computer science, also from UW–Madison. His research interests include sensory marketing, social influence, and complex systems. In 2006 he was inducted into UW–Madison's Teaching Academy for excellence in teaching, and in 2008 he was selected as the 2007–2008 recipient of the Henry C. Naiman Teaching Award.

Melissa G. Bublitz is a doctoral student at the University of Wisconsin–Milwaukee. Melissa received her B.S. in marketing and her M.B.A. from the University of Wisconsin–Oshkosh. Melissa's research interests are focused on consumer judgment and buyer behavior in the areas of food, nutrition, and health decision making. She is interested in the public policy implications of the marketing of food, health products/services, and financial products/services as well as marketing to children. She is a member of the Society for Consumer Psychology and the Association for Consumer Research.

Cindy Caldara is a Ph.D. student in consumer behavior at the University of Grenoble 2 (Pierre-Mendés-France) in France. She belongs to the CERAG laboratory of research. She received a grant from Rhône-Alpes region in 2007 and has been a visiting scholar at the Ross Business School

(University of Michigan). Her areas of research interest are focused on the processing of visual information, touch, and the interactions of senses.

Marina Carnevale is a Ph.D. candidate in marketing at Baruch College, City University of New York. She received a bachelor's and a master's degree in business administration from Bocconi University. Her research interests include consumer decision behavior, choice-making preferences, and brand equity. Particularly, she studies psychological aspects of brand relationships, psycholinguistic and symbolic characteristics of brand names, and the way emotions and experiences may influence the consumption and evaluation of luxury brands.

Pierre Chandon is associate professor of marketing at INSEAD (with tenure), which he joined in 1999. He was a visiting assistant professor of marketing at the Wharton School (2005–2006) and at the Kellogg School of Management (2004–2005). He holds a Ph.D. from HEC Paris and an M.B.A. from ESSEC. His research examines how perceptual biases influence food consumption decisions, attention, and consideration decisions at the point of purchase and the validity of marketing surveys. He has published articles in the *Journal of Marketing Research*, *Journal of Marketing*, and *Journal of Consumer Research*. He is a member of the editorial boards of the *Journal of Consumer Research*, *Journal of Marketing*, *International Journal of Research in Marketing*, and *Recherche et Applications en Marketing*, the journal of the French Marketing Association. His research and case studies have won numerous awards, including an honorable mention in the 2005 Marketing Science Institute /H. Paul Root Award and the ECCH prize for the fastest-selling case in 2006 (marketing category), 2007 (marketing category and overall award), and 2008 (overall award).

Amitava Chattopadhyay is the L'Oreal Chaired Professor in marketing-innovation and creativity and professor of marketing at INSEAD. He is an expert on branding and his research has appeared in leading journals, including the *Journal of Marketing Research*, *Journal of Consumer Research*, *Journal of Marketing*, *Marketing Science*, and *Management Science*. His participation in editorial review boards includes the *Journal of Consumer Psychology*, *Journal of Consumer Research*, *International Journal of Research in Marketing*, and *Long Range Planning*. For his research, he has been the recipient of the Robert Ferber Award. He has developed and taught courses on branding, marketing strategy, communication strategy, and consumer behavior for M.B.A. and Ph.D. students. He has taught in executive programs in Europe, the Americas, Asia, Australia, and Africa. He is on the advisory boards of several companies and a consultant to leading multinational firms. He holds a Ph.D. from the University of Florida, a P.G.D.M. from the Indian Institute of Management, Ahmedabad, and a B.Sc. from Jadavpur University, India.

Jean-Charles Chebat holds the ECSC Research Chair of Retailing at HEC-Montreal. He was the first marketing researcher ever elected to the Royal Society of Canada, the first professor of management ever elected as the president of the Academy I (humanities and social sciences), and the first to receive a research medal from the Royal Society (the Sir Dawson Medal for the best interdisciplinary researcher). He was recently knighted by the prime minister of Quebec for his academic contribution, the highest recognition for this province of Canada. He is on the board of several marketing journals (*Journal of Retailing, Journal of Business Research, Journal of the Academy of Marketing Science*) and psychology journals (*Journal of Economic Psychology, Journal of Applied Social Psychology*). He is the associate editor of *Perceptual and Motor Skills* and *Psychological Reports*. He received various fellowships in the United States (American Psychological Association, Society for Marketing Advances, Academy of Marketing Science) and Japan (Japan Society for the Promotion of Science) and 12 best paper awards. He was recently elected to the board of the Academy of Marketing Science. He has published about 130 refereed journal articles, many conference papers, four books, and 10 book chapters.

Terry L. Childers is the Dean's Chair in Marketing at Iowa State University, Ames, where he will teach graduate courses at the Ph.D level in measurement and M.B.A. and undergraduate marketing research. He was previously on the faculty at the University of Kentucky and the University of Minnesota and has a Ph.D. in marketing from the University of Wisconsin–Madison. He was formerly director of the Von Allmen Center for E-Commerce and is director of the Advertising and Interactive Marketing (AIM) Research Laboratory. In 2005 he was selected as a fellow of the Association for Psychological Science and Consumer Psychology Division of the American Psychological Association. His research has been published in a number of journals, including the *Journal of Marketing Research, Journal of Marketing, Journal of Consumer Research, Journal of Consumer Psychology, Journal of Retailing, Journal of Business Research, Public Opinion Quarterly, Journal of the Academy of Marketing Science, Journal of Advertising Research, Journal of Risk and Insurance*, and *Journal* *of Mental Imagery.* He serves on the editorial review boards at the *Journal of Consumer Research* and *Journal of Consumer Psychology.*

Hae Eun Chun is currently a doctoral candidate of marketing at the University of Southern California's Marshall School of Business and will join the Cornell School of Hotel Administration as assistant professor in the fall of 2009. She completed her bachelor's (1999) and master's (2001) degrees in consumer studies from Seoul National University. Her primary research interests focus on consumers' savoring of an anticipated future consumption experience and its impact on consumption enjoyment, the ways for a firm to manage consumers' savoring of new products or experiences, and affective forecasting. She is an AMA-Sheth Doctoral Consortium Fellow and a Houston Doctoral Symposium Fellow.

Darren Dahl is the Fred H. Siller Professor in applied marketing research at the University of British Columbia. His research interests are in the areas of new product design and development, creativity, consumer product adoption, the role of social influence in consumer behavior, and understanding the role of self-conscious emotions in consumption. His research has been presented at numerous national and international conferences and published in various texts and such journals as the *Journal of Marketing Research, Journal of Marketing, Journal of Consumer Research, Management Science, Journal of Consumer Psychology, Marketing Letters, Journal of Business Research,* and the *Journal of Advertising Research.* He teaches courses in consumer behavior, marketing research, and strategic marketing analysis at the undergraduate, M.B.A., and executive education levels. Before coming to UBC he held a faculty appointment at the University of Manitoba for 4 years. He also has been a visiting professor at Columbia University, Stanford University, Hong Kong University of Science and Technology, and the Thammasat University in Thailand. He received his Ph.D. from the University of British Columbia.

Peter R. Darke is currently an associate professor of marketing in the Schulich School of Business at York University in Toronto, Canada. He received his doctoral degree in psychology from the University of Toronto. His current work focuses on consumer attitudes, judgment, and decision making. He has published articles in the *Journal of Applied Psychology, Journal of Applied Social Psychology, Journal of Consumer Psychology, Journal of Consumer Research, Journal of Economic Psychology, Journal of Marketing, Journal of Marketing Research, Journal of Personality and*

Social Psychology, Journal of Research in Personality, Journal of Retailing, Marketing Letters, and *Personality and Social Psychology Bulletin.*

Xiaoyan Deng is a doctoral candidate of marketing at the Wharton School, University of Pennsylvania. She will join Fisher College of Business, at the Ohio State University, as an assistant professor of marketing in July 2009. Her research interests focus on consumer responses to visual designs of product and packaging, consumer codesign and cocreation in the context of mass customization, and consumer aesthetics. Her research on packaging design has been accepted for publication in the *Journal of Marketing Research.* Prior to her Ph.D., she received a B.E. and an M.A. in industrial design, both from Hunan University, China, and an M.S. in advertising from the University of Illinois at Urbana–Champaign. She enjoys fine and applied arts, movies, and traveling.

Ryan S. Elder is a doctoral candidate in marketing at the Ross School of Business, University of Michigan. His research explores the impact of sensory marketing communications on product evaluations. Specifically, he is interested in both the cognitive and affective processing of sensory advertising and its subsequent impact on sensory perceptions. He is currently working on projects exploring the impact of sensory advertising on taste perceptions, the interaction of haptic and olfactory stimuli on product evaluations, as well as the link between sensory descriptions and hedonic consequences. Further, he works in the area of visual persuasion, examining the usage of images in advertising, and the impact of design aesthetics on consumption experiences.

Claire Gélinas-Chebat is a full professor of linguistics at the University of Quebec in Montreal. Her research interests are related to messages' perception and integration: more specifically phonetics and psycholinguistics. She is also involved in computer text analysis. She had published some 30 refereed journal articles and as many conference papers. She received several best paper awards for her research, in Canada, the United States, and France.

Gerald Gorn is professor of marketing at the University of Hong Kong and formerly chair professor of marketing at the Hong Kong University of Science and Technology. He received his Ph.D. from Pennsylvania State University and his M.Sc. from the London School of Economics. He previously was advisory council professor of consumer behavior at the University of British Columbia from 1983 until 1996. He has been a visiting professor at the Copenhagen Business School and held the Nabisco Chair as a visiting professor at McGill University. His research focuses on understanding consumer perceptions, attitudes, and behaviors and the factors that influence them. He is primarily interested in understanding and shaping consumer reactions to communications in areas of concern to marketers and public policy makers. His research has been published in marketing, health, and psychology journals, including in the *Journal of Marketing Research, Journal of Consumer Research, Management Science, Journal of Consumer Psychology, Marketing Letters*, and *American Journal of Public Health*. His most recent publication in the *Journal of Consumer Research* (June 2008) is titled "Babyfaces, Trait Inferences, and Company Evaluations in a PR Crisis." For his *Journal of Public Policy and Marketing (JPPM)* article "Heightening Adolescent Vigilance Toward Alcohol Advertising to Forestall Alcohol Use," he and his coauthors received the 2007 Thomas C. Kinnear *JPPM* Award. This award recognizes articles that have made a significant contribution to the understanding of marketing and public policy within the past 3 years. His editorial board memberships include the *Journal of Consumer Research, Journal of Consumer Psychology, International Journal of Research in Marketing*, and *International Journal of Internet Marketing and Advertising*. He also has been associate editor of the *Journal of Consumer Psychology*. He has taught a variety of courses at both the graduate and undergraduate levels in business schools and also in a psychology department. He has won an award for M.B.A. teaching (University of British Columbia) and for undergraduate teaching (Hong Kong University of Science and Technology).

Eric A. Greenleaf is professor of marketing at the Leonard N. Stem School of Business, New York University. He has a long-standing interest in issues of consumer aesthetics and design, the fine arts, and the art market. He also has published research in the areas of consumer perceptions of prices, auctions, why consumers delay making purchase decisions, and marketing research and survey methods. He has published articles in numerous journals including *Empirical Studies of the Arts, Journal of Consumer Research, Journal of Marketing Research, Management Science, Marketing Letters, Marketing Science*, and *Public Opinion Quarterly*.

Rachel Herz is a visiting professor in the Department of Psychiatry and Human Behavior at the Warren Alpert Medical School of Brown University. She has been conducting research on the sense of smell for 19 years and is considered one of the world's leading experts in olfactory psychology and psychobiology. She is the author of the first popular book about olfactory psychology *The Scent of Desire: Discovering Our Enigmatic Sense of Smell* (William Morrow, HarperCollins, 2007), which has received numerous accolades including being selected as a finalist for the 2009 AAAS/Subaru Prize for Excellence in Science Books. She serves on several advisory boards, including the Fragrance Foundation, and consults for many of the world's leading multinational flavor and fragrance companies.

Julia M. Hormes, M.A. completed her undergraduate degree at Princeton University and is currently a Ph.D. candidate in clinical psychology at the University of Pennsylvania. Her research interests are in the field of psychology of preference, with a particular focus on attitudes to food. She is currently conducting studies on food cravings, specifically perimenstrual chocolate craving, and on ambivalence or conflicting attitudes to food. Her clinical interests are in the area of behavioral medicine, including the treatment of eating disorders and obesity, and the psychosocial complications associated with chronic illnesses, such as cancer.

Barbara Kahn is currently the dean and professor of marketing at the School of Business Administration at the University of Miami. Previously, she spent 17 years at the Wharton School, University of Pennsylvania, where she was most recently the Dorothy Silberberg Professor of Marketing and the vice dean of the undergraduate division of the Wharton School. While at University of Pennsylvania, she was also a senior fellow of the Leonard Davis Institute of Health Economics (LDI) and a faculty member of the graduate group in the psychology department. She received a B.A. in English literature at the University of Rochester and an M.B.A. in marketing and statistics and a M.Phil. and Ph.D. in marketing from Columbia University. Her research focuses on customer decision making and creating customer value. She has over 50 articles on these topics in major journals in marketing, consumer research, public policy, retailing, and statistics. She is coauthor of the book *Grocery Revolution: New Focus on the Consumer*. She is currently on or has been on the editorial boards of *Journal of Marketing Research*, *Journal of Marketing*, *Marketing Science*, *Journal of Consumer Research*, and *Marketing Letters* and is a past president of the policy board of *Journal of Consumer Research*. She has been an area editor of *Marketing Science* and an associate editor of *Journal of Consumer Research* and *Journal of Consumer Psychology*. She has served as an academic trustee of the Marketing Science Institute and as president of the Association for Consumer Research.

Roberta Klatzky is professor of psychology and human–computer inter-action at Carnegie Mellon University, where she is also on the faculty of the Center for the Neural Basis of Cognition. She received a B.S. in mathematics from the University of Michigan and a Ph.D. in experimental psychology from Stanford University. Her research interests are in human perception and cognition, with special emphasis on perception by touch. She has done extensive research on how people recognize objects and their properties through vision and touch and on how perception guides action. Her work has application to haptic virtual environments and interface design, exploratory robotics, telemanipulation, and image-guided surgery. She is the author of over 200 articles and chapters, and she has authored or edited seven books.

Dawn B. Lerman received her Ph.D. from Baruch College, City University of New York and is associate professor of marketing at Fordham University. Her main research interests include psycholinguistic, sociolinguistic, and cross-cultural aspects of consumer behavior, advertising, and branding. Her work has appeared in journals such as the *Journal of Consumer Research*, *Journal of Advertising Research*, *Psychology and Marketing*, and *European Journal of Marketing*. She has chapters in *Managing Tourism Firms*, *Best Practices in International Marketing*, *European Perspectives in Marketing*, and *Cross-Cultural Marketing: Contexts, Concepts, and Practices*. She is a member of the editorial board for the *Journal of Business Research* and *International Marketing Review*.

Chan Jean Lee is a Ph.D. student in marketing at the Haas School of Business, University of California–Berkeley. She received a bachelor's and a master's degree in Consumer Studies from Seoul National University and a master's degree in Information Management and Systems from University of California at Berkeley. Her research examines how emotions affect various judgments such as aesthetic and financial judgments.

David Luna received his Ph.D. from the University of Wisconsin–Milwaukee and is an associate professor of marketing at Baruch College (City University of New York). His main research interest is marketing communications. In particular, he has investigated how culture and language influence the effectiveness of marketing messages targeting the end consumer, both online and using traditional media. He has studied the consumer behavior of U.S. Hispanic consumers. Other interests include imagery processing, mental representation, and the role of automatic processes on judgment formation. His work has been published in academic journals such as the *Journal of Consumer Research*, *Journal of Consumer Psychology*, *Journal of the Academy of Marketing Science*, and *Journal of Advertising*, among others. His research has also been published in several books and his papers appear regularly in the proceedings of national and international conferences, such as the *Society for Consumer Research* and the *Association for Consumer Research* proceedings. He has cochaired two major consumer research conferences: the first Latin American Consumer Research Conference and the Society for Consumer Psychology Conference.

May Lwin is an associate professor and a division head with the Wee Kim Wee School of Communication and Information in Nanyang Technological University, Singapore. Her research interests are mainly in the areas of olfactory and auditory communications and health and social communications. She has published in many international journals and authored numerous books, including the best-selling Clueless Series and a leading textbook on advertising in the Asia Pacific.

Joan Meyers-Levy is the Holden-Werlich Professor of Marketing at the Carlson School of Management, University of Minnesota. Her research interests encompass a variety of consumer-related issues such as persuasion, people's processing of visual, verbal, and other sensory information, their use of alternative types or styles of information processing, and how ad or environmental contextual factors (e.g., music, architectural elements) as well as various individual difference factors (e.g., gender, self-construal) affect people's processing and responses. She has published her work in premier outlets such as the *Journal of Consumer Research*, *Journal of Marketing Research*, and *Journal of Marketing*. In addition, her work has been featured extensively in the business and popular media. She has been actively involved in numerous marketing-related professional organizations and conferences, including chairing a major conference, serving on several editorial boards, and serving as guest editor for a major journal. She also has been recognized for her extensive research contributions with the Society for Consumer Psychology Fellow Award.

Gina S. Mohr is a doctoral candidate in marketing at the Leeds School of Business, University of Colorado–Boulder. Her research interests include understanding the effects of multisensory external cues on the processing, evaluation, and identification of olfactory stimuli in the consumer environment. She also studies the relationship between negatively correlated choice environments and decision conflict, with an emphasis on the role that compromise products play in mitigating decision conflict. Additional research projects examine various consumer welfare issues such as social influences on eating behavior, brand placement in television, and the effects of nutrition labeling on guilt and purchase intentions. She received her B.A. in economics at the University of Colorado in 2002 and is expected to receive her Ph.D. in 2009.

Andrea Morales is associate professor of marketing at the W. P. Carey School of Business at Arizona State University. She received her Ph.D. from the Wharton School of Business at the University of Pennsylvania, her M.S. in marketing from the University of Pennsylvania, and a B.A. in economics and liberal arts from the University of Texas–Austin. Before joining ASU, she was assistant professor of marketing at the Marshall School of Business at the University of Southern California, where she received their Golden Apple Award for teaching excellence. She teaches the core marketing management class in the M.B.A. program in the W. P. Carey School of Business. Her research interests include the role of emotions in a consumer context, specifically disgust and gratitude, and consumer responses to retail and service environments. Her work has been published in the *Journal of Consumer Research, Journal of Marketing Research, Journal of Marketing, Journal of Consumer Psychology*, and *Journal of Retailing*. For her dissertation article she received an honorable mention for the Robert Ferber Award, an award given annually to the best interdisciplinary dissertation article published in the *Journal of Consumer Research*. In 2007 she was selected to participate in the Marketing Science Institute's Young Scholars Program, an honor extended every 2 years to the top 25 untenured marketing professors in the world based on their research productivity and impact.

Maureen Morrin, an associate professor of marketing at Rutgers University, conducts research on a variety of topics that impact the consumer decision-making process, including branding, atmospherics (e.g., scent and touch), and financial decision making. Her dissertation, which examined the impact of brand extensions on parent brand memory retrieval, was awarded an honorable mention by the American Marketing Association and was subsequently published in the *Journal of Marketing Research*. Her research has been published in several other journals such as the *Journal of Consumer Research, Journal of Consumer Psychology*, and *Journal of Public Policy and Marketing*. She is the recipient of a grant from the NASD

Investor Education Foundation to explore the effects of plan structure on investing for retirement. She won the Rutgers School of Business Superior Achievement Awards in both Teaching and Research and Provost's Award for Teaching at Rutgers Camden. She is a graduate of New York University (Ph.D.), where she was a consortium fellow and won an outstanding teaching award as a Ph.D. student. She also is a graduate of Thunderbird, the American Graduate School of International Management (M.B.A.), and Georgetown University (B.S.F.S.). Her corporate work experience includes 5 years in packaged goods advertising and brand management.

Joann Peck is an assistant professor of marketing at the University of Wisconsin–Madison. Peck received her Ph.D. from the University of Minnesota and also holds a B.S. in secondary education from the University of Michigan and an M.B.A. from the University of Wisconsin–Madison. Prior to joining the UW marketing department, she was a visiting professor at the University of Chicago. Her primary research interests are in the consumer behavior area, particularly involving the sense of touch or haptics. Her work looks at aspects of the object (some objects encourage touch more than others), aspects of the situation (in various media such as the internet touch is unavailable), and individual differences (some people prefer haptic or touch information more than others) to examine motivations for haptic exploration. Her recent published research includes "The Effect of Mere Touch on Perceived Ownership" (with Suzanne Shu) forthcoming in the *Journal of Consumer Research*, "The Effects of Sensory Factors on Consumer Behaviors" (with Terry Childers), in F. Kardes, C. Haugtvedt, and P. Herr (Eds.), *Handbook of Consumer Psychology* (Mahwah, NJ: Erlbaum), "It Just Feels Good: Consumers' Affective Response to Touch and Its Influence on Persuasion" (with Jennifer Wiggins), in the *Journal of Marketing*, "To Have and to Hold: The Influence of Haptic Information on Product Judgments" (with Terry L. Childers), in the *Journal of Marketing*, and "Individual Differences in Haptic Information Processing: On the Development, Validation, and Use for the 'Need for Touch' Scale" (with Terry L. Childers), in the *Journal of Consumer Research*. When she is not studying touch, she enjoys triathlons, bicycling, running, and drinking wine.

Laura A. Peracchio is professor of marketing at the University of Wisconsin–Milwaukee. She received her Ph.D. from Northwestern University and a dual B.A. and B.S.E. from the Wharton School and the College of Arts and Sciences at the University of Pennsylvania. Her areas of research interest are focused on consumer information processing including visual persuasion, language and culture, and food and nutrition issues. Her work has appeared in the *Journal of Consumer Research*, *Journal of Marketing Research*, *Journal of Consumer Psychology*, *Journal of Public Policy and Marketing*, and *Journal of Advertising*. She is an associate editor of the *Journal of Consumer Psychology* and has served as an associate editor of the *Journal of Consumer Research*. She is immediate past president of the Society for Consumer Psychology.

Priya Raghubir is a Professor of Marketing and the Mary C. Jacoby Faculty Fellow at the Stern School of Business, New York University. Prior to joining NYU Stern, she was a Professor at the Haas School of Business, University of California at Berkeley and at the Hong Kong University of Science and Technology. Professor Raghubir's research interests are in the areas of consumer psychology, including survey methods, psychological aspects of prices and money; risk perceptions; and visual information processing. She has published over 50 articles in journals and books, including the *Journal of Marketing Research*, *Journal of Consumer Research*, *Journal of Marketing*, *Journal of Consumer Psychology* and *Marketing Science*. She is on the editorial boards of five journals, and has delivered more than 100 presentations of her research at major universities, symposia and conferences around the world. She received her undergraduate degree in Economics from St. Stephen's College, Delhi University; her M.B.A from the Indian Institute of Management, Ahmedabad; and her Ph.D. in Marketing from New York University.

Paul Rozin was born in Brooklyn, New York. He attended the University of Chicago, under the Hutchin's General Education System, receiving an A.B. in 1956, and received a Ph.D. in both biology and psychology from Harvard, in 1961. His thesis research was sponsored by Jean Mayer. He spent two subsequent years working with Jean Mayer as an NIH post-doctoral fellow at the Harvard School of Public Health. Since then, he has been a member of the psychology department at the University of Pennsylvania, where he is currently professor of psychology. Past scholarly interests included food selection in animals, the acquisition of fundamental reading skills, and the neuropsychology of amnesia. Over the past 25 years, the major focus of his research has been human food choice, considered from biological, psychological, and anthropological perspectives. During this period, he has studied the psychological significance of flavorings placed on foods in different cuisines, the cultural evolution of cuisine, the development of food aversions, the development of food preferences, family influences in preference development, body image, the acquisition of liking for chili pepper, the weaning process, addiction, chocolate craving, and attitudes toward meat and water. Most recently, major foci of attention have been the emotion of disgust, the entry of food issues (e.g., meat, fat) into the moral domain in modern American culture, and the growing American tendency to worry more about food and enjoy it less. Much of the recent research is carried out in France, Japan, and India, as well as the United States. In the past few years, he has also investigated forgiveness, aversions to ethnic groups, and ethnic identity. He is a member of the Society of Experimental Psychologists, has twice been a fellow at the Center for Advanced Study in the Behavioral Sciences, a visiting scholar for Phi Beta Kappa, and a visiting scholar for 1 year at the Russell Sage Foundation. He is a member of the American Academy of Arts and Sciences. He is a recipient of the American Psychological Association Distinguished Scientific Contribution Award for 2007. He was an editor of the journal *Appetite* for 10 years. He has been teaching introductory psychology for about 30 years, has chaired the psychology department at the University of Pennsylvania, directed the university-wide undergraduate honors program, and has been involved in developing policies and teaching materials to guarantee a minimal competence in quantitative skills and critical thinking in University of Pennsylvania undergraduates. He was also a founding director of the Solomon Asch Center for the Study of Ethnopolitical Conflict.

Antonios (Adoni) Stamatogiannakis is a marketing doctoral candidate at INSEAD, France. He is linked to sensory marketing through his research on visual perception and product design. He is also doing research on the areas of consumer goals and consumer memory. Part of his research has been presented at leading conferences, including the Association for Consumer Research, Society for Consumer Psychology, and European Marketing Academy conferences. He holds B.Sc. and M.Sc. degrees from the Athens University of Economics and Business.

Brian Wansink is the John Dyson Professor of Consumer Behavior at Cornell University, where he directs the Cornell Food and Brand Lab. He is author of over 100 academic articles and books, including the best-selling *Mindless Eating: Why We Eat More Than We Think* (2006) along with *Marketing Nutrition* (2005), *Asking Questions* (2004), and *Consumer Panels* (2002). From 2007–2009 he was granted a leave of absence from Cornell to accept a presidential appointment as executive director of

USDA's Center for Nutrition Policy and Promotion, the federal agency in charge of developing the 2010 Dietary Guidelines and promoting the Food Guide Pyramid (MyPyramid.gov). His award-winning academic research on food psychology and behavior change has been published in the world's top marketing, medical, and nutrition journals. It contributed to the introduction of smaller "100 calorie" packages (to prevent overeating), the use of taller glasses in some bars (to prevent the overpouring of alcohol), and the use of elaborate names and mouth-watering descriptions on some chain restaurant menus (to improve enjoyment of the food). It has been presented, translated, reported, and featured in television documentaries on every continent but Antarctica.

Mindawati Wijaya is a graduate student in Wee Kim Wee School of Communication and Information, Nanyang Technological University, Singapore. Her research interests include children, health communication, market research, and computer-mediated communication.

Eric Yorkston is associate professor of marketing at the Neeley School of Business, Texas Christian University. His research focuses on how consumers' language and information processing affect brand decisions. His work has appeared in the *Journal of Consumer Research*, *Journal of Retailing*, and others.

1

An Introduction to Sensory Marketing

The Sensuality of Products

I consider myself to be a sensuist. I enjoy the pleasure that my senses bring me when I drink second flush Darjeeling tea in porcelain cups, view the figurative art prints I have collected over the years, listen to a-tonal jazz, cook foods with strong aromas, or garden without gloves. Each of these activities gratifies at least one of my senses—taste, vision, sound, smell, and touch, respectively. The word *sensory* means relating to sensation or the senses, and the word *sensual* is similar in meaning, relating to a gratification of the senses, as is the word sensuous. This book highlights what I perceive managers and business school professors to have missed—the fact that products are sensual in nature; that the more firms can create, accentuate, or highlight the sensuality of their products, the more appealing these products can be for consumers. This book provides many examples of products' sensuality and I begin with an example where a completely new sensation is created in a consumer experience—a spa environment.

Creating a New Sensation

When I visited Singapore in August 2008, people urged me to go to a fish spa. While I comprehended ice creams and birthday parties for dogs, I did not quite understand spas for fish. The explanation, rather than assuaging my concerns, made the concept seem quite bizarre. It was not, after all, a spa for fish, but was instead an alternative pedicure method where one inserted one's feet into a fish tank and hundreds of tiny fish made a dash for their fish food of your dead skin. Many phone calls from the concierge got me an appointment along with every tourist who wanted to try it. I reached the spa to see two dozen people with their calves and feet in a fish tank either screaming or grinning widely. Apparently, after three minutes of initial screaming, which was the period of getting used to the fish bites, most people settled down and really enjoyed the experience. Was it just the thrill of fish giving a pedicure or was it also the absolutely novel haptic sensation of hundreds of fish incessantly biting the feet with tiny, harmless bites until all the dead skin was gone? I would argue that the novel haptic sensation of the fish bites enhanced the whole experience. If consumers were used to another pedicure product with the same sensation, getting it from fish would not have been nearly as appealing.

Haptic feel and other sensory perceptions affect what we like and what we buy. The example of the fish spa is just one among several that demonstrates that our senses are innately linked to our perception of products and services. This important role of the senses in consumer marketing is, however, only just being acknowledged. But this recognition will change how products are created and sold. The links between marketing and the senses relate to a battery of questions. How do our senses affect which products we like and which ones we don't like? Can products be designed more sensorially so that they stand out from others? Can sensory properties of products be enhanced to make them more memorable? Can one sensory aspect of a product impact how a person perceives a different sensory aspect of the product? For instance, will a person drink more wine when the glass is less sleek and more squat? Will the haptic feel of an appeals brochure from the botanical gardens impact how much one donates to them? Why are hotels coming up with their own toiletries that have signature smells? Why does a computer emit a particular strange music each time it is turned on? These are the types of questions that are addressed in this book. I now put sensory marketing in perspective.

Sensory Marketing in Perspective

What is sensory marketing, and why is it interesting and also important? I define it as marketing that engages the consumers' senses and affects their behavior. In this book, several experts discuss how sensory aspects of products (i.e., the touch, taste, smell, sound, and look of products) affect our emotions, memories, perceptions, preferences, choices, and consumption of these products. We see how creating new sensations or merely emphasizing or bringing attention to existing sensations can increase a product's or service's appeal. The book provides an overview of sensory marketing research that has taken place thus far. It should facilitate sensory marketing by practitioners and also research by academics.

An analysis of the recent history of product marketing indicates that the 1940s to 1960s, the post-Depression era, was also the no-nonsense era in terms of products. People looked carefully at price and what the product offered. They lived frugally, purchasing inexpensive products and making lower-priced stores popular. However, the no-nonsense era was lost when the economy started to prosper again.

The 1970s started the popularity of the branded good. In the 1970s, jeans, especially Levis, became ubiquitous, and "brand" became a new concept. Firms realized that brands could command a premium, and the marketing focus shifted to creating brand names. In that decade, much money was spent on advertising, and marketing researchers came up with many methods of measuring brand equity and better ways to create it.

In the past, most firms ignored the sensory aspects of products; it was invisible in the no-nonsense era, hardly being mentioned if at all, and the focus on the brand later on detracted from other aspects of the product. Only recently, in the new millennium, are firms actively looking at the sensory aspects of products. If one considers advertising for food alone, in the past year, many food items have started touting themselves as being multisensory. The chewing gum "5 Gum" is called that because it proposes to stimulate all five senses (the tagline is "5 gum Food—Stimulate your senses"). Ads for Magnum 5 Senses Ice Cream and Denny's breakfast ("taste it with all five senses") are similar. There are also new advertisements that sell to one sense but try to also stimulate a totally different one. Thus, Axe Dark Temptation deodorant's new ad features a man made of chocolate that the girls cannot get enough of ("Become as irresistible as chocolate"). Even technical products want to evoke our senses adopting names like BlackBerry, Chocolate, and Touch.

In saying that the focus on sense is a very recent phenomenon I am not implying that marketers previously did not know about the power or the idiosyncrasies of our senses—clearly some did. Let's consider lemon dishwashing detergent, which has been around for decades. The lemon scent makes people feel the detergent works better, even though there often is no real lemon in the product, and if there is, it is minimal. Someone first came up with the idea of using a lemon scent for dishwashing detergent. This entrepreneur knew about and exploited the connection between lemon scent and a feeling of cleanliness. The early connection may have been established based on lemon's acidity and its use in earlier times to cut through grease, to polish silver, and to generally make things cleaner.

When people started associating the lemon scent with a feeling of cleanliness, even the demise of the relationship could not preclude the perceived link from persisting, so that a lemon scent still indicates "cleaner." Sensory feelings are difficult to eliminate. Reversing the relationship (making a lemon scent indicate unclean) will be near impossible to do.

As styles change, such as jean types moving in cycles from bell bottoms to straight legs to skinny jeans and back again, so too brands come and go and certain features become more or less desirable. But our senses remain an elemental part of us, and if we make a product more positively sensorial, it is more likely to stay that way. Our senses being primal, we react immediately and subconsciously to them, unlike to a brand name or an attribute, both of which are learned.

Sensory marketing will persist since senses can affect the marketing of products in many ways. For instance, sense can be used as a symbol (e.g., Tiffany's blue color bag), for arousal about the product (e.g., when artificial smells are sprayed by cookie and pizza stores to entice shoppers into the store), and for directing imagery. In fact, sensory aspects of products affect us in ways we had never imagined. We also react immediately and subconsciously to sensory inputs (the smell of cookies baking), unlike to a brand name alone (e.g., McDonald's). The rest of the book explains the many ways in which sensory marketing can be done. We begin by discussing a product's sensory signature, which provides evidence for the inevitability of sensory marketing.

Sensory Signature

Is there something about your brand that leaves a sensory impression in people's minds? Do people remember a certain sensory aspect of your product that helps them recall the product and remember it fondly? Are you emphasizing a sensory aspect of your product or creating a new sensory aspect where none existed before? How strong is your sensory signature and why is it important?

One of the most frequently cited examples of sensory marketing by the few consultants who work in the area is that of Singapore Airlines. While the consultants call it sensory marketing or sensory branding, I like to call it a sensory signature. The fleet has used a signature aroma, Floridian waters, specially mixed for them, which is infused into the hot towels, sprayed in the planes, and worn by flight attendants. When frequent-flyers on Singapore Airlines smell this aroma, they feel more at home, enhancing their flying experience and increasing their satisfaction.

For another example of sensory signatures, do the following imagination exercise. Close your eyes and think of the color pink. Keep your eyes closed for 10 seconds. What comes to mind? Now, add a ribbon. If you are reading this book in the United States, there is a very strong chance that you thought of breast cancer with just the color pink alone and a near perfect chance that you thought of it when the ribbon was added. Susan G. Komen for the Cure was started in 1982 and is now the largest nonprofit devoted to breast cancer. They initiated the use of the pink ribbon for breast cancer and also the message of hope. Most people will not know Susan G. Komen but will know the pink ribbon.

Why is this pink ribbon different from other product logos, say the McDonald's arch? The most important difference is that logos are visual, whereas sensory signatures can encompass any set of the five senses. If a product or brand can claim a vivid and somewhat unique color and link it to an emotion, then not only is the color memorable, but one can also lay claim to the emotion. Then when one sees the color, the emotion is also evoked along with the brand name. Logos that are typically multicolored and bring visual attention to the shape, as opposed to the color, are less able to evoke such strong emotions. Susan G. Komen has managed to connect the pink to "goodness, giving, and hope." The "pink for cancer" link is now so strong that hundreds of pink products (not just ribbons) are automatically recognizable as donating to breast cancer research. Tiffany's blue bag, Christian Louboutin's red lacquer soles, and ING bank's orange also reveal a color–brand name link, with ING's being less strong. Pink is breast cancer's sensory signature, and it has allowed them to raise more money than would have been possible without the color association.

Susan G. Komen is a nonprofit that asks for donations and does not even have a specific product to sell; however, it has created a "positive" sensory aspect around the notion of breast cancer and products linked to breast cancer, and it has done this so strongly that pink is now automatically linked with breast cancer awareness; if pink is not the normal color for an object, people instinctively assume that the product is related to breast cancer. When that happens (i.e., when the signature triggers a brand name), a very strong sensory signature has indeed been created. Recently, some companies (e.g., Frito-Lay) have started investing a lot of money and resources to develop their brands' sensory signatures. They have come to understand its importance.

Emphasizing a Sense

We discussed the fish spa earlier and how a new sensation can increase a product's appeal. Another sensorial way to increase product appeal is by merely emphasizing the existing sensorial aspects of a product. An excellent example of this is provided by iPod's Touch, or iTouch as it is more commonly known, launched by Apple in 2008. Here, the product name itself brought attention to a sensory aspect of the product and gave ownership to iTouch of that sense, the sense of "touch." The product name iTouch has connotations for the way the product feels when we use it and for the way it responds to our fingers. This was yet another prescient move made by Apple to play up the senses when few other competitors were doing so. The product descriptions for iTouch further rides on the brand name by pointing out the "Revolutionary Multi-Touch interface," "So much to touch," and "Touch your movies, photos, and more."

Sensory Imagery

Will everyone be affected by the senses in the same way? Sheehan (1967) pointed out that not just vision but all senses can be imagined (i.e., we can imagine smell, touch, sounds, and taste besides sights). However, he also argued that there may be a difference in people's ability to imagine different senses (i.e., he argued for individual differences in sensory imagery ability). Some prior literature has shown how this difference in sensory imagery results in different responses to sensory stimuli. Thus Elder and Krishna (2008) show that an individual's imagery ability can interact with the presentation of an ad and consequently affect perceived taste. Similarly, Petrova and Cialdini (2005) show that the individual's imagery ability can interact with the presentation of an ad and consequently affect brand attitudes.

People may also have differences in sensory arousal (i.e., How likely is a sensory stimuli to arouse an individual or affect their mood?). So far, work on mood manipulations has assumed that all individuals are affected by the mood manipulation in the same way (such as when music is used to manipulate food). This would be a good topic for researchers to study.

Thus far I have provided a definition of sensory marketing, its place within marketing, how products can create a new sense or emphasize an existing one, and the concept of sensory signatures. I now provide an outline for the rest of this book.

What This Book Contains

The book is divided into six sections, one for each sense and one for future research on sensory marketing. I received tremendous help in putting together each of the five sense sections by coordinators for each of the five senses. These people were also the coordinators for each sense at the sensory marketing conference held in 2008 at the Ross School of Business in Michigan. Other conference participants provided additional chapters for each sense. As for the future of the field, the doctoral students who attended the conference collaborated to write the final chapter, discussing what remains to be researched. While the book is a compilation of chapters submitted by conference participants, it is not a haphazard or uncoordinated effort in any way. It is very systematically organized. Even before they came to the conference, participants were required to submit chapters along specific lines. In keeping with the focus of an organized and useful book, the coordinators for each sense have written an overview of literature related to that sense. These overviews are fairly comprehensive and involve many years of reading by the authors. They are shared with readers with the hope of facilitating future work in the area. Other chapters within each sense show recent and ongoing research pertaining to that sense, and the section coordinators and I debated at great length about what to include here.

The book starts with the haptic sense and an overview by Joann Peck, who is the most active consumer behavior researcher working on haptics. In this overview, Peck provides a taxonomy of touch showing the difference between various kinds of instrumental touch (touch with a functional purpose behind it) and hedonic touch (touch for sheer pleasure). Situational, individual, and product-related reasons for touching are discussed and incorporated into a cohesive framework. The chapter that follows by Roberta Klatzky, who is undoubtedly one of the best neuropsychologists working on haptics, unravels the mysteries of our skin and the role of various haptic receptors that lie within it. While Joann presents more about the effects of touch with a purpose, Andrea Morales's chapter focuses on the effects of incidental touch, such as people touching the front-most package on a shelf of cereals. She discusses possible positive and negative effects of incidental person-product, and product-product touch. The last chapter on haptics by Terry Childers and Joann Peck is centered on haptic product evaluation (i.e., what feels good haptically) and whether this haptic evaluation is best measured by self-report or by an alternative behavioral measure.

After haptics, we turn to olfaction and an overview by Maureen Morrin discussing the extant literature on olfaction organized by the various consequences of scent. Morrin is one of the first people in marketing to study olfaction and she continues to do so. In the next chapter, Rachel Herz discusses the close connection between odor, emotion, and the brain. If one wants to read more of her work, her book *The Scent of Desire* (2007) is excellent. In the book, one also gets a better understanding of the importance of studying the smell–emotion connection. She mentions how she is often called upon by lawyers to put a value on someone losing their sense of smell through an accident. May Lwin and Mindawati Wijaya offer a cross-cultural perspective on scents. They look at the feelings that scents evoke and whether these are similar or dissimilar across cultures; for instance, what smells do Chinese versus Indians versus Americans associate with a clean and an unclean place? The olfaction section ends with a chapter by Maureen Morrin, Jean-Charles Chebat, and Claire Gelinas-Chebat that discusses that not only does scent affect mood, memory, and emotion, but also that scent can impact perceptions of time duration.

Audition has had little research devoted to it by marketing researchers. While people have studied radio and television ads, not much research has examined the effect of the sound itself, as opposed to the meaning the words carry. As such, Joan Meyers-Levy, Melissa Bublitz, and Laura Peracchio had a difficult job writing an overview for the area. But their overview is a revelation; instead of merely focusing on research that has been done on audition, they show the connection between words, language, and sound (e.g., that sound is symbolic, such as the Ex in FedEx connoting the idea of speed), then review research on music that is pertinent to marketing, and finally discuss audition and the multisensory experience. Eric Yorkston expands on this by highlighting the effects of auxiliary sounds or sounds that are not a focal aspect of a product or service, such as the sound of a car horn indicating information about its size. Darren Dahl moves away from products and service sounds to voices of spokespeople in broadcast advertising: How do voice characteristics affect perceptions of the speaker? What do speech rate and frequency convey about the speaker? Marina Carnevale, Dawn Lerman, and David Luna go back to phonetic symbolism and look at the auditory processing of novel brand names. Between the joint effort of the different chapters in this section, one gets a fairly broad view of possible auditory effects within the marketing toolbox.

Priya Raghubir and I started working together on visual perception in 1990. I was walking back from the health clinic to my office at Columbia one day when I realized that I always took one of two possible paths. I roughly sketched the Columbia map and asked eight colleagues which of the two paths they would choose. Seven systematically chose one. I wondered why, dug through literature on the topic, and came up with some theories. To make the project more enjoyable, I asked Priya, an old friend and then a doctoral student at NYU, whether she would join me on the project, resulting in a decade-long productive collaboration on spatial perception biases. Priya has continued to work on visual perception since then and her overview demonstrates her expertise in the area. She provides a typology of visual properties of objects and a framework for how these are processed and affect consumer judgments. Amitava Chattopadhyay, Gerald Gorn, and Peter Darke provide the second cross-cultural chapter in the book. They look at the similarities and differences between Chinese and Caucasians in their preference for color. Eric Greenleaf's chapter reflects the virtuoso art historian and art critic in him. He provides a history of using black and white (monochrome) versus color in photography, fine art, and communications in general. Eric also considers how monochrome images can influence emotion and mood, defines when it is perceived as highbrow versus lowbrow, and if there are individual differences in preference for monochrome. The last chapter under visual perception by Barbara Kahn and Xiaoyan Deng explores the connection between the visual images on a package and its perceived heaviness. However, this issue is considered within a broader context so that the authors examine the more comprehensive role of visual package imagery, specifically layout decisions regarding the use of a product image on the package.

The overview on taste also provides a framework of the antecedents and consequences of taste, an aspect of taste that is emphasized in this overview by Aradhna Krishna and Ryan Elder. In the chapter by Paul Rozin and Julia Hormes, several ideas are presented for marketing academics (e.g., duration of neglect of sensory pleasures, benign masochism, the low predictability of sensory pleasure, the disparity between experience and remembered pleasure, and many others), and it literally drips with extremely deep insights (I love the following: "Older people have the same potential experience anticipating a positive event that will occur in the near future, but will have less opportunity to consume the memory because of a shorter lifespan. The utility of building memories declines with age, even assuming the acuity of memory remains intact!"). It also makes us question the current norm of experimental research and publishing. Pierre Chandon provides a summary of all the extant research on estimating food quantity, including psychophysical models of consumers' quantity perception with the resultant consequences for obesity. Nilufer Aydinoglu, Aradhna Krishna, and Brian Wansink show how size labels, even newly constructed ones (e.g., super-quencher), become an accepted part of the consumer vocabulary with a common meaning, so that people think similarly about relative sizes (Is super-quencher bigger or smaller than an extra large?).

We end with a chapter on future directions in sensory marketing. One important take-away from this chapter is that while there has been some research on individual senses, there has been little research to date on the interaction between senses.

We now briefly turn our attention to a few other issues before we dive into the book itself. Since we have at least two chapters, those by Herz and Klatzky, devoted to the neuropsychology of the senses, it is important to discuss, at least briefly, the relationship between sensory marketing, psychology, and neuroscience.

Sensory Marketing, Psychology, and Neuroscience

One important thing to note in the evolution of neuroscience research is the relationship between psychology and neuroscience research. This is exemplified in an article by Rozin (1982) that demonstrates that olfaction is the only dual sensory modality, sensing objects both in the external world orthonosally and also sensing them retronasally from within the mouth (the back of the throat connect to the nose). He then suggests that the same olfactory stimulation may be perceived and evaluated in two qualitatively different ways, depending on whether it is referring to the mouth (smelled orthonasally) or the external world (smelled retronasally). For instance, aged cheese may taste good but smell bad. This is odd since smell is the largest component of the taste of this cheese. Similarly, we like the smell of many foods but dislike the taste (e.g., coffee). He ends with three possible explanations for this duality: "(i) The olfactory input to the brain could be gated differently depending on whether the input is processed as in-mouth or out-there. The differential gating could lead to qualitatively different sensations, ... (ii) The olfactory input may not be gated but, rather, combined with available oral inputs into an emergent percept in which the olfactory component loses its separate identity, ... and (iii) The stimulus input to the olfactory mucosa may be very different in the in-mouth vs. out-there situations." This raises an interesting research question for neuroscientists. They can then do magnetic resonance imaging (MRI) to see which explanation is the valid one. In fact, Rolls (2005) has recently found support for Rozin's second explanation.

Indeed, much neuroscience research is done to investigate some intriguing finding of psychologists. Thus, the norm is *not* to do a few MRIs within the psychology paper, but to keep the MRIs for neurologists to conduct in later research. There are reasons for this; one reason is that a paper can be complete, rigorous, and intriguing when one shows an interesting effect. Demonstrating why that effect occurs, from the brain's perspective, is sometimes better left to a team of neuroscientists trained in different skills. So, the role I see for psychology, neuroscience, and marketing in "sensory marketing" research is for psychologists and marketing researchers to come up with interesting experimental results that are then probed by neuroscientists for a neurological explanation. Neuroscience research can also yield findings that raise interesting questions for marketing academics and psychologists to study. As such, the three fields would also inform one another in determining important topics to study and what results should be expected in the experiments (i.e., in developing hypotheses and conceptual frameworks).

Cross-Cultural Differences in Sensory Response

While two chapters in this book (by Lwin and Wijaya and by Chattopadhyay, Gorn, and Darke), as well as part of Herz's chapter, are devoted to cross-cultural research in sensory marketing, there is vast scope for more work in this area. Sound preferences, for instance, could vary across cultures and are not well understood. Similarly, while it is obvious that taste preferences vary across cultures (Indians like more spicy food than Scandinavians), it would be interesting to study differences in basic (sweet, salty, sour, bitter) taste preferences across cultures.

Problems in Sensory Marketing Research

One needs to understand the difficulties in conducting sensory marketing researcher. A good example is the study of smell. Studies on scent need to control for many factors. First, if one is studying the effect of a scent on something else, typically one needs to have a manipulation that includes a sense, and it cannot be a simple paper-pencil study. For instance, if one is looking at the effect of scent on memory, one needs to have at least two conditions, one with scent and one without. If there are additional variables within the scent condition (e.g., high or low load), then the conditions with scent need to ensure that all subjects get the stimuli with the same degree of scenting—not more and not less—so that there is no amount of scent and load confound. That means that in all the scent conditions, the stimuli needs to be infused with the scent to the same degree (with the same amount of scent, in the same way, and for the same amount of time). Thus, to infuse the scent into stimuli, one needs, for example, to drop exactly the same amount of essential oils on or into the stimuli and then put the stimuli into an airtight container (e.g., a double zipping bag so that the smell is infused and does not get lost) for a specified period. Subjects then take the stimuli out of the airtight container. If one is examining the effects of a specific scent, one has to be additionally careful to ensure that when subjects are given the scent stimulus, it (and also the environment) is not contaminated by any other olfactory stimuli. Where subjects are asked to evaluate multiple scent stimuli, respondents should clear their nasal passage of the previous scent before moving on to the next one. This is done to minimize contamination from one scent to the next—an accepted practice in the fragrance industry to clear the nasal passage is to smell coffee beans. In studies where a scent cue is provided to subjects as a retrieval cue for aided recall, the cue often consists of a small glass bottle (or zipping bag) that contains a blotter paper infused with several drops of the essential oil and participants who receive the scent retrieval cue are asked to uniformly take at most two breaths. One can thus see the time-consuming nature in order for sensory studies to be done in a meticulous manner. Besides the amount of effort involved, sample sizes for scent studies typically also need to be large to get significant effects, since the effects tend to be subtle in nature.

Conclusion

I end this chapter by reminding the reader that the consumer marketplace is inundated with different brands. For example, we have hundreds of cereals, shampoos, personal computers, hotels, and airlines to choose from. While marketers have focused on trying to make their products and services more attractive to consumers, I believe that sensory aspects of products and services have not been emphasized enough. This book demonstrates how enhancing a product sensorially can make a big difference in product and service appeal, its memorability, and the emotional attachment that consumers feel with it.

References

Elder, R. S., & Krishna, A. (2008). *The effect of advertising copy on sensory thoughts and perceived taste.* University of Michigan Working Paper.

Herz, R. (2007). *The scent of desire: Discovering our enigmatic sense of smell.* New York: William Morrow.

Petrova, P. K., & Cialdini, R. B. (2005, December). Fluency of consumption imagery and the backfire effects of imagery appeals. *Journal of Consumer Research, 32*, 442–452.

Rolls, E. T. (2005, May 1). Taste, olfactory, and food texture processing in the brain, and the control of food intake. *Physiology and Behavior, 85*, 45–56.

Rozin, P. (1982). "Taste-smell confusions" and the duality of the olfactory sense. *Perception and Psychophysics, 31*(4), 397–401.

Sheehan, P. W. (1967). A shortened form of Betts's questionnaire upon mental imagery. *Journal of Clinical Psychology, 23*, 386–389.

Section I

Haptics

2

Does Touch Matter? Insights From Haptic Research in Marketing

Joann Peck

Remember "Mr. Whipple ... Please don't squeeze the Charmin!"? And how often when shopping do you hear parents telling their children "Please don't touch!"? Touch can be an almost irresistible urge for children and adults, yet despite its ubiquity, this fascinating sense has not been studied in marketing. In this chapter, I provide some background on the sense of touch and introduce a taxonomy of touch in marketing. Next I discuss object/product attributes and individual differences that have been considered in touch research. Finally, I end with recent developments in this exciting area of sensory research.

The importance of the sense of touch has been recognized for centuries. Aristotle believed that touch mediated all sense perception, even vision (Siegel, 1970). It was thought that invisible particles bombarded the surface of the body to convey smell, taste, and sound. During the Renaissance, immense power was attributed to touch. In the fresco *The Creation of Man* (Sistine Chapel, Vatican), Michelangelo painted God stretching out a hand toward the hand of Adam in order to transmit life. As discussed by Weber (1978), this is notable in that touch is depicted as not only necessary for the survival of the human race, but for a person to become whole. Since Adam's body was already formed, what touch added was the soul and spirit, without which the body could not function.

The historical prominence of touch is also reflected in language (Ackerman, 1990; Katz, 1925; Montagu, 1986; Williams, 1976). The use of various touch terms is prevalent in the English language. Some words convey affect such as a *"touching" story*, while others are more concerned with cognition, as in *did you "catch" that mistake* and *can you "handle" the problem*? Personality is also described through touch terms such as a *"touchy" person*, an *"abrasive" personality*, or a *"handy" person*. Some people are *"hard" to deal with* and they may be *out of "touch" with reality* because they tend to *lose their "grip."* Communication includes touch words such as *on the other "hand"* and *keep in "touch."* Finally, familiar branding includes touch terms, as evidenced by *reach out and "touch" someone* from AT&T and *"touching" is believing* from Apple.

Although studies of touch may involve any tactile surface on the human body, in marketing, research has centered on the hands as the primary source of input to the perceptual system. The hand has been called a person's "outer brain" (Klatzky & Lederman, 1987) and Lederman and Klatzky (1987) describe the "intelligent hand." Gibson (1966) adopted the term "haptics" to refer to the functionally discrete system involved in the seeking and extraction of information by the hand. This term, first introduced in 1931 by Révész (cited in Révész, 1950), comes from the Greek word *haptikos*, which means "able to lay hold of." The term *haptics* is also used by Klatzky and Lederman (e.g., Klatzky & Lederman, 1992, 1993) and incorporates both cutaneous (affecting the skin) and kinesthetic (muscle tissue) information. The term haptics in marketing generally refers to the active seeking and perception by the hands.

Touch and Other Senses

How is the sense of touch different from other senses? The sense of touch is often called the near sense or the proximal sense. The other senses act through some medium; vision, smell, and hearing all operate through the air, while for taste the wetness of saliva must be present. Only with the sense of touch do people usually only feel things that actually come into contact with them. Touch can be extended beyond its normal body bounds with special tools such as a cane. However, for the most part, if a stimulus is to be perceived by touch, it must come in contact with the skin. Unlike hearing, smell, and vision, the idea of an ambient touch is not relevant.

Besides being a proximal sense, perception by touch is sequential in nature. While some other senses like vision can take in a vast array of sensory information simultaneously, the sense of touch can generally perceive only one input at a time. This sequential perception has led some researchers to note its limitations, especially compared to vision (Révész, 1950). A long-standing question has been whether the senses of vision and touch give the same information about objects, and if not, which sense tends to dominate. Vision and touch seem to be differentially suited for different events and interact in various ways depending on the nature of the perceptual performance that is involved (Warren & Rossano, 1991).

Information Available to Touch

Research has demonstrated that haptic explorers can be remarkably fast and accurate at recognizing real objects (Klatzky, Lederman, & Metzger, 1985). Lederman and Klatzky (1987) explain the special perceptual abilities of the hands by calling attention to particular hand movements that they call exploratory procedures (EP). An EP is a stereotypical hand movement that maximizes the sensory input corresponding to a certain object property (Lederman & Klatzky, 1987). The haptic system is particularly adept at encoding the object properties corresponding to texture, hardness, temperature, and weight information, and a separate EP has been found to correspond to each object dimension. For example, when an individual wants to assess the weight of an object, you can observe him or her hefting the object, often repeatedly. Lederman and Klatzky (1987) term this the "unsupported holding" exploratory procedure. They have documented strong linkages between stereotypical hand movements, or "exploratory procedures," and the haptic perception of specific object properties (Klatzky & Lederman, 1992, 1993; Lederman & Klatzky, 1987). Texture, hardness, temperature, and weight information, which are best gleaned by touch, have been termed material properties by Klatzky and Lederman (1992, 1993). Roberta Klatzky's chapter in this book further discusses the haptic perceptual system and EPs.

Taxonomy of Touch in Marketing

In consumer behavior, products are touched for many different reasons, not necessarily to ascertain material properties. The taxonomy of touch presented here was facilitated by a formal observational study I did in the produce department at a local grocery store as well as more informal observations at several art fairs and various retail establishments. In developing a taxonomy of touch in consumer behavior, four distinct types of touch are evident (see Figure 2.1). The first three types of touch assume a consumer is engaged in goal-directed, problem-solving, prepurchase behavior. The classification of instrumental touch is used to indicate that consumers are touching products as a means to an end, possibly purchase. The actions of

Instrumental Touch (touch as a means to an end)

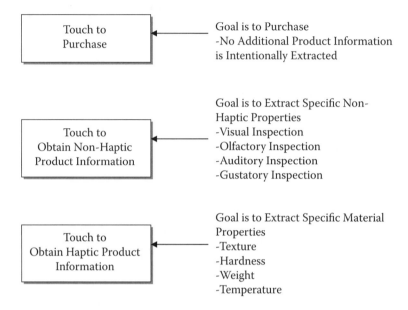

Hedonic Touch (touch as an end in itself)

Figure 2.1 A taxonomy of touch in consumer behavior.

the consumer are directed toward product evaluation and making purchase decisions. In contrast, the fourth type is hedonic touch, where touch is an end in itself with the focus being the sensory experience of touch. Hedonic touch may or may not ultimately result in product purchase.

Instrumental Touch

At the simplest level, a consumer may touch a product only to make a purchase. For example, a consumer may wish to purchase a particular type of cereal and touch it merely to place it in the cart for purchase. A simple repeat purchase heuristic such as "purchase the same brand as last time" may be operating. At this level of touch, the haptic perceptual system is not intentionally extracting relevant purchase decision information about the product.

At the next level, a consumer may touch a product with the goal of obtaining information that is not best ascertained by the haptic perceptual system. The most frequent type of touch where nonhaptic information is desired is that of visual inspection. For example, a consumer undecided about which brand of cereal to purchase may touch a package in order to rotate it so that the nutrition information can be read. After visual inspection, the consumer may or may not decide to make the purchase depending on his or her evaluation.

Similarly, a consumer may touch a product to make an olfactory inspection. In grocery stores, shoppers can be seen smelling cantaloupe and pineapple, presumably to assess the ripeness of the fruit. Other forms of nonhaptic information are auditory and gustatory sources of sensory input. An example of auditory inspection would be a consumer pushing a button to listen to information provided at a kiosk. Gustatory input may be obtained by sampling products at a grocery store prior to purchase.

It is important to note that in both touch to purchase and touch to obtain nonhaptic information, haptic information may be available to the consumer, yet the consumer is not attending to the haptic information. In picking up a box of cereal to visually inspect the label, the weight of the cereal box, a haptic or material property, is available to the consumer, yet the goal of the consumer is to obtain some sort of nonhaptic information, so the haptic information may be overlooked.

Finally, a consumer may wish to touch a product to gain product knowledge that can best be gleaned by touch, such as the material properties of texture, hardness, temperature, and weight. The goal of a consumer in touching to gain haptic product information is to extract specific material properties. Evidence has been found for a "visual preview model," which states that vision provides a quick "glance" that results in broad but coarse information on the haptic properties of an object, information that is useful in directing further processing (Klatzky, Lederman, & Matula, 1993). When encoding properties of familiar objects, vision is often sufficient because it triggers the retrieval of information stored in memory, eliminating the need for direct perceptual encoding by haptic exploration. However, vision may also reveal that more detailed information about a material property is desired. For example, a visual glance at a sweater may determine that the texture (a property best explored and encoded haptically) should be touched to obtain more detailed information on the texture or weight of the material.

Hedonic Touch

The instrumental categories of touch to purchase, touch to gain nonhaptic information, and touch to gain specific haptic information match the view of the consumer as a problem solver engaged in goal-directed activities, searching for information, retrieving cues from memory, and arriving at careful product judgments. In contrast, the hedonic touch category suggests that some touch is done as an end in and of itself. This hedonic touch is oriented toward pleasant sensory experiences.

For some categories of touch, a barrier to touch such as shopping online or through catalogs is not as problematic as other types of touch. For example, touch to purchase and touch to gain nonhaptic information, especially visual information, are easily compensated for when shopping online. Instead of touch to purchase, a consumer simply adds an item to the shopping cart with a mouse click. Touch to obtain visual information can also be provided in nontouch media such as online or catalogs. In the cereal example above, nutrition information can be conveyed in text form online.

However, touch to obtain material property information and hedonic touch are not easily provided in a nontouch context. Perhaps the rise in online shopping can partially account for the increasing interest in touch by marketing academics. The research done on touch in marketing has been concerned with touch to gain specific haptic information as well as hedonic touch. The next section will examine both informational and hedonic touch and the research that has been done in marketing.

Object and Product Factors

Informational Touch

Some objects encourage touch more than others. Often consumers want to touch products to ascertain specific product information that only touch can provide. As discussed, touch excels at obtaining texture, hardness, temperature, and weight information (Klatzky & Lederman, 1992, 1993). If a product category varies in a diagnostic way on one or more of these attributes, also termed material properties, consumers will be more motivated to touch the product prior to purchase. For example, clothing varies on texture and weight and will likely encourage prepurchase touch more than books, which do not vary on material properties in a diagnostic manner.

Holbrook (1983), when using sweaters as stimuli for a study, noted the strong role played by tactile cues when participants were evaluating a product. He encouraged using, or at least being aware of using, actual products instead of visual representations (e.g., pictures of products) in research. McCabe and Nowlis (2003) varied whether products differed on material properties and whether participants had the actual product to evaluate a picture of the product, a list of attributes, or some combination of these. The primary dependent variable was purchase likelihood. Results showed that product categories that varied in the diagnosticity of touch (e.g., bath towels, carpeting) were more likely to be preferred in shopping environments that allow physical inspection than in those where touch is unavailable. However, there was no difference in the preference of products across shopping environments (touch, no touch) when a product category did not vary on material properties (e.g., videotape, rolls of film), since for these categories, vision was diagnostic. Results also showed that differences in preferences between the two environments were reduced when the material properties of the products were verbally described. In effect, compensation for lack of touch was possible with a written description (see Peck & Childers, 2003a).

Grohmann, Spangenberg, and Sprott (2007) also examined product factors. They found that tactile input had a positive effect on the evaluation of products that varied in the material properties of softness and texture, especially for products high in quality. When evaluating high and low quality levels at the same time, tactile input had a negative effect on product evaluations for low quality products. The authors argue that their results are best explained by an information processing mechanism and not an affective one, as had been used in some touch studies (Peck & Wiggins, 2006). The chapter by Childers and Peck in this book examines more closely information processing and affective processes.

Noninformational or Hedonic Touch

What about touch that has no informational value? For example, GlaxoSmithKline's Alli, the fat-blocking pill used to help individuals lose weight, is accompanied by a pill carrying package that is shaped like a finger. When this package is opened, the texture inside feels somewhat rubbery, a bit like skin. The idea was that the package would allow the consumer to feel as if he or she were holding the hand of a friend or an ally who would be accompanying him or her on the weight-loss journey. Although this type of touch carries no informational value, this example suggests that it may nonetheless be persuasive.

For touch to influence marketing decisions and evaluations, does it have to provide product attribute information? Or can hedonic aspects of touch alone be persuasive? Peck and Wiggins (2006) examined touch unrelated to a product in the context of a persuasive advertisement. They varied the valence of a touch element attached to a pamphlet (negative, neutral, and positive) as well as the fit of the touch element with the message in the pamphlet. They found that adding a touch element that felt good (e.g., a feather on a pamphlet requesting donations to a local arboretum) increased persuasion, measured as attitude toward the ad, as well as the likelihood of donating time or money to the organization. An unexpected finding was that the fit of the touch element with the message did not matter for individuals who prefer touch information; any touch element was better than no touch element for these participants. However, for people who are not as motivated to touch, it was important that the touch element fit with the message; otherwise, it had no influence on persuasion.

Peck and Shu (2009) also examined the role of noninformational touch, linking touch to the notion of psychological ownership. They found that touching an object, compared to an inability to touch, resulted in greater feelings of psychological ownership and also a greater willingness to pay. They also employed ownership imagery to increase psychological ownership when the ability to touch was absent, and this too resulted in increased psychological ownership and the amount a person was willing to pay.

Similarly, Peck and Barger (2008) investigated haptic imagery to determine whether imagining touching an object is as good as actually touching an object as far as psychological ownership and valuation. They found that if a person closes his or her eyes and imagines touching, this is as effective as actual touch. They conjecture that a person closing his or her eyes while imagining touching focuses cognitive resources. They then added haptic interference and varied whether the stimuli fit the object being imagined (i.e., touching a soft swatch while imagining touching a soft blanket) or did not fit (i.e., touching sandpaper while imagining touching a soft blanket). They found that when a person's eyes are open, the presence or absence of haptic stimuli does not affect haptic imaging. However, when a person's eyes are closed, the presence or absence of haptic stimuli does significantly impact haptic imagining if the stimulus is incongruent. A cognitive resource explanation is used to support the findings.

In other research not related to attributes ascertained by product touch, Hornik (1992) examined touch as nonverbal communication in an interpersonal touch context. In three field settings (a bookstore, a restaurant, and a supermarket), he found that unobtrusive touch by an employee on the arm of a customer enhanced positive feelings for the external stimuli (e.g., the bookstore) as well as the touching source (the employee). Customers touched by a requester tended to comply more than those customers who were not touched.

Does touch by another person always result in a positive outcome? In several studies (Argo, Dahl, & Morales, 2006; Morales & Fitzsimons, 2007), researchers have found that consumers react less favorably to products touched by other consumers. Manipulating contamination cues such as proximity to contact varied the salience of the contamination and the time elapsed since contact. Results for the proximity to contact only held when participants believed that other consumers had recently come in contact with the product. Disgust was found to be the underlying mechanism explaining the negative effects of contamination on product evaluation. The chapter by Andrea Morales in this book gives more details on this concept.

Touch and Individual Differences

Peck and Childers (2003a) examined whether compensation for lack of touch was possible, taking into account the type of material properties to be compensated for as well as an individual difference in the preference for touch information. They conjectured that not all material properties create the same type of response in consumers. Specifically, pleasant sensory feedback experienced when assessing softness may differentially influence the person touching compared to a more functional material property such as weight. In addition, they considered an individual difference in the preference for touch information. Peck and Childers (2003b) developed the need for touch (NFT) scale and tested the scale in seven studies. NFT is defined as a preference for the extraction and use of information obtained through touch. It includes two dimensions: instrumental touch and autotelic touch. The instrumental dimension of NFT refers to those aspects of touch that reflect outcome-directed touch with a salient purchase goal. The image of a consumer involved in instrumental touch is that of a problem solver consciously engaged in the goal-directed activity of searching for information and arriving at a final judgment. In contrast, autotelic touch involves a consumer seeking fun, sensory stimulation and enjoyment with no purchase goal necessarily salient. The autotelic factor is defined as the enjoyment and affect of touch along with the compulsive or irresistible urge to explore via touch.

Peck and Childers (2003a, 2003b) found that NFT moderated the relationship between direct experience and confidence in product judgments. For individuals higher in NFT, a lack of direct experience (an inability to touch) resulted in less confidence in the judgment. For low NFT individuals, confidence in judgment was unaffected by a barrier to touch provided there was a clear visual of the product. The researchers also found that for individuals high in NFT, compensation for an inability touch was not always possible. For more functional haptic information, such as weight, a written description compensated for the inability to touch. However, for a material property with pleasant sensory feedback (softness), a written description did not provide this compensation. In effect, there are certain types of product attributes for which there is no substitute for actual touch. The authors conjecture that visual information compensated for actual haptic exploration.

Citrin, Stem, Spangenberg, and Clark (2003) developed an individual difference scale they called need for tactile input that was similar to the instrumental dimension of NFT. They found that it was negatively related to products purchased over the Internet, especially those categories that vary with respect to material properties. They also found that women showed a higher need for tactile input than men.

An individual difference in the preference for touch information has been found to moderate the time spent touching products to ascertain information (Peck & Childers, 2004). Specific stereotypical hand movements or exploratory procedures have been linked to the haptic perception of material properties as discussed earlier. These researchers found that for all material properties except texture, high NFT individuals spent less time exploring with their hands than individuals low in NFT. The authors note that since touch information is more accessible for high NFT individuals, they are more efficient at extracting this information. Higher accessibility of haptic information for high NFT individuals was exhibited through a free recall exercise and through a timed response measure (Peck & Childers, 2003b). However, since texture provided a pleasant sensory feedback (a soft sweater), high NFT individuals spent a longer time assessing texture than their low NFT counterparts.

Besides product category differences and an individual difference in the preference for touch information, situations vary as to whether touch is salient. In some situations, such as online or catalog purchases, there is no opportunity to touch. In other situations, the salience of touch has been altered. For example, Peck and Childers (2006) manipulated the environment in a study in a grocery store to examine impulse purchase behavior and environmental stimuli encouraging touch. They varied point of purchase signs (either no sign or "feel the freshness") to increase the salience of touch in the grocery store environment and found that the sign encouraging touch resulted in more unplanned purchases than the no sign condition. In addition, there was a main effect of individual difference in autotelic NFT. Individuals high in autotelic NFT made more unplanned purchases than individuals low in autotelic NFT.

To summarize, object or product differences, individual differences, and situational differences all interact to determine the motivation of a consumer to touch a product prior to purchase. Besides these three factors, there may be a mechanism in place that would compensate a consumer for the inability to haptically examine a product prior to purchase. For example, as discussed, a clear written description or a picture may compensate for some types of material properties for some individuals (e.g., McCabe & Nowlis, 2003; Peck & Childers, 2003a). Figure 2.2 is a summary of the motivation to touch.

What's Next?

During this sensory conference, it was clear that more research on the interaction of the senses is needed. There has been some movement in this direction in the area of haptic research. For example, Krishna (2006) investigated the elongation bias and showed that sensory modality (touch or vision) affects the extent and direction of the elongation bias. The elongation bias predicts that with two containers of equal volume, the taller of the two is judged to have a larger volume. The author hypothesized that in a visual perception task, height is the salient dimension, and thus the taller container would appear larger. However, in another condition, when the participants had only haptic cues (they handled the objects blindfolded), width became the salient dimension and there was a reversal in the elongation bias (wide containers appeared bigger).

Krishna and Morrin (2008) asked whether nondiagnostic touch-related cues can influence the taste of a product. They varied the nondiagnostic

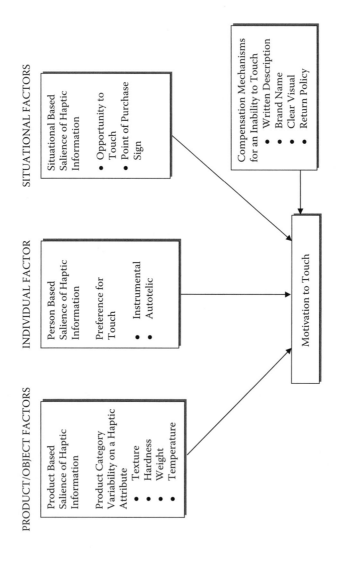

Figure 2.2 Motivation to touch.

haptic qualities of a product's package or serving container and found that nondiagnostic haptic cues influenced the perceptions and evaluations only of individuals lower in NFT. In other words, higher NFT individuals are better at determining when touch information is informative and do not use this information when making product evaluations if the information is nondiagnostic.

Although multisensory research is important, there are other areas that are also worthy of further investigation. To this end, the final chapter of this volume is devoted to the future of sensory research.

References

Ackerman, D. (1990). *A natural history of the senses.* New York: Random House.

Argo, J. J., Dahl, D., & Morales, A. C. (2006, April). Consumer contamination: How consumers react to products touched by others. *Journal of Marketing, 70,* 81–94.

Citrin, A. V., Stem, D. E., Spangenberg, E. R., & Clark, M. J. (2003). Consumer need for tactile input: An Internet retailing challenge. *Journal of Business Research, 56*(11), 915–922.

Gibson, J. J. (1966). Observations on active touch. *Psychological Review, 69,* 477–490.

Grohmann, B., Spangenberg, E. R., & Sprott, D. E. (2007). The influence of tactile input on the evaluation of retail product offerings. *Journal of Retailing, 83*(2), 237–245.

Holbrook, M. B. (1983). On the importance of using real products in research on marketing strategy. *Journal of Retailing, 59*(1), 4–23.

Hornik, J. (1992). Tactile stimulation and consumer response. *Journal of Consumer Research, 19*(3), 449–458.

Katz, D. (1925). *The world of touch.* (L. E. Krueger, Trans. in 1989). Hillsdale, NJ: Lawrence Earlbaum.

Klatzky, R. L., & Lederman, S. J. (1987). The intelligent hand. In G. Bower (Ed.), *The psychology of learning and motivation* (pp. 121–151). San Diego, CA: Academic Pres.

Klatzky, R. L., & Lederman, S. J. (1992). Stages of manual exploration in haptic object identification. *Perception and Psychophysics, 52*(6), 661–670.

Klatzky, R. L., & Lederman, S. J. (1993). Toward a computational model of constraint-driven exploration and haptic object identification. *Perception, 22,* 597–621.

Klatzky, R. L., Lederman, S. J., & Matula, D. E. (1993). Haptic exploration in the presence of vision. *Journal of Experimental Psychology: Human Perception and Performance, 19*(4), 726–743.

Klatzky, R. L., Lederman, S. J., & Metzger, V. A. (1985). Identifying objects by touch: An expert system. *Perception and Psychophysics, 37*(4), 299–302.

Krishna, A. (2006). Interaction of senses: the effect of vision versus touch on the elongation bias. *Journal of Consumer Research, 32*(4), 557–567.

Krishna, A., & Morrin, M. (2008). Does touch affect taste? The perceptual transfer of product container haptic cues. *Journal of Consumer Research, 34*(6), 807–818.

Lederman, S. J., & Klatzky, R. L. (1987). Hand movements: A window into haptic object recognition. *Cognitive Psychology, 19,* 342–368.

McCabe, D. B., & Nowlis, S. M. (2003). The effect of examining actual products or product descriptions on consumer preference. *Journal of Consumer Psychology, 13*(4), 431–439.

Montagu, A. (1986). *Touching: The human significance of the skin.* New York: Harper and Row.

Morales, A. C., & Fitzsimons, G. J. (2007, May). Product contagion: Changing consumer evaluations through physical contact with "disgusting" products. *Journal of Marketing Research, 44,* 272–283.

Peck, J., & Barger, V. (2008). *In search for a surrogate for touch: The effect of haptic imagery on psychological ownership and object valuation.* Working Paper.

Peck, J., & Childers, T. L. (2003a, April). To have and to hold: The influence of haptic information on product judgments. *Journal of Marketing, 67*(2), 35–48.

Peck, J., & Childers, T. L. (2003b). Individual differences in haptic information processing: The "need for touch" scale. *Journal of Consumer Research, 30*(3), 430–442.

Peck, J., & Childers, T. L. (2004). *Self-report and behavioral measures in product evaluation and haptic information: Is what I say how I feel?* Association for Consumer Research Working Paper Track.

Peck, J., & Childers, T. L. (2006). If I touch it I have to have it: Individual and environmental influences on impulse purchasing. *Journal of Business Research, 59,* 765–769.

Peck, J., & Shu, S. (2009). The effect of mere touch on perceived ownership. *Journal of Consumer Research,* Oct.

Peck, J., & Wiggins, J. (2006). It just feels good: Consumers' affective response to touch and its influence on attitudes and behavior. *Journal of Marketing, 70*(4), 56–69.

Révész, G. (1950). *Psychology and the art of the blind* (H. A. Wolff, Trans.). London: Longmans Green.

Siegel, R. E. (1970). *Galen on sense perception. His doctrines, observations and experiments on vision, hearing, smell, taste, touch and pain, and their historical sources.* Basel and New York: Karger.

Warren, D. H., & Rossano, M. J. (1991). Intermodality relations: Vision and touch. In M. A. Heller & W. Schiiff (Eds.), *The psychology of touch* (pp. 119–137). Hillsdale, NJ: Lawrence Erlbaum.

Weber, E. H. (1978). *The sense of touch* (English trans. of De Tactu [1834] and Der Tastsinn [1846]; E. H. Ross & D. J. Murray, Trans.) London: Academic Press.

Williams, J. M. (1976). Synaesthetic adjectives: A possible law of semantic change. *Language, 52,* 461–478.

3

Touch

A Gentle Tutorial With Implications for Marketing

Roberta L. Klatzky

Advertising pervasively appeals to vision and hearing. Print and pictures are ubiquitous in newspapers and magazines, commercials resound from radio and television, and the Web combines both the visual and auditory modalities. More recently, scent technology has made it possible to deliver precise mixtures to closed areas, enabling businesses to enhance surroundings and even brand themselves through olfaction. Pity, then, the marketer who wants to exploit touch. Unlike vision, hearing, and smell, which can sense the distal world, touch is the proximal sense. With rare exceptions, like the warmth of the sun, we must physically contact a surface or object to sense it through touch. Consumers must be seduced into touching an object before its tactual properties can be communicated.

In this chapter I will recount some basic scientific findings about the sense of touch, with the goal of drawing implications for its exploitation in marketing. Certain properties of touch make it quite different from other senses for that purpose. As was just noted, touch receives information about the immediately surrounding world, not distant objects and events. Furthermore, touching goes beyond mere contact. Tactual perception is inextricably linked to action; what we feel depends on how we explore. Touch informs us about the properties of surfaces and objects in the world. Along with touching may come, as well, positive or negative affective responses, such as pleasure or repulsion. The sense of touch also encompasses the negative sensations of itch and pain.

The chapter begins with the neurophysiological building blocks of touch, the sensory receptors underneath the skin. When describing touch, starting out with the first layer is important, because primitive sensory responses are tightly linked to full-blown conscious experience of the

world. Visual science, in contrast, tells us the story of a long processing chain from eye to perceived surroundings. Photons of light are represented successively as points, edges, regions, volumes, and ultimately,
coherent objects. We can be informed quite directly about the properties
of the world, however, by receptors in skin, muscles, tendons, and joints.
For example, the perception of a surface as warm or cool comes to us with
minimal processing intervention: Specialized nerve endings underneath
the skin respond to the flow of heat from a warm surface into the cooler
body of the person contacting it, and these early neural responses convey
an impression of warmth to the brain. Not all of the properties of objects
and surfaces are perceived with so little mediation; some information
requires complex neural computations. The immediacy of touch, however,
constitutes one of its principal features.

The Receptors of Touch

The common conception of five senses is, of course, a fallacy. Consider
vision, which encompasses systems for objects (what) and space (where),
and within the object system has distinct modules for shapes, colors, and
motion, among other attributes. Smell, in many terrestrial animals, sepa-
rates gustatory appetite from sexual appetite, both anatomically and neu-
rally. Touch, too, is polysensory.

An initial division can be made between two subsenses of touch, called
cutaneous and *kinesthetic*. The cutaneous system responds to stimulation
of the skin and conveys information about the surface being contacted. The
kinesthetic system responds to signals from muscles, tendons, and joints;
it conveys a sense of the positions that limbs take in space. Kinesthesis also
informs us about the properties of objects, as, for example, when we determine how large an object is by enclosing it in our hand. When we actively
explore the world, we are drawing information from both the cutaneous
and kinesthetic subsystems, and the combination is called *haptics*, or haptic perception. Of the two haptic subsystems, scientists arguably better
understand the cutaneous system at a basic neurophysiological level, and
the present discussion will concentrate on that component of touch.

To understand the polysensory nature of touch, we must refer to the
concept of a receptor. The term *receptor*, as applied to touch, refers to a
neural fiber, the axon of a neuron, which in some cases has a specialized
ending. Stimulation of a receptor causes the neuron to fire, sending a signal to a subsequent neuron across a synaptic connection. These electronic

transmissions constitute the language of the nervous system and underlie our conscious responses to objects and events.

In the cutaneous subsystem of touch, several populations of receptors have been identified, differing according to the type of stimulation that causes the neuron to fire. Some receptors, called *mechanoreceptors*, respond to stimulation in the form of pressure applied to the skin. These receptors terminate in special endings. Other neurons are "naked" at their terminus. These include the thermoreceptors, which respond to ambient and changing temperature. There are separate thermoreceptors to detect warmth and coolness. Still other neural fibers have been identified that correspond to itch and different types of pain.

Two features characterize the mechanoreceptors, which are pressure sensitive. One is adaptation rate; that is, how quickly the receptors stop firing when the world remains constant. The receptors may be fast adapting (FA), in which case they cease firing in the presence of unchanging stimulation, or they may be slow adapting (SA), in which case they fire throughout the application of a single continuous stimulus (within limits). To make FA receptors respond repeatedly, a mechanical source must be applied, removed, and reapplied, as is the case with a vibrating surface. FA receptors tend to have preferred vibratory frequencies, where the stimulus amplitude (strength) needed to invoke a response is minimized.

The second feature used to categorize the cutaneous mechanoreceptors is the receptive field. A receptive field is the area of skin to which a receptor is sensitive. Stimulation anywhere in a receptor's receptive field will cause it to fire, as long as the source is strong enough to exceed a minimum (called the threshold). Some mechanoreceptors have small receptive fields. As a result, groups or populations of these receptors divide up the skin's real estate into small regions, much like the pixels on a computer monitor. The smaller their receptive fields, the more capable a neural population is of resolving pressure on the skin into distinct points. On the other hand, a large receptive field means that a single receptor fires when a stimulus is applied anywhere over a relatively large region of the skin. Receptors with larger fields tend to lie relatively deeply under the skin, whereas those with spatial acuity tend to be nearer the skin surface. This makes sense, in that it seems necessary to be close to the skin surface to partition it finely.

It turns out that the two features just described—adaptation rate and receptive field size—act as a 2 × 2 partitioning that categorizes mechanoreceptors into four types. There are fast adapting receptors with small and large receptive fields, called FA I and FA II, respectively. And there are likewise SA I and SA II classes, that is, slowly adapting receptors with small and large fields, respectively. The different fibers, when stimulated in isolation, induce different sensations, like flutter versus buzz.

The distribution of different types of receptors across the skin of the body is far from uniform. In particular, spatially acute receptors are packed into the fingertips. You can demonstrate this for yourself with a home-grown approximation to measuring the "two-point threshold." Bend a bit of wire (like a paper clip) into a U-shape and touch the tips of the U into your skin. Determine the minimal separation of the tips where they feel like two distinct points. Tips of a U that are close together may be perceived as separate on the fingertips, but the same U-shape will blend and seem like one point when placed on the back.

A recent addition to the catalog of touch receptors is a class associated with pleasant touch; they respond, for example, to mild stroking of the skin. These seem particularly to occur within skin surfaces that are hairy; that is, *not in* the most sensitive areas of the skin such as the fingertips or lips (McGlone, Vallbo, Olausson, Loken, & Wessberg, 2007).

A take-away message of this section, with potential relevance for marketing, is that the world of objects sensed through touch begins with contact. By virtue of different receptors, contact alone can arouse a variety of sensations. Those initial responses are converted by the perceptual system into a representation of object properties, as is described next.

From Receptors to Surface Properties

Why bother with neurophysiology when considering the role of touch in marketing? The answer has already been given: For some aspects of touch, the receptors deliver an immediate depiction of the contacted surface, with relatively little mediating processing. Apparent warmth and coolness have already been alluded to as features that are delivered so directly. Others include the presence of pressure discontinuities; for example, edges and holes or the instantaneous prick of a sharp point.

In addition to discontinuities, which are essentially binary signals (smooth or uneven), details of the shape of a surface contacted by the skin can also come from the primary responses of the receptors. Consider curvature: Just touch the surface of your pen with your fingertip and you have a clear impression of how it is curved. This happens because less pressure is produced by a surface as it curves away from the center of contact. The less the pressure, the lower the neural output from slowly adapting receptors. If those receptors have small receptive fields (as with SA I mechanoreceptors), from their outputs it is possible for the sensory system to assign a given sensation of pressure to a particular spatial location. The result is a sensory map of the pressure differential across the fingertip, and from this follows (with some additional brain processing) the perception of curvature.

A take-away message of this section, with potential relevance for marketing, is that mere contact with an object tells us quite a bit about its local properties: thermal, punctate, and geometric. That first touch by itself might have implications for consumer response. Yet, if we were to stop at mere contact, even with our spatially sensitive fingers, we would learn only a limited amount. The world sensed by touch expands dramatically when we go beyond contact to active exploration, as discussed next.

Haptic Exploratory Procedures and the Properties of Objects

Touch a table tennis ball and the outside of an egg. Which is rougher? It is likely you have done more than simply contacted the objects; you have rubbed them. Rubbing is what Lederman and Klatzky (1987) call an "exploratory procedure." It is a principled, stereotyped action pattern that is linked to an object property, in this case surface texture. Lederman and Klatzky showed that rubbing is not an isolated instance of purposive exploration. In general, when blindfolded people were asked to compare objects along some named dimension, like roughness or hardness, they moved their hands in systematic ways. The researchers constructed a catalog of these exploratory procedures and their associations with object properties.

For example, when asked to judge hardness, people exhibited an exploratory procedure called "pressure," which could take the form of pressing or twisting, but always exerted force on the object against a resisting force. Rubbing is a version of the exploratory procedure they called "lateral motion," which can be done with the finger, toe, or tongue, but always produces a sideways or shearing force against a surface. Why these patterns? It turns out that generally, the observed pattern of purposive exploration optimizes the neural signals that are used to compute the object property. Take temperature, for example. People judging the warmth or coolness of an object use "static contact"; that is, they place a large skin surface against the object and hold it steady. The large surface excites the maximum number of thermoreceptors, and signals from which converge. That is, static contact is effective to sense temperature because it creates signals from many thermal sensors distributed across space, which are summed by "downstream" neurons.

Experiments by Lederman and Klatzky (1987) confirmed that in general, the exploratory procedure that is spontaneously produced in conjunction with an object property is also the optimal one. If you want to know the roughness of a surface, you should rub, not use static contact.

Nevertheless, suboptimal exploration still turned out to be informative. By careful analysis, these researchers were able to show how well each exploratory procedure delivered information about each object property in their tested set. Some exploratory procedures turned out to be the most generally informative in that they provided at least a crude amount of information about several object properties. The winning exploratory procedures in this informativeness competition were enclosing an object (optimal for gross shape and size), lifting it (optimal for weight), and exploring its contours with the fingers (optimal for precise shape). Unfortunately, the last procedure, contour following, was very slow to execute, rendering it less useful.

It turns out, then, that simply enclosing and lifting an object is the most efficient way to learn about it quickly. And that is what people are observed to do when they are asked to quickly ascertain some feature. Only after the first grasp and lift do they tend to perform further, more specialized, exploration (Lederman & Klatzky, 1990). Grasping and lifting tell us a lot about an object, and when followed with specialized exploration as needed, the object leaps into life as a whole within the hand. It may be surprising to learn that people are able to recognize common objects by touch alone with virtually perfect accuracy, most often within a couple of seconds of exploration (Klatzky, Lederman, & Metzger, 1985).

There is an important flip side of effective exploration, namely, *ineffective* exploration. Some exploratory procedures are not generally informative; to the contrary, they are specialized. This specialization of exploration means that it is possible to handle an object without learning about some of its properties. If you touch an object with an exploratory procedure specialized for property X, you will not get information about properties Y and Z. Klatzky, Lederman, and Reed (1989) showed, for example, that people who explored a wafer-shaped object around its edges, in an effort to determine its precise shape, knew relatively little about its surface roughness.

A take-away message of this section, with potential relevance for marketing, is that it is important to think not only about seducing people into touching a product, but getting them to touch *in the right way*. Active exploration can enhance or limit what is learned about an object.

Touch in Relation to Vision

Decades ago, the sense of touch was considered by many as a weak form of vision. The pixel power of touch in comparison to vision is very coarse. The Braille symbol, which when seen in a public elevator is easy for our eyes to resolve into dots, is near the spatial limits of touch. (People with diabetes-induced blindness tend to suffer from loss of acuity in the fingertip as well, and generally they cannot easily learn Braille.) The poor-cousin view of touch in relation to vision was mistaken, however. The senses have complementary roles. They are not generally competing for the same information, with touch the loser.

To understand this point better, let's think about the properties of objects. It is useful to divide them into two broad classes: material and geometry. Material properties are generally defined as not depending on the shape of any particular sample. They include surface properties like roughness or stickiness or friction and other properties like compliance or elasticity. Geometric properties pertain to size and shape, although measures of shape in particular have proven difficult to define (pointiness? curviness?).

As a general rule, touch is most informative about material, and vision about geometry. The relative specializations of vision and touch have been demonstrated with a variety of experimental methods (see Klatzky & Lederman, 2007, for a review). By way of summary, material properties are more quickly accessed by touch relative to vision, and they are discriminated more precisely. The same applies to geometric properties for vision. I will describe two demonstrations of this specialization that have particular relevance to marketing.

The first demonstration of vision versus touch specialization comes from a task in which subjects were asked to judge which of two visible objects was greater along some scale (Klatzky, Lederman, & Matula, 1993). For example, they might be shown a pen and a toothbrush and asked which was heavier. The objects were physically placed just in front of the subjects so that they could see them and touch or not, as they pleased. However, they were asked to respond as quickly as possible, so that idle touching was discouraged. The experimental manipulations then comprised two variables: (a) the specific property being judged, and (b) difficulty of the comparison, as determined by the difference between the stimuli. With regard to judged property, on some trials, material properties such as weight, roughness, or hardness were queried; on others, the comparison pertained to geometric properties of size and shape complexity. With regard to difficulty, some judgments were easy, like the roughness of silk versus sandpaper, and others were difficult, like the relative size of a grape versus a marble.

The results were very clear: People did not bother to touch the objects when the judgment was easy, in which case they could see the difference or simply make their judgment on the basis of prior knowledge about the objects. They also did not tend to touch the objects when the judgment was difficult and the dimension of interest was geometric. However, when making difficult judgments about material, the participants tended to touch the objects, and in those cases, to explore them appropriately to ascertain the desired property. In short, this experiment shows a clear specialization of the haptic modality: It is used for difficult discriminations of material properties. If vision is effective, as with geometric and easy material comparisons, it is preferred, and why not? Touch, the proximal and active sense, is effortful, whereas vision, being distal, is cheap.

Interestingly, the same distribution of utility was observed in a mental-imagery version of the object-comparison task (Klatzky, Lederman, & Matula, 1991). In this case, the objects were presented verbally rather than tangibly on each trial. After answering a question as to which of two named objects was rougher, harder, or so on, the subject was asked about any mental images that had been present. (Each subject in the experiment was asked just one question, so as to maintain the spontaneity of the imagery.) Visual images of the objects were commonly reported, but in addition, when making difficult judgments about material, subjects frequently mentioned seeing their hand in the image, generally making appropriate exploratory procedures. Haptic imagery was reported in over 30% of difficult material judgments and in less than 5% of geometric ones. This intriguing finding suggests that imagined hand movement may somehow facilitate the processing of material object properties that are retrieved from memory. A follow-up brain-imaging study with the same task (Newman, Klatzky, Lederman, & Just, 2005) supported the distinction between material and geometric properties in imagery by showing that different patterns of brain activation were observed in the two types of judgments. Comparisons of geometric features differentially activated the intraparietal sulcus, associated with visual imagery, whereas questions about material features differentially activated the inferior extrastriate region, associated with processing of semantic object representations.

The second demonstration of visual versus touch specialization is a bit subtler. It concerns the mental salience of object properties; that is, their impact on imagination and thought (Klatzky, Lederman, & Reed, 1987). Participants in this experiment were asked to sort a large collection of hand-sized objects into three bins, so that similar objects were placed together. Before sorting, they were allowed to explore the set of objects, which revealed to them the nature of the problem: The objects had been designed so that they could be sorted into three groups by any of four features: size (small, medium, large), texture (coarse, medium, fine), compliance (soft, medium, rigid), or shape complexity (oval, hourglass, clover). These features were combined in all possible ways across the full set of objects, so that sorting by shape, for example, meant that a bin of exclusively oval objects would have to mix together objects having different size, texture, and compliance.

In short, participants had to choose what it meant for objects to be "similar" and hence to be aggregated or differentiated in sorting. The assumption behind the research is that the feature that partitions the objects is the most salient, perceptually and cognitively. As a further manipulation, participants were instructed as to the meaning of similarity. Some subjects were simply blindfolded and given no instruction. Others were blindfolded but told to think of what the objects looked like, and yet another group could see the objects. The intention was to determine how these instructions affected the relative salience of the different features.

The effects were very clear: When people had vision, they sorted exclusively by shape, and they touched the objects minimally, just enough to toss them into the bins. When people were blindfolded and had no biasing instructions, they tended to sort by surface texture and explored accordingly. But when they were blindfolded and told to think about what the objects looked like, they shifted to exploring the contours and sorting by shape. The implication is that when objects are touched but not seen, what comes to mind is their material more than their shape. When they are seen, even if touched, shape predominates in the impression of the objects, and visual imagination tilts toward shape salience in the same way.

Vision, and its preference for shape, may have dominated in the sorting task, but it is important to note that dominance of one sense over another is not universal. A more general model appears to apply when two senses both contribute information about the same feature of an object. Consider, for example, pinching a raised edge in space while looking at it. Both touch and vision tell you how big the edge is. According to the model, the two senses each contribute estimates of the edge's size, and the perceptual outcome is a weighted sum of the two together. One specific version of this model says that if people integrate optimally, they weight the contribution of each modality according to its statistical reliability. This model, called maximum-likelihood estimation, has been found to hold for some judgments involving vision and touch (Ernst & Banks, 2002). As a general rule, whether or not the weightings are optimal, vision should be weighted more than touch in judgments of geometry, with the reverse weighting for judgments of material.

A take-away message of this section, with potential relevance for marketing, is that it is important to think about what touch can add to people's interest in a product. Touch may offer relatively little added value when a product's utility or interest is determined by its geometry. On the other hand, invoking touch may be invaluable for products where material is key.

Eliciting or Inhibiting Touch: Speculations for Marketing

What follows are speculations about a role for eliciting touch in marking. I conceive of two stages of customer involvement where touch might be usefully induced. The first is when customers are exposed to a product, which they may or may not elect to touch. Seduce people into touching the object, and this alone might increase the potential to buy it. If the product has marketable material properties, eliciting an initial touch provides the opportunity for enhancing its attractiveness by conveying information and inducing pleasure. The second stage at which one might manipulate touch during marketing is postcontact. At this point, the goal would presumably be to guide customers to perform appropriate exploratory procedures, with the intention of optimizing the impact of the product's properties.

The goal of eliciting touch leads to the questions of when do people touch and when do they avoid it? The study of haptic perception from the perspective of cognitive science and neuroscience can give us insights, although the scientific perspective clearly does not tell the whole story. Here, supported by previous research, observation, and a bit of *chutzpah*, I suggest distinguishing among five types of elicited touch, as follows:

> *Information-Seeking Touch*: This is the touch that is exhibited when people are asked which is softer, a rose petal or a piece of velvet. It is intended to deliver discriminative information about object properties. Touch is necessary because the discrimination is relatively difficult, and the information desired pertains to an object's material. Occasionally, informative touching is post hoc rather than anticipatory; for example, a surface that looks slick, but on first contact is found to inhibit slip, may invite further exploration.

Hedonically Elicited Touch: Touching may be regulated by biological mechanisms related to emotion. Obviously, people avoid touching stimuli that they associate with pain; for example, objects that look very hot or sharp. Conversely, people may seek touch for its positive hedonic value. The receptors for pleasant touch, which respond to light stroking, may lead to a desire for certain kinds of contact, as when people stroke a fur coat. People may also anticipate positive emotions from touch. For example, oral touch could be elicited from the prospective pleasure of chewing or mouthing. The feel of fat constitutes an important dimension of gustatory enjoyment.

Aesthetics-Elicited Touch: Some objects in the world seem to invite touching: the soft skin of a baby, the smooth curve of a sculpture. In comparison to the biologically directed hedonic touch just described, the aesthetic pleasure in this contact is relatively subjective and variable across people (Peck & Childers, 2003). The spontaneity and variability of exploration in aesthetic contexts would make it difficult to predict or control for scientific study.

Compulsive Touching: Special cases involve the irresistible impulse to touch. The most important example is itch. Light, localized contact, as occurs when a mosquito lands on the skin, may also command touch.

Socially Elicited Touch: People touch others to communicate support or sympathy, in social rituals such as hand shaking, and in sex. This type of touch lies far from the scope of this chapter.

Of the foregoing categories of elicited touch, informative, aesthetic, and positively valenced hedonic touching appear to be the best candidates for marketing. Considering first informative touch, there are various avenues that might be pursued to elicit it. We know that people exhibit information-seeking touch when they wish to make difficult material discriminations. Offering tangible comparisons of material (the smoothness of two fine-grit sandpapers or the softness of two paper towels) is a potential means to elicit touching. Another avenue might be to devise products that have novel or unusual surfaces, particularly having extreme values along some tangible dimension. Because people have in mind a notion of the usual range of haptically accessible object properties, seeing an object that looks extreme or exceptional might elicit touch. We might reach for a piece of velvet because it looks so soft or a pebbly texture to feel its extreme bumpiness.

The elicitation of aesthetic or positive hedonic touch is more challenging. To my knowledge, there is no principled work on the attributes of objects that invite contact in pursuit of pleasurable sensation; this is an exciting area for research. There may be some form of haptically appealing geometry, for example. Observation suggests that people voluntarily feel objects with smooth, curved contours that fall within scope of the hand, for example. It would be very useful to experimentally explore the dimensions of objects that lead to aesthetic appeal. It is also possible that aesthetic interest could be elicited by having another person serve as a model. Seeing someone else enjoy touching is likely to pique one's own desire to touch.

Work of Peck and Childers (2003) suggests an important constraint on any general principles for eliciting touch, namely, that there are likely to be individual variations. People differ in their tendency to touch for both aesthetic or informational reasons, which Peck and Childers call autotelic and instrumental touch, respectively (although autotelic touch goes beyond aesthetic or hedonic goals to include impulse and compulsion). So-called high need for touch (NFT) individuals contact objects more, think about objects more, rely more on touch for evaluation, and process touch-related information more quickly.

Haptic Display Technology and Market Applications

Sights, sounds, and even scents can be readily simulated for marketing purposes. The physical object that corresponds to these events need not be present; it can be evoked by a picture, a recording, or an aerosol spray. In contrast, it is not easy to create haptic experience in the absence of a physical object. A picture of a terry-cloth towel does not substitute for the sensory experience of rubbing its textured surface. As we have seen, discriminating finely along material dimensions demands haptic input.

The difficulty of creating a haptic simulation represents a handicap for marketers of products whose value is based on their material properties. Obviously, technologies that rendered virtual objects for haptic exploration would have great value in marketing.

The desired level of simulation is far from attainable at present, but the technology for creating virtual tangible objects has been rapidly advancing (see Lin & Otaduy, 2008, for a review). Several commercial devices are available, such as the PHANTOM and a new magnetic-levitation device called Butterfly Haptics. These devices work by producing resisting forces according to a computer-generated model. For example, a simulated wall corresponds to "infinite" resistance (actually, the maximum stiffness of the device) along a continuous line in the workspace. Typically, the user guides a handle or thimble within a workspace, and when the location of a surface is encountered, the user experiences a resisting force generated according to the model. Simulations can be very complex. Force-feedback devices have been used for virtual object worlds, textures, spinal cords, or gallbladders, for example.

A drawback to most of these devices is that they simulate not the act of touching the world directly, but rather contact through some rigid intermediary, like a thimble or a stick. This situation eliminates the pressure map on the skin that is provided by the SA I mechanoreceptors, as well as eliminating an impression of the thermal properties of objects. Hence force-feedback devices rely heavily on kinesthetic signals to the positions of the limbs as they encounter forces from the virtual world rendered by the computer.

The limitations notwithstanding, force feedback provides a rich sense of the tangible surround. David Katz (1925) observed decades ago that when one feels the world through a stick, one feels the world, not the stick. Think of stirring a pot to keep something from sticking or burning; the impression is that the bottom of the pot is directly being explored. To some extent, at least, it seems that the requirement of a rigid barrier between object and skin may not be an insurmountable obstacle to creating virtual objects that people really feel. Lederman and Klatzky (1999) systematically evaluated people's ability to make perceptual judgments when their fingers were covered with a rigid sheath, which essentially eliminated the array of pressure sensation on the fingertip. What was lost was the ability to perceive pattern information, like the direction in which an edge was oriented. What was preserved on the skin was overall force and vibration, from which people retained an excellent ability to judge and discriminate texture. Force-feedback devices would preserve vibratory-based features, then, as well as providing kinesthetic cues to object contours.

There have been efforts to design fingertip array stimulators; for example, small pins driven by motors that force them into the skin to simulate a pattern. Such efforts have generally been problematic. Two specific difficulties are restrictions on the density with which pins can be packed and limits on the robustness of the stimulator. Augmenting force-feedback displays with heating or cooling devices has also simulated thermal signals. However, commercial devices with array or thermal stimulation do not seem to be a near-term possibility.

As for the marketing utility of commercially available force-feedback devices, a major problem at present is the tradeoff between quality and price. A vibrating joystick is cheap, but it will be low in temporal and spatial precision and not amenable to programming realistic models. Costs of high-bandwidth force-feedback devices at present are in the tens of thousands of dollars. Their expense and size preclude the idea of attaching haptic devices to the home computer for purposes of high-fidelity e-commerce. It should also be noted that every virtual world requires a model, generally of considerable complexity. Building the model constitutes a significant part of the cost of an application.

Conclusions

Touch-based advertising is in its infancy relative to use of sight and sound, and it lags behind scent. Touch presents unique problems but also unique possibilities. The purpose of this chapter was to improve understanding of the potential niche for touch in marketing. To summarize particularly salient points:

1. From the first moment of contact, touch provides a rich array of properties of the proximal surface, including temperature, local geometry, and material.
2. Active touching greatly expands the available information and creates a vivid impression of the object as a whole.
3. Touch is complementary to vision, offering fast and precise access to material relative to geometry. This distinction plays out even when objects are imagined.
4. People touch for a variety of reasons, some of which may be controllable by marketing.
5. Technology for virtual touch is a growing field, but at present it is limited by the types of cues it can present, the size of the apparatus, and the expense of the device.

References

Ernst, M. O., & Banks, M. S. (2002). Humans integrate visual and haptic information in a statistically optimal fashion. *Nature, 415*, 429–433.
Katz, D. (1925). *The world of touch.* (L. Krueger, Translation in 1989). Hillsdale, NJ: Erlbaum.
Klatzky, R. L., & Lederman, S. J. (2007). Object recognition by touch. In J. Rieser, D. Ashmead, F. Ebner, & A. Corn (Eds.), *Blindness and brain plasticity in navigation and object perception* (pp. 185–207). Mahwah, NJ: Erlbaum.
Klatzky, R. L., Lederman, S. J., & Matula, D. E. (1991). Imagined haptic exploration in judgments of object properties. *Journal of Experimental Psychology: Human Learning, Memory and Cognition, 17*, 314–322.

Klatzky, R. L., Lederman, S. J., & Matula, D. E. (1993). Haptic exploration in the presence of vision. *Journal of Experimental Psychology: Human Perception and Performance, 19*, 726–743.

Klatzky, R. L., Lederman, S. J., & Metzger, V. (1985). Identifying objects by touch: An "expert system." *Perception and Psychophysics, 37*, 299–302.

Klatzky, R. L., Lederman, S. J., & Reed, C. (1987). There's more to touch than meets the eye: The salience of object attributes for haptics with and without vision. *Journal of Experimental Psychology: General, 116*, 356–369.

Klatzky, R. L., Lederman, S. J., & Reed, C. (1989). Haptic integration of object properties: Texture, hardness, and planar contour. *Journal of Experimental Psychology: Human Perception and Performance, 15*, 45–57.

Lederman, S. J., & Klatzky, R. L. (1987). Hand movements: A window into haptic object recognition. *Cognitive Psychology, 19*, 342–368.

Lederman, S. J., & Klatzky, R. L. (1990). Haptic classification of common objects: Knowledge-driven exploration. *Cognitive Psychology, 22*, 421–459.

Lederman, S. J., & Klatzky, R. L. (1999). Sensing and displaying spatially distributed fingertip forces in haptic interfaces for teleoperator and virtual environment systems. *PRESENCE: Teleoperators and Virtual Environments, 8*, 86–103.

Lin, M., & Otaduy, M. (Eds.). (2008). *Haptic Rendering: Foundations, algorithms, and applications* (pp. 7–19). Wellesley, MA: A. K. Peters.

McGlone, F., Vallbo, A. B., Olausson, H., Loken, L. S., & Wessberg, J. (2007). Discriminative touch and emotional touch. *Canadian Journal of Experimental Psychology, 61*(3), 173–183.

Newman, S. D., Klatzky, R. L., Lederman, S. J., & Just, M. A. (2005). Imagining material versus geometric properties of objects: An fMRI study. *Cognitive Brain Research, 23*, 235–246.

Peck, J., & Childers, T. L. (2003). Individual differences in haptic information processing: The "Need for Touch" scale. *Journal of Consumer Research, 3*, 430–442.

4

Understanding the Role of Incidental Touch in Consumer Behavior

Andrea C. Morales

When thinking about how the five senses in general and touch in particular relate to marketing, one immediately thinks about how consumers use their senses to acquire information about products and services in a retail environment. Consumers actively engage different senses or combinations of senses to help inform their purchase decisions. For instance, consumers clearly rely on their sense of smell when choosing which perfume to buy, but sight could also play a key role by influencing perceptions and preferences for one bottle shape over another (Folkes & Matta, 2004; Raghubir & Greenleaf, 2006; Raghubir & Krishna, 1999). Likewise, the way a bottle feels when touched might also impact product choice. Indeed, researchers have shown that information gathered through touch can have a significant influence on product evaluations (Mooy & Robben, 2002; Peck & Childers, 2003) and even hinder online shopping precisely because it does not provide consumers with tactile information (Alba et al., 1997; Citrin, Stem, Spangenberg, & Clark, 2003; McCabe & Nowlis, 2003). But what about cases where touch is not used for information seeking about products? Will it still have an impact on consumer behavior? This is the focus of the current chapter.

In Joann Peck's chapter in this book, she proposed a taxonomy of touch in marketing that divided consumer touch into two broad categories: (a) instrumental touch—"touch as a means to an end," and (b) hedonic touch—"touch as an end in itself." Although these two categories accurately describe the different ways and reasons consumers touch products, the taxonomy leaves out a third category of touch that can also have a significant influence on consumer behavior—*incidental touch*. In addition to actively touching products, when shopping in a retail environment, consumers may also observe other consumers or other products touching the items for which they are shopping. These observed forms of physical contact between consumers and products are two categories of incidental touch. In this chapter I describe how these two categories of incidental touch, until recently ignored by the marketing literature, can have powerful effects on consumers by altering their evaluations and purchase intentions.

Incidental Touch by Other Consumers

We have all seen it happen and many of us are culprits ourselves. Instead of taking the outer-most cereal box, we reach behind for another one; we try on one shirt in the dressing room, but purchase another from the bottom of the stack that is still neatly folded and in the protective packaging. It is clear from these examples that consumers prefer to buy products that appear untouched by others, but why is this the case? When consumer touching actually damages a product (i.e., crushed cereal inside a well-handled box or makeup stains on a shirt), it is just a desire for quality driving the preference for untouched items. But what about cases where the product is completely unaffected by consumer touching? Why do consumers still prefer to buy products that no one else has touched? Research in anthropology provides some answers.

The Law of Contagion

In studying the beliefs and practices of primitive cultures and how they view the physical world, anthropologists discovered the laws of sympathetic magic (Mauss, 1902/1972; Tylor, 1871/1974). Although these "laws" are not necessarily explicit, they govern how people think the world works, and as such, have a strong influence on behavior. The law of contagion is the idea that when a person or object (the source) touches another person or object (the target), the source will continue to influence the target even after contact has ceased (Rozin & Nemeroff, 1990). This is because the source is believed to transfer some or all of its essential properties to the target upon contact (Nemeroff & Rozin, 1994).

Although anthropologists identified the law of contagion as the basis for many of the magical practices and rituals observed in traditional cultures such as voodoo and strict hierarchical rules for meal preparation (Meigs, 1984), work in psychology (Rozin, Millman, & Nemeroff, 1986) showed that modern, Western cultures also behave in ways that suggest they, too, follow the law of contagion and believe that "once in contact, always in contact." For example, they found that once a sterilized cockroach had touched a drink or a person they disliked had worn a shirt, nothing could be done to make these items more desirable; the contact with a negative object or person permanently altered perceptions. Notably, participants in these studies often could not or would not explain what was driving their lowered perceptions of touched items, since acknowledging a belief in the law of contagion might make them seem foolish or silly. Nevertheless, this work clearly demonstrates that contagion beliefs exist and influence behavior in both primitive as well as advanced societies.

So how might contagion effects change evaluations of products touched by other consumers? The law of contagion argues that when a source touches a target, the source has a permanent influence on the target. Thus, evaluations of the touched product will depend completely on the source doing the touching. If the source is negative, evaluations of the target product should be lower, but if the source is positive, evaluations of the target product should be higher. Although both forms of contagion are theoretically possible, outside of a consumer context, previous research has indicated that negative contagion effects, where contact with a source devalues a target, are more powerful than positive contagion, where contact with a source enhances the value of the target (Rozin & Kalat, 1971). Indeed, until recently, no experimental evidence in either the psychology or marketing literature had supported a significant, positive contagion effect. However, recent work in marketing has demonstrated significant effects for both negative and positive contagion in a consumer context. Both are described in detail below.

Negative Contagion Effects

Evidence for negative contagion effects is relatively easy to find. Anecdotal evidence and articles in the trade press provide numerous examples of the strong aversion consumers tend to exhibit toward touched products. In what can only be called a bittersweet consumer paradox, consumers really like touching products (e.g., towels are touched on average six times before purchase; Underhill, 2000), but they really dislike other people touching products they plan to buy. As mentioned previously, consumers often bypass the first item on a rack or stack of products and instead reach for the fresh one behind or below. O'Reilly, Rucker, Hughes, Gorang, and

Hand (1984) found that 76% of survey participants indicated they would not buy used underclothing and 20% refused to purchase used overcoats. And in his bestselling book *Why We Buy* (2000), Paco Underhill talks about the problems retailers face with consumers touching display products and how they can effectively manage the negative effects. In all of these examples, the person touching or originally owning the products is anonymous, so the lower perceptions of the touched products cannot be attributed to specific negative associations with the contact source, but instead demonstrate a general fear of contamination; touched products are less desirable simply because they have been in physical contact with someone else. But why?

The reason evaluations of products touched by other consumers are lower is because physical contact leads to feelings of disgust toward the contaminated items (Argo, Dahl, & Morales, 2006). Disgust has been defined as "revulsion at the prospect of (oral) incorporation of an offensive substance" (Rozin & Fallon, 1987, p. 23; see also Angyal, 1941), emphasizing the strong relationship between disgust and physical contact with the human body. However, this does not mean that physical contact is necessary to evoke disgust; oftentimes people experience disgust just thinking about touching or even being near certain objects. Disgust evokes a feeling state of revulsion, and this feeling state leads to an implicit action tendency to distance oneself from surrounding objects (Rozin, Haidt, & McCauley, 1993). Thus, when another shopper touches the product a consumer is planning to purchase and elicits disgust, evaluations of the touched product will decrease as the consumer tries to pull away from the cause of disgust. As such, disgust mediates consumer evaluations for products that are touched by others. In addition to the consumer context, disgust has been identified as the underlying mechanism driving contagion effects in food rejection, disease, and moral taint (Rozin et al., 1993).

Argo et al. (2006) examined specifically how other shoppers can trigger feelings of disgust in consumers simply by touching products before them. Building off of the law of contagion, they developed a theory of consumer contamination that shows when consumers become cognizant that another shopper has previously touched a product, their evaluations of and purchase intentions for that same product decrease. This occurs even when a product is objectively unharmed by the physical contact, indicating an underlying contamination process at work. In order to be more certain that the theory they were testing held true in the "real world," instead of documenting these effects in the lab, the researchers instead conducted three field studies in an actual retail shopping environment during regular store hours. Despite the complexity this added to the investigation, the contagion effects they documented were large in magnitude and quite robust.

Previous research on contagion and disgust had shown that contagion effects were stronger when contamination was made more salient (Angyal, 1941). Thus, Argo et al. (2006) followed up on this result by varying the degree to which a T-shirt appeared to have been touched by another shopper. In doing so, they were able to demonstrate how different "contamination cues," including proximity to contact, time elapsed since contact, and the number of contact sources, could exacerbate or mitigate contagion effects in a retail setting by making contamination more or less apparent.

In all of these consumer contamination studies, participants were instructed to find a particular T-shirt (the target shirt) and try it on. The researchers then manipulated proximity to contact by changing the location in the store where participants found the target shirt. Consistent with social impact theory (SIT; Latané, 1981), which proposes a force will have the greatest impact on a target when it is in close proximity as opposed to farther away (Latané & Wolf, 1981), the idea was that when the shirt was closer to the point of contact with another shopper, contamination would be more salient, and evaluations of the shirt would be lower. Depending on condition, participants found the shirt either hanging on a rack in the regular clothing section of the store, on the return rack of the dressing room, or inside the dressing room. As predicted, evaluations of the shirt were higher the farther away it was from the point of contact; evaluations were highest when it was on the regular rack, lower when it was on the return rack of the dressing room, and lowest when it was inside the dressing room. In all cases, however, the target shirt was in perfect condition and untouched by others. It was only the *perception* of contact with another shopper that led to it seeming contaminated and drove the drop in evaluations across conditions.

In a second study, the researchers manipulated time since contact to see whether the "once in contact, always in contact" belief about permanent contagion effects also held true in a consumer context (Rozin, Markwith, & McCauley, 1994). Arguing for more temporary contagion effects, in their research on construal level theory, Trope and Liberman (2003) show that temporal distance systematically alters the way individuals mentally construe future events with people forming high-level construals (i.e., abstract representations) for things in the distant future and low-level construals (i.e., more concrete and vivid details) for events in the near future. Although this work has focused only on future events, the same construal theory principles should apply to past events as well, thereby reducing the salience of contamination when more time has passed after contact. Indeed, in this study, contagion effects were only found when participants were told that the target shirt "had just been tried on," but were not significant when the shirt "had not been tried on for a few days." In contrast to other contexts, this finding suggests that in an interpersonal, retail context, contagion effects dissipate over time.

Finally, Argo et al. (2006) examined how consumer contagion effects vary depending on the number of contact sources. According to SIT (Latané, 1981), the more sources, the stronger the impact on the target; therefore, more sources of contact predict stronger contamination effects and lower evaluations of the target shirt. However, in this context, the more sources of contact (i.e., the more people who tried on the same shirt), the more popular the shirt may appear to be. Thus, even though being touched by another shopper generally lowers evaluations due to contamination effects, having a lot of people try it on may also serve to heighten evaluations by signaling popularity. Although plausible, no support was found for the popularity argument. When participants believed that lots of other people had tried on the target shirt, contamination effects were significantly stronger (with product evaluations and purchase intentions being significantly lower) than when participants believed only one other person had tried on the shirt.

It is important to note that in the Argo et al. (2006) consumer contamination studies, consumers did not observe the target product being touched by another shopper but instead inferred that contact had taken place through the different contamination cues. This suggests that by default consumers infer that the anonymous other who touched the target product before them is an individual who elicits disgust. Given that these studies took place on a college campus, in reality it is just as likely that rather than being a disgusting person, the anonymous other shopper was an average-looking college student or even a highly attractive co-ed. Yet, when faced with contamination cues that imply previous touching has occurred, consumers naturally think the worst of the other shopper and feel disgusted by any unobserved touching. It appears that when it comes to incidental touch, our imaginations are often more disgusting than reality. These feelings of disgust then lead to lower evaluations and purchase intentions for the touched products.

But what would happen if instead of inferring contact had occurred through contamination cues, consumers actually saw the other shopper who touched a product before they had? Would the same effects still hold?

According to the law of contagion, if a positive source comes in contact with a target object, the value of the target object will be enhanced. By this reasoning, if consumers believe that an extremely attractive shopper has touched a product before they had, evaluations of the product might increase rather than decrease. To test this hypothesis, in a second paper described below, Argo and her colleagues ran a similar set of studies, but this time manipulated precisely who the contact source was. Specifically, they examined whether the effects of incidental touch by consumers are different when other shoppers of varying levels of attractiveness touched products.

Positive Contagion Effects

Research in psychology has provided mixed support for the existence of positive contagion effects. Although the law of contagion predicts positive effects resulting from contact with positive sources, demonstrating such effects has proven difficult in response to questionnaires. In two different studies where participants were asked to imagine different positive sources (e.g., a lover, an admired religious figure) coming in contact with various target objects (e.g., a blouse, a toothbrush), only a few sources resulted in significant increases in value for the target objects and some showed no change or even decreases in value (Nemeroff & Rozin, 1994; Rozin et al., 1986). Whenever evidence for positive contagion has been found, the contact source was a liked or aspirational other, suggesting that positive contagion is largely dependent on precisely who is doing the touching.

Building on this previous research, Argo, Dahl, and Morales (2008) ran several studies where they varied the attractiveness of the contact source, successfully providing the first experimental support for the existence of positive contagion effects. The results of their studies demonstrate consumer evaluations of a target product are actually higher when male consumers believe that a highly attractive (vs. average) female has touched the product before they had, as well as when female consumers believe that a highly attractive (vs. average) male has touched the product before they had. Thus, positive contagion effects exist in a retail context but only when the contact source is highly attractive *and* the opposite gender of the target consumer. When the contact source and the gender of the target consumer are the same (either female/female or male/male), consumer evaluations are unaffected by the contact source trying on the target shirt. Moreover, in a third study, they show that these positive contagion effects go away when the target shirt previously worn by a highly attractive source of the opposite gender is dry cleaned. Consistent with a physical model of contagion (Rozin et al., 1986), cleaning the garment reduces the positive nature of the contagion by wiping away the physical trace or "essence" that the highly attractive other left on the shirt when he or she touched the product. In this case, leaving products dirty is actually better, as it leads to higher evaluations and purchase intentions when highly attractive consumers touch them.

Incidental Touch by Products

Contact between other consumers and products is one form of incidental touch that can impact consumer behavior, but shoppers also frequently observe contact between products. For example, as a practice, grocery stores strive to utilize every square inch of shelf space; consequently, almost every product in stock is likely to be touching the product next to it on the shelf. Even in cases where contact between products is minimized at the retail level, once consumers place items inside a basket or cart, a second stage of contact occurs between products when they brush against one another or are stacked upon each other in a tighter, more confined space.

Despite the frequency with which incidental touch between products is likely to occur, in order for the contact to result in contagion effects, at least one of the products involved needs to elicit disgust. As discussed previously, the law of contagion suggests that negative sources are able to contaminate target objects through direct, physical contact with them. Applying this law to the current context, product contagion occurs when disgusting products come in contact with other products, making them less desirable. Because people believe disgusting products (as opposed to products that induce other forms of negative affect) transfer general or specific offensive properties to the target products they touch, they alone will contaminate products upon contact. If a product does not initially have offensive properties to transfer to a target, it cannot contaminate another product through touch alone.

If disgust-inducing products are necessary for contagion effects to occur between products, a natural question to ask is how many products actually induce disgust? Are such products readily available in the marketplace, or are there so few that contagion is not an issue worth studying? Morales and Fitzsimons (2007) answered these questions by having consumers report the level of disgust they experienced when thinking about the top 100 supermarket sellers (as defined by the Food Institute's Food

Industry Review 2004). Their study found that consumers rate 6 of the top 10 nonfood supermarket sellers, as well as many other top selling food and nonfood items, at least moderately disgusting (a mean disgust rating of 5 or higher on a 10-point scale). These items are not obscure products that consumers rarely purchase or see in the store, but are instead things such as trash bags, cat litter, diapers, mayonnaise, shortening and oil, cigarettes, and feminine napkins; products that are frequently purchased, common household items. Rather than being a trivial issue for consumer behavior, these results suggest that disgust and contagion are likely to impact behavior even on routine shopping trips and warrant further attention from researchers.

Consumers Touching Products

Before looking at the effects of incidental touching between products, with so many of the top selling products evoking disgust in consumers, it is first important to establish how consumers themselves react to direct, physical contact with such products. Indeed, if consumers feel contaminated when they touch disgusting products, they may also believe the same contamination process occurs between products. Morales and Fitzsimons (2007) examined this issue by having participants either carry a disgusting product (feminine napkins) in its protective packaging back to their seats, thereby touching the product, or look very closely at, but not touch it before reporting evaluations on a survey. As the law of contagion would predict, they found that consumers reported feeling more dirty, gross, revolted, and disgusted when they actually had contact with the disgusting product versus when they were only looking at, but not touching it. Although most would be reluctant to state it explicitly, consumers responded as though the disgusting product contaminated their hands by passing its offensive properties to them upon contact. Looking at the disgusting product and thinking about the negative associations it evokes were not enough to elicit such a strong response; physical touch was necessary for consumers to experience feelings of contamination. Although in reality the product (still in its package and sterilized) was not harmful in any way, because it elicits disgust, it was perceived as having the power to contaminate. The study above shows this to be true for products contaminating consumers, but do products also have the ability to contaminate one another? And if so, to what degree?

Products Touching Other Products

Building on the idea of disgusting products having the power to contaminate, Morales and Fitzsimons (2007) developed a theory of product
contagion that demonstrates how disgust-inducing products can influence evaluations by touching other products. They ran a series of studies
where participants observed four products either inside a grocery cart or
on a shelf, with the middle two products either touching or separated by a
6-inch space. One of the middle products was a source product that elicits
disgust, and the other was a neutral target product, so in all cases, the
disgusting product was either touching or not touching the neutral target product. Across studies, they found that when the source product was
next to, but not touching, the target product, perceptions of contamination
did not occur and evaluations of the target product remained unchanged.
However, when the source product was touching the target product, participants believed the disgusting product contaminated the target product,
thereby lowering evaluations of it. These effects were found at a general
level, making a target product overall less desirable, as well as at a specific level, where a source product (e.g., lard) could contaminate a target
product (e.g., rice cakes) by passing on its undesirable attribute (e.g., fat) to
the target (e.g., fattening rice cakes). Originally, they also expected product contagion effects to be stronger in cases where the target product was
consumable (e.g., cookies) versus nonconsumable (e.g., notebook paper),
as prior work has established a powerful relationship between disgust and
contact with one's own body (Angyal, 1941; Rozin & Fallon, 1987), but
they found no difference in contagion effects across target products. Being
touched by a disgusting product led to contamination regardless of the
degree of contact a product had with consumers' bodies.

Based on the above results it is clear that incidental touching between
products can alter evaluations of the touched products, but how long do
these changes last? To address this question, Morales and Fitzsimons (2007)
had participants look at the four products with the source and target product either touching or not touching, but then waited to ask evaluations of
the products for more than an hour. Not only did contact still lead to lower
ratings of the touched product, but it also resulted in a significant difference
in choice. Participants were given the choice of sampling a cookie from the
target box of cookies (which were rated higher on taste) or from a different box of cookies (which were rated lower on taste). In the nontouching
condition, a larger percentage of participants chose the higher rated, target cookies than those in the touching condition, where the target cookies

were higher rated but also thought to be contaminated by the disgusting product. These results indicate that product contagion can not only have a significant impact on product evaluations, but that this impact persists across time and can have an enduring effect on consumer behavior.

Morales and Fitzsimons (2007) also highlight the unique nature of disgust with regard to contagion effects by showing that contamination does not occur for products that induce other nondisgusting, negative feelings. When the source product was one that induces frustration and anger (e.g., income tax software) instead of disgust, ratings of the target product did not differ whether the source product was touching or not touching the target product. Since disgusting products are believed to have contaminating properties that they can pass to other products upon contact, only disgusting source products generate contagion effects. Moreover, since disgust alone is associated with the implicit action tendency to pull away from surrounding objects, contamination will only occur in situations where disgust is evoked.

Finally, this work also shows that product contagion and experiences of disgust more generally have a strong visual component. When target products were in opaque rather than transparent packages and consumers literally could not see the source product touching the target, no contamination was perceived to have occurred. This finding has important implications for marketers with regard to product packaging and managing contagion effects in the retail environment, but it also speaks to the interaction between touch and vision that Roberta Klatzky discusses in depth in her chapter in this book and provides an interesting avenue for future research. In order for contagion to occur in this case, consumers have to see the source product coming in contact with the target product. As mentioned previously, however, contamination cues alone are enough to trigger contagion effects between other consumers and products. Consumers do not have to see another shopper touching a product for consumer contamination to occur; they only have to know that it has been previously touched. Thus, it seems there is a difference in the way touch and vision interact for the two forms of incidental touch, with vision being optional for touch by other consumers to have an impact on evaluations but necessary for touch between products.

Conclusions and Future Research

Though relatively new to the marketing literature, studies show that incidental touch can have a significant impact on consumer behavior. Whether a consumer decides at the last second not to buy a pair of jeans because the price tag has been ripped off, indicating that someone else had purchased and returned it, or puts the loaf of bread back on the shelf after it touches a box of trash bags inside the grocery cart, the effects of incidental touch are widespread and far-reaching. To date, researchers have identified and examined two forms: incidental touch by other consumers and incidental touch between products. However, clearly there are additional forms and combinations that deserve consideration, with touch between consumers, touch between employees, touch between products and consumers, and touch between consumers and employees being obvious contenders. When it comes to incidental touch involving consumers, future work should also look more closely at how contagion effects differ depending on the roles and individual characteristics of the consumers. Prior work has already examined touch by other shoppers and sales associates, as well as the positive effects of physical attractiveness, but there are numerous factors that might also influence the way consumers respond to incidental touch. In addition, more research should investigate how incidental touch interacts with the other senses. As mentioned above, vision and touch have a complicated relationship when it comes to the effects of incidental touch, but it is likely that there are also interesting interactions with the other senses just waiting to be discovered. Stay tuned.

References

Alba, J., Lynch, J., Weitz, B., Janiszewski, C., Lutz, R., Sawyer, A., et al. (1997, July). Interactive home shopping: Consumer, retailer, and manufacturer incentives to participate in electronic marketplaces. *Journal of Marketing, 61*, 38–54.

Angyal, A. (1941). Disgust and related aversions. *Journal of Abnormal and Social Psychology, 36*, 393–412.

Argo, J. J., Dahl, D. W., & Morales, A. C. (2006, April). Consumer contamination: How consumers react to products touched by others. *Journal of Marketing, 70*, 81–94.

Argo, J. J., Dahl, D. W., & Morales A. C. (2008, December). Positive consumer contagion: Responses to attractive others in a retail context. *Journal of Marketing Research, 45*(6), 690–701.

Citrin, A. V., Stem, D. E., Spangenberg, E. R., & Clark, M. J. (2003). Consumer need for tactile input: An Internet retailing challenge. *Journal of Business Research, 56*(11), 915–922.

Folkes, V. S., & Matta, S. (2004, September). The effect of package shape on consumers' judgments of product volume. *Journal of Consumer Research, 31*, 390–401.

The Food Institute. (2004). *The Food Institute's food industry review 2004*. Elmwood Park, NJ: Author.

Latané, B. (1981). The psychology of social impact. *American Psychologist, 36*(4), 343–356.

Latané, B., & Wolf, S. (1981). The social impact of majorities and minorities. *Psychological Review, 88*(5), 438–453.

Mauss, M. (1972). *A general theory of magic* (R. Brain, Trans.). New York: Norton. (Original work published in 1902).

McCabe, D. B., & Nowlis, S. M. (2003). Effect of examining actual products or product descriptions on consumer preference. *Journal of Consumer Psychology, 13*(4), 431–439.

Meigs, A. S. (1984). *Food, sex, and pollution: A New Guinea religion*. New Brunswick, NJ: Rutgers University Press.

Mooy S. C., & Robben, H. S. J. (2002). Managing consumers' product evaluations through direct product experience. *Journal of Product and Brand Management, 11*(6–7), 432–445.

Morales, A. C., & Fitzsimons, G. J. (2007, May). Product contagion: Changing consumer evaluations through physical contact with "disgusting" products. *Journal of Marketing Research, 44*, 272–283.

Nemeroff, C. J., & Rozin, P. (1994). The contagion concept in adult thinking in the United States: Transmission of germs and of interpersonal influence. *Ethos. Journal of the Society for Psychological Anthropology, 22*, 158–186.

O'Reilly, L., Rucker, M., Hughes, R., Gorang, M., & Hand, S. (1984). The relationship of psychological and situational variables to usage of a second-order marketing system. *Academy of Marketing Science Journal, 12*(3), 53–76.

Peck, J., & Childers, T. L. (2003, April). To have and to hold: The influence of haptic information on product judgments. *Journal of Marketing, 67*(2), 35–48.

Raghubir, P., & Greenleaf, E. (2006, April). Ratios in proportion: What should be the shape of the package? *Journal of Marketing, 70*(2), 95–107.

Raghubir, P., & Krishna, A. (1999, August). Vital dimensions: Biases in volume estimates. *Journal of Marketing Research, 36*(3), 313–326.

Rozin, P., & Fallon, A.E. (1987). A perspective on disgust. *Psychological Review, 94*(1), 23–41.

Rozin, P., Haidt, J., & McCauley, C. (1993). Disgust. In M. Lewis, and J. Haviland (Eds.), *Handbook of emotions* (pp. 575–594). New York: Guilford.

Rozin, P., & Kalat, J. W. (1971). Specific hungers and poison avoidance as adaptive specializations of learning. *Psychological Review, 78*, 459–486.

Rozin, P., Markwith, M., & McCauley, C. (1994). Sensitivity to indirect contacts with other persons: AIDS aversion as a composite of aversion to strangers, infection, moral taint, and misfortune. *Journal of Abnormal Psychology, 103*(3), 495–504.

Rozin, P., Millman, L., & Nemeroff, C. (1986). Operation of the laws of sympathetic magic in disgust and other domains. *Journal of Personality and Social Psychology, 40*(4), 703–712.

Rozin, P., & Nemeroff C. (1990). The laws of sympathetic magic: A psychological analysis of similarity and contagion, in *Cultural psychology: Essays on comparative human development,* James E. Stigler, Richard A. Shweder, and Gilbert Herdt, eds. New York: Cambridge University Press, 205–232.

Trope, Y., & Liberman, N. (2003). Temporal construal. *Psychological Review, 110*(3), 403–421.

Tylor, E. B. (1974). *Primitive culture: Researches into the development of mythology, philosophy, religion, art, and custom.* New York: Gordon Press. (Original work published in 1871).

Underhill, P. (2000). *Why we buy: The science of shopping.* New York: Simon and Schuster.

5

Informational and Affective Influences of Haptics on Product Evaluation
Is What I Say How I Feel?

Terry L. Childers and Joann Peck

The role of touch in product evaluation is emerging as an important area of study in marketing and consumer behavior (Peck & Childers, 2003a, 2003b; Peck & Childers, 2008). The chapter by Peck in this book provides a comprehensive review of the role of touch, and thus we focus our discussion in this chapter on haptic product evaluation. The studies in marketing conducted to date on haptic product evaluation have used questionnaire-oriented responses and scales that are subject to a number of limitations produced through various forms of response biases (cf., Viswanathan, 2005). When utilized, responses of a self-report nature are potentially more accurate at capturing the more cognitive informational influences of touch. In contrast, self-report measures may be more seriously challenged in representing affective-based influences of touch. This has become more significant as several recent studies have examined in greater depth how touch may influence product evaluation through a more affective route to persuasion (Krishna & Morrin, 2008; Peck & Wiggins, 2006). Thus, current studies that find support for haptic product evaluation through both informational and affective or hedonic forms of touch have assumed that self-report methodologies converge with how individuals actually behave in the marketplace. The primary purpose of this chapter is to report on research that examines this correspondence for both informational and affective forms of haptic product evaluation.

Haptic Attributes and Product Evaluation

Whether a consumer feels the need to explore a product haptically will partially depend on the salience of haptic attributes of the product. One factor that may affect the salience of haptic properties has been referred to as stimulus-set discriminability. Simply, this states that if all stimuli or products in a category have similar values along a dimension, then this dimension should not be highly salient (Klatzky, Lederman, & Reed, 1987). For example, most consumers perceive that the product category of clothing varies on material attributes such as texture (or perhaps softness) and weight, and consequently it is more probable that consumers would want to touch these products prior to purchase.

In contrast, for a product category such as compact disks or books, most people would not perceive product category discriminability of a haptic attribute. McCabe and Nowlis (2003) demonstrate this finding through a self-report-based increased likelihood of purchase. Products varying on haptic attributes (e.g., carpeting or bath towels) were directly examined through touch relative to products that emphasized geometric (shape) discriminability (e.g., videotapes and containers of motor oil or soup). Similarly, these informational influences of touch should be reflected in alternative behaviors, such as the time spent touching products during product evaluation. Even more important, a behavioral indicator should be sensitive enough to capture variations in discriminability of the material attributes across different products. Lastly, a behavioral measure may be useful in differentiating haptic responses of a diagnostic informational nature from a more affective oriented evaluation.

Informational Touch: Self-Report Versus Behavioral Measures

"If investigators are to make inferences about touch on the basis of such measures (self-report), it seems necessary to validate these claims by comparing scores on questionnaires and behavioral data" (Jones & Brown, 1996, p. 148). Given the predominance of self-report methodologies and the recency of touch to marketing, the correspondence between self-report measures and behavioral measures is important to verify.

> **H1:** For product categories lower (higher) in a self-report-based discrimination of their material properties, less (more) time will be spent touching during product evaluation.

Exploratory Procedure Hand Movements and "Need for Touch"

The nature of the time spent haptically evaluating products should also be informative. Klatzky and Lederman (1992, 1993; Lederman & Klatzky, 1987) have documented linkages between hand movement profiles (exploratory procedures [EPs]) and the haptic perception of specific material properties. When individuals need to assess texture, they engage in the *lateral motion* EP, which consists of rubbing the fingers back and forth across the surface of an object; for hardness, individuals engage in the *pressure* EP, which consists of squeezing or poking the object; for temperature, they engage in the *static contact* EP (laying the hand on the object without moving it); for weight, individuals use the *unsupported holding* EP, which consists of resting the object flat in the hand and lifting it away from any supporting surface, often repeatedly. This research suggests that consumers will use specific haptic EPs depending on the product evaluated and the information to be assessed. For instance, when evaluating a sweater consumers will use the lateral motion EP to assess the sweater's texture.

We conjecture that persons higher in their need for touch (NFT) are more likely to have chronic information accessible and to seek haptic information and to use it as they form judgments. Research has found that chronically accessible categories are used more efficiently, allowing one to encode relevant information in less time than people who are non-chronic (Bargh & Thein, 1985). At first glance, this may suggest that persons higher in their NFT may spend less time performing the haptic EPs when evaluating a product compared to those low in their NFT. However, a useful distinction needs to be made concerning the type of information extracted. High NFT individuals may spend *less* time extracting haptic information, such as weight (of a computer or cell phone using the unsupported holding EP) or the responsiveness of the keys of a calculator or microwave (using the pressure EP), of an object.

In contrast, the softness of an object (assess by the lateral motion EP) has been associated with a pleasant sensory feeling (Bushnell & Boudreau, 1991; Essick, James, & McGlone, 1999). This pleasant sensory feedback may encourage high NFT persons to forgo their efficiency in processing haptic information, and it turn, to enjoy this pleasant feedback. Peck and Wiggins (2006) recently demonstrated a related outcome of this predicted effect using self-report methods. Participants received a pamphlet that contained a manipulation eliciting positive haptic associations associated with softness (a feather). The pamphlet containing this positive haptic manipulation elevated attitudes toward the message (pamphlet) for individuals high in NFT. Similarly at the behavioral level, we expect individuals higher in their NFT will engage in the lateral motion EP (to assess softness) for a longer period of time than their low NFT counterparts. This leads to a hypothesis concerning the times of EPs performed and the interaction with the individual difference NFT.

> **H2:** Individuals high in their "need for touch" will perform the lateral motion exploratory procedure (softness) longer than those low in their "need for touch" while the reverse is expected for the unsupported holding (weight) and the pressure (hardness) exploratory procedures.

Study

Overview

This experiment tests H1 and H2 and documents the various haptic exploratory procedures used by consumers. This study has two primary objectives. The first is to demonstrate that product categories differ in their salience of haptic information as measured by the time spent extracting haptic information (by using EPs) during product evaluation. Also, this experiment examines the correspondence between the self-report measure (that touch is important to product evaluation in certain product categories) and the behavioral measure (actual hand movements and time touching). In addition, this study looks at the individual difference NFT as a moderator of time extracting different types of material properties. The experiment was a 3 (product-based salience of haptic attributes) × 2 (product replicates) × 2 (need for touch) design with product-based salience of haptic attributes within subjects factor and product replicates and need for touch between subjects factors.

Procedure

One hundred and seventy-five undergraduate students were videotaped as they evaluated three products. A warm-up procedure was used (cf., Bettman & Park, 1980; Biehal & Chakravarti, 1982) consisting of individuals evaluating a pen. Following this, each product (participants evaluated three products in total) drawn from three categories differing in potential haptic attribute salience was positioned on a raised table. Two replicates were used and the order of product presentation was counterbalanced between participants. Each participant was told that he or she should evaluate the product. After each product was evaluated, the participant went to a nearby cubicle while the experimenter set up the next product for examination.

Following the product examinations, participants filled out a questionnaire that included the NFT scale, among other measures. After completion, participants were asked whether they knew the purpose of the study. No subject realized that the focus of the camera was to videotape the participants' hand movements.

Independent Variables

Need for Touch
NFT was measured with a 12-item scale (reliability = .96). The possible range of the 12-item NFT scale was from –36 to +36 and the entire range was represented in this sample. Low and high NFT were determined by a median split with participants scoring above the median (a score of 7) classified as high NFT ($n = 85$) and those scoring at or below the median classified as low in NFT ($n = 88$).

Product-Based Salience of Haptic Attributes
Product-based salience of haptic attributes was manipulated and consisted of three levels: those products where prepurchase touch is most important (level A), those in which prepurchase touch is moderately important (level B), and finally, those in which prepurchase touch is less important (level C). The three levels of product-based salience of haptic properties were determined by two pretests using self-report measures. In the first pretest, participants were asked to "list any products, services, and/or consumer experiences in which touch plays an important role in your decision process." From these results, 11 products were selected and rated in a second pretest using the question "It is important to touch (product) before deciding whether to purchase" on a 7-point scale (7 = strongly agree). From these ratings two products were selected for each of the three categories. The ratings were as follows: Category A—sweater = 6.5 and tennis racquet = 6.4 ($t = .22, p > .05$), Category B—calculator = 5.3 and cordless telephone = 5.6 ($t = .68, p > .05$), and Category C—cereal = 1.5 and toothpaste = 1.2 ($t = 1.78, p > .05$). Collapsing the ratings across products indicated that all were significantly different and in the expected direction (Category A, $m = 6.5 >$ Category B, $m = 5.4, t = 4.0, p < .05$; Category A, $m = 6.5 >$ Category C, $m = 1.3, t = 29.5, p < .05$; and Category B, $m = 5.4 >$ Category C, $m =$

1.3, $t = 16.3$, $p < .05$). Thus, one replicate of products consisted of a tennis racket (level A), a cordless telephone (level B), and a bag of cereal (level C). The second replicate consisted of a sweater (level A), a calculator (level B), and a tube of toothpaste (level C).

Dependent Measures

Behavioral Measures of Salience of Haptic Properties—Time Touching

Behavioral measurement of the salience of haptic properties was based on the time spent performing haptic EPs. Videotaping was used to assess the participant's hand movements as they evaluated the products. An independent judge, blind to the conditions, viewed a sample of the participants (two participants from each of the seven tapes) and recorded the time evaluating each product, the time touching each product, and the time each exploratory procedure was performed. Eighty-four percent of the time, the two judges agreed to within 1 second. Differences were subsequently reconciled prior to the analyses.

Examination for Outliers

In order to examine for outliers, z-scores were calculated for the time each individual spent touching each of the three products. Seven of the subject's times included variables with z-scores greater than 3. The videotapes of seven of the total participants were then examined and all seven participants were found to be nonnative English speakers. Their times were higher than the native English speakers because it appeared the right word or phrase could not always be found. For this reason, those seven participants were dropped from further analysis. Alternatively, a log transformation was applied to the touch time scores. Both the raw scores with the seven cases omitted and the log transformation scores with the seven cases omitted yielded the same results, for simplicity of exposition the raw data were reported.

Results

Behavioral Measure of Salience of Haptic Properties

Hypothesis 1 predicted that as the salience of material properties of a product increased as measured in a self-report measure, more time would

TABLE 5.1   Means and Standard Deviations for EPs

	A1 Tennis Racket	B1 Telephone	C1 Cereal	A2 Sweater	B2 Calculator	C2 Tooth paste
EPs Time (seconds)	6.14 (7.24)	3.76 (4.50)	0	6.59 (5.72)	5.24 (6.60)	0

be spent performing EPs to extract haptic product information. A limited number of EPs were found for product categories with the least haptic attribute salience and thus Category C was excluded from the first analysis (Table 5.1). Hypothesis 1 was supported by a main effect ($F_{1,164} = 13.76, p < .05$) for product salience with products in Category A eliciting longer times for EPs than products in Category B (mean of 6.37 vs. 4.49, respectively).

Haptic Extraction and Exploratory Procedures
As previously mentioned, separate haptic exploratory procedures have been reported to correspond to specific object attributes (Klatzky & Lederman, 1992, 1993; Lederman & Klatzky, 1987). Hypothesis 2 predicted that participants would vary in the time in which they performed various EPs depending on the EP performed and their NFT. Because of their increased efficiency in extracting haptic information, individuals higher in the NFT are expected to perform the more informational oriented EPs for a shorter length of time than their low NFT counterparts. The exception to this is the lateral motion EP since this is used to extract softness, and provides pleasant sensory feedback.

Table 5.2 illustrates the product categories, the types of EPs, and the times that EPs were performed by high and low NFT individuals. Only individuals that performed specific EPs during product evaluations were included in this analysis. As predicted, for the sweater, the lateral motion EP was performed longer for high versus low NFT individuals (mean of 7.13 vs. 4.99 seconds, $t_{72} = 2.16, p < .05$). For all other diagnostic haptic informational extraction, high NFT individuals performed EPs for less time than low NFT individuals due to their efficiency at processing this information.

Conclusions and Future Research

Results indicated that the salience of haptic product properties converge for self-report and behavioral measures of actual time spent touching products during their evaluation. Results were consistent across the three

TABLE 5.2 Type of Exploratory Procedures Performed by NFT

| Product | Exploratory Procedure (EP) | Time Performing EP (seconds) | | Significance |
		High Need-for-Touch	Low Need-for-Touch	
Sweater	Lateral motion (texture)	7.13	4.99	$t_{72} = 2.16, p < .05$
	Unsupported holding (weight)	1.98	3.50	$t_{11} = 2.02, p = .07$
Tennis racket	Unsupported holding (weight)	1.63	4.36	$t_{39} = 3.63, p < .01$
	Pressure (hardness)	2.24	4.41	$t_{46} = 2.50, p < .05$
Telephone	Unsupported holding (weight)	2.89	4.51	$t_{20} = 2.08, p < .05$
	Pressure (hardness-feel of keys)	3.63	5.01	$t_{36} = 2.61, p < .05$
Calculator	Pressure (hardness-feel of keys)	4.99	7.13	$t_{55} = 2.60, p < .05$

product categories differing in haptic attribute salience and for the two product replicates. Products containing salient haptic properties with greater stimulus-set discriminability were evaluated longer than those products lacking in this distinctive haptic type of information.

This study also explored matching specific haptic exploratory procedures or stereotypical hand movements with specific products. When a particular type of product attribute was assessed (such as texture), a matching exploratory procedure was observed (such as lateral motion). These results underscore the importance of haptic information to product evaluations and the variation between products in the importance of this haptic information. Results also validate the use of the behaviorally based EPs in a marketing context. Differential time performing EPs by high and low NFT individuals was predicted and supported depending on the type of information extracted. Although persons high in NFT are generally more efficient at extracting haptic information, they also enjoy the pleasant, sensory feedback more than those low in NFT.

These results also provide insight regarding the underlying drivers of haptic product evaluation. Recently, Grohmann, Spangenberg, and Sprott (2007) offered two theoretical explanations; the first related to the *informational* nature of haptic product evaluation versus a second, *affective*-based explanation. They conclude that haptic product evaluation is driven by an information-processing mechanism focused on extracting the diagnostic attributes of a product. Our results demonstrate this conclusion to be partially supported. Individuals do assess the informational haptic qualities of a product, but there seems to be a more affective evaluation at work as well. This also appears to differ based on a greater need to touch products. The latter evaluate products' diagnostic attributes to a greater degree (e.g., weight), but also spend time assessing the more hedonic aspects of products (e.g., the softness of a product's texture). Thus, additional examination is needed to better understand the role of haptic information on product evaluation and how this relates to the material properties corresponding to the informational attributes of a product. This needs to be contrasted with the affective nature of haptic evaluation and the conditions under which the two forms of touch impact product evaluation. Preliminary results of this study indicate that individual differences play an important role in this distinction. As noted, Peck and Wiggins (2006) found that the influence of affectively oriented positive haptic information varied by individual differences in NFT. Recently, Krishna and Morrin (2008) reported there was a negative impact of a nondiagnostic haptic cue for product evaluations for individuals lower in NFT. Synthesizing, there may be an asymmetry in the influence of haptic information on products across individuals, and how this relates to NFT needs further assessment.

The literature on the role of touch in marketing continues to mount toward supporting the importance of this sensory related cue in understanding how individuals assess products for their purchase. Our next challenge will be to pursue the conditions and mechanisms operating in haptic product evaluation and integrate these issues with the role of touch in relation to all of our basic sensory systems.

References

Bargh, J. A., & Thein, R. D. (1985). Individual construct accessibility, person memory, and the recall-judgment link: The case of information overload. *Journal of Personality and Social Psychology*, 49, 1129–1146.

Bettman, J. R., & Park, C. W. (1980). Implications of a constructive view of choice for analysis of protocol data: A coding scheme for elements of choice processes. In J. C. Olson (Ed.), *Advances in consumer research* (vol. 7, pp. 148–153). Ann Arbor, MI: Association for Consumer Research.

Biehal, G. J., & Chakravarti, D. (1982). Experiences with the Bettman-Park verbal protocol coding scheme. *Journal of Consumer Research, 8*, 442–448.

Bushnell, E. W., & Boudreau, J. P. (1991). The development of haptic perception during infancy. In M. A. Heller & W. Schiff (Eds.), *The psychology of touch* (pp. 139–161). Hillsdale, NJ: Lawrence Erlbaum.

Essick, G. A., James, A., & McGlone, F. P. (1999). Psychophysical assessment of the affective components of non-painful touch. *Neuroreport, 10*(10), 2083–2087.

Grohmann, B., Spangenberg, E. R., & Sprott, D. E. (2007). The influence of tactile input on the evaluation of retail product offerings. *Journal of Retailing, 83*(2), 237–245.

Jones, S. E., & Brown, B. C. (1996). Touch attitudes and behaviors, recollections of early childhood touch, and social self-confidence. *Journal of Non-Verbal Behavior, 20*(3), 147–163.

Klatzky, R. L., & Lederman, S. J. (1992). Stages of manual exploration in haptic object identification. *Perception and Psychophysics, 52*(6), 661–670.

Klatzky, R. L., & Lederman, S. J. (1993). Toward a computational model of constraint-driven exploration and haptic object identification. *Perception, 22*, 597–621.

Klatzky, R. L., Lederman, S. J., & Reed, C. (1987). There's more to touch than meets the eye: the salience of object attributes for haptics with and without vision. *Journal of Experimental Psychology General, 116*, 356–369.

Krishna, A., & Morrin, M. (2008). Does touch affect taste? The perceptual transfer of product container haptic cues. *Journal of Consumer Research, 34*(6), 807–818.

Lederman, S. J., & Klatzky, R. L. (1987). Hand movements: A window into haptic object recognition. *Cognitive Psychology, 19*, 342–368.

McCabe, D. B., & Nowlis, S. M. (2003). The effect of examining actual products or product descriptions on consumer preference. *Journal of Consumer Psychology, 13*(4), 431–439.

Peck, J., & Childers, T. L. (2003a, April). To have and to hold: The influence of haptic information on product judgments. *Journal of Marketing, 67*(2), 35–48.

Peck, J., & Childers, T. L. (2003b). Individual differences in haptic information processing: On the development, validation, and use of the 'need for touch' scale. *Journal of Consumer Research, 30*(3), 430–442.

Peck, J., & Childers, T. L. (2008), "If it tastes, smells, sounds, and feels like a duck, then it must be a …": Effects of sensory factors on consumer behaviors. In C. Haugtvedt, P. Herr, & F. Kardes (Eds.), *Handbook of consumer psychology* (pp. 193–219). Mahwah, NJ: Lawrence Earlbaum.

Peck, J., & Wiggins, J. (2006). It just feels good: Consumers' affective response to touch and its influence on attitudes and behavior. *Journal of Marketing, 70*(4), 56–69.

Viswanathan, M. (2005). *Measurement error and research design*. Thousand Oaks, CA: Sage.

Section II

Olfaction

6

Scent Marketing
An Overview

Maureen Morrin

Scent has long influenced human behavior, indicating objects that should either be approached (e.g., food, flowers, potential mates) or avoided (e.g., predators, poisons, gas leaks; Axel, 1995). Studies have shown, however, that individuals generally undervalue their sense of smell (Martin, Apena, Chaudry, Mulligan, & Nixon, 2001). Although the sense of smell, or olfaction, is generally considered less important to human survival and progress than are other senses, such as vision and hearing, it nevertheless plays an important role in day-to-day living.

The sense of smell is critical to the perception of flavors, for example. Without a sense of smell, Coke and Sprite would taste the same (Herz, 2007, p. 196). The sense of smell also plays an important role in mate selection. Young women recently ranked a man's scent as the most important physical factor in deciding on a potential lover (Herz, 2007). And losing one's sense of smell, a condition known as anosmia (e.g., from brain injury), is often associated with feelings of depression and a world described as "dull and colourless" (Douek, 1988, p. xviii). Research shows that anorexics can suffer from an impaired sense of smell, making it even more difficult for them to savor their food and eat healthfully (Fedoroff, Stoner, Andersen, Doty, & Rolls, 1995). Interestingly, loss of the sense of smell has been found to be one of the earliest indicators of the onset of Alzheimer's disease (Svoboda, 2007).

In the past decade or so, marketers have become more aware of the potential role that scent can play in differentiating brands in the marketplace as well as improving consumers' satisfaction levels and sense of well-being in marketplace settings. The phrase *scent marketing* has been used to describe using scents "to set a mood, promote products or position a brand" (Vlahos, 2007, p. 70). This definition hints at the myriad ways that marketers utilize scents.

Most obviously, marketers can use scents as a *primary product attribute*, such as in personal fragrances or room deodorizers. In these instances, the scent itself is the primary reason a consumer purchases the product.

Marketers probably more often use scents as a *secondary product attribute*. There are many scent-infused products whose primary attributes are something other than the smell of the product. The scents associated with many of these products come to be uniquely associated with specific brands. For example, most consumers, if blindfolded, could probably correctly identify the scent of Play-Doh modeling clay or Ivory soap. For such products, the unique scents are not usually the primary reason for product purchase. However, use of the scent as a secondary product attribute helps to distinguish the brand from competitive offerings.

Marketers also use scents as part of *advertising and sales promotion* efforts. For example, the California Milk Producer Board recently scented bus shelters in San Francisco with the scent of chocolate chip cookies in conjunction with the Got Milk campaign. The scents were removed within days, however, due to consumer complaints (Gordon, 2006). Another example consists of a joint promotion between Starbucks and Omni hotels involving peel-n-sniff patches applied to *USA Today* newspapers. The guests at Omni hotels received the papers with the patches smelling of blueberry muffins to encourage muffin purchases at the Starbucks located in the hotel lobbies (Elliott, 2007). In other efforts, direct marketers are adding scents to their direct mail pieces via a microencapsulation process that activates when the mail is opened (Pfanner, 2007).

Perhaps the greatest growth in scent marketing in recent years has taken place with regard to the use of *ambient* scent, that is, emitting scent into the atmosphere of hotels, retail stores, casinos, or restaurants as an element of an environment's atmospherics (Kotler, 1973). Ambient scent is popularly believed to have the potential to create positive mood states, which will then translate into more favorable store and product evaluations and eventually into higher sales revenues.

Applications of ambient scenting have been reported by a variety of retailers such as Bloomingdale's, Sony, Samsung, and Thomas Pink (Byron, 2007; Mui, 2006), by hotels such as Westin and Omni (Elliott, 2007; Stellin, 2007), by banks such as Credit Suisse (McGregor, 2008), and by real estate developers such as Toll Brothers (Vlahos, 2007). A small industry has developed in recent years to meet the demand for such ambient scenting efforts (e.g., firms such as AirAroma, AromaSys, Prolitec, and ScentAir, as well as a professional association, the Scent Marketing Institute). Unique combinations of scents are increasingly being sought to create what are called "signature scents" to serve as potentially competitive differentiators in a crowded retail marketplace (Davies, Kooijman, & Ward, 2003).

To what extent does empirical research bear out these notions? That is, does scent really have the capacity to influence consumers in the marketplace? If so, how, and under what conditions? The purpose of this chapter is to review the empirical results published to date largely by researchers in marketing on the effects of scent in order to consider what we have learned and what we still need to know about scent's capacity to alter consumer behavior.

In terms of a theoretical framework, most of the literature assumes a simple S-O-R (Stimulus–Organism–Response) model, wherein pleasant ambient scents (S) should lead to a pleasant [unpleasant] affective response within the consumer (O), which in turn should lead to approach [avoidance] behavior mediated by the emotional response (R) on the part of the consumer (such as a positive mood state; Mehrabian & Russell, 1974). In this way, environmental stimuli, such as scents, serve a functional role in helping us to survive. In a marketing context, approach behaviors could manifest as more positive consumer evaluations, more time spent within the store, intentions to revisit the store, the spending of more money in the store, and so forth.

Here I explore whether and under what conditions such approach behaviors do indeed tend to result from scent marketing efforts. First, I discuss some of the characteristics of the sense of smell and then provide a summary of the empirical research regarding the effects of scent. I also discuss the factors that moderate such effects and end by suggesting areas for future research.

Scent Characteristics

Scents Are Hard to Label but Easy to Recognize

Research has shown that we often find it difficult to attach a verbal or semantic label to scents, a phenomenon called the "tip-of-the-nose" effect (Lawless & Engen, 1977). Nevertheless, we are able to distinguish among many different scents that we have smelled previously. There are over 5 million olfactory neurons in our nasal cavity with which we are able to detect over 10,000 different scents (Axel, 1995; Buck, 2004).

Scent Preferences Are Learned

Studies have shown that our liking or disliking for scents is learned over time (Engen, 1988; Herz, Beland, & Hellerstein, 2004). Our scent preferences are thus not innate or hardwired. So, if you experience a particular scent while a pleasant activity or event occurs, you will likely end up liking that scent for the rest of your life. Additional evidence for the acquired nature of scent preferences is seen in the differences among cultures in scents that are liked or disliked. For example, the scent of cheese, which is generally liked in Western countries, is often considered putrid in East Asian countries (Herz, 2007).

Scent Processing Is Slow but Persistent

It takes us a relatively long time to perceive the presence of a scent in our surroundings. Thus, while it takes only 45 milliseconds (i.e., thousandths of a second) for humans to detect a visual object, it takes about 450 milliseconds, or 10 times as long, to detect an odor (Herz & Engen, 1996). Researchers believe the reason for this is because olfactory neurons are unmyelinated, which means that the information travels from the olfactory neurons to neurons in the brain more slowly (Herz & Engen, 1996). The sense of smell can also be considered the slow sense in that it takes twice as long to retrieve an autobiographical memory that is cued with a scent cue compared to one cued with a visual or verbal cue (Goddard, Pring, & Felmingham, 2005).

However, we are able to recognize and recall scents we have smelled long after the encoding episode has passed (Aggleton & Waskett, 1999; Lawless & Engen, 1977). Information encoded along with scent information also appears to be very persistent over time, exhibiting relatively flat forgetting curves over time (Krishna, Lwin, & Morrin, n.d.).

Effects of Scent on Consumer Behavior

Although smell is a relatively underresearched sense in the field of consumer behavior, it has begun to generate increased interest over the past decade or so. These studies will be summarized below according to the types of effects scent has had on various aspects of consumer behavior.

The review is meant to be representative rather than comprehensive or exhaustive in nature.

Mood

Although it is commonly assumed that scent, if it has an impact on consumers, probably does so via its ability to alter consumers' moods, there is actually little in the way of empirical evidence to support this notion. Bone and Ellen (1999) reviewed 22 studies on scent that contained 206 tests of olfactory effects. They found that only 16.1% of the tests of the effect of scent on mood or physiological arousal were statistically significant. Similar results have been obtained in scent studies published in marketing since the publication of the Bone and Ellen review paper (e.g., Bosmans, 2006; Morrin & Ratneshwar, 2000, 2003; Spangenberg, Crowley, & Henderson, 1996). Moreover, where mood or arousal effects have been found, they have been mixed. Some researchers have found scents to be physiologically arousing (e.g., Mattila & Wirtz, 2001), whereas others have found them to be calming (Gould & Martin, 2001). More research is needed to establish the conditions under which scent has a demonstrable and reliable effect on mood and arousal levels.

Research *has* found that emotional states can *interact* with scents to have significant effects on memory. For example, Herz (1997) found that scent as a retrieval cue was more effective if respondents were put into an anxious (vs. normal) mood at the time of encoding. On the whole, however, the evidence to date suggests the direct effects of ambient scent on consumer mood are weak.

Evaluation

The effects of scent on product and store evaluation, on the other hand, are more robust. Probably the earliest published study to assess the potential impact of scent on consumer evaluations was that of Laird (1932), who found that silk stockings, which otherwise emitted a mildly unpleasant odor, when scented with a floral scent, were evaluated more positively by housewives in a door-to-door survey.

More recently, the effects of ambient scent on consumer evaluations were examined by Spangenberg et al. (1996), who found, in a simulated store setting, that ambient scents generally improved both store and product evaluations. In this study, over 26 different scents were pretested, but the authors interestingly found that scent type did not moderate the results. A later study by Spangenberg, Grohmann, and Sprott (2005) found that a pleasant ambient scent improved evaluations, but only when it was seasonally congruent with the background music played in the environment (e.g., Christmas music paired with a Christmas scent). Bosmans (2006) similarly investigated the effect of scent and scent congruency on evaluations. This author also found that pleasant scents generally resulted in more positive evaluations, largely because consumers tended to misattribute the effects of the liked ambient scent to the products that were being evaluated.

As an exception to the stream of research that has found generally positive effects of scent on evaluations, Ellen and Bone (1998) found that scratch-n-sniff patches attached to print advertisements had no positive effect on evaluations and actually had negative effects when the scent was perceived to be incongruent with the product that was advertised. On the whole, this line of research suggests that pleasant scents will generally enhance consumer evaluations; however, scent congruency may be required to elicit such effects.

Spending

Researchers have begun to explore whether a pleasant ambient scent in purchase settings increases the amount of money spent in the environment. The results have generally suggested that yes, under certain conditions, adding a pleasant scent can increase revenues. Spangenberg, Sprott, Grohmann, and Tracy (2006) found that shoppers spent more in a store selling clothing when the scent that was emitted in a particular department was congruent with the type of clothing being sold (i.e., a feminine [masculine] scent emitted into the women's [men's] department). Morrin and Chebat (2005) found that emitting a pleasant scent into a shopping mall increased expenditures, but only among more contemplative shoppers or those who did not make unplanned purchases. The more impulsive shoppers, in contrast, spent more when pleasant music was playing in the background. Importantly, shoppers spent the least when both scent and music were present, suggesting marketers need to be careful not to overstimulate their clientele with too many environmental stimuli.

Memory

It is widely believed that scent has a unique capacity to enhance human memory, due in part to the famous story about the French author Marcel Proust. Upon smelling a madelèine cake he had not eaten since childhood, Proust was flooded with memories that formed the basis of his famous writings. Empirical evidence regarding the ability of scent to enhance memory is only beginning to emerge, however. Herz (1998, 2000) has found that scent cues tend to evoke memories that are more emotional in nature than those that are evoked by verbal, visual, auditory, or tactile cues. Other research suggests that information encoded with scents may be very long lasting (Aggleton & Waskett, 1999). Morrin and Ratneshwar (2000, 2003) found that consumers look longer at product packaging on a computer screen when there is a pleasant scent in the room, which later manifests in superior brand recall and recognition. Other research shows that scent improves memory performance, especially after a time delay (Krishna et al., n.d.). Thus, there would appear to be emerging evidence in favor of the notion that scent can indeed enhance consumer memory.

Lingering

In a field study, Gueguen and Petr (2006) found that the scent of lavender (but not lemon) increased actual time spent in a pizzeria by about 15% compared to an unscented control condition. Mitchell, Kahn, and Knasko (1995) found that consumers spent more time processing product information when there was a congruent versus an incongruent scent in the environment. Spangenberg et al. (1996) found that a pleasantly scented environment increased only perceptions of time elapsed, not actual time spent, in a simulated store environment. Thus, the results regarding the effects of ambient scent on actual and perceived time spent in an environment are somewhat mixed. Additional research is called for to explore the effects of scent on actual and perceived time durations.

Moderators

Congruency
Beyond the main effects of scent on the various dependent measures discussed above, potential moderators have been explored. By far, the

moderator investigated more than any other with regard to the effects of scent on consumer behavior is congruency. Scent congruency has been conceptualized and operationalized in many ways. Scent has been conceptualized as being congruent with the actual product being purchased (e.g., Bosmans, 2006; Mitchell et al., 1995; Morrin & Ratneshwar, 2000, 2003), with the gender-based type of product being purchased (Spangenberg et al., 2006), with the arousal level of background music (Matilla & Wirtz, 2001), and with the seasonality of background music (Spangenberg et al., 2005). As a whole, the studies suggest that evaluations tend to be more positive under conditions of scent congruency, however defined.

Individual Differences
Individual difference variables such as impulsivity (Morrin & Chebat, 2005) and age (Chebat, Morrin, & Chebat, 2009) have also been found to have moderating effects. For example, the ability of ambient scent to enhance consumer expenditures in a shopping mall was found to significantly diminish among older shoppers (Chebat et al., 2009). Such a finding reflects the fact that the acuity of our sense of smell begins to deteriorate as early as our 20s (Hoffman, Ishii, & MacTurk, 1998).

Other moderating variables should be explored at this point. Interactions with the other senses would prove a fertile ground for exploration, as would cross-cultural or subcultural effects. Another possibility would be the development of a valid scale to measure the individual propensity to acquire and utilize scents to evaluate and purchase products or services. Thus, similar to the need for touch (NFT) scale developed by Peck and Childers (2003), a need for scent scale could be useful. Initial attempts in this direction have been made (Martin et al., 2001; Wrzesniewski, McCauley, & Rozin, 1999). However, a fuller, more multidimensional effort would be worthwhile. It would be interesting to see whether a consumer's need for scent is correlated positively or negatively with olfactory function, which can be tested with existing batteries, such as the University of Pennsylvania Smell Identification Test (UPSIT) (Doty, Newhouse, & Azzalina, 1985).

Suggestions for Future Research

Some intriguing developments in the basic disciplines have emerged that may have implications for consumer researchers. For example, one recent study found evidence for the possibility of an olfactory imagery (Bensafi et al., 2003). These researchers note that when we are asked to remember a scent we have previously smelled, we sniff in more air. Furthermore, if we are prevented from sniffing while trying to remember a scent (e.g., via a nose clip), the vividness of the scent memory is reduced. How does olfactory imagery contribute to the accuracy and emotional potency of consumption experiences?

Another intriguing study (Rasch, Buchel, Gais, & Born, 2007) found that emitting an ambient scent during periods of deep sleep improves memory performance. This result suggests that scent may play a role in memory consolidation, even without conscious awareness. In this study, participants played a memory game involving card pair locations on a computer screen while a pleasant scent was (or was not) emitted into the room. Later, during periods of deep sleep, the same scent was emitted (or not). The next day, those who had the scent present at both learning and during sleep showed improved recall accuracy (85.8% vs. 97.2%). Do consumers remember more about their consumption experiences when they take place repeatedly in scented environments?

Beyond incorporating the latest findings from the basic disciplines, the area of scent marketing can make additional progress by moving beyond mood-mediated theoretical frameworks. Interesting questions that do not necessarily implicate mood include the ability of scent to prime a promotion or prevention focus among consumers. Would a pleasant ambient scent prime a promotion focus and an unpleasant scent prime a prevention focus?

Researchers should also explore moderators other than scent congruency. Cross-cultural differences might be interesting to explore. Construction of a need for scent scale might also be of use, as mentioned previously. The interactive effects of other senses on the effects of scent would be interesting to explore. For example, can inhibiting the sense of smell reduce the pleasure associated with taste sensations and thus obesity? Can enhancing or restoring an individual's sense of smell alleviate depression? Researchers have many potentially fruitful avenues to investigate given the relatively unexplored terrain of scent marketing.

References

Aggleton, J. P., & Waskett, L. (1999). The ability of odours to serve as state-dependent cues for real-world memories: Can Viking smells aid the recall of Viking experiences? *British Journal of Psychology, 90*(1), 1–7.

Axel, R. (1995, October). The molecular logic of smell. *Scientific American, 273*, 154–159.

Bensafi, M., Porter, J., Pouliot, S., Mainland, J., Johnson, B., Zelano, C., Young, N., Bremner, E., Aframian, D., Kahn, R., & Sobel, N. (2003). Olfactomotor activity during imagery mimics that during perception. *Nature Neuroscience*, 6, 1142–1144.

Bone, P. F., & Ellen, P. S. (1999). Scent in the marketplace: Explaining a fraction of olfaction. *Journal of Retailing, 75*(2), 243–262.

Bosmans, A. (2006, July). Scents and sensibility: When do (in)congruent ambient scents influence product evaluations. *Journal of Marketing, 70*, 32–43.

Buck, L. (2004, January 23). The search for odorant receptors. *Cell, (116)*, S117–S119.

Byron, E. (2007, September 4). How P&G led also-ran to sweet smell of success. *Wall Street Journal*, p. B2.

Chebat, J. C., Morrin, M., & Chebat, D. R. (2009, March 1). Does age attenuate the impact of pleasant ambient scent? *Environment and Behavior, 42*(2), 258–267.

Davies, B. J., Kooijman, D., & Ward, P. (2003). The sweet smell of success: Olfaction in retailing. *Journal of Marketing Management, 19*, 611–627.

Doty, R. L., Newhouse, M. G., & Azzalina, J. D. (1985). Internal consistency and short-term test-retest reliability of the University of Pennsylvania smell identification test. *Chemical Senses, 10*(3), 297–300.

Douek, E. (1988). Abnormalities of smell. In S. Van Toller & G. H. Dodd (Eds.), *Perfumery: The psychology and biology of fragrance* (pp. xvii–xx). London: Chapman and Hall.

Ellen, P. S., & Bone, P. F. (1998). Does it matter if it smells? Olfactory stimuli as advertising executional cues. *Journal of Advertising, 27*(4), 29–39.

Elliott, S. (2007, April 2). Joint promotion adds stickers to sweet smell of marketing. *New York Times*, p. C5.

Engen, T. (1988). The acquisition of odour hedonics. In S. Van Toller & G. H. Dodd (Eds.), *Perfumery: The psychology and biology of fragrance* (pp. 79–90). London: Chapman and Hall.

Fedoroff, I. C., Stoner, S. A., Andersen, A. E., Doty, R. L., & Rolls, B. J. (1995). Olfactory dysfunction in anorexia and bulimia nervosa. *International Journal of Eating Disorders, 18*(1), 71–77.

Goddard, L., Pring, L., & Felmingham, N. (2005). The effects of cue modality on the quality of personal memories retrieved. *Memory, 13*(1), 79–86.

Gordon, R. (2006, December 17). At bus stops, scents of dissent. *The Philadelphia Inquirer*, p. A29.

Gould, A., & Martin, G. N. (2001). A good odour to breathe? The effect of pleasant ambient odour on human visual vigilance. *Applied Cognitive Psychology, 15*, 225–232.

Gueguen, N., & Petr, C. (2006). Odors and consumer behavior in a restaurant. *International Journal of Hospitality Management, 25*, 335–339.

Herz, R. S. (1997). Emotion experienced during encoding enhances odor retrieval cue effectiveness. *American Journal of Psychology, 110*(4), 489–505.

Herz, R. S. (1998, November 30). Are odors the best cues to memory? A cross-modal comparison of associative memory stimuli. *Annals of New York Academy of Science, 855,* 670–674.

Herz, R. S. (2000, July–August). Scents of time. *The Sciences,* 34–39.

Herz, R. S. (2007). *The scent of desire: Discovering our enigmatic sense of smell.* New York: HarperCollins.

Herz, R. S., Beland, S. L., & Hellerstein, M. (2004). Changing odor hedonic perception through emotional associations in humans. *International Journal of Comparative Psychology, 17,* 315–338.

Herz, R. S., & Engen, T. (1996). Odor memory: Review and analysis. *Psychonomic Bulletin and Review, 3*(3), 300–313.

Hoffman, H. J., Ishii, E. K., & MacTurk, R. H. (1998). Age-related changes in the prevalence of smell/taste problems among the United States adult population: Results of the 1994 disability supplement to the national health interview survey (NHIS). *Annals of the New York Academy of Sciences, 855,* 716–722.

Kotler, P. (1973). Atmospherics as a marketing tool. *Journal of Retailing, 49*(4), 48–65.

Krishna, A., Lwin, M. O., & Morrin, M. (n.d.). *Beyond the Proustian phenomenon: The effect of product-embedded scent on memory for product information.* Working paper. University of Michigan.

Laird, D. A. (1932, June). How the consumers estimate quality by subconscious sensory impressions: With special reference to the role of smell. *Journal of Applied Psychology, 16,* 241–246.

Lawless, H. T., & Engen, T. (1977). Associations to odors: Interference, mnemonics, and verbal labeling. *Journal of Experimental Psychology: Human Learning and Memory, 3,* 52–59.

Martin, G. N., Apena, F., Chaudry, Z., Mulligan, Z., & Nixon, C. (2001). The development of an attitude towards the Sense of Smell Questionnaire (SoSQ) and a comparison of different professions' responses. *North American Journal of Psychology, 3*(3), 491–502.

Matilla, A. S., & Wirtz, J. (2001). Congruency of scent and music as a driver of in-store evaluations and behavior. *Journal of Retailing, 77,* 273–289.

McGregor, J. (2008, April 7). The sweet smell of … deposits. *BusinessWeek,* p. 26.

Mehrabian, A., & Russell, J. A. (1974). *An approach to environmental psychology.* Cambridge, MA: Massachusetts Institute of Technology.

Mitchell, D. J., Kahn, B. E., & Knasko, S. C. (1995, September). There's something in the air: Effects of congruent or incongruent ambient odor on consumer decision making. *Journal of Consumer Research, 22,* 229–238.

Morrin, M., & Chebat, J. C. (2005). Person-place congruency: The interactive effects of shopper style and atmospherics on consumer expenditures. *Journal of Service Research, 8*(2), 181–191.

Morrin, M., & Ratneshwar, S. (2000). The impact of ambient scent on evaluation, attention, and memory for familiar and unfamiliar brands. *Journal of Business Research, 49*, 157–165.

Morrin, M., & Ratneshwar, S. (2003, February). Does it make sense to use scents to enhance brand memory? *Journal of Marketing Research, 40*, 1–25.

Mui, Y. Q. (2006, December 19). Dollars and scents: Retailers use technology to get shoppers by nose. *Washington Post*, p. D1.

Peck, J., & Childers, T. L. (2003). Individual differences in haptic information processing: On the development, validation, and use of the "need for touch" scale. *Journal of Consumer Research, 30*(3), 430–442.

Pfanner, E. (2007, November 15). Sending a scent by snail mail. *The New York Times*, p. C9.

Rasch, B., Buchel, C., Gais, S., & Born, J. (2007, March 9). Odor cues during slow-wave sleep prompt declarative memory consolidation. *Science, 315*, 1426–1429.

Spangenberg, E. R., Crowley, A. E., & Henderson, P. W. (1996, April). Improving the store environment: Do olfactory cues affect evaluations and behaviors? *Journal of Marketing, 60*, 67–80.

Spangenberg, E. R., Grohmann, B., & Sprott, D. E. (2005). It's beginning to smell (and sound) a lot like Christmas: The interactive effects of ambient scent and music in a retail setting. *Journal of Business Research, 58*, 1583–1589.

Spangenberg, E. R., Sprott, D. E., Grohmann, B., & Tracy, D. L. (2006). Gender-congruent Ambient scent influences on approach and avoidance behaviors in a retail store. *Journal of Business Research, 59*, 1281–1287.

Stellin, S. (2007, September 11). Eau de hotel. *The New York Times*. Retrieved May 28, 2009, from www.nytimes.com/2007/09/11/business/11scents.html?ex=1 190174400&en=9b3f284fadf7ecba&ei=5070&emc=eta1

Svoboda, E. (2007, August 14). Sniff test may signal disorders' early stages. *New York Times*, p. F5.

Vlahos, J. (2007, September 9). Scent and sensibility: Can smell sell? *New York Times*, Key insert, pp. 69–73.

Wrzesniewski, A., McCauley, C., & Rozin, P. (1999). Odor and affect: Individual differences in the impact of odor on liking for places, things and people. *Chemical Senses, 24*, 713–721.

7

The Emotional, Cognitive, and Biological Basics of Olfaction
Implications and Considerations for Scent Marketing

Rachel S. Herz

Olfaction is our phylogenetically oldest and most primitive sense, yet it is highly involved in every aspect of our lives. In particular, the sense of smell influences our emotions, memories, and motivations with singular intensity. This chapter presents a scientific overview of the emotional, cognitive, and biological basics of olfaction. How odors come to be liked or disliked, acquire meaning, influence moods, elicit memories, and motivate behavior will be explained through a comprehensive review of the literature. The most recent data and theories in the psychobiology of olfaction and the neuroanatomical and evolutionary basis for the connection between scent and emotion will be elucidated. In the final section of this chapter, how the unique associative, emotional, and motivational properties of olfaction can be useful for scent marketing will be explored with special attention to several cognitive, physiological, and logistical factors that are critical considerations for manipulations involving the sense of smell.

Olfactory Preferences

Hedonic perception is an affective evaluation that centers on liking. The most immediate and basic response we have to a scent is not analytical (What is it?), but hedonic, whether we like the scent or not. Pleasantness, familiarity, and intensity are the three factors most often evaluated when examining odor hedonic perception. Pleasantness and familiarity are positively correlated in odor preference perception (Moskowitz, Dravnieks,

& Klarman, 1976). Familiar odors tend to be better liked than unfamiliar odors, and pleasant odors are frequently perceived as familiar. Intensity has a more complex relationship to odor liking and either shows an inverted-U or linear function. For example, a lilac scent may be evaluated as more positive with increasing intensity, up to a point; where the function reverses, and as the scent becomes stronger, it is judged to be more disagreeable. By contrast, a weak fishy odor may be acceptable; but as intensity increases, its hedonic value becomes steadily more negative. It is also the case that genetic individual differences in the number and type of olfactory receptors expressed may influence one's sensitivity to a particular odorant and hence the predisposition to experience specific odors along a pleasantness continuum (Menashe, Man, Lancet, & Gilad, 2003).

A long-standing debate in olfactory perception is whether hedonic responses to odors are innate or learned. The *innate view* of odor preference claims that we are born with a predisposition to like or dislike various smells; that rose is inherently a good smell and skunk is inherently a bad smell. Though widely believed, this view has not been empirically validated in humans and is largely due to extrapolations from taste perception, which is predominantly hardwired. A drop of quinine on a newborn's tongue will instantly elicit a grimace and a drop of sucrose will trigger a smile. By contrast, the *learned view* states that we are born merely with a predisposition to learn to like or dislike smells, and whether we have a preference for a certain odor or not is due to our acquired emotional associations to that scent (Engen, 1991; Herz, Beland, & Hellerstein, 2004).

Associative Learning and Odor Hedonic Perception

Associative learning is the basis of the *learned view* of odor hedonic perception. Associative learning is the process by which one event or item comes to be linked to another as a function of an individual's past experiences (Wasserman & Miller, 1997). Imagine there is a stimulus called "A." Your response to A is A+. Imagine there is another stimulus called "B." Your response to B, however, is nothing. Next A and B are paired together and the following occurs. When you are presented with A again your response to it is still A+. However, when you are presented with B again, your response to it is now A+ as well. That is, through association, B, which was formerly meaningless, has taken on the properties of A. Associative learning is responsible for a large part of human cognition and behavior and is also the basis of classical conditioning.[1]

The associative learning theory of odor hedonic perception states that an odor is the meaningless B stimulus and an emotion is the A stimulus. Therefore, as a function of associative learning, an odor can: (a) elicit an emotional state connected with prior exposure and have a general impact on mood, and (b) attach to the odor itself and imbue it with hedonic meaning (through the emotional response evoked by the odor), thus determining odor hedonic perception.

Developmental and cross-cultural research provides strong evidence that associative learning with emotion as the mediating variable governs odor hedonic perception. Mennella and Beauchamp (1991) found that infants of mothers who consumed distinctive smelling volatiles (e.g., garlic, alcohol, cigarette smoke) during pregnancy or lactation showed preferences for these smells compared to infants who had not been exposed to these scents. It has further been shown that early learned odor preferences influence food and flavor preferences in later childhood (Mennella & Garcia, 2000) and adulthood (Haller, Rummel, Henneberg, Pollmer, & Koster, 1999).[2] In a study of infant formula acceptance, it was found that if neonates were exposed to an "offensive" formula flavor, they not only accepted this flavor in later childhood, but showed preferences for it compared to the standard more "pleasant" formula (Mennella & Beauchamp, 2002). Similarly, infants who had been fed a vanilla-flavored formula preferred vanilla-adulterated ketchup to traditional ketchup when tested as adults more than 20 years later (Haller et al., 1999).

Feeding, in addition to providing nutrition, is an opportunity for close physical contact and emotional bonding. Thus feeding is a perfect situation for emotional associations to odors to develop. Association through affectionate cuddling also induces preferences for specific (yet arbitrary) scents, such as cherry oil or mother's perfume (Lott, Sullivan, & McPherson, 1989).

In contrast, when there has been no prior learning, the responses of young children to unfamiliar odors either do not adhere to adult norms, for instance liking the odors of sweat and feces (Stein, Ottenberg, & Roulet, 1958), or are nondiscriminative, for example showing the same response to butyric acid (found in rancid foods) and to amyl acetate (banana-like scent) (Engen, 1988). Only one published study has reported that young children (3-year-olds) had adultlike responses to certain odors (Schmidt & Beauchamp, 1988). However, this experiment has been criticized on methodological grounds (Engen & Engen, 1997). In sum, the developmental literature demonstrates both the lack of a priori hedonic responses to odors, as well as the readiness of the olfactory system to learn the significance of odors or flavors based on associative learning and the emotional valence of the associated experience.

Cross-cultural data provide further evidence that associative learning, rather than hardwired responses, dictates olfactory preferences. No empirical data have shown cross-cultural consensus in odor evaluations for either common "everyday" odors (Schleidt, Hold, & Attila, 1981) or even "offensive" scents. Indeed, in a study undertaken by the U.S. military to create a "stink bomb" it was impossible to find an odor (including "U.S. army issue latrine" scent) that was unanimously considered unpleasant across various ethnic groups (Dilks, Dalton, & Beauchamp, 1999). The following example illustrates how associated emotion is at the root of these effects.

In the mid-1960s, in Britain, Moncrieff (1966) asked adult respondents to provide hedonic ratings to a battery of common odors. A similar study was conducted in the United States in the late 1970s (Cain & Johnson, 1978). Included in both studies was the odor methyl salicylate (wintergreen). Notably, in the British study, wintergreen was given one of the lowest pleasantness ratings, whereas, in the U.S. study it was given the highest pleasantness rating. The reason for this difference can be explained by history. In Britain, the smell of wintergreen is associated with medicine and, particularly for the participants in the 1966 study, with analgesics that were popular during World War II, a time that these individuals would not remember fondly. Conversely, in the United States, the smell of wintergreen is exclusively a candy mint smell and one that has sweet and positive connotations. Thus, the key to olfactory associative learning is the experience that occurs when the odor is first perceived and in particular the emotional connotation of that experience (Engen, 1982; Herz et al., 2004).

Odor, Emotion, and the Brain

Neuroanatomy explains the unique emotional and associative potency of odor stimuli. Only two synapses separate the olfactory nerve from the amygdala, a structure critical for the expression and experience of emotion (Aggleton & Mishkin, 1986) and human emotional memory (Cahill, Babinsky, Markowilsch, & McGaugh, 1995); and only three synapses separate the olfactory nerve from the hippocampus, involved in the selection and transmission of information in working memory, short-term and long-term memory transfer, and in various declarative memory functions

(Eichenbaum, 2001). Moreover, olfactory information is not mediated through the thalamus (a principal integration locus for sensory information) as all other sensory information is, but rather is directly and immediately relayed to the amygdala-hippocampal complex. Classical conditioning of specific cues to emotion is also mediated by the amygdala (LeDoux, 1998), and the olfactory cortex and amygdala have been shown to play a major role in stimulus reinforcement association learning (Rolls, 1999). None of our other senses have this direct and intimate connection with the areas of the brain that process emotion, associative learning, and memory.

In addition to the distinctive neuroanatomical connection between olfaction and emotion, olfaction and emotion are deeply connected by neuroevolution. The structures of the limbic system (e.g., the amygdala and hippocampus) evolved out of tissue that was originally olfactory cortex. That is, the emotional and associative learning substrates of the brain grew out of tissue that was first dedicated to processing the sense of smell. Something to ponder is whether or how we would experience emotion if we did not have a sense of smell. Furthermore, the informational significance of emotion and olfaction is functionally the same. The most immediate responses we have to an odor are simple binary opposites: like or dislike, approach or avoid. Emotions convey the same message: approach what is good, joyful, loving; avoid what is bad, fearsome, or liable to cause grief. Thus emotions and olfaction are functionally analogous. Both enable the organism to react appropriately to its environment, maximizing its chances for basic survival and reproductive success. It is my opinion that the human emotional system may be a highly evolved, cognitive version of the basic behavioral motivations instigated by the olfactory system in animals (Herz, 2000, 2007).

Experimental Evidence for Odor-Associative Learning in Preference Formation

Indirect evidence supporting the central role of emotion in odor-associative learning has been shown in several studies. For example, in an experiment assessing autonomic emotional responses to odors it was found that eugenol ("clove" odor used in dental cement) was rated as very unpleasant and elicited autonomic reactions indicative of fear among patients who were afraid of dental procedures. While, by contrast, participants who did not have a history of negative dentistry experiences evaluated eugenol positively and showed neutral autonomic responses (Robin, Alaoui-Ismaili, Dittmar, & Vernet-Mauri, 1998).

To more powerfully and directly assess the *learned view* of odor hedonic perception, my laboratory recently conducted two experiments to test whether odor hedonic responses could be changed by association with specific emotional states (Herz et al., 2004). The experiments varied with regard to whether a novel "target" odor was preexperimentally pleasant or unpleasant and the emotion that was linked to it was negative or positive. In each experiment, participants were randomly assigned to an experimental group (odor + emotional association) or various control groups. Evaluations of the target odor and several "anchor odors" that were not explicitly part of the association procedures were made several times throughout the study: at baseline prior to the manipulation; postmanipulation; 24 hours after the manipulation; and 1 week from the first session.

The results from both experiments showed that evaluation of the target odor by all participants was comparable at the baseline ratings prior to the manipulations. However, in each experiment, postemotional manipulation ratings to the target odor were significantly altered in the experimental group and showed that odor perception had changed in accord with the emotional valence of the associated experience. When a "pleasant" target odor was paired with a negative emotional experience, subsequent evaluations of that odor were more negative, and when an "unpleasant" target odor was paired with a positive emotional experience, subsequent evaluations of that odor were more favorable. No effects were seen in the control groups, and no change in ratings to the anchor odors was observed. Importantly, changes in odor preferences in the experimental group remained throughout the week of testing. This implies that simple manipulations can produce changes in odor preference perception that are highly enduring. When a novel odor is paired with an emotional event, hedonic perception of that odor is altered in accord with the associated emotion. Odor novelty is important in these manipulations, because if the odor were familiar it would by necessity already have acquired associative meaning, and due to the strong proactive interference effects known in olfaction (Lawless & Engen, 1977), it would be difficult (especially in a laboratory context) to reassociate it to a new experience. Although our study could not rule out the possibility of innate responding to odors, when joined with past empirical work and developmental and cross-cultural data it appears that emotion in conjunction with odor exposure is a powerful manipulator of odor preference formation.

The Connection Between Odor Perception, Mood, and Behavior

Following from the establishment of odor hedonic responses are the down-stream consequences of how these responses influence mood. Several studies have found that pleasant fragrances (e.g., baby powder, perfume) used in both laboratory and "real life" settings improved mood and even alleviated some of the symptoms associated with unpleasant physical conditions (Schiffman, Sattely-Miller, Suggs, & Graham, 1995; Villemure, Slotnick, & Bushnell, 2003). In contrast, participants exposed to unpleasant odors, such as dimethyl disulfide (cabbagelike smell), report being in a less pleasant mood (Knasko, 1992).

Tracking the sequence of action from perception to mood is the well-observed finding that mood affects cognition. For example, mood has been shown to influence creativity with the typical finding that individuals in a positive mood exhibit higher levels of creativity than individuals in a negative mood (Isen, Daubman, & Nowicki, 1987). Similar cognitive effects are seen when ambient odor environments are manipulated. Ehrlichman and Bastone (1992) demonstrated that the presence of a pleasant ambient odor (muguet or almond) improved creative problem solving relative to an unpleasant odor condition (thiophene or butyric acid). Similarly, pleasant ambient odors were found to enhance vigilance during a tedious task (Warm, Dember, & Parasuraman, 1991) and improve performance on anagram and word completion tests (Baron & Bronfen, 1994).

From the effects of mood on cognition are the ways in which mental states are translated into observable behaviors. A large body of psychological literature indicates that mood influences behavior. In general, positive mood is linked to an increase in productivity and the tendency to help others (Clark, 1991; Isen, 1984; Wright & Staw, 1999), while negative mood reduces pro-social behavior (Underwood, Froming, & Moore, 1997). Notably, pro-social behavior and productivity are also enhanced in the presence of positive ambient odors. For example, people exposed to pleasant ambient odors in a shopping mall (baking cookies, roasting coffee) were more inclined to help a stranger than people not exposed to an odor manipulation (Baron, 1997). Baron (1990) also found that participants who worked in the presence of a pleasant ambient odor (air freshener) reported higher self-efficacy, set higher goals, and were more likely to employ efficient work strategies than participants who worked in a no-odor condition. Conversely, Rotton (1983) found that the presence of a malodor (ethyl mercaptan) reduced participants' subjective judgments and lowered their tolerance for frustration. Participants in these studies also reported concordant mood changes.

The cognitive and behavioral effects reported in the presence of ambient odors are proposed to be due to the individual's past history with the odors in question and can be explained by associative learning mechanisms. Specifically, through prior associative pairing with emotional events, odors become conditioned stimuli for the emotional events and consequently exert the same type of cognitive influences and behavioral outcomes that the emotional events themselves would produce.

Experimental Evidence for Emotional Odor-Associative Learning Effects on Behavior

In an early study that suggested how emotional odor-associated learning could produce mood consistent outcomes, it was observed that female participants who were exposed to low levels of a novel odor while they worked on a stressful task later reported feeling anxious when exposed to the same odor in a nonstressful setting (Kirk-Smith, Van Toller, & Dodd, 1983). Based on this finding, my laboratory has tested the idea that odors can become associated to emotions and then act as conditioned stimuli for the emotions themselves, consequently altering behavior in accord with the conditioned (associated) emotion (Epple & Herz, 1999; Herz, Schankler, & Beland, 2004).

In our first study (Epple & Herz, 1999) we asked 5-year-olds to complete an "impossible maze" while they were in a room scented with an unfamiliar smell. The maze involved trying to move a toy troll around concentric rings with the goal of getting to the center of the maze without crossing a line. However, the maze was designed such that this was impossible to do. The children worked on the maze for 5 minutes and from videotaping their facial expressions and remarks it was evident that they became very frustrated by the impossibility of this task. The children were then given a break in an unscented area and 20 minutes later were brought to a different room and given a new task to perform.

The new task involved finding and circling drawings of "puppies missing their tails" from a sheet containing 120 animal illustrations.[3] The key manipulation was that the room they did this test in was either scented with the same smell as the room where they had done the maze task, scented with a different scent, or not scented at all. We found that children who did the worksheet test in a room scented with the same smell as the maze circled far fewer puppies correctly than children in any other setting. We changed the odors around and got the same results. No matter what the ambient aroma was, if it was the same one that had been present during the impossible maze the children did not do well. In other words, the odor that was present during the maze task had become linked to the feeling of frustration, such that later exposure to that scent elicited frustration and consequently the children behaved in an unmotivated manner and did not perform well. In addition to the odor-associative effects observed in this study, this finding has important implications for school environments and underscores how children's ability and performance may not be the same, the latter being strongly influenced by motivational state.

We repeated a version of this experiment with college students and obtained the same results (Herz et al., 2004). For the college students, their frustrating emotional experience was to play a computer game that was rigged to be very annoying and make them "lose" in the end. They played the computer game in a room that was scented with an unfamiliar odor. Then, after a short break, the students entered another room that was either scented with the same smell as the annoying computer game room, a different smell, or unscented and here they had to work on a series of difficult word puzzles. An example problem was "log rail" *change the order of the letters to make one word.*[4] As a measure of odor-emotional conditioning, we recorded how long the students persisted at solving the word puzzles before giving up.

We found that students who did the word puzzles in a room that was scented with the same odor as the computer game gave up more quickly than the students who did the word puzzles in the presence of a different odor or no odor. More specifically, they spent significantly less time on the problems that they ended up skipping and leaving blank than participants in the other groups. That is, when confronted with particularly challenging word problems, the behavior of participants exposed to the computer game exemplified a lack of motivation. To make sure that the effects were due to the elicitation of frustration by the ambient odor and not a nonassociative effect, such as boredom, we tested another group of students who experienced the same odor present during a neutral waiting room initial experience and then again at the test task. These data showed that the group who had prior exposure to the odor under neutral mood conditions spent the same amount of time trying to solve the problems as participants in the no-odor or different odor conditions. Only the group who had the same odor present both times, where it had first been associated to the frustrating computer game, showed lower persistence on the problems they ended up leaving blank.

These experiments indicate that after an odor has become associated to an emotional experience, that odor is able to elicit the associated emotions when later encountered, which can alter thoughts and behavior accordingly. Our experiments involved negative emotional manipulations because we were unable to produce sufficiently motivating positive circumstances in the laboratory. People are generally in relatively positive mood states, and to make them especially happy is much more difficult than to make them annoyed. Nevertheless, the theoretical mechanisms underlying the effects of odor-emotional conditioning should exist for positive manipulations just as much as for negative ones.

Odor Associations, Memory, and the Brain

Odors elicit liking, mood, and behavioral responses as a function of the emotional associations that have been made to them. Most of the time these associations are generalized and cannot be precisely linked to one past episodic event. However, there are occasions where both liking and memory events are precisely linked to an odor; a woman once told me that she hated the scent of roses because the first time she ever smelled a rose was at her mother's funeral. Thus, the scent of rose for this woman was both highly disliked and a specific recollection of a very upsetting past event.

There have been many anecdotal and literary accounts of the special resonance of odor-evoked memories. The most famous example is the one described by Marcel Proust at the start of his seven-volume opus on memory (*The Remembrance of Things Past*) where he recounts the experience of dipping a madelèine biscuit into linden tea and the triggering of a long-forgotten recollection that ensued from the aroma. From the fame of this description, the common term for these special smell-evoked memories has become known as the "Proust phenomenon." Proustian memories are characterized as emotionally rich, vivid, and sudden autobiographical recollections that are triggered by a scent. Stemming from this conception, odors have also earned the reputation of being the "best" cues to memory. But what "best memory cues" refers to is not clear. My laboratory has spent nearly two decades elucidating this claim.

The most comprehensive method for assessing the special character-istics of odor-evoked memories is with a cross-modal approach, where memories elicited by stimuli presented in various sensory modalities are compared. For example, a series of familiar source objects (cues) are pre-sented to participants in either olfactory, verbal, visual, or tactile form (e.g., the smell of popcorn, the word "popcorn," seeing popcorn, or feeling popcorn) while participants' view emotionally evocative pictures. In these experiments, participants are told that we are interested in the effects of different environmental cues on the perception of pictures. No mention of memory or memory testing is ever made. Two days later, however, when participants return to the lab, they are given a surprise cued recall test for their picture experiences, and the accuracy and emotionality of their memories are assessed.

In every experiment, we find that memories of the pictures evoked by the various cue types do not differ in accuracy (the ability to correctly recall which picture went with which cue or the details of the picture). However, memories recalled to odors are always experienced as signifi-cantly more emotional than memories triggered by any other sensory cue. Across a range of cross-modal experiments designed to elicit both experimentally constrained and personal autobiographical memories, we found that memories associated to odors are distinguished by their emo-tional potency and are also more evocative; people feel more brought back to the original time and place, compared to memories associated to cues perceived through other modalities (visual, tactile, verbal, music) (Herz, 1998, 2004; Herz & Cupchik, 1995; Herz, Eliassen, Beland, & Souza, 2003; Herz & Schooler, 2002). Others have recently replicated these findings (e.g., Willander & Larsson, 2007).

We have furthered these results using functional magnetic resonance imaging (fMRI) and compared regions of activation during recall trig-gered by olfactory and visual versions of cues that were connected to a personally meaningful memory (elicited by a personally selected perfume for each individual) or a comparable control cue (an unmarketed perfume that was the same for all participants) (Herz et al., 2003). In this study, fMRI analyses revealed significantly greater activation in the amygdala during recall to the odor of the personally significant perfume than to any other cue, and self-report responses confirmed that emotional responses were greatest to the personally meaningful odor cue. These findings are the first neurobiological evidence that the subjective experience of the emotional potency of odor-evoked memory is specifically correlated with heightened activation in the amygdala during recall.

Mediating Factors: Context, Expectation, and Visual-Verbal Priming

Several factors mediate odor-associative learning and the subsequent memories, moods, and behaviors that are elicited. Context, expectation, and visual-verbal schemas are the most powerful influences. A context is a state or situation (mental or physical) or environment that induces a set of preconceptions and expectations and has been shown to be a very powerful mediator of odor hedonic perception. Visual scenes and physical context prime expectations for odors, and the effects have been clearly demonstrated in experiments involving color and odors or flavors. Zellner, Bartoli, and Eckard (1991) found that flavored water was evaluated differently depending on the color of the solution. For example, when a lemon-flavored solution was colored yellow, it received much higher liking scores than when that exact same solution was colored red. More embarrassingly, a French panel of trained enologists gave specific red wine descriptions to a white wine that had been adulterated with red food coloring (Morrot, Brochet, & Dubourdieu, 2001). This phenomenon is also well known in the nonalcoholic beverage industry. When the occasional mistake occurs and the purple colored "grape" drink is accidentally flavored with cherry, there are almost never any complaints.

My laboratory has further found that verbal expectation effects are so great that they can cause olfactory illusions (Herz & von Clef, 2001). Using the definition that an illusion is created when a physical stimulus remains invariant but its context alters perception, we investigated whether verbal context could produce olfactory illusions. We examined five ambiguous odors:[5] violet leaf, patchouli, pine oil, menthol, and a 1:1 mixture of isovaleric + butyric acid. Participants sniffed each odor at two sessions separated by 1 week. At each session an odor was given a different verbal label, either positive or negative (for example, isovaleric + butyric acid was alternately called "vomit" or "parmesan cheese," and pine oil was called "disinfectant" or "Christmas tree"). Participants then gave ratings to the odors on several hedonic scales and provided motivational and interpretative responses to them.

Results showed that the label provided could significantly influence the hedonic perception of all the odors. When the label was positive, each odor was evaluated as more pleasant and familiar than when that same odor was given a negative label. Moreover, motivational responses were entirely different as a function of label. For example, when isovaleric + butyric acid was called "parmesan cheese," it inspired participants to say they would like to eat it, while when it was given the negative label ("vomit"), it provoked the wish to escape from it. The effect was so strong for certain odors that participants would not believe that the same odor had been presented to them at both sessions. Thus, the connotation of words can have a tremendous impact on how an odor will be liked, independent of how it was originally learned, which has obvious implications for scent marketing.

Visual and verbal contexts are more influential in olfactory perception than any other sensory modality because odors are so devoid of information in themselves. Moreover, in contrast to other sensory stimuli, odors are invisible and they cannot be precisely localized in physical space, thus the drive to seek meaning from external context is especially high (Engen, 1982; Herz, 2003). The shrewd sensory marketer could use these factors to elicit maximum impact in product labeling and branding.

Considerations for Scent Marketing

From the present review it would seem that there are numerous straightforward implications and applications of odor-emotional manipulations that can be used in scent marketing. Emotional associations to odors should be able to influence the perception of product value, moods elicited by the product, and purchase behavior. However, there are several cognitive, physiological, and logistical aspects of olfaction that need to be taken into account before any implementation of scent marketing methods should be carried out.

Congruence

With respect to the psychological impact of the odor itself, the most important issue is not actually odor liking (hedonics), but rather the degree to which the odor is perceived to be thematically congruent and embellishing of the retail product or the retail environment. It has long been established that humans are positively predisposed to congruency and react negatively when expectations are violated (Mandler, 1982). This has been directly shown with odor and flavor experiences. As mentioned earlier, Zellner et al. (1991) found that when flavors did not match the expected sensation based on color (e.g., yellow liquid tasted like grape), liking ratings were much lower than if the sensation matched the color expectation (yellow liquid tasted like lemon). In the domain of scent marketing several studies have also shown that when a pleasant scent did not match expectations based on product theme, lower responses to merchandise were obtained than when no scent was used at all (Mattila & Wirtz, 2001). This indicates that there is a real cost to using the wrong scent, which is independent of simple odor hedonics. Conversely, when the "correct" scent was used in a specific retail environment, purchase behavior and sales were found to increase (Spangenberg, Sprott, Grohmann, & Tracy, 2006).

The correct thematically congruent scent is not always obvious and indeed can be quite difficult to ascertain. For retailers with scent-literal products (e.g., a coffee shop) the choice of a thematically congruent scent is easy (coffee), and many coffee shop chains use artificial air-diffused coffee scents. However, the majority of retailers sell products that do not have an obviously translatable scent. What is the correct scent of a ski store? An electronics store? A clothing store? The choice of the "right" scent is further complicated by store logistics, such as indoor or contained air flow, size and space, proximity to other scented areas, whether more than one type of merchandise is sold, and varied customer demographics, including age, culture, education, socioeconomic status, and gender. For any success in using scent marketing, retailers need to actually test what responses their customers, from a range of backgrounds or at least their preferred target demographic, have to various scent-product matches and also must be mindful of and address several physical and environment olfactory issues.

The Physical Behavior of Odors

Olfaction is our slowest sense. The lag time between sniffing and the brain's registering a smell varies, averaging approximately 400 milliseconds (almost half a second). By contrast, it takes 45 milliseconds for the visual cortex to register an image presented to the retina. This half-second duration for odor registration does not take into account the time required to react to a scent, which effectively doubles the perceptual time, making olfaction an especially slow sense. In addition to being slow to detect, odors are slow to leave. Odors linger for varying lengths of time depending on ambient air flow and temperature. Odors are also sticky (hydrophobic molecules). The walls of a store will become impregnated with whatever scent is being piped in, and the only way to get rid of it will be to paint the store; the same principle applies to the store furniture, not to mention the merchandise.

Olfaction is also a synthetic sense; when you mix two odors together the resulting whole is not the same as the sum of the parts. The mixture of chocolate and licorice does not smell like "chocolatey licorice," it would smell like something new; and that "something new" is unpredictable. Indeed the fact that it is impossible to predict the perceptual experience of a scent based on its chemical composition is a major barrier to technological advancements in the fragrance industry (Turin, 2006). Another concern relates to overodorizing and odor intensity. As previously mentioned, the stronger the scent, the more unpleasant it becomes. Stores, such as Abercrombie and Fitch, that overwhelm the senses of their customers have very limited viability beyond the sensation-seeking teenage demographic. Further, exposure to an odor, regardless of intensity, produces the physiological fact of adaption.

Odor adaptation can be likened to too much of a good thing. For example, you walk into your favorite delicatessen and smell the smoked meat, the pickles, and all the condiments, and your mouth begins to water. To your dismay, however, you discover that once your sandwich finally arrives, you can barely smell the heaping hot corned beef slathered in mustard on the plate in front of you. This phenomenon is due to **receptor adaptation**.

The precise length of time for receptor adaptation to occur varies as a function of both the individual (Dalton, Doolittle, & Breslin, 2002) and the odor (Pierce, Wysocki, Aronow, Webb, & Boden, 1996). On average it takes about 15 to 20 minutes of continuous exposure to an odor for the molecules to stop eliciting an olfactory response, but adaptation can also occur in less than a minute. Fortunately, receptor adaptation can be undone relatively quickly. Adaptation occurs when odor molecules bind to their corresponding receptors. The receptors are then internalized into their cell bodies and are no longer physically available to respond to an aroma (Firestein, 2001). Inside the cell body the receptors become unbound from the odor and are then recycled through the cell and emerge again. Stepping outside the deli for a few minutes gives unbound olfactory receptors a chance to accumulate on the cell surface, so that when you walk back in you can enjoy the appetizing scents once more.

One way to prolong the effect of smelling a scent before adaptation kicks in is to dispense an odor intermittently rather than continuously. The magnitude of adaptation is also affected by odor intensity (Kadohisa & Wilson, 2006). The higher the intensity, the longer it takes us to adapt. For example, it will take longer to adapt in an Abercrombie and Fitch store than in a Sony Style store.

It is also the case that exposure to one odor can raise the odor detection threshold for a second, completely different odor. You have probably noted that when sniffing perfumes in a department store you become fairly use-less at differentiating them after several samples. This phenomenon is due to **cross-adaptation**, and it is presumed to occur when the odors in question rely on similar sets of olfactory receptors. However, this simple explanation is complicated by the fact that most cross-adaptation relation-ships are nonreciprocal. For example, smelling pentanol (a chemical used in some paints) has a strong cross-adapting effect on subsequently smell-ing propanol (used as an antiseptic and solvent), whereas smelling propa-nol first has only a small cross-adapting effect on then smelling pentanol (Cain & Engen, 1969). Furthermore, exposure to the first odor can some-times *enhance* sensitivity to the second odor.

Adaptation and cross-adaption have clear consequences for scent mar-keting. First, if a customer lingers in your store for more than 15 minutes, any intended effects of the ambient scent will disappear. When one can-not perceive an odor, it will not have any psychological effect. There is no subliminal odor perception. Unlike in vision, where a millisecond flash of a Camel cigarette package can cause "unexplained" interest in smoking Camel's cigarettes, when an odor is below the level of perceptual detec-tion it cannot have any behavioral or psychological consequences. Fear of unknown odor manipulations is therefore groundless. Note, however, that this is different from the case where a customer is *unaware* that the presence of a detectable odor has increased his or her impression that the store's clothing is of particularly high quality. When odors are above their detection threshold, one often has to attend to them in order to "smell" them. Lack of attention to odors actually decreases odor detection ability (Plailly, Howard, Gitelman, & Gottfried, 2008; Zelano et al., 2005).

Summary

Substantial evidence indicates that through association with emotional experiences the hedonic perception of odors can be formed and changed. Odors also elicit more emotional and evocative memories than any other sensory cues, and through association with emotional experiences odors can trigger specific emotions that have a direct impact on mood and behavior. Further, there is a privileged and unique connection between the neural substrates of emotion and the sense of smell. I have developed a model to illustrate these relationships and their effects (Figure 7.1). Emotion and a novel odor are experienced together; through amygdala-hippocampal mediation the odor becomes associated to the emotion,

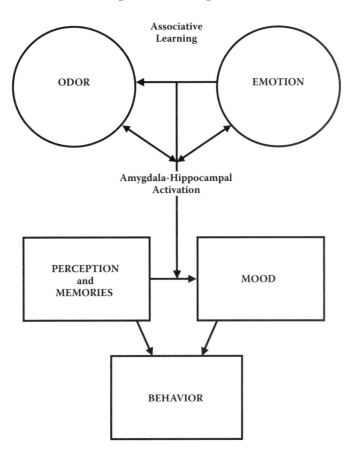

Figure 7.1 Emotion and a novel odor are experienced together. Through amygdala-hippocampal mediation the odor becomes associated to the emotion which produces the hedonic responses and memories that are elicited by the odor. As a function of the acquired hedonic valence and emotional associations, subsequent exposure to that odor impacts mood and concordantly influences behavior.

which produces the hedonic responses and memories that are elicited by the odor; as a function of the acquired hedonic valence and emotional associations, subsequent exposure to that odor impacts mood and concordantly influences behavior.

An ambient fragrance that is emotionally and thematically associated to a product should be able to alter perception, cognition, and behavior with positive consequences for revenue. However, *caveat venditor*, there are many practical, physiological, and psychological factors that need to be considered.

Notes

1. Pavlov's dogs inherently salivated to meat, but a bell meant nothing to them. After a bell had been paired with the presentation of meat several times, the bell alone was sufficient to make the dogs salivate.
2. Flavor is primarily produced by odor; taste contributes only the sensations of salt, sour, sweet, bitter, and savory (*umami*).
3. There were 20 puppies missing tails, and 20 puppies with tails.
4. Answer is gorilla.
5. Ambiguous odors are those with minimally fixed sources and thus can be interpreted with various hedonic connotations.

References

Aggleton, J. P., & Mishkin, M. (1986). The amygdala: Sensory gateway to the emotions. In R. Plutchik & H. Kellerman (Eds.), *Emotion: Theory, research and experience.* Vol. 3: *Biological foundations of emotion* (pp. 281–299). Orlando, FL: Academic Press.

Baron, R. A. (1990). Environmentally-induced positive affect: Its impact on self-efficacy, task performance, negotiation and conflict. *Journal of Applied Social Psychology, 20,* 368–384.

Baron, R. A. (1997). The sweet smell of helping: Effects of pleasant ambient fragrance on prosocial behavior in shopping malls. *Personality and Social Psychology Bulletin, 23,* 489–503.

Baron, R. A., & Bronfen, M. I. (1994). A whiff of reality: Empirical evidence concerning the effects of pleasant fragrances on work-related behavior. *Journal of Applied Social Psychology, 24,* 1179–1203.

Cahill, L., Babinsky, R., Markowilsch, H. J., & McGaugh, J. L. (1995). Amygdala and emotional memory. *Nature, 377,* 295–296.

Cain, W. S., & Engen, T. (1969). Olfactory adaptation and the scaling of odor intensity. In C. Pfaffman (Ed.), *Olfaction and taste III* (pp. 127–141). New York: Rockefeller University Press.

Cain, W. S., & Johnson, F. Jr. (1978). Lability of odor pleasant-ness: Influence of mere exposure. *Perception, 7,* 459-465.

Clark, M. S. (Ed.). (1991). *Mood and helping: Mood as a motivator of helping and helping as a regulator of mood.* Newbury Park, CA: Sage.

Dalton, P., Doolittle, N., & Breslin, P.A. (2002). Gender specific induction of enhanced sensitivity to odors. *Nature Neuroscience, 5,* 199–200.

Dilks, D. D., Dalton, P., & Beauchamp, G. K. (1999). Cross-cultural variation in responses to malodors. *Chemical Senses, 24,* 599.

Ehrlichman, H., & Bastone, L. (1992). The use of odour in the study of emotion. In S. van Toller & G. H. Dodd (Eds.), *Fragrance—the psychology and biology of perfume* (pp. 143–159). London and New York: Elsevier Applied Science.

Eichenbaum, H. (2001). The hippocampus and declarative memory: Cognitive mechanisms and neural codes. *Behavioural Brain Research, 127*, 199–207.

Engen, T. (1982). *The perception of odors.* New York: Academic Press.

Engen, T. (1988). The acquisition of odour hedonics. In S. van Toller & G. H. Dodd (Eds.), *Perfumery—the psychology and biology of fragrance* (pp. 79–90). London: Chapman and Hall.

Engen, T. (1991). *Odor sensation and memory.* New York: Praeger.

Engen, T., & Engen, E. A. (1997). Relationship between development of odor perception and language. *Enfance, 1*, 125–140.

Epple, G., & Herz, R. S. (1999). Ambient odors associated to failure influence cognitive performance in children. *Developmental Psychobiology, 35*, 103–107.

Firestein, S. (2001). How the olfactory system makes sense of scents. *Nature, 413*, 211–218.

Haller, R., Rummel, C., Henneberg, S., Pollmer, U., & Koster, E. P. (1999). The influence of early experience with vanillin on food preference in later life. *Chemical Senses, 24*, 465–567.

Herz, R. S. (1998). Are odors the best cues to memory? A cross-modal comparison of associative memory stimuli. *Annals of the New York Academy of Sciences, 855*, 670–674.

Herz, R. S. (2000, July–August). Scents of time. *The Sciences*, 34–39.

Herz, R. S. (2003). The effect of verbal context in olfactory perception. *Journal of Experimental Psychology General, 132*, 595–606.

Herz, R. S. (2004). A comparison of autobiographical memories triggered by olfactory, visual and auditory stimuli. *Chemical Senses, 29*, 217–224.

Herz, R. S. (2007). *The scent of desire: Discovering our enigmatic sense of smell.* New York: William Morrow/HarperCollins.

Herz, R. S., Beland, S. L., & Hellerstein, M. (2004). Changing odor hedonic perception through emotional associations in humans. *International Journal of Comparative Psychology, 17*, 315–339.

Herz, R. S., & Cupchik, G. C. (1995). The emotional distinctiveness of odor-evoked memories. *Chemical Senses, 20*, 517–528.

Herz, R. S., Eliassen, J. C., Beland, S. L., & Souza, T. (2003). Neuroimaging evidence for the emotional potency of odor-evoked memory. *Neuropsychologia, 42*, 371–378.

Herz, R. S., Schankler, C., & Beland, S. (2004). Olfaction, emotion and associative learning: Effects on motivated behavior. *Motivation and Emotion, 28*, 363–383.

Herz, R. S., & Schooler, J. W. (2002). A naturalistic study of autobiographical memories evoked to olfactory versus visual cues. *American Journal of Psychology, 115*, 21–32.

Herz, R. S., & von Clef, J. (2001). The influence of verbal labeling on the perception of odors: Evidence for olfactory illusions? *Perception, 30*, 381–391.

Isen, A. M. (1984). Toward understanding the role of affect in cognition. In A. L. Wyer & T. K. Scrull (Eds.), *Handbook of social cognition* (pp. 179–236). Hillsdale, NJ: Lawrence Erlbaum.

Isen, A. M., Daubman, K. A., & Nowicki, G. P. (1987). Positive affect facilitates creative problem solving. *Journal of Personality and Social Psychology, 52,* 1122–1131.

Kadohisa, M., & Wilson, D. A. (2006). Olfactory cortical adaptation facilitates detection of odors against background. *Journal of Neurophysiology, 95,* 1888–1896.

Kirk-Smith, M. D., Van Toller, C., & Dodd, G. H. (1983). Unconscious odour conditioning in human participants. *Biological Psychology, 17,* 221–231.

Knasko, S. C. (1992). Ambient odor's effect on creativity, mood and perceived health. *Chemical Senses, 17,* 27–35.

Lawless, H., & Engen, T. (1977). Associations to odors: Interference, mnemonics and verbal labeling. *Journal of Experimental Psychology: Human Learning and Memory, 3,* 52–59.

LeDoux, J. (1998). Fear and the brain: Where have we been and where are we going? *Biological Psychiatry, 44,* 1229–1238.

Lott, I. T., Sullivan, R. M., & McPherson, D. (1989). Associative olfactory learning occurs in the neonate. *Neurology, 39,* 110.

Mandler, G. (1982). The structure of value: Accounting for taste. In M. S. Clark & S. T. Fiske (Eds.), *Affect and cognition: The 17th annual Carnegie symposium on cognition* (pp. 3–36). Hillsdale, NJ: Erlbaum.

Mattila, A. S., & Wirtz, J. (2001). Congruency of scent and music as a driver of in-store evaluations and behavior. *Journal of Retailing, 77,* 273–289.

Menashe, I., Man, O, Lancet, D., & Gilad, Y. (2003). Different noses for different people. *Nature Genetics, 34,* 143–144.

Mennella, J. A., & Beauchamp, G. K. (1991). The transfer of alcohol to human milk: Effects on flavor and the infant's behavior. *New England Journal of Medicine, 325,* 981–985.

Mennella, J. A., & Beauchamp, G. K. (2002). Flavor experiences during formula feeding are related to preferences during childhood. *Early Human Development, 68,* 71–82.

Mennella, J. A., & Garcia, P. L. (2000). Children's hedonic response to the smell of alcohol: Effects of parental drinking habits. *Alcoholism: Clinical and Experimental Research, 24,* 1167–1171.

Moncreiff, R. W. (1966). *Odour preferences.* New York: Wiley.

Morrot, G., Brochet, F., & Dubourdieu, D. (2001). The color of odors. *Brain and Language, 79,* 309–320.

Moskowitz, H. R., Dravnieks, A., & Klarman, L. A. (1976). Odor intensity and pleasantness for a diverse set of odorants. *Perception and Psychophysics, 19,* 122–128.

Pierce, J. D., Jr., Wysocki, C. J., Aronov, E. V., Webb, J. B., & Boden, R. M. (1996). The role of perceptual and structural similarity in cross-adaptation. *Chemical Senses, 21,* 223–237.

Plailly, J., Howard, J. D., Gitelman, D. R., & Gottfried, J. A. (2008). Attention to odor modulates thalamocortical connectivity in the human brain. *Journal of Neuroscience, 28*, 5257–5267.

Proust, M. (1919). *Du côté de chez Swann.* Paris: Gaillimard.

Robin, O., Alaoui-Ismaili, O., Dittmar, A., & Vernet-Mauri, E. (1998). Emotional responses evoked by dental odors: An evaluation from autonomic parameters. *Journal of Dental Research, 77,* 1638–1946.

Rolls, E. T. (1999). *The brain and emotion.* Oxford: Oxford University Press.

Rotton, J. (1983). Affective and cognitive consequences of malodorous pollution. *Applied Social Psychology, 4,* 171–191.

Schiffman, S. S., Sattely-Miller, E. A., Suggs, M. S., & Graham, B. G. (1995). The effect of pleasant odors and hormone status on mood of women at midlife. *Brain Research Bulletin, 36,* 19–29.

Schleidt, M., Hold, B., & Attila, G. (1981). A cross-cultural study on the attitude towards personal odors. *Journal of Chemical Ecology, 7,* 19–31.

Schmidt, H. J., & Beauchamp, G. K. (1988). Adult-like odor preferences and aversions in three-year-old children. *Child Development, 59,* 1136–1143.

Spangenberg, E. R., Sprott, D. E., Grohmann, B., & Tracy, D. L. (2006). Gender-congruent ambient scent influences on approach and avoidance behaviors in a retail store. *Journal of Business Research, 59,* 1281–1287.

Stein, M., Ottenberg, M. D., & Roulet, N. (1958). A study of the development of olfactory preferences. *Archives of Neurological Psychiatry, 80,* 264–266.

Turin, L. (2006). *The secret of scent.* New York: HarperCollins.

Underwood, B., Froming, W. J., & Moore, B. S. (1997). Mood, attention and altruism. *Developmental Psychology, 13,* 541–542.

Villemure, C., Slotnick, B. M., & Bushnell, M. C. (2003). Effects of odors on pain perception: deciphering the roles of emotion and attention. *Pain, 106,* 101–108.

Warm, J. S., Dember, W. N., & Parasuraman, R. (1991). Effects of olfactory stimulation on performance and stress in a visual sustained attention task. *Journal of the Society of Cosmetic Chemistry, 42,* 199–210.

Wasserman, E. A., & Miller, R. R. (1997). What's elementary about associative learning? *Annual Review of Psychology, 48,* 573–607.

Willander, J., & Larsson, M. (2007). Olfaction and emotion: The case of autobiographical memory. *Memory and Cognition, 35,* 1659–1663.

Wright, T. A., & Staw, B. M. (1999). Affect and favorable work outcomes: Two longitudinal tests of the happy-productive worker thesis. *Journal of Organizational Behavior, 20,* 1–23.

Zelano, C., Bensafi, M., Porter, J., Mainland, J., Johnson, B., Bremner, E. et al. (2005). Attentional modulation in human primary olfactory cortex. *Nature Neuroscience, 8,* 114–120.

Zellner, D. A., Bartoli, A. M., & Eckard, R. (1991). Influence of color on odors identification and liking ratings. *American Journal of Psychology, 104,* 547–561.

8

Do Scents Evoke the Same Feelings Across Cultures?
Exploring the Role of Emotions

May O. Lwin and Mindawati Wijaya

Introduction

Scent has been a part of human civilization since the beginning of time. Throughout history, the possession of scent, in the forms of perfumes and incense, had been the mark of distinction, wealth, and affluence. Among the royal gifts in Ancient Egypt were incense and perfumes, the wealthy Romans were famous for perfumed bathwater, the Chinese had their scented joss sticks and red paper, while the Indians prized their sandalwood incense and jasmine flowers. In the religious circles, scented oils of varying origins are used during rites and for anointing the faithful. As time passed, the methods of dispensing scents have also been refined, and scents of every possible combination have been captured, bottled, and used at various occasions by different cultures.

Culture and Perception

Culture influences individuals in many ways, shaping thoughts, values, and even behaviors, often without conscious realization. The importance and uniqueness of culture, which varies from society to society, is captured in its definition as described by the United Nations Educational, Scientific, and Cultural Organization (UNESCO, 2002): "the set of distinctive spiritual, material, intellectual, and emotional features of society or a social group, and that it encompasses, in addition to art and literature, lifestyles, ways of living together, value systems, traditions and beliefs."

According to Hall's (1976) culture-context theory, people in different cultures communicate differently, and as a result, see the world differently. For instance, people from the United States are detailed oriented, meaning they need detailed background information when they interact with others, and they look for explicit messages because they value logic and directness (Hall & Hall, 1990). Among Asians, on the other hand, information is transmitted either in the physical context or through implicit means of which very little is imparted explicitly in the message (Hall, 1976). Hall further argues that the whole communication process was affected by the nature of "context," which helped explain the difference in meanings and perceptions from culture to culture.

Cultures not only function as a set of norms and a way of life but also help us make sense of everything that our five senses can recognize—through sight, touch, hear, taste, and smell—by giving meaning to them. In visual communication, for example, culture is an important determinant of how people comprehend and decipher messages. Several past studies have demonstrated that to understand a visual message in an advertisement, the audience must first deconstruct the signs and symbols embedded in the message based on their cultural knowledge (Barthes, 1972; Hall, 1976; Fiske, 1989; Frith & Tsao, 1998). For instance, Hedberg and Brown (2002) showed that in a classroom setting with students from different cultures, educators needed to develop Web site interfaces that matched with the students' cultures in order to maximize their learning process.

Smell, however, is unique because olfactory responses are generally autonomic, meaning that it influences humans physiologically before actually influencing cognition. In general, little, if any, cognitive effort is required to experience scents (Ehrlichman & Bastone, 1992), and scents result in emotionally laden memory associations when recalled. Although research in olfaction has emerged extensively in areas like services and retailing (e.g., Chebat & Michon, 2003), few researchers have looked at how cultures shape perceptions through scents. We therefore address this gap in this chapter by exploring how people from different cultures associate scents with emotions and meanings.

Literature Review

The Emotional Role of Olfaction

Humans are exposed to many kinds of scents every day from which individual human responses are formed. Consumers prefer certain perfumes, room fragrances for the home, or choose to patronize certain service outlets because of the preferred ambient scent. Many of our olfactory preferences are based purely on emotional associations (Fox, 2008). Meaning, how humans feel about a particular scent, depends on how they relate the scent with certain emotions. This primarily has to do with the scent linkages within the limbic system of the brain. When coming into contact with smells, these scents act as inducing agents that stimulate these connections. The limbic system has a role in processing and expressing emotions. Of all the five senses, scent is most closely linked to emotion rather than "facts" (Herz & Cupchik, 1992).

Scents have personal meaning and a very high propensity to be associated with events, surroundings, experiences, objects, and even people (Kirk-Smith & Booth, 1987). Pleasant scents are associated with those that are able to elicit some positive emotions, such as being happy or feeling loved, while unpleasant scents are those which evoke negative emotions, such as being sad or feeling lonely, and this association serves as a requirement for an odor to attract us or warn us (Hummel & Nordin, 2005). Humans are partial to the smell of good food because it provides the cue that the food is delicious. People can receive a feeling of satisfaction just by smelling, and some fragrances are even effective in reducing stress and creating positive moods for those who smell it (Ehrlichman & Bastone, 1992; Parasuraman, 1984; Warrenburg, 2005). On the other hand, we tend to avoid garbage smell because of its negative associations. The stronger the emotional experience when smelling a scent, the greater the potential for the scent in eliciting associations with things (Herz, 1997).

Culture and Scents

Culture also influences our perceptions of scents. Researchers have found that babies learn about smells early but are indifferent to scents until they are about 8 years old. For example, infants like the smell of feces and are equally indifferent to what adults consider to be positive or negative scents (Herz, 2007). There is much evidence for what has been termed odor-associative learning whereby how one feels when first encountering the scent determines one's perception of the scent. Hence, it is the cultural differences in experiences that establish how a particular individual responds to an array of olfactory stimuli.

In many cultures scents are clearly defined as having certain qualities, be they desirable or undesirable. This influences the aesthetic experiences related to the scent. For example, the Dassantch of Ethiopia find the odor of cattle (which connotes fertility and social status) attractive and hence wash their hands with cow urine and smear their bodies with manure (Classen, Howes, & Synnott, 1997). For the Chinese, certain scents have corresponding meanings in a comprehensive system of interrelated sensory codes. For example, the burnt smell is related to the element fire, as well as the bitter taste, the color red, and so on. Other cultures, such as the Suya Indians of Brazil and the Serer Ndut of Senegal even have their own scent classifications that enable them to distinguish different scents and give meaning to each of them. For example, in Suya Indians' culture, a bland smell was associated with adult men, small mammals, and birds, while a strong smell was associated with adult women, children, and carnivorous mammals and birds (Seeger, 1981). The Serer Ndut perceived ducks, camels, and pigs as rotten, while donkeys as acidic (Dupire, 1987).

Research Question: Cross-Cultural Responses to Contexts in Sensory Perception

Interestingly, there are certainly many areas whereby various cultures have overlapped the meanings they imbue to certain scents. The concept and the use of scent can be viewed as both universally similar or indigenous and dissimilar. For example, the smell of Mom's home-cooked meal is usually universally viewed as being inviting. However, when it comes to a more specific detail of the meal itself, individual associations of the scent come into play and differ from culture to culture. For example, the smell of salted fish may represent a delicious home-cooked meal for some, while for others it can be unappetizing, depending on associations in that particular culture. This reiterates how emotions influence the meaning given to scents, as the strength of scent associations is related with the emotional experience (Herz, 1997). Furthermore, if scent is indeed influenced by emotional experience, different emotive contexts may therefore elicit different responses.

Would the emotiveness of context influence how culture shapes scent associations? That is, when scent associations are formed within a cultural context, whether those experiences were in the context of strong emotion may create differences in how scent associations occur. We sought to explore scent-attribute association among different cultures and to examine the universality of scent preferences in different contexts. With this study, we attempted to answer this specific research question: Does the emotiveness of contexts play a role in the cultural association of scents?

Method

We conducted eight focus groups, involving 8 to 10 respondents from eight different cultural backgrounds, which were grouped into four sub-groups (Indian subcontinent, Chinese, European, and American). These four groupings were combined to form two main groups of Easterners and Westerners, respectively. The participants were evenly split between males and females and age grouped between 20 to 43 years old, with at least a high school education.

During the focus group discussion, we asked participants to think of situations in two types of experiences: one lower emotive and the other high emotive. For the low-emotive context, we asked two questions that we considered were set in neutral situations that did not evoke a high level of emotions and had commonality across cultures. We felt that a "clean place" was something everyone would have experienced but would be low in emotional intensity. Hence our first set of questions revolved around what was considered a clean or an unclean place. For high-emotive context, we considered situations such as something that was emotive in nature and commonly experienced across cultures. We felt that a joyful celebration was something everyone would have experienced but would be higher in emotional intensity. Hence our second set of questions revolved around what was considered a happy or sad occasion.

Results

In analyzing the results, we were interested in scent associations and the recall of experiences that were related to the scent. Findings will be explained comprehensively in each context and then summarized in Table 8.1.

Low-Emotive Context

What smells would you associate with a clean place?
All groups had a few participants who named citrus scents such as lime being associated with a clean place/house. These participants noted smells like "lime, lemon, grapefruit, orange" as denoting cleanliness. Some of these scents were further associated with brands. A female German participant commented "I know a place is clean when it has the freshly

TABLE 8.1   Cultural Associations of Scents in Low and High Emotive Contexts

Context	Germans/U.K./French	U.S.	Pakistanis and Indians	Chinese Singaporeans, Chinese, Chinese Malaysians
Low emotive: Clean Place	lemon, mint, VIM, freshly washed clean sheets, mountain smell, Alps, ventilated, freshly cooked food, GLADE	pine, chlorides, detergents like TIDE and CHEER, fresh air, lemon, strawberry, orange, grape fruit, mountain breeze, ocean breeze	Citrus, airy, meadows and mountains, lemon and lime; orange; sunny smell, VIM, TIDE detergent, paint, flowers	lemon, lime, lavender, floral, DETTOL, TIDE, sunned, citrus; mint, lime, woody, running water, Alpine mountains, air freshener, fresh paint, fresh paint, detergent, KIWI, GOOD MAID, air fresheners
Low emotive: Not Clean Place	garbage, old food, musty, stale air, dirty clothes	garbage, spoiled food, sewage, stuffy, stale	garbage, stale, spoilt food	garbage, salted fish, smoke, sour, burnt, still, dust, rotten food, stuffy
High emotive: Happy/Celebratory	Christmas smell, forest, candles, beer, wine, cookies, Christmas food, warm, homely, fireplace, sausages	pie, ham, Christmas tree, pine, cake, candles, turkey, chocolate, eggnog, snow, champagne	curry, spices, sweet smell, cake, herbs, oil lamps, incense, whisky	fresh notes, Chinese cookies, barbecue pork, coconut oil, cake, fried chicken, oranges, money smell, liquor, carbonated drinks, fireworks, herbs
High emotive: Sad/Funereal	church smell, flowers, stones	flowers, candle, earth	burning, Bhopal leaves, incense	joss stick, floral, ash, incense, burnt paper, porridge

Note: n = 76, 19, 18, 19, and 20.

scrubbed lemon detergent smell, like Lemon Vim." In another group, a male Chinese Malaysian commented that it was the "lemon soap smell at my mother's sink" that he associated with cleanliness.

Again for every group, there was a strong cleanliness association with "nature smells," such as what an Indian male described as the "airy smell" and an American male described as "fresh air." The Europeans appeared to share a similar association with air/wind, as a British female talked about "clean rooms are well ventilated, or have windows where you can feel (and smell) the breeze." In particular, participants appeared to conceptualize mountains like the Alps, what a Chinese Malaysian male described as "the smell of the mountains in *Sound of Music*," and an Indian female described as "beautiful grassy meadows and high mountains." The concept of nature extended further for participants like a female Chinese Singaporean who said "When you are in a clean place, you can smell natural things like wood and fresh running streams." Among Europeans and American participants, this concept of air, altitude, and nature was also clearly visualized as they relate cleanliness to "mountain breeze and ocean breeze."

A number of participants in each group also had associations with synthetic scents. For example, an American male and a few Chinese Singaporeans and Chinese participants offered "detergents," while another American male associated "chlorides" as being associated with clean. A Malaysian participant mentioned "fresh paint smell" in this regard. Participants from all groups also recounted the scent brands that offered cleaning products as Kiwi and Vim.

In particular, Chinese Malaysian and Chinese Singaporean participants put the smell of Dettol (an antiseptic typically used in high dosage in hospitals) as being an ultimate reflector of cleanliness. As one Chinese Singaporean female commented, "You know it is a clean place when you can smell Dettol." Similarly, there appeared to be universal agreement that the smell of laundry detergent brands (such as Tide and Cheer) and household cleaning agents (such as Vim) stood for cleanliness. The final set of clean product associations relates to air fresheners. Again all groups had participants who presented the smell of air fresheners in a variety of scent types as connoting a clean place.

What smells would you associate with an unclean place?
When participants were asked about the lack of cleanliness, there were a large number of participants who mentioned "Garbage!" in unison. The concept of smells emitting from undesirable items of discard was foremost in the minds of participants from every group. A Pakistani female

likened "rubbish bins and anything that is thrown away in the rubbish" as being unclean. There was also a unison agreement pertaining to smells from spoiled foods. A Chinese Singaporean felt that "salted fish and other old food stuff" smells did not seem clean, while an American male recalled that "sometimes I forget to put my leftovers in the fridge and the rotten food stinks up my whole kitchen the next day!" In addition, it was the antithesis smells to what was earlier discussed as cleanliness that appeared to contribute to unclean association, namely staleness of air, stuffy rooms, and lack of air movement. Like most, a Dutch participant felt that something that smells like "musty mildewy room" must lack cleanliness.

High-Emotive Context

What smells would you associate with a happy celebration?
When participants were asked about smells associated with celebrations, food appeared to be a primary factor in the scent considerations. However, the food smells evoked were highly culture specific. In the European group, a female German participant thought about "Sausages and beer smells," while a British male remembered "Christmassy foods and the smells of candles and fireplace." The American group also had a number of participants who associated Christmas smells like pies and Christmas trees, but many Americans also recalled Thanksgiving smells, "To me, a celebration is when I smell the turkey in the oven!"

In the Chinese group "barbeque pork" (also known in variants like char siew and bak qwa) ranked high on smells associated with celebrations, while Indian/Pakistanis associated "the smells of sweets and spices and curry." Liquor smells also appeared to figure strongly in evoking the celebratory mood; these range from mentions of beer (Europeans) to champagne (Americans) to hard liquor smells (Asia).

In terms of the nonfood items, for every group, there was a strong festive association with occasion-specific scents like "oil-lamp smell at Deepavali" that an Indian male described. Similarly, the Chinese had occasion-related smells, what many Chinese Malaysians and Chinese Singaporeans called the "joyous smell of money" or "new notes," referring to "ang-pows" or notes stuffed in red packets that are exchanged at almost every celebration and the Chinese New Year. Some Europeans appeared to have a similar type of association with snow and mistletoe, as a British female talked about "The smell of fresh cut mistletoes makes me think of Christmas parties."

What smells would you associate with a very sad place or occasion?
When this question was asked, most of the participants were reminded of funerals and such occasions of farewell. For the Indian participants, burning smells were foremost in their mental imagery of a sad occasion. An Indian female likened "the smell of burning wood and burning cloth and burning flesh" to be the most painful and sad smell she could remember. In this regard, many of the associations were related to funerals, and once that smell was experienced in this highly emotionally charged context, it seemed that the participants remembered it vividly. A Chinese Singaporean female remembered that "My grandmother's funeral, her body lay in my house for the wake for three days, and the smell of the flowers from the wreaths was strong. ... I don't know how to describe it but when I smell that in a market or anywhere, I start tearing." For the Asians, there was a general consensus of the smells of burning, certain types of flowers and culture-specific items like joss stick and Bhopal leaves as smells associated with sadness.

For both Europeans and Americans, the smell experiences lie more in church and cemetery environments. Churches were related to "church smell" that evoked sad feelings. An American male recalled that "I said goodbye to my friend at a soggy cemetery which smelled of the earth and rain, and when it rains and I smell the earth I feel sad." Many participants agreed that if one attended a funeral of someone close in that church, the smells experienced on that sad occasion remained a haunting reminder.

Discussion

Our objective was to explore how higher or lower contexts of emotion relate with scent perceptions across cultures. The focus group discussions yielded some interesting findings of how strong scent associations prevail in different cultures. First, in line with past studies on olfaction, we found that scents evoke a host of past experiences, regardless of the cultures. There appeared to be greater descriptions from all participants with "positive" or "happy" contexts and lesser types of scents being evoked for the negative situations.

Second, our focus group responses showed that for low emotive context, scent linkages tend to be rather universal. When asked about scent associations to a clean room, three similar items emerged: (a) citrus smells, (b) detergent/synthetic air fresheners, and (c) mountain/nature scents. Almost all groups connected the scent of a clean room with smells of nature, specifically lemon and lime, and synthetic smell from various brands of cleaning products, antiseptics, or synthetic air freshener scents. What was also striking was that almost all groups talked about nature smells, like the smell of the Alps, the mountains, the rivers, even if they had not themselves experienced smelling those in real life.

In Kaiser's (2006) examination of the world geography in relation to scents, most were classified as tropical, savanna, or desert, and only a very small percentage of habitats were really considered "high mountain area" and few habitats in the world would thus be exposed to such smells. The fact that the city dwellers from Calcutta, Singapore, Kuala Lumpur, and Bangkok mentioned this universal ideal of the clean room implies that perhaps advertising and media images have successfully influenced scent associations internationally. When queried, we found that none of the participants from Asia had visited the Alps or lived in a mountainous place. Few had been to any mountain above 1,000 feet. This seems to imply that the concepts of citrus scents or Alpine mountains being associated with cleanliness were gained from exposures to mass media rather than cultural experiences, which typically use these themes to market their household products.

For the unclean house, garbage was mentioned unanimously in all groups. Although many types of negative scents exist in different cultures (for example, the smell of pork, which is disliked by Muslims; the smell of tobacco, disliked by Singaporeans; the smell of rancid cheese, disliked by the Chinese; the smell of durian, a spiky fruit native to Southeast Asia that has a distinctive and very strong odor, which is disliked by Westerners), the universal commonality of "garbage" or "rubbish" smells appears to be evoked rather than these culture-specific smells. The finding again seems to suggest that in low emotive context, people need not depend much on their cultural knowledge to give meaning to the pleasant or unpleasant scents, but rather through common meaning associated with the context. Perhaps participants tend to agree with these universal associations of certain scents, or with what is being communicated in the media, because of the less involved nature of the context.

On the other hand, our findings clearly showed that highly culture-specific scent associations are evoked in high emotive contexts, emphasizing the importance of cultures in making sense of these scents. Our participants were clearly brought back to the joyous or the sad experiences they themselves experienced in the past together with friends and family. Scents that are associated with happy occasions came mostly from memories of culturally bound celebrations, such as Christmas and Chinese New

Year. This is in agreement with Roubin's (2006) argument that fragrances can take on the role of messenger to herald a festive time and communicate the festiveness of the season. On the other hand, unhappy occasions are associated with different rituals in funerals (i.e., flowers for Westerners, joss stick and Bhopal leaves for Easterners), and these smells were strongly evoked for our participants. Several studies have recognized that people from different cultures do associate the smell of a sad occasion with funerals. For example, the Kuswar of Nepal believe that certain fragrant plants can open up communication between the villagers and the world of the deceased and the divinities (Roubin, 2006). Because the smell of these fragrant plants is ubiquitous during the funeral rites, unpleasant feelings are evoked for the Kuswarese whenever the smell is present. The same cultural associative explanation goes for the smell of porridge, which is typically served at the Chinese funeral wakes. The smell of burnt paper may not be meaningful to Westerners, but to Easterners, especially Chinese, the smell can evoke a sad feeling when it is reminiscent of (a) the Hungry Ghost Festival, where souls are believed to revisit the earth and (b) All Souls Day, when the Chinese visit their ancestral grave sites. For the Indians, the burning smells connote the sadness of funeral pyres. These are all highly culture specific.

To conclude, our findings suggest that culture does play an important role in shaping scent perception, especially in highly emotive contexts. In the high-emotive contexts, people do associate their past experiences strongly with the scents involved in them. In the low-emotive contexts, the meanings of the scent are more universal and appear to be adopted not just from experiences but from what has been communicated in the mass media. We note that there is much to be explored in examining culture and scent. Future research can examine when and how the acculturation process actually takes place. According to Hirsch (2006), scent preferences shift from generation to generation even within the same culture. For example, people born in the 1920s felt that the smell of flowers, grass, and roses could evoke the feelings of nostalgia, while those born in 1960s named baby powder, mother's perfume, and window cleaner as evoking similar emotions. However, there is a lack of longitudinal data that examine this phenomenon across cultures. Second, it will be useful to examine whether scent associations are additive as people get exposed to other cultural experiences, or if early emotive linkages remain most dominant throughout one's life. Third, research can examine how marketers can create scent attribute associations for their brands or products much like house cleaning products have done for mountain smells.

Finally, there is scope for research to examine how overall the cultural lens can shape mental approaches to scents. Cognitive psychologists have argued that Asians tend to view the world through wide-angle lens, or pay more attention to the environment, and to be more holistic by understating the context of the problem, whereas Westerners have tunnel vision and tend to focus on solving specific problems (Nisbett, 2003). Would differences in the two cultures result in differences in the way they perceive scents, such as Easterners paying attention to "holistic" scents and Westerners paying more attention to "individual" scents? More interesting avenues lie ahead to study smell cultural universes, smell consumption classifications, and smell-sensory associations within cultures.

References

Barthes, R. (1972). *Mythologies* (A. Lavers, Trans.). London: Jonathan Cape.

Chebat, J. C., & Michon, R. (2003). Impact of ambient odors on mall shoppers' emotion, cognition, and spending: A test of competitive causal theories. *Journal of Business Research, 56*, 529–539.

Classen, C., Howes, D., & Synnott, A. (1997). *Aroma: The cultural history of smell.* London and New York: Routledge.

Dupire, M. (1987). Des goûts et des odeurs: Classifications et universaux. *L'Homme, 27*(4), 11–14.

Ehrlichman, H., & Bastone, L. (1992). The use of odour in the study of emotion. In S. V. Toller & G. H. Dodd (Eds.), *Fragrance: The psychology and biology of perfume* (pp. 143–159). London: Elsevier Applied Science.

Fiske, J. (1989). *Understanding popular culture.* Boston, MA: Unwin Hyman.

Frith, K. T., & Tsao, J. (1998). Advertising and cultural China: Challenge and opportunities in Asia. *Asian Journal of Communication, 8*(2), 1–17.

Fox, K. (2008). The smell report: An overview of facts and findings. Social Issues Research Centre. Retrieved May 29, 2009, from http://www.sirc.org/publik/smell_emotion.html

Hall, E. T. (1976). *Beyond culture garden city.* New York: Doubleday Anchor Books.

Hall, E. T., & Hall, M. R. (1990). *Understanding cultural differences.* Yarmouth, ME: Intercultural Press.

Hedberg, J. G., & Brown, I. (2002). Understanding cross-cultural meaning through visual media. *Education Media International, 39*(1), 23–30.

Herz, R. S. (1997). The effects of cue distinctiveness on odor-based context-dependent memory. *Memory and Cognition, 25*, 375–380.

Herz, R. S. (2007). *The scent of desire: Discovering our enigmatic sense of smell.* New York: William Morrow.

Herz, R. S., & Cupchik, G. C. (1992). An experimental characterization of odour-evoked memories in humans. *Chemical Senses, 17*, 519–528.

Hirsch, A. R. (2006). Nostalgia, the odors of childhood and society. In J. Drobnick (Ed.), *The smell culture reader* (pp. 187–189). Oxford: Berg.

Hummel, T., & Nordin, S. (2005). Olfactory disorders and their consequences for quality of life. *Acta Oto-Laryngologica, 125*(2), 116–121.

Kaiser, R. (2006). *Meaningful scents around the world: Olfactory, chemical, biological, and cultural considerations.* Weinheim: Wiley.

Kirk-Smith, M. D., & Booth, D. A. (1987). Chemoreception in human behavior: Experimental analysis of the social effects of fragrances. *Chemical Senses, 12*(1), 159–166.

Nisbett, R. E. (2003). *The geography of thought: How Asians and Westerners think differently … and why.* New York: Free Press.

Parasuraman, R. (1984). Sustained attention in detection and discrimination. In R. Parasuraman & D. R. Davies (Eds.), *Varieties of attention* (pp. 243–271). Orlando, FL: Academic Press.

Roubin, L. A. (2006). Fragrant signals and festive spaces in Eurasia. In J. Drobnick (Ed.), *The smell culture reader* (pp.128–137). Oxford: Berg.

Seeger, A. (1981). *Nature and society in central Brazil: The Suya Indians of Mato Grosso.* Cambridge: Harvard University Press.

United Nations Educational, Scientific and Cultural Organization (UNESCO). (2002). United Nations Educational, Scientific and Cultural Organization universal declaration on cultural diversity. Retrieved May 29, 2009, from http://www.unesco.org/education/imld_2002/unversal_decla.shtml

Warrenburg, S. (2005). Effects of fragrance on emotions: Moods and Physiology. *Chemical Senses, 30*(1), 248–249.

9

The Impact of Scent and Music on Consumer Perceptions of Time Duration

Maureen Morrin, Jean-Charles Chebat, and Claire Gelinas-Chebat

What impact do ambient scent and background music have on shoppers' perceptions of how much time has elapsed or how much distance was traveled during a shopping episode? Retail managers are interested in the effects of store atmospherics on such perceptions because they can be an important determinant of customer satisfaction levels.

If a particular customer activity is a pleasant one, for example, if enjoyment is derived from the act of shopping (Guiry, Magi, & Lutz, 2006), a retailer may want to increase shoppers' duration perceptions in order to enhance satisfaction levels. Alternatively, if a customer activity is an unpleasant one, such as having to wait in line for service, a retailer may instead want to decrease shoppers' perceived durations to avoid causing dissatisfaction (Katz, Larson, & Larson, 1991). Thus, a clearer understanding of how specific store atmospherics influence perceived time durations is of critical importance to retailers.

Store atmospherics refer to the various background elements found in retail settings, such as lighting, scent, music, color, and crowding, all of which can influence shopper perceptions and behaviors (Baker & Cameron, 1996; Donovan & Rossiter, 1982; Kotler, 1973; Turley & Milliman, 2000). Theoretical frameworks for understanding the effects of store atmospherics are usually based on formulations of Mehrabian and Russell's (1974) approach/avoidance model of environmental psychology. This model suggests that affective reactions such as mood or arousal, which are created by store atmospherics, result in either approach or avoidance behaviors on the part of consumers. Approach behaviors include lingering longer and exploring items in the environment, whereas avoidance behaviors include attempts to exit the environment more rapidly.

In the current research, we are interested in how the atmospheric elements of ambient scent and background music influence consumers' perceptions of time duration and distance traveled in a retail setting. There are several streams of research that help to explain the effects of environmental variables on duration and distance perceptions. The two areas most relevant to the current research are a chronobiological approach known as the internal clock model (e.g., Treisman, 1963), and a memory-based approach known as the storage-size model (e.g., Ornstein, 1969). We discuss these streams of research in more detail below and build our hypotheses for the expected effects of scent and music on duration perceptions.

Music and the Internal Clock Model

Kellaris and Kent (1992) examined the effect of music on consumers' perceptions of the duration of a time period. They found that perceived duration was longest (shortest) for those exposed to positively (negatively) valenced music. Thus, in the presence of more liked music, perceived time durations increased. These researchers employed a retrospective approach to duration estimates, that is, one in which the participants were not told ahead of time that they would be asked to estimate how much time passed during the task, as in the present research. Based on these results, the authors concluded that time does not necessarily fly when having fun. Similarly, Hui, Dubè, and Chebat (1997) found that positively valenced music triggers both a positive emotional response as well as longer perceived wait durations. These results are in accord with chronobiological models of perceived duration, such as the internal clock model.

The internal clock model of perceived duration (Treisman, 1963) suggests that feelings of stress, anxiety, or physiological arousal can speed up the "ticking" of an individual's internal clock and thus make more time seem to pass during a given interval. Thus, colors that induce feelings of relaxation would be expected to slow down the internal clock and reduce perceived time durations (Gorn, Chattopadhyay, Sengupta, & Tripathi, 2004). This is indeed what Gorn et al. (2004) found when they manipulated background colors of Web sites (e.g., blue vs. yellow or red) during downloads.

In the present experimental context, we expect that pleasant background music will increase consumers' affective response to the environment. Considerable evidence exists to suggest that background music can positively impact consumers' moods and physiological arousal levels as well as their overall affective response to the environment (Bruner, 1990).

If background music does indeed impact consumers' affective responses in this way, it could serve to speed up their internal clocks and make it seem as if more time has passed. Such a result would be in accord with the results obtained by Kellaris and Kent (1992), as well as with the internal clock model of perceived duration. The foregoing leads us to expect that the presence of pleasant background music will increase consumers' affective responses as well as their perceptions of perceived time duration:

> **H1:** Background music will increase perceptions of time duration and distance traveled.

> **H2:** Background music will enhance consumers' environmental affective response.

Scent and the Storage-Size Model

One study that specifically measures the effects of ambient scent on perceived time durations is that of Spangenberg, Crowley, and Henderson (1996). These authors found that while the presence of pleasant ambient scents did not affect the actual time spent in a simulated shopping environment, it did reduce the perception of how much time had passed, from 11.0 minutes when no scent was present to 9.6 minutes when there was a scent present. Based on this prior research, we expect to observe a similar effect of ambient scent in the present research, namely, we expect scent to reduce perceptions of time duration. Furthermore, we explore whether such a result can be explained using an alternative model of duration estimation: the storage-size model.

Although prior research has found that pleasant music influences consumers' affective responses, as discussed above, research does not suggest the same is true of ambient scent (Chebat & Michon, 2003). Instead, ambient scents have been found to impact responses such as lingering (Knasko, 1995), attention (Morrin & Ratneshwar, 2000, 2003), variety seeking (Mitchell, Kahn, & Knasko, 1995), and memory (Herz, 2004). The evidence is considerably weaker regarding the effects of scent on mood, arousal, and other types of affective response. Thus, we might not expect scent to alter consumers' internal clocks. Chronobiological models of time duration may be less helpful in understanding the effects of scent on consumer response in this domain because of the limited evidence that it impacts consumers' moods and arousal levels. Instead, a more cognitively based model such as the storage-size model, which is based on memory processes, may be more appropriate.

The storage-size model (Ornstein, 1969) focuses on the amount of information that is stored and later recalled from an elapsed time period. When asked how long an episode lasted, individuals may try to recall information from memory related to the episode and use the amount of information retrieved as a cue for how long the episode lasted. Therefore, if more information is processed, stored, and later retrieved, longer duration estimates will result. If less information is processed, stored, and retrieved, shorter duration estimates will result. In accord with this line of thought, Mantel and Kellaris (2003) found that perceived durations of radio ads depended, in part, on the amount of information recalled. The limited evidence available regarding the effect of scent on perceived durations suggests that the presence of ambient scent tends to reduce such perceptions (Spangenberg et al., 1996). However, no process evidence has been offered to support the underlying drivers of such a result. Thus, we explore whether scent does indeed reduce duration and distance estimates. We also explore whether scent reduces the amount of cognitive processing engaged in by consumers, which could explain reduced duration and distance estimates, if they are observed. We thus hypothesize:

> **H3:** Pleasant ambient scent will reduce perceptions of time duration and distance traveled.

> **H4:** Pleasant ambient scent will reduce the depth of cognitive processing.

To summarize, we expect that background music will create an affective response in consumers such that consumers' internal clocks will be sped up, resulting in longer perceived time durations, in accord with the internal clock model of perceived duration. Ambient scent, on the other hand, may reduce consumers' cognitive processing efforts, resulting in shorter perceived time durations, in accord with the storage-size model of perceived duration.

A study designed to test these hypotheses is discussed next.

Method

Sample

One hundred sixty graduate students of a major business school volunteered to participate in the study in return for course credit. Ages ranged from 18 to 39 years (mean = 22.5), 46.5% were male.

Design

The study was a 2 (ambient scent, no ambient scent) × 2 (background music, no background music) full factorial design. Participants were randomly assigned to one of four treatment groups. For those in the scented conditions, the scent of geranium was emitted into the room's atmosphere with an electric diffuser into which several drops of geranium essential oil had been placed. This scent has been pretested and successfully used in prior consumer research (Morrin & Ratneshwar, 2000). The diffuser itself was hidden from view to minimize the salience of the scent manipulation. For those in the background music conditions, the music consisted of a piece of classical music (Mozart's Allegro for Horn Concerto No. 3 in E Flat Major), which was played on a music player, also hidden from view.

Procedure

Participants entered the laboratory and were informed that they would be viewing a videotaped "walk" through a shopping center. They were informed, "While you are watching this video, we would like you to imagine that you are actually walking around this shopping mall, experiencing your surroundings, as you normally would, while visiting a real shopping mall. When the video is finished, we are going to ask you some questions."

The participants were not informed that the experiment concerned perceptions of time duration or distance traveled, and thus the study consists of an examination of retrospective estimations of duration. After viewing the video, participants were first asked to provide duration estimates, described in more detail below, and then list their thoughts, completing the 7-item Fisher (1974) scale for environmental quality, the 5-item pleasure and 4-item arousal dimensions of the PAD (Pleasure Arousal Dominance) Emotion Scale (Mehrabian & Russell, 1974), as well as manipulation checks and demographic questions such as age and gender.

Measures

Two questions were used to assess perceived time duration. The first question asked was, "How long do you think you were 'walking around' in this mall? That is, how long were you watching this video? Please be as precise as possible, even if you are not certain." The open-ended answer stated, "I estimate that I was walking around in this mall for _____ minutes and _____ seconds." This question was modeled on prior research (Kellaris, Mantel, & Altsech, 1996).

The second measure used to estimate duration was, "How much distance did you cover, while 'walking around' in this mall? Please estimate how many meters you walked while in this simulated mall experience." The open-ended answer stated, "I estimate that I walked _____ meters." We included this item as a measure of perceived pace, or "how rapidly the succession of events within a time interval seems to take place" (Kellaris et al., 1996). The sequence of events or changes within a time period may be perceived to take place at a more rapid pace than that at which they actually happen. Perceived pace will generally be positively correlated with perceived duration and either may be used as an inference for the other (Kellaris et al., 1996). Then participants were asked to "Recall all of the thoughts that were going through your head while the video was playing." After completing the closed-ended questions, participants were debriefed and thanked for their participation.

Results

A series of analyses of variance (ANOVAs) were conducted on the measures as a function of the two manipulated factors (scent and music) with covariates for age, gender, liking of the music, and liking of the scent included for control. Prior research suggests that both age (Yalch & Spangenberg, 1990) and gender (Kellaris & Mantel, 1994) can influence perceived duration.

Perceived Time Duration

On average, participants estimated that 504 seconds, or about 8.4 minutes, had elapsed while watching the video (range = 150 to 2,718 seconds, standard deviation = 386). The true video duration was 320 seconds, or about 5.3 minutes. Because the seconds' measure exhibited a long right-tailed distribution, we transformed this measure via the natural log function. We conducted an ANOVA on the natural log of perceived time elapsed as a function of the music and scent conditions, plus the covariates. The covariate for age ($F(1, 151) = 4.61$, $p < .05$) was significant, with older participants providing longer time estimates. The only other significant effect was that of music ($F(1, 151) = 4.33, p < .05$). When there was no music present, participants estimated that 396 seconds, or about 6.6 minutes, had elapsed. When music was present, their time estimates increased to 475 seconds, or about 7.9 minutes, about a 20% increase in estimated duration. This result supports H1.

Perceived Distance Traveled

On average, participants estimated that they had traveled 502 meters while watching the video (range = 20 to 20,000 meters, standard deviation = 407). Again, because the meters measure exhibited a long right-tailed distribution, we transformed this measure with the natural log function. We conducted an ANOVA on the natural log of the estimated number of meters traveled in the mall as a function of scent, music, and the covariates.

The covariates of age ($F(1, 151) = 4.16, p < .05$) and liking of the scent ($F(1, 151) = 5.35, p < .05$) were significant. Older participants tended to provide longer distance estimates. Also, those who did not like the scent tended to provide longer distance estimates. Two main effects were also significant: both music ($F(1, 151) = 4.69, p < .05$) and scent ($F(1, 151) = 5.38, p < .05$). The presence of music increased the perception of distance traveled, from 300 (no music) to 413 (music) meters, in support of H1. The presence of scent, on the other hand, decreased the perception of meters traveled, from 418 (no scent) to 296 (scent) meters, in support of H3.

Affective Responses

Affective response to the environment was measured using Fisher's (1974) 7-item scale, which measures the degree to which the environment is perceived to be relaxing, comfortable, cheerful, colorful, stimulating, lively, and bright (coefficient alpha = .88). We conducted an ANOVA on affective response to the environment as a function of scent and music plus the covariates. Two of the covariates were significant: the degree to which the scent was liked ($F(1, 151) = 8.35, p < .01$) and the degree to which the music was liked ($F(1,151) = 9.32, p < .01$). Not surprisingly, the environmental quality of the mall was rated more positively if either the scent or music was liked. The only other effect that was significant was music condition ($F(1, 151) = 5.09, p < .05$). Affective response to the environment was greater when there was music present ($M = 4.10$) versus absent ($M = 3.64$).

This result supports H2. We also measured respondents' levels of happiness and arousal using dimensions of the PAD scale, but neither analysis was significant.

Cognitive Responses

Number of Words

We first simply counted the number of words written in the cognitive response section as an overall measure of amount of cognitive processing. We conducted an ANOVA on the number of words as a function of scent, music, and the covariates. The covariate of age was significant ($F(1, 151)$ = $17.49, p < .0001$), with older participants listing more words. Scent also had a significant effect ($F(1, 151) = 8.57, p < .005$), with the number of words falling from 30.5 to 24.4 when scent was present. This result supports H4. This effect is qualified, however, by a significant interaction between scent and music ($F(1, 151) = 15.55, p < .0001$). Inspection of the means shows that the presence of scent reduces the number of words (from 34.0 in the no scent/no music condition to 19.7 in the scent only condition), unless there is also music present ($M = 27.2$ music only condition, $M = 29.1$ in scent and music condition).

Number of Thoughts

We then conducted a more rigorous analysis of the thoughts listed. We relied on MacInnis and Jaworski's (1989) typology for categorizing cognitive responses to advertisements according to the attention and processing capacity allocated to the information, as determinants of the depth of information processing. Six levels of processing are involved:

1. feature analysis,
2. basic categorization,
3. meaning analysis,
4. information integration,
5. role-taking,
6. constructive processes.

In the MacInnis and Jaworski (1989) framework, level 1 typically occurs when motivation, ability, or opportunity to process is very low. In such a situation, attention will be focused primarily on feature analysis or encoding salient features of the environment. At a slightly higher level of motivation, ability or opportunity to process, basic categorization will occur, such as that involving assigning a semantic label to an element of the environment. Meaning analysis involves interpreting salient cues to derive some basic understanding; information integration involves synthesizing meanings assigned to several stimuli; and constructive processes and role-taking involve relating the information to the self (MacInnis & Jaworski, 1989). The types of responses linked to these processing operations are then classified as message related (1, 2), execution related (3, 4), or context related (5, 6).

For the present research, which concerned processing of retail environments rather than of ads, we interpreted these categories from a linguistic point of view as follows. According to the respondent's written cognitive responses, the individual reached one of the six levels of information processing when he or she (a) recalled contextual elements, (b) evaluated contextual elements, (c) made explicit inferences, (c) made implicit inferences, (d) made statements of personalization or identification, and (d) exhibited imaginative constructs. Thus, levels 1 and 2 refer to context, levels 3 and 4 refer to content, and levels 5 and 6 refer to the actor. After categorizing the thoughts into one of the six categories, we summed across the first three categories and the second three categories to differentiate between lower order and higher order thoughts. We conducted an ANOVA on the number of lower order thoughts (categories 1 to 3) as a function of scent, music, and the covariates, but none of the effects were significant, except for age, which indicated that older participants listed more lower order thoughts.

Then we conducted an ANOVA on the number of higher order thoughts (categories 4 to 6) and found that the covariate of age was significant ($F(1, 151) = 4.76$, $p < .05$), with older participants listing more higher level thoughts. In addition, scent was significant ($F(1, 151) = 4.25$, $p < .04$). The presence of scent reduced the number of higher order thoughts listed by participants, from 1.74 (no scent) to 1.27 (scent). This result supports H4.

Discussion

In this study we find that music improves shoppers' affective response to the environment and increases their perceptions of both elapsed time as well as distance traveled in the mall. This result is in accord with the findings of Kellaris and Kent (1992) as well as with the affectively based internal clock model of duration estimation.

The presence of ambient scent, on the other hand, had an opposite effect on perceptions of distance traveled in the mall. When a scent was present, participants perceived that they had traveled a shorter distance. The presence of scent also reduced the level of cognitive processing, as evidenced by fewer words and fewer higher-level thoughts listed. The perceived distance results are consistent with the duration estimation results reported by Spangenberg et al. (1996). The results regarding the reduced processing efforts suggest the cognitively based storage-size model of duration estimation may be a more appropriate framework for understanding the effects of scent on perceived durations or distances traveled. It should be noted, however, that the presence of a pleasant ambient scent did not alter perceptions of time duration, only of distance traveled in the mall. Thus, the effects of scent on duration and distance perceptions as well as on the level of cognitive processing require further testing, as the evidence is more tentative in this regard.

Overall the results indicate that it cannot be concluded that simply adding pleasant atmospheric elements to a retail environment will necessarily result in shorter perceived time durations. That is, retailers should not simply assume that making their environments more pleasant will make shoppers perceive they have spent less time in the store or mall. Instead, the type of effect that a particular atmospheric element will have on consumers' perceptions of time duration or distance traveled may be a function of whether it elicits primarily affective or cognitive responses. When a pleasant atmospheric element elicits a positive affective response, such as positive environmental affect, physiological arousal, or pleasant mood, then it may tend to speed up the consumer's internal clock and make it seem as if more time has passed and more distance has been traveled. This may be a desirable effect in instances where the shopping activity is considered pleasant.

If, on the other hand, a pleasant atmospheric element elicits a cognitive type of response, such as shallower processing, then it may impact the amount of information that can be recalled about the elapsed time period and result in the perception that less time has passed. This would be a desirable effect in instances where the shopping activity is considered unpleasant, such as waiting for service. Future research is needed not only to document the effects of other types of atmospheric elements on perceived time durations (e.g., noise, crowding, lighting, humidity, etc.) but also on whether the element tends to have a greater impact on affective or cognitive responses of the consumer.

References

Baker, J., & Cameron, M. (1996). The effects of the service environment on affect and consumer perception of waiting time: An integrative review and research propositions. *Journal of the Academy of Marketing Science, 24*(4), 338–349.

Bruner, G. C. (1990). Music, mood, and marketing. *Journal of Marketing, 54*, 94–104.

Chebat, J. C., & Michon, R. (2003). The impact of ambient odors on mall shoppers' emotions, cognition, and spending: A test of competitive causal theories. *Journal of Business Research, 56*(7), 529–539.

Donovan, R. J., & Rossiter, J. R. (1982, Spring). Store atmosphere: an environmental psychology approach. *Journal of Retailing, 58*, 34–57.

Fisher, J. (1974, August). Situation-specific variables as determinants of perceived environmental esthetic quality and perceived crowdedness. *Journal of Research in Personality, 8*, 177–188.

Gorn, G. J., Chattopadhyay, A., Sengupta, J., & Tripathi, S. (2004, May). Waiting for the Web: How screen color affects time perception. *Journal of Marketing Research, 41*, 215–225.

Guiry, M., Magi, A. W., & Lutz, R. J. (2006). Defining and measuring recreational shopper identity. *Journal of the Academy of Marketing Science, 34*(1), 74–83.

Herz, R. S. (2004). A naturalistic analysis of autobiographical memories triggered by olfactory visual and auditory stimuli. *Chemical Senses, 29*, 217–224.

Hui, M. K., Dubè, L., & Chebat, J. C. (1997). The impact of music on consumers' reactions to waiting for services. *Journal of Retailing, 73*(1), 87–104.

Katz, K. L., Larson, B. M., & Larson, R. C. (1991, Winter). Prescription for the waiting-in-line blues: Entertain, enlighten, and engage. *Sloan Management Review, 32*, 44–54.

Kellaris, J. J., & Kent, R. J. (1992). The influence of music on consumers' temporal perceptions: Does time fly when you're having fun? *Journal of Consumer Psychology, 1*(4), 365–376.

Kellaris, J. J., & Mantel, S. P. (1994). The influence of mood and gender on consumers' time perceptions. *Advances in Consumer Research, 21*, 514–518.

Kellaris, J. J., Mantel, S. P., & Altsech, M. B. (1996). Decibels, disposition, and duration: The impact of musical loudness and internal states on time perceptions. *Advances in Consumer Research, 23*, 498–503.

Knasko, S. C. (1995). Pleasant odors and congruency: Effects on approach behavior. *Chemical Senses, 20*(5), 479–487.

Kotler, P. (1973). Atmospherics as a marketing tool. *Journal of Retailing, 49*(4), 48–65.

MacInnis, D. J., & Jaworski, B. J. (1989, October). Information processing from advertisements: Toward an integrative framework. *Journal of Marketing, 53*, 1–23.

Mantel, S. P., & Kellaris, J. J. (2003, March). Cognitive determinants of consumers' time perceptions: The impact of resources required and available. *Journal of Consumer Research, 29*, 531–538.

Mehrabian, A., & Russell, J. A. (1974). *An approach to environmental psychology.* Cambridge, MA: MIT Press.

Mitchell, D. J., Kahn, B. E., & Knasko, S. C. (1995, September). There's something in the air: Effects of congruent or incongruent ambient odor on consumer decision making. *Journal of Consumer Research, 22*, 229–238.

Morrin, M., & Ratneshwar, S. (2000). The impact of ambient scent on evaluation, attention, and memory for familiar and unfamiliar brands. *Journal of Business Research, 49*, 157–165.

Morrin, M., & Ratneshwar, S. (2003, February). Does it make sense to use scents to enhance brand memory? *Journal of Marketing Research, 40*, 10–25.

Ornstein, R. E. (1969). *On the experience of time.* New York: Penguin.

Spangenberg, E. R., Crowley, A. E., & Henderson, P. W. (1996, April). Improving the store environment: Do olfactory cues affect evaluations and behaviors? *Journal of Marketing, 60*, 67–80.

Treisman, M. (1963). Temporal discrimination and the indifference interval: Implications for a model of the "internal clock." *Psychological Monographs, 77*(13), 1–31.

Turley, L.W., & Milliman, R. E. (2000, August). Atmospheric effects on shopping behavior: A review of the experimental evidence. *Journal of Business Research, 49*, 193–211.

Yalch, R. F., & Spangenberg, E. (1990). Effects of store music on shopping behavior. *Journal of Consumer Marketing, 7*, 55–63.

Section III

Audition

10

The Sounds of the Marketplace
The Role of Audition in Marketing

*Joan Meyers-Levy, Melissa G. Bublitz,
and Laura A. Peracchio*

Each day we are all exposed to a cacophony of auditory information. A good part of what we hear comes from the world of marketing operating around us. Consider a typical scenario. You wake up to the blaring tune of an ad jingle on your clock radio. As you get ready for work, you turn on the television to hear the morning's news and weather forecast. Your drive to work is punctuated by the percussive sound of jackhammers and a construction worker alerting you of a traffic detour. Shortly after entering your office, the familiar Microsoft tones greet you as you boot up your computer. Later, a sales call from a vendor interrupts your focus. On your drive home from work, you stop at a store where a salesperson explains all the must-have features of the latest iPhone. Finally, when you stop at a grocery store to purchase food for dinner, the store's continuously looped advertising messages drone in your ears. How much of your day is spent listening to marketing-related audio information? If you are like most people, you probably spend hours being exposed to auditory material delivered by marketers aimed at shaping your thoughts, judgments, and behaviors.

In virtually all consumer domains, marketers use sound to communicate and attempt to persuade consumers. In some instances, sound is a crucial aspect of the product experience, as with the pop you hear when uncorking a bottle of champagne. Retailers have long used sound to enhance the nature of a venue's experience. From the cranked up pulsing music in teen-targeted stores to the soothing sound of flowing water at luxurious spas, sound may be a core and valued part of the consumption experience. Advertisers too pay much heed to sounds that may attract your attention, impact your mood, or help you to remember a brand name or key information. Yet, despite the important role that sound plays in a wide range of consumption experiences, researchers have only just begun to examine how sound influences consumer psychology and marketing. This chapter highlights a smattering of selected research that sheds light on how sound influences marketing and the consumption experience. We begin with a discussion of how sound symbolism and language can influence consumer perceptions. Next, we examine the multifaceted role of music in marketing and consumption. We then consider how auditory stimuli interact with the other four senses. Our hope is that this overview will stimulate new ideas and directions that help address the fascinating question of what roles audition may play in marketing and the way that consumers process information.

Words, Language, and Sound

Words and language represent the primary means by which marketers engage in auditory communication. In this section, we focus on research that sheds light on some of the unique ways that words, language, and sound can influence consumers, thereby illustrating the central role that such auditory communication plays in marketing.

Sound Symbolism

There is widespread belief that language is inherently arbitrary. That is, although people may combine sound units or phonemes to form words, no connection actually exists between the sound of a word and its meaning (Hockett, 1966). Yet, a significant body of research challenges this assumption, revealing that in many languages, the sound of a phoneme embedded in a word can indeed contribute to people's semantic understanding of the word. This work is important as it builds a case for sound symbolism (see Nuckolls, 1999, for a review). To illustrate, consider research that investigates the symbolism associated with two vowels sounds on the opposite end of the speech production spectrum, /i/ and /a/. When you form the /i/ sound, as in kiss, your mouth is closed and the high frequency sound is formed at the front of your mouth. By contrast, you form the /a/ sound, as in palm, near the back of your mouth with your mouth open. In an exploration of possible sound symbolism, Sapir (1929) studied nonwords like mil and mal, which employ the /i/ and /a/ sounds. Such nonwords were used to ensure that any inferences people might derive from the stimuli could only be attributed to their sound, not any preexisting semantic meaning. When people were asked to choose which word, mil or mal, represented either a small or a large table, Sapir found that more people associated the short, front /i/ sound in mil with smaller items, as compared to the open back /a/ sound in mal. As such, research like this demonstrates that the sound of a word can influence the specific associations that are triggered as language is processed.

Several consumer researchers have built on this early sound symbolism evidence by examining how the sound of a word can influence people's product perceptions. Klink (2000) found that the /i/ vowel sound, which has been connected with diminutive symbolism (Nuckolls, 1999), can also elicit related notions such as lighter, thinner, and softer. On the other hand, long, back vowels sounds, such as /a/ in father and /o/ in bought, are associated with larger items (Newman, 1933; Sapir, 1929). Further, the symbolic associations triggered by how a word sounds may not be language specific. Tanz (1971) examined six different families of languages and found that the /i/ and /a/ sounds are used fairly consistently in words that represent temporal distance, with /i/ used to capture the concepts of here or near, and /a/ associated with there or far. This provides further evidence of sound symbolism in language.

Sound symbolism seems to play a role in helping consumers infer product benefits derived from a brand name. Yorkston and Menon (2004) showed that a brand name with an /ä/ sound, as in chop, versus a shorter /i/ sound, as in kiss, influenced consumers' perceptions of a fictitious brand of ice cream. Specifically, consumers rated a Frosh brand of ice cream (using /ä/) as smoother, creamier, and richer than a Frish (/i/) brand. They also indicated that they were more likely to choose the former brand for purchase. Klink (2000) also investigated sound symbolism effects on brand perceptions, but did so for a larger set of phonemes. Table 10.1 summarizes these effects on consumers' ratings of fictitious brand names across a variety of product categories and attributes. Again, this work speaks to the potential for marketers to influence brand associations and perceptions by strategically choosing brand names with particular sounds.

Lowrey and Shrum (2007) expanded on the preceding work by demonstrating the widespread effect of sound symbolism on product perceptions across product categories. These researchers found that brand evaluations were generally positive when the perceptions or features elicited by a phoneme in a brand name were congruent with the expectations of the

TABLE 10.1   Summary of Klink's 2000 Investigation of Sound Symbolism in Brand Names

Linguistic Property	Phonemes Manipulated	Product Perceptions
Front vs. Back Vowel Sounds	**Front:** ē (bee) i (hit) ā (hate) e test **Back:** ü (food) ō (home) ö (caught) ə (dusk) ä (father)	Front vowel sound elicit ideas like smaller, lighter (relative to darker), milder, thinner, softer, faster, colder, more bitter, more feminine, friendlier, weaker, lighter (relative to heavier), and prettier
Fricatives vs. Stop Consonants*	**Fricatives:** f, s, v, and z **Stops:** p, t, b, d, g, and k	Fricatives elicit ideas such as smaller, faster, lighter (relative to heavier), and more feminine.
Voiced vs. Voiceless** Stop Consonants	**Voiced Stops:** b, d, and g **Voiceless Stops:** p, t, and k	Voiceless stops elicit ideas such as smaller, faster, lighter (relative to heavier), sharper, and more feminine.
Voiced vs. Voiceless Fricatives Consonants	**Voiced Fricatives:** v and z **Voiceless Fricatives:** f and s	Voiceless fricatives elicit ideas such as smaller, softer, and more feminine.

*Fricatives are phonemes where the sound enunciated can continue, compared to stops where the mouth stops the airflow to create the sound.

**Voiced phonemes are produced by vibrating the vocal cords, while voiceless phonemes are produced by pushing air with the vocal cords apart.

evaluated product. Adding to these sound symbolism effects, other aspects of brand names also can evoke desired attributes or other positive connotations. For example, because FedEx stands for Federal Express, consumers may associate the abbreviated Ex in the brand name with ideas of speed, which has positive connotations for this service company. Further, Keller, Heckler, and Houston (1998) demonstrated that for new products, brand names that suggest a product's benefits can conjure up initially advertised benefit claims that are consistent in meaning with the brand name. All in all, this line of research implies that the use of sound symbolism and word associations in brand names can be a valuable way to convey particular product attributes that consumers desire.

Research suggests that these kinds of perceptions engendered by sound symbolism are automatic in nature, meaning that they occur without awareness, effort, or intention (Yorkston & Menon, 2004). Further, judgments based on sound symbolism appear to be updated if consumers encounter more diagnostic information about the brand (Yorkston & Menon, 2004). This updating process presumably occurs via the two-stage or dual processing model of cognition, which posits that after initial judgments are formed automatically, they may be subsequently updated based on additional information acquired from interaction with or prolonged exposure to the item (Chaiken & Trope, 1999). Thus, the effects of sound symbolism may be short-lived if the product fails to live up to the expectations created by these associations. Returning to Yorkston and Menon's (2004) ice cream brands, if consumers buy Frosh ice cream because its brand name sounds thick and creamy, but upon consuming it find its texture to be light and inconsistent with their expectations, their initial perceptions of the brand are likely to be modified. In sum, the research reviewed in this section suggests that effects spawned by sound symbolism are likely to emerge automatically, but they may not be enduring. Still, they offer a useful way to understand consumers' reactions and their choices that are often based on the marketing messages encountered every day.

Language

The spoken word typically relays meaning beyond just the symbolism of the word's individual sounds or phonemes. That is, the particular words or language employed in a persuasive message can directly influence product perceptions and attitudes. For example, a brand name identified in a message may act as a summary cue that helps consumers recollect the product's features and persuasive message or infer the product's benefits. It also is true that memory for a brand name itself can be influenced by specific aspects of the language, such as the frequency with which the brand name word(s) is used in the language and the number of associations elicited by the word(s). Meyers-Levy (1989) demonstrated this, showing that when brand names were comprised of high frequency words, recall of the names was greater when the brand name words evoked a small versus a large set of associations. Yet when brand names were composed of low frequency words, the number of associations to the words had no effect on brand name recall.

The manner in which language is used also influences how consumers process and access information. Words or phrases can activate schemas that influence how the presented information is categorized and used to form judgments. Along these lines, Meyers-Levy and Tybout (1989) showed that compared to either congruity or extreme incongruity, a moderate level of incongruity between how a product was described and its claimed product category schema can actually enhance product attitudes. This occurs because moderate incongruity prompts consumers to elaborate extensively on the product and message with the goal of resolving the incongruity. Hence, when a consumer hears a message that partially violates expectations, he or she is challenged to think extensively about all of the data, which not only can resolve the incongruity but also render people's attitudes more extreme in favorableness. Still, not all consumers appear to respond to moderate incongruity in this way. Studies suggest that relative novices, those who lack in-depth familiarity with the product category, show the aforementioned effect. Yet consumers who are category experts and thereby possess much relevant and elaborate knowledge about the category may be able to resolve such moderate incongruity without much elaboration (Peracchio & Tybout, 1996). Thus, experts' product attitudes may not be enhanced by such moderate incongruity.

Other research suggests that consumers' attitudes also can be affected by the magnitude of the cognitive resources that are devoted to versus required for processing a message. Provided that consumers are fairly motivated to process a message, studies reveal that they form more favorable attitudes toward a target good when the cognitive resources they allocate to processing are commensurate with, rather than either fall short of or exceed, those that are required to process the message (Meyers-Levy & Peracchio, 1995; Peracchio & Meyers-Levy, 1997).

To recapitulate, the preceding findings point to a myriad of factors that can be influenced by the language used in marketing communications, all of which affect the success of the communications. These include inherent aspects of the language such as word frequency and the number of associations activated by the chosen words, the extent to which incongruities are suggested by implicated product categories or terms used in message language, and the resource demands that are imposed on consumers by variables that may be linked to language.

At the same time, these as well as other complexities associated with language confront marketers who enter the global arena. There, the prevailing languages may differ in structure, and consumers are often bicultural or multilingual. Indeed, research suggests that the very structure of language can impact the extent to which auditory information will be encoded and remembered. Because of the logographic writing system of Chinese characters, studies find that Chinese consumers exhibit superior recall for brand names that are presented visually (Schmitt, Pan, & Tavassoli, 1994). On the other hand, due to the sound-based writing system of English, native speakers of English generally display better recall for brand names that they hear. Similarly, logos or visual elements elicit stronger branding connections in memory for Chinese-speaking consumers, while sounds that are linked to brand images produce better encoding and recall among English-speaking consumers (Tavassoli & Lee, 2003). The branding of Microsoft provides a compelling example of how these differences might be manifested in the marketplace. Chinese consumers are likely to associate the Microsoft brand more strongly with its multicolored checkered flag. Yet, English speakers should be more likely to link the brand with the harmonizing tones that air when booting up a Microsoft program. Of course, other structurally grounded differences in processing may also exist. Pan and Schmitt (1996) found that Chinese consumers showed heightened sensitivity to visual elements such as typeface, but English consumers were more sensitive to auditory cues like an announcer's voice. These visual and auditory processing differences also may explain why Chinese-speaking consumers are more greatly disrupted by visual distraction, say Web site graphics, while English-speaking consumers' processing is more disturbed by background sounds (Tavassoli & Han, 2001; Tavassoli & Lee, 2003). Such observations clearly indicate that marketers should be mindful of how language structure can affect processing as they attempt to tailor their ads to global targets.

Another body of research provides crucial insights into how bilingual consumers process information. Bilingual consumers' processing of information appears to depend on both characteristics of the consumer and the message. Not surprisingly, these individuals' processing is sensitive to how proficient they are in the nondominant or second language. Zhang and Schmitt (2004) found that bilingual consumers who are less proficient in their second language tend to process data presented in their dominant first language semantically and holistically. However, they process material in their second language phonologically, piecing together word meanings to interpret the message. Alternatively, bilinguals who are proficient in both languages access semantic as well as phonological meanings, exhibiting sensitivity to the meaning and the sound of a message.

Appreciating the unique way that bilingual-bicultural consumers process information also may enable marketers to use language strategically to heighten elaboration or influence the semantic associations that consumers attach to messages. Not only do bicultural audiences speak multiple languages, but they also tend to possess extensive experience with the cultural systems associated with those languages. Accordingly, such bicultural consumers are apt to possess different sets of schemas and product associations for each language and culture (Krishna & Ahluwalia, 2008). When bicultural consumers hear a brand name in one language, they may evoke a very different set of associations than they would if the same brand name were presented in another language (Luna, Ringberg, & Peracchio, 2008). Further, hearing messages in a particular language can cause bicultural consumers to switch cultural frames and align their preferences with those of the focal cultural system, thereby triggering inferences about corresponding values and influencing both consumers' product perceptions and choices (Briley, Morris, & Simonson, 2005).

Frequently, advertisers choose to switch cultural frames within a single message, employing what is known as code switching. Code switching aims to induce consumers to elaborate on specific elements within an ad by presenting a key word or phrase in a second language. Hence, code switching within an ad can prompt consumers to take particular note of the code-switched element (Luna & Peracchio, 2001). A broader goal of code switching could be to activate schemas from another language and thereby favorably influence attitudes toward a brand. Luna and Peracchio (2005) found that if people hold positive attitudes toward the second language employed in a code-switched phrase, their positive attitudes can transfer to the brand. Alternatively, if attitudes toward the second language are negative, directing attention to the code-switched expression can heighten elaboration of the code-switched language's schema, and in this case negative attitudes linked to that schema can be transferred to the brand. Appreciation for how language can influence the perceptions of bicultural or bilingual consumers promises to grow as international markets continue to expand and more consumers exhibit intimate knowledge of more than one language and its corresponding cultural system.

Another challenge confronted by global marketers is that of choosing a brand name and developing advertising for international markets. Among the pertinent issues here is how the schemas activated by a language will influence product perceptions and attitudes. Some languages such as French and Spanish contain formal gender markers. For example, in French, the article *the* is expressed by either *le* or *la*, depending on the item's gender. In such languages, gender markers of brand names have been shown to activate schemas and influence encoding, storage, and recall of the brand name (Yorkston & De Mello, 2005). Consumers also use gender markers when deriving meanings for unfamiliar brand names (Yorkston & De Mello, 2005). Yet even consumers who do not speak a particular language may hold beliefs or be influenced by cultural stereotypes based on the perceived language of origin of a brand name. To exemplify, by varying the pronunciation of brand names so that they sounded either French or English, Leclerc, Schmitt, and Dubé (1994) were able to alter the cultural stereotypes that were activated, which in turn affected consumers' product evaluations. Hence, consumers' attitudes toward a hedonic product, such as fragrances, were more positive when the spoken brand name sounded French rather than English. Such findings demonstrate that the sound of a brand name associated with a particular country can activate schemas that shape product perceptions.

In sum, the research in this section demonstrates that selecting a brand name or designing an ad involves far more than simply choosing words to impart a message. Marketers also must consider the symbolism and associations triggered by the sound of the chosen words and the schemas activated by such words. Further, as marketers set their sights on global targets, new challenges arise, such as the influence of language structure on consumers' processing of information and the potential of using code switching to strategically foster or highlight desired associations among bilingual or bicultural consumers. Other important concerns in international markets center on the sound of a brand name, the precise meaning of a translated word, and the visual or auditory representation of the brand name. In short, a broad spectrum of language related variables can affect the persuasiveness of global communications.

Music

Although words and language comprise the major auditory devices used
to convey purposeful or central material in marketing communications,
marketers also have long made use of music as an ancillary auditory
device, for it too can exert a potent influence on consumers. When used
in advertising, music may set a mood, invoke particular brand perceptions, or influence the favorableness of attitudes and consumption more
generally. Further, in retail environments, music is often used to alter the
ambiance of the shopping experience or even modify the pace of consumers' behavior. In this section, we focus on some of the alternative ways by
which music can shape persuasion and the consumption experience.

Music in Advertising

Music accompanies much of the radio and television advertising that we
are exposed to each day, and it is increasingly used in Internet advertising
to attract browsers' attention. Park and Young (1986) suggested that music
may act as a peripheral persuasion cue in advertising, triggering affective
feeling states or moods that can spill over and shape consumers' ad or brand
attitudes. Indeed, substantial research in marketing can be explained by
the link between music and one's mood. For example, Gorn (1982) found
that after hearing liked or disliked music while viewing a pen in one of
two different colors, individuals more frequently chose a pen of the color
that was associated with liked music, but they chose the alternative color
pen when the featured pen had been associated with the disliked music.
Although the author attributed these findings to simple classical conditioning, the outcomes also could be explained in terms of music-induced
mood effects. The liked or disliked music may have affected individuals'
mood, which in turn guided their product choices. This sort of influence of
music as a peripheral cue typically occurs when consumers' involvement
with the target item is low (Petty, Cacioppo, & Schumann, 1983).

   Although background music in an ad typically exerts a positive influence on attitudes, Park and Young (1986) found that sometimes music can
interfere with a consumer's ability to process a brand's featured attributes.
Apparently, here, music operates as a distracter, usurping people's attention or cognitive resources and thereby undermining the processing of the
ad message. Such interference is unlikely to occur under low involvement
conditions because uninvolved individuals tend to be far more attentive

to peripheral cues like music rather than message data. Yet, under high involvement, there is potential for music to interfere with consumers' natural inclination to focus on and deeply process the ad message. MacInnis and Park (1991) suggested music may prompt such interference due to its propensity to trigger memories of powerful prior emotion-laden experiences associated with the music, and they tested the preceding reasoning. They found that music actually increased message processing among low involvement consumers, ostensibly because the highly evocative music prompted such consumers to devote some incidental attention to the message. But, as anticipated, the music interfered with the message processing of high involvement consumers, presumably because these individuals became so consumed by the music-triggered emotional memories that they were unable to process the ad message.

The preceding findings suggest that consumers' involvement with a message plays an important role in how music affects consumers' processing of information. Yet some research indicates that music itself can alter such involvement. Along these lines, MacInnis and Park (1991) found that music heightened consumers' involvement with an advertisement, stimulating an increase in both message and nonmessage processing. In most ads, though, music is intended to serve as an effective accompaniment for a message that itself is designed to convey pertinent meaning. Music is rarely chosen in a vacuum, but instead it is often selected to work synergistically with the message by conveying either a similar or complementary meaning (Scott, 1990). Supporting this goal, research shows that when the meaning ascribed to ad music is congruent, rather than incongruent, with the ad message, music benefits message processing, producing enhanced brand and message recall (Kellaris, Cox, & Cox, 1993).

Although much of the work discussed to this point assumes that music plays a subservient or ancillary role in promotion, in some instances it can serve as a rather central element of an ad, perhaps conveying the ad's essence. This might be so if an ad message is intricately woven into the music, as in a signature ad jingle. In this case, consumers may need to commit sizable cognitive resources to it to understand and encode the musical material. Indeed, Anand and Sternthal (1990) found that advertising messages embedded in music's lyrics were more difficult for consumers to process compared to ads that employed either music as a backdrop for a spoken message or no music. In practice, however, advertisers often set messages to music where the music serves primarily as a memory device that can facilitate recall of a key benefit or attribute of the advertised product. Although, like ad jingles, these messages may require substantial resources to process, the musical format may help consumers better tolerate ad repetition, enabling the repeated ad to generate positive attitudes and increase brand recall (Scott, 1990).

Beyond setting a specific mood or providing a structure for messages, music also can evoke rather general hedonic feelings. These feelings have been referred to as music's embodied meaning, for they are independent of the setting and result simply from the sounds that embody the music, such as its tempo, rhythm, percussive elements, key, or novelty of sound (Meyer, 1994; Zhu & Meyers-Levy, 2005). For example, faster tempo energetic music elicits more positive feelings than does sedate music (Stout & Leckenby, 1988), music performed in either a major versus minor key or a higher pitch stimulates more favorable feelings (Bruner, 1990), and music dynamics like increasing rather than decreasing volume or tempo elicit more optimistic climactic feelings (Bruner, 1990). Notably, regardless of listeners' musical training, they reveal substantial agreement in their interpretations of such embodied meanings (Rigg, 1937).

Coexisting with such purely hedonic embodied meaning, music also can evoke semantic or designative interpretations, which are referred to as its referential meaning. Unlike embodied meaning, referential meanings are learned, context dependent, and arise from the external world's networks of descriptive concepts that music may bring to mind based on past experience (Meyer, 1960, 1994; Zhu & Meyers-Levy, 2005). To exemplify such referential meanings, consider how exposure to the tune of a nursery rhyme can evoke concepts related to childhood, or how hearing an unfamiliar yet energetic song may stir up thoughts about mindless carefree frivolity, while the same song performed in a sedate manner might conjure up notions of undisturbed reflection or thoughtful meditation.

Zhu and Meyers-Levy (2005) theorized that it should be more cognitively demanding to infer the referential rather than the embodied meaning of fairly muted background music in ads. Hence, they tested this by exposing motivated ad recipients to a radio ad where the ad's message format was varied to alter how resource demanding it was to process the ad message, and the energetic versus sedate style of the background ad music was also manipulated. Prior work suggested that messages should be more taxing to process if they are presented in an interactive drama format versus a monologue-like lecture format. Based on the premise that motivated ad recipients would first devote their cognitive resources to processing the ad message and then expend their remaining resources processing the background ad music, clear predictions were derived. As hypothesized, motivated processors of the ad discerned and based their assessments of the featured product on the music's embodied meaning when the ad message was presented in a cognitively taxing drama format. But they inferred and based their assessments on the music's referential meaning when the ad message was aired in a less onerous lecture format. As a result, these individuals' perceptions of the same product were shown to differ predictably depending on both the presentation format of the ad message and the style of the ad's background music. This research underscores the importance of considering both consumers' motivation or involvement level as well as the cognitive demands of the task that consumers will pursue when anticipating how the music presented in marketing communications will influence responses.

Music in the Consumer Environment

Music also can shape the very behaviors or actions that consumers display, a finding that clearly follows from the idea that motion may be the most primal sensorial response to music (Lacher & Mizerski, 1994). Consider how an up-tempo tune on your iPod can inspire you to pick up the pace as you walk or run. Adding to this, the symbolism conveyed by musical lyrics may stimulate corresponding visual imagery (Holbrook & Grayson, 1986). Music also may foster cognitive stimulation if listeners categorize the music or analyze its technical aspects (Lacher & Mizerski, 1994). In light of this, it is hardly surprising that music often affects consumers' actions, decision making, and choices in retail environments. Milliman (1982) found that background store music with a slow versus fast tempo altered both the pace of shopping and total sales volume; slower music prompted more leisurely in-store traffic, which in turn elevated sales volume. Slow-tempo music also has been found to lead diners to spend more time at a restaurant. As a result, they ate the same amount as did patrons in a faster-paced outlet, but they drank more, which heightened their average expenditure (Milliman, 1986). Also, although music may not shorten the perceived duration that consumers wait, it can make the waiting more pleasant, producing more positive evaluations of wait times (Antonides, Verhoef, & van Aalst, 2002; Kellaris & Kent, 1992).

In conclusion, although the inherently complex and dynamic nature of music renders it challenging to study, research attests that music can exert a potent influence on consumers' perceptions, attitudes, and behavior. Existing research points to a number of factors that are likely to qualify the way that music affects us, including our motivation or involvement level (e.g., the effortfulness of our processing), the demands of the task that we perform when hearing the music, and the demands of the marketing message itself. Nevertheless, further inquiry is needed to add to our understanding of how the music we hear can influence when and what we will buy.

Audition and the Multisensory Experience

Just as music possesses many complex and dynamic elements that operate in unison to create unique musical experiences, auditory stimuli represent only one of the many elements that are often used in marketing communications. Neuroscience and psychology researchers have sought to tease apart the effect of the auditory stimuli from other sensory modalities, with research by Eimer (1999) suggesting that a single system may control people's visual and auditory attention. If so, individuals may be impeded from simultaneously directing their attention to visual and auditory stimuli in opposite locations. Further, when visual and verbal stimuli compete for attention, it may be that consumers must divide their attention among such stimuli (Bonnel & Hafter, 1998).

Consumer researchers have long been interested in the relationship between visual and verbal elements in persuasive communications. In an examination of product placements, Russell (2002) found that unless the placement was integral to the plot of the televised program, viewers remembered auditory placements better than visual ones. Presumably when viewers divide their attention between visual images and auditory stimuli in a television program, priority is given to processing auditory stimuli because dialogue tends to be critical to understanding the television show plots. Still, it seems possible that visual rather than verbal product placements may be more impactful if visual stimuli are especially noteworthy, as in, say, travel documentaries. Most of the current research that has contrasted visual with verbal stimuli has compared print images with text. Although valuable insights are offered by such research, it remains unclear to what extent conclusions from these studies apply to the processing of visual and auditory stimuli. Future research needs to explore both differences in the processing of such stimuli in persuasive communications and corresponding synergies.

In many product categories, sound itself may provide important diagnostic data, as in the case of, say, stereo speakers. Consumers have been shown to place substantial weight on their own evaluation of sensory attributes like sound, taste, or touch when these attributes are critical to the product experience. Still, rich descriptions of the crucial sensory experience may compensate for a consumer's desire for direct sensory experience (McCabe & Nowlis, 2003). This implies that radio advertisers may benefit by including rich product descriptions in their messages, for these descriptions might compensate for the absence of visual data. Also, to the extent that verbal or auditory stimuli engage the listener in visual imagery, heightened elaboration may promote more successful persuasion (Unnava, Agarwal, & Haugtvedt, 1996). As consumers consider buying more product categories online, it is likely to become critically important that consumers are provided with elaborate descriptions of sensory attributes that the medium simply prevents them from experiencing directly. Future research is needed that explores the extent to which one sense may compensate for another in online settings.

Sensory perception frequently involves the integration of complex stimuli from multiple senses. Provocative work by Zampini and Spence (2004, 2005) examined how the perception of one sensory attribute, sound, can influence product perceptions involving a different sensory dimension, taste. These researchers found that the sound heard when eating or pouring a food product can influence consumers' perceptions of the product's freshness or taste. Thus, when biting a potato chip, a louder crunch enhanced perceptions of the product's crispness and freshness. Similarly, consumers perceived that a beverage was more carbonated when they heard loud bubbling when the drink was poured into a container. Extending on this, imagine what your perceptions of Rice Krispies would be if you failed to hear *Snap, Crackle, Pop* the next time you poured milk on them? Indeed, the loud rumble heard when a Harley-Davidson motorcycle passes by was viewed as so crucial to brand identification that the company attempted to trademark the low, guttural growl of the motorcycle's engine and exhaust system in an effort to prevent competitors from copying the bike's signature sound (Wilde, 1995). There is little doubt that sound represents a critical part of the consumer experience for many products. Future research must further explore how the senses jointly influence product perceptions and which product attributes are viewed as diagnostic for particular types of evaluations.

Conclusions

This chapter provided an overview of some of the intriguing research in marketing that has investigated the ways in which sound can affect consumers. While important headway has been made in understanding how sound symbolism, aspects of both language and music, and multi-sensory experiences that involve sound can influence consumers' memory, evaluations, and behaviors, more work is needed. Ironically, although radio is both a very real and dominant advertising medium that focuses almost entirely on sound, it has received quite limited research attention. An interesting exception is some work by Chattopadhyay, Dahl, Ritchie, and Shahin (2003), which showed that faster syllable speed, but not interphrase pausation, impaired attention to and recall of radio ad messages. The heightened syllable speed reduced listeners' motivation to process the radio ad message. Forehand and Perkins (2005) also conducted some work that is noteworthy for its realism, although it was done in the context of television ads. These researchers found that when audiences were able to identify celebrity voice-overs in ads, their explicit brand attitudes were negatively influenced by their attitude to the celebrity. Yet the opposite outcome emerged when ad recipients were unable to identify the celebrity voice-overs.

Most of the auditory research presented in this chapter investigated the intentional use of sound by marketers. Yet in today's media environment, where much exposure occurs when consumers are out of the home, ambient or environmental sounds in the broader environment also may influence how consumers' process and are persuaded by marketing communications. Research is needed that examines how ambient sound, say a barking dog or the omnipresent ring of a passerby's cell phone, might serendipitously affect persuasion. Finally, as investigators explore the role of sound in consumer behavior, it seems that much more research is needed that examines information processing from a multisensory perspective. Such work could shed important light on our understanding of how the senses work together in influencing persuasion.

References

Anand, P., & Sternthal, B. (1990, August). Ease of message processing as a moderator of repetition effects in advertising. *Journal of Marketing Research, 27,* 345–353.

Antonides, G., Verhoef, P. C., & van Aalst, M. (2002). Consumer perception and evaluation of waiting time: A field experiment. *Journal of Consumer Psychology, 12*(3), 193–202.

Bonnel, A. M., & Hafter, E. R. (1998). Divided attention between simultaneous auditory and visual signals. *Perception and Psychophysics,* 60 (2), 179–190.

Briley, D. A., Morris, M. W., & Simonson, I. (2005). Cultural chameleons: Biculturals conformity motives, and decision making. *Journal of Consumer Psychology, 15*(4), 351–362.

Bruner, G. C. (1990, October). Music, mood, and marketing. *Journal of Marketing, 54,* 94–104.

Chaiken, S., & Trope, Y. (1999). *Dual process theories in social psychology.* New York: Guilford.

Chattopadhyay, A., Dahl, D. W., Ritchie, R. J. B., & Shahin, K. N. (2003). Hearing voices: The impact of announcer speech characteristics on consumer response to broadcast advertising. *Journal of Consumer Psychology, 13*(3), 198–204.

Eimer, M. (1999). Can attention be directed to opposite locations in different modalities? An ERP study. *Clinical Neurophysiology, 110*(7), 1252–1259.

Forehand, M. R., & Perkins, A. (2005, December). Implicit assimilation and explicit contrast: A set/reset model of response to celebrity voice-overs. *Journal of Consumer Research, 32,* 435–441.

Gorn, G. J. (1982, Winter). The effects of music in advertising on choice behavior: A classical conditioning approach. *Journal of Marketing, 46,* 94–101.

Hockett, C. F. (1966). The problem of universals in language. In J. H. Greenberg (Ed.), *Universals of language* (2nd ed., pp. 1–29). Cambridge, MA: MIT Press.

Holbrook, M. B., & Grayson, M. W. (1986, December). The semiology of cinematic consumption: Symbolic consumer behavior in *Out of Africa. Journal of Consumer Research, 13,* 374–381.

Kellaris, J. J., Cox, A. D., & Cox, D. (1993, October). The effect of background music on ad processing: A contingency explanation. *Journal of Marketing, 57,* 114–125.

Kellaris, J. J., & Kent, R. J. (1992). The influence of music on consumers' temporal perceptions: Does time fly when you're having fun? *Journal of Consumer Psychology, 1*(4), 365–376.

Keller, K. L., Heckler, S. E., & Houston, M. J. (1998, January). The effects of brand name suggestiveness on advertising recall. *Journal of Marketing, 62,* 48–57.

Klink, R. R. (2000, February). Creating brand names with meaning: The use of sound symbolism. *Marketing Letters, 11,* 5–20.

Krishna, A., & Ahluwalia, R. (2008). Language choice in advertising to bilinguals: Asymmetric effects for multinationals versus local firms. *Journal of Consumer Research, 35*(4), 692–705.

Lacher, K. T., & Mizerski, R. (1994, September). An exploratory study of the responses and relationships involved in the evaluation of, and in the intention to purchase new rock music. *Journal of Consumer Research, 21,* 366–380.

Leclerc, F., Schmitt, B. H., & Dubé, L. (1994, May). Foreign branding and its effects on product perceptions and attitudes. *Journal of Marketing Research, 31,* 263–270.

Lowrey, T. M., & Shrum, L. J. (2007, October). Phonetic symbolism and brand name preference. *Journal of Consumer Research, 34,* 406–414.

Luna, D., & Peracchio, L. A. (2001, September). Moderators of language effects in advertising to bilinguals: A psycholinguistic approach. *Journal of Consumer Research, 28,* 284–295.

Luna, D., & Peracchio, L. A. (2005, March). Advertising to bilingual consumers: The impact of code-switching on persuasion. *Journal of Consumer Research, 31,* 760–765.

Luna, D., Ringberg, T., & Peracchio, L. A. (2008, August). One individual, two identities: Frame switching among biculturals. *Journal of Consumer Research, 35,* 279–293.

MacInnis, D. J., & Park, C. W. (1991, September). The differential role of characteristics of music on high- and low-involvement consumers' processing of ads. *Journal of Consumer Research, 18,* 161–173.

McCabe, D. B., & Nowlis, S. M. (2003). The effect of examining actual products or product descriptions on consumer preference. *Journal of Consumer Psychology, 13*(4), 431–439.

Meyer, L. B. (1960, May). Universalism and relativism in the study of ethnic music. *Ethnomusicology, 4,* 49–54.

Meyer, L. B. (1994). Emotion and meaning in music. In R. Aiello & J. A. Sloboda (Eds.), *Musical Perceptions* (pp. 3–39). New York: Oxford University Press.

Meyers-Levy, J. (1989, September). The influence of a brand name's association set size and word frequency on brand memory. *Journal of Consumer Research, 16,* 197–207.

Meyers-Levy, J., & Peracchio, L. A. (1995, September). Understanding the effects of color: How the correspondence between available and required resources affects attitudes. *Journal of Consumer Research, 22,* 121–138.

Meyers-Levy, J., & Tybout, A. M. (1989, June). Schema congruity as a basis for product evaluation. *Journal of Consumer Research, 16,* 39–54.

Milliman, R. E. (1982, Summer). Using background music to affect the behavior of supermarket shoppers. *Journal of Marketing, 46,* 86–91.

Milliman, R. E. (1986, September). The influence of background music on the behavior of restaurant patrons. *Journal of Consumer Research, 13,* 286–289.

Newman, S. S. (1933, January). Further experiments in phonetic symbolism. *American Journal of Psychology, 45,* 53–75.

Nuckolls, J. B. (1999). The case for sound symbolism. *Annual Reviews Anthropology, 28,* 225–252.

Pan, Y., & Schmitt, B. H. (1996). Language and brand attitudes: Impact of script and sound matching on Chinese and English. *Journal of Consumer Psychology, 5*(3), 263–277.

Park, C. W., & Young, S. M. (1986, February). Consumer response to television commercials: The impact of involvement and background music on brand attitude formation. *Journal of Marketing Research, 23,* 11–24.

Peracchio, L. A., & Meyers-Levy, J. (1997, September). Evaluating persuasion-enhancing techniques from a resource-matching perspective. *Journal of Consumer Research, 24,* 178–191.

Peracchio, L. A., & Tybout, A. M. (1996, December). The moderating role of prior knowledge in schema-based product evaluation. *Journal of Consumer Research, 23*, 177–192.

Petty, R. E., Cacioppo, J. T., & Schumann, D. (1983, September). Central and peripheral routes to advertising effectiveness: The moderating role of involvement. *Journal of Consumer Research, 10*, 135–146.

Rigg, M. G. (1937). An experiment to determine how accurately college students can interpret intended meanings of musical compositions. *Journal of Experimental Psychology, 21*, 223–229.

Russell, C. A. (2002, December). Investigating the effectiveness of product placements in television shows: The role of modality and plot connection congruence on brand memory and attitude. *Journal of Consumer Research, 29*, 306–318.

Sapir, E. (1929). A study in phonetic symbolism. *Journal of Experimental Psychology, 12*(3), 225–239.

Schmitt, B. H., Pan, Y., & Tavassoli, N. T. (1994, December). Language and consumer memory: The impact of linguistic differences between Chinese and English. *Journal of Consumer Research, 21*, 419–431.

Scott, L. M. (1990, September). Understanding jingles and needledrop: A rhetorical approach to music in advertising. *Journal of Consumer Research, 17*, 223–236.

Stout, P., & Leckenby, J. D. (1988). Let the music play: Music as a nonverbal element in television commercials. In S. Hecker & D. W. Stewart (Eds.), *Nonverbal communication in advertising* (pp. 207–233). Lexington, MA: Lexington Books.

Tanz, C. (1971). Sound symbolism in words relating to proximity and distance. *Language and Speech, 14*(3), 266–276.

Tavassoli, N. T., & Han, J. K. (2001, December). Scripted thought: Processing Korean Hancha and Hangul in a multimedia context. *Journal of Consumer Research, 28*, 482–493.

Tavassoli, N. T., & Lee, Y. H. (2003, November). The differential interaction of auditory and visual advertising elements with Chinese and English. *Journal of Marketing Research, 40*, 468–480.

Unnava, H. R., Agarwal, S., & Haugtvedt, C. P. (1996, June). Interactive effects of presentation modality and message-generated imagery on recall of advertising information. *Journal of Consumer Research, 23*, 81–88.

Wilde, A. D. (1995, June 23). Harley hopes to add Hog's roar to its menagerie of trademarks [Eastern Edition]. *Wall Street Journal*, p. B1.

Yorkston, E., & De Mello, G. E. (2005, September). Linguistic gender marking and categorization. *Journal of Consumer Research, 32*, 224–234.

Yorkston, E., & Menon, G. (2004, June). A sound idea: Phonetic effects of brand names on consumer judgments. *Journal of Consumer Research, 31*, 43–51.

Zampini, M., & Spence, C. (2004). The role of auditory cues in modulating the perceived crispness and staleness of potato chips. *Journal of Sensory Studies, 19*, 347–363.

Zampini, M., & Spence, C. (2005). Modifying the multisensory perception of a carbonated beverage using auditory cues. *Food Quality and Preference, 16,* 632–341.

Zhang, S., & Schmitt, B. H. (2004, June). Activating sound and meaning: The role of language proficiency in bilingual consumer environments. *Journal of Consumer Research, 31,* 220–228.

Zhu, R., & Meyers-Levy, J. (2005, August). Distinguishing between the meanings of music: When background music affects product perceptions. *Journal of Marketing Research, 42,* 333–345.

11

Auxiliary Auditory Ambitions
Assessing Ancillary and Ambient Sounds

Eric Yorkston

As far as the role of the five senses in marketing, sound has probably been given its due notice. However, when sound is examined across the range of marketing areas in which one would expect it to play a decisive role, such as product design and development, it quickly becomes apparent that the literature has too often been quiet. The study of sound in marketing has often been relegated to the role of sound in advertising, both in speech and in music (see Harris, Sturm, Klassen, and Bechtold [1986] for a review of language in advertising and Oakes [2007] for the role of music in advertising).

Granted, marketing communications is a natural focus for the study of sound. To some extent all traditional communication in English involves sound. All radio advertisements must convey the entirety of their messages aurally, and sound is a seminal component of almost all television advertisements. Indirectly, even print ads that involve the English language utilize sound; words are "heard" in the mind when read. In order to process a phonetic written language, read words enter a *phontactic loop*, similarly to spoken words, before being encoded in the mind (Pinker, 1994). This phenomenon has been nicely examined in marketing cross-culturally by comparing languages with phonetic-based writing systems with logographic-based writing systems (Schmitt, Pan, & Tavassoli, 1994). Researchers have also documented the interplay of music and language as embodied in the ever-lilting jingle. This melodious inclusion has been shown to increase memory, attention, and affect for the brand and commercial message (Scott, 1990; Wallace, 1991).

In all these cases, sound is considered an essential part of the message and plays a purposeful role in communication. But what about when the sounds attached to a product, service, or communication only play an auxiliary role? Just because sound may not be a focal aspect of the consumer decision process does not mean that it does not play a valuable role for companies or consumers. In fact these auxiliary sounds can exert a strong influence on the consumer. This chapter focuses on these auxiliary sounds and the role they play. It proposes a new framework for auxiliary sounds containing two distinct categories: ancillary sounds and ambient sounds.

Ancillary Sounds

In most products or services, sound in and of itself is not the attribute of interest to the consumer. However, that does not mean that sound does not play a pivotal role. Sound often plays an ancillary role by providing a cue to how a product performs on some desirable dimension. For example, the slam of a car door is often considered a signal of the quality of the car (Kuwano, Fastl, Namba, Nakamura, & Uchida, 2006) and the sound of the horn can reveal information regarding its size and personality. These ancillary sounds provide essential support to the perceptions of an object's attributes and function.

Individuals expect that the sound an object emits will reveal something about the properties of that object. For example, in animals, it is expected that volume and pitch correlate to animal size; large dogs should have loud, low barks and small dogs should have high-pitched, softer, yippy barks. This natural correlation between sound and size is behind much of the work on *sound symbolism*, where the sounds of the word connote the object it represents (Yorkston & Menon, 2004). But humans have also been able to notice patterns occurring in man-made objects and in inanimate objects in the natural world. When hearing unknown sounds, people are able to recognize features of the source such as shape, material, and hollowness (Rocchesso, Ottaviani, Fontana, & Avanzini, 2003). For example, Kunkler-Peck and Turvey (2000) found that individuals were able to identify shape and material properties upon hearing impact sounds. Lederman (1979) demonstrated that in judging the roughness of a surface, judgments based on auditory information were almost identical to those based on the corresponding tactile information.

The converse is also true; individuals are able to predict what sounds an object will make from its physical properties. If this relationship is violated, then not only are individuals taken aback, but they negatively transfer this auditory betrayal to the objects themselves. Ludden and Schifferstein

(2007) examined what happens when an object's sound is incongruent with consumers' expectations. Consumers watched an experimenter operate a "flimsy" juicer (i.e., it was relatively small, had simple rounded shapes, and was made out of white and transparent plastic) or a "robust" juicer (i.e., it was tall, had a vertical main form, was shaped with smooth curves, and had a silver metallic and black color combination). Sounds were digitally manipulated to emphasize or attenuate their specific expressive characteristics. If the flimsy (robust) juicer produced robust (flimsy) sounds, then consumers reported amazement and surprise. Interestingly, consumers seemed equally surprised both when a product negatively underperformed and when a product positively over performed. Ludden and Schifferstein (2007) found similar results when comparing a "tough" dust buster (i.e., was large, had sharp edges, and silver metallic color) to a "cute" dust buster (had a round, curved shape and a creamy white and orange color combination).

When sound does not match our expectations, it not only fails to elicit surprise, but it can mold our perceptions of the physical characteristics of the object. Zampini and Spence (2004) demonstrated that a sound's characteristics can influence the perceived characteristics of the representative product. In their studies, participants heard real-time manipulated sound through headphones as they bit into potato chips. The participants' mastication was recorded and the overall sound level was either amplified or attenuated and fed back into their headphones. As the overall sound level increased, so did participants' perceptions of the crispness and staleness of the potato chips. Further, Zampini and Spence (2004) demonstrated that it was the high frequency sounds traditionally associated with the "snap" of biting into fresh and crisp foods that were driving perceptions. When only high frequency sounds (in the range of 2 kHz to 20 kHz) were amplified, the chips once again were perceived to be crisper and fresher. Selectively amplifying the lower frequency sounds had no discernable effect on judgments of crispness or freshness.

Zampini and colleagues have continued to explore this relationship across a multitude of product categories and found that manipulating the overall sound levels and frequencies can make electric toothbrushes less pleasant or rougher (Zampini, Guest, & Spence, 2003) and sodas more carbonated (Zampini & Spence, 2005). Finally, Lageat, Czellar, and Laurent (2003) investigated how gestalt perceptions of luxury can be produced for lighters. For a classic flip-open lighter, they found that luxury was associated with either sounds that were full-bodied, even, and low in pitch, or with sounds that were clear, resonant, and clicking.

Although there has been much talk regarding multisensory experiences, especially in the hedonic consumption paradigm (Lageat et al., 2003), the role of sound is often overlooked in favor of the more "exotic" senses of smell, touch, and taste. The study of ancillary sounds and the processes by which their influence manifests is still in its infancy and there is great room for future research.

Ambient Sounds

Of course not all sounds are even indirectly related to an object's or a service's attributes. Atmospheric sounds, which may occur naturally, at random in a particular environment, or at a particular time, need not provide information. Instead, these background, or *ambient* sounds may set the pervading tone or mood of a place, service, or object. Sounds are heard continually and continuously and there is almost no time when true "silence" is experienced. For every event there is an auditory component, and control of this component can take on great importance.

Work on ambient sounds in marketing has appropriately focused on a company's primary point of contact with the consumer: the retail or service space. Service spaces often intentionally control ambient sounds. The most common method of control is through the inclusion of music in the consumption experience, for the retail or service experience often occurs in its own physical space and under company control. Not surprisingly, background music has been widely studied to see how it can affect the mood, attitudes, and behavior of the consumer. This research appears to center around three music dimensions: music tempo, music type, and music volume.

Music Tempo

Studies have shown that the tempo of music in stores is often correlated with the pace of shopping (Milliman, 1982, 1986). Consumers who hear music with a slower tempo complete tasks at a slower pace. Because slower pace translates into a longer service encounter and time in a store, it is not surprising that slower music provides consumers with greater consumption opportunities and influences quantity purchased. When music tempo was manipulated in a supermarket, shoppers spent more time and money in the slow tempo retail environments and sales correspondingly increased by 38% (Milliman, 1982). Similar results have been observed for music tempo in a restaurant (Milliman, 1986). Customers in the slow music condition took more time to eat their meals compared to those in the fast-music condition. And although the pace of music did not change which foods were ordered or the amount spent on food, the extra time spent at the table did translate into more drinks being consumed and a 41% increase in beverage revenue.

Not only does music tempo help determine the pace of shopping, but it also provides greater context and associative information about what sorts of products, schemas, and ultimately purchases are most appropriate. These associations can influence consumers by influencing unconscious thought processes. For example, people do not consciously think that they should take their time in a store if slow background music is playing. Studies have repeatedly demonstrated that consumers cannot recall the properties of the music playing and in many cases report being unaware of music playing at all (Milliman, 1986; North, Hargreaves, & McKendrick, 1999). Rather, consumers most likely unconsciously associate slow music with a more relaxed pace. The relaxed tempo can also produce a calming effect. In a study that examined the effects of ambient music on customers' response to bank lines, McDonnell (2007) documented that ambient music can reduce queue rage.

Just as slow tempo music relaxes consumers, fast tempo music can create states of arousal in its listeners. Dubé, Chebat, and Morris (1995) demonstrated that music-induced arousal, independent of pleasure, had a positive effect on consumers' affiliation behaviors in a banking context. The faster tempo music heightened arousal and increased positive consumer attitudes of friendliness toward the bank personnel. Additionally, consumers exposed to fast tempo music reported greater behavioral intentions to smile, say hello, and chat with the bank employees.

Music Type

Yalch and Spangenberg (1990) conducted research that built on the Milliman studies regarding music and its effect on perceptions of time. They manipulated the type of music played. In a department store setting, they compared the effects of foreground music (Top 40), and background music (instrumental and easy listening), to a no music control group. In that study, younger shoppers (under 25) thought that they had spent more time shopping in the easy listening condition, whereas older shoppers perceived that they had shopped longer when Top 40 music was played. The authors concluded that encountering atypical environmental factors (e.g., unfamiliar music) might adversely influence consumers' time perceptions.

The specific type of ambient store music not only influences pace and time perceptions, but it also affects product choice through the associations generated. In a study involving wine purchases, North et al. (1999) investigated the extent to which stereotypically French and German music influenced supermarket customers' selections of French and German wines. Music with strong national associations activated customers' related knowledge and resulted in customers buying wine from the respective country. Over a 2-week period, French and German music was played on alternate days in a store that had in-store displays for both French and German wines. French music led to French wines outselling German ones, whereas German music led to the opposite effect on sales of French and German wine. Responses to a questionnaire suggested that customers were unaware of these effects of music on their product choices. Music can also generate associations regarding class, status, and price. Another study found that wine shoppers purchased more expensive wines when classical music was playing than when the store played Top 40 hits (Areni & Kim, 1993).

The type of ambient music is often chosen to appeal to the target demographic's particular taste and establish connections between a company, its brand, and its customer. Music's powerful ability to establish rich, deep connections is a valuable branding tool, and companies are going further and further to make this meaningful connection between brand and consumer. Proctor and Gamble, maker of TAG body spray, recently teamed up with Jermaine Dupri, president of Island Def Jam's Urban Music division, to start Tag Records, a new label that will specialize in hip-hop music. It is hoped that this collaboration will make TAG body spray resonate with its young target audience (Levine, 2008).

Similarly, retailers have established connections with a target demographic by playing, promoting, and selling musical genres that appeal to that target demographic in their stores. In these cases, retailers act as a music distribution channel or engage in typical cross-promotion strategies. For example, Starbucks, the Seattle coffee chain, sells a range of music including Alicia Keys, Kenny G, and James Blunt. Starbucks reported selling 4.4 million compact disks in North America in 2007, up some 22% from the year before (Leeds, 2008). Although the additional revenue that the sales provide is an added benefit, Starbucks' main interest is how the music selections give them credibility with their audience by promoting and introducing new artists. When Starbucks stocked *Careless Love*, a compact disk of sophisticated pop-jazz songs by Madeleine Peyroux, who had attracted only a modest following in the United States, Peyroux soon found herself at number 81 on the Billboard chart and has since become a mainstay of jazz (Leeds, 2008).

Music can also be an excellent cross-promotional tool that can link brands with similar target audiences and strengthen brand identities. For example, in November 2007, the lingerie and beauty retailer Victoria's Secret exclusively released the compact disk version of *Spice Girls: Greatest Hits*, which featured 13 of the best-selling British girl-group's chart-topping smash singles. The two brands share a mutual goal of projecting an image of sexy and empowered women, and both brands benefit from these connections. Further cementing the Spice Girls partnership with Victoria's Secret, the group made their reunion television debut at Victoria's Secret's annual fashion show.

Of course the type of music chosen does not have to drive sales or even drive customers to the store. Music type can just as easily drive people away. The aversive power of music has a long and storied history. In the U.S. military, loud music is utilized by *psyops*, or psychological operations, and is considered a tried and true method to repel, harass, and bring down the enemy. In 1989, when Manuel Noriega, a noted opera buff who reportedly hated rock music, was ensconced in the Vatican embassy in Panama City, U.S. soldiers assailed Noriega's ears with Guns and Roses and Van Halen (McFadyen, 2006). He quickly surrendered. Less drastically, empirical evidence also suggests that sound can dissuade individuals not in the target demographic from actions such as entering retail spaces. For example, the use of classical music to alienate youth is widespread. To clear out undesirables, opera and classical music have been piped into Canadian parks, Australian railway stations, English seaside shops, 7-Eleven parking lots and, most recently, London Underground stops. For example, a McDonald's in Camberwell, England, has used the sonic approach of playing classical music outside its restaurant to stop youths from gathering there (Morris, 2005).

According to figures released in January 2005 from Transport for London, the local government agency responsible for the London Underground, a test of classical music in select London subway stations showed robberies in the subway down by 33%, assaults on staff down by 25%, and vandalism of trains and stations down by 37% (Morris, 2005). Additional sources have reported fewer muggings and drug deals. London authorities now plan to expand the playing of Mozart, Vivaldi, Handel, and opera (sung by Pavarotti) from three subway stations to an additional 40 (Fisher, 2008).

Music Volume

Youths and hooligans are not the only ones to be deterred by music. Abercrombie and Fitch is famous for dissuading adults from entering the store through the use of loud music (Thornton, 2007). A recent television news exposé measured the sound in one Portland, Oregon, Abercrombie and Fitch store at 90 decibels (peaking out at 98 decibels). This is as loud as a chain saw and right on the threshold of the Occupational Safety and Health Administration's permissible occupational noise exposure for an 8-hour shift (U.S. Department of Labor, 2008). Similar noise levels were observed in Nordstrom's teen section (mid-80 dB) and Hollister (90 dB) (Thornton, 2007). Thornton (2007) reports that audiologists say prolonged exposure to sounds above 85 dB could cause permanent hearing loss and that everyone working at the observed Abercrombie and Fitch should be wearing hearing protection. Employees reported that they were not allowed to turn down the music due to corporate policy.

Loud music has also been shown to affect the amount of time spent in a store. Smith and Curnow (1966) found that customers spent significantly less time in stores when the music was loud compared to when the music was soft, although there was no significant difference in sales or in the customers' reported levels of satisfaction.

Unexpected Effects

To this point we have addressed the intentional application of ancillary and ambient sounds. Yet auxiliary sounds are not always under the control of the marketer. Ancillary sounds may be an unintended or uncontrollable consequence of a product feature. There may also be difficulties caused by sounds corresponding to correlated attributes. The reassuring thump of the new Volkswagen Beetle's door may signal high quality, but it also identifies the door's hefty weight, which could lead to concerns regarding the automobile's peppiness or fuel efficiency. Ancillary sounds also interact with the environment and the consumption context. The refreshing "pop" heard when opening a can of Coca-Cola might be desirable in most instances, but it is surely unappreciated (and a dead giveaway of impermissible behavior) in a quiet library.

Ambient sounds also face these constraints. Atmospherics are not always under a company's control, especially with sound's pesky reluctance to obey property lines. Street noises, construction, and customers' themselves are not only sources of competing sounds, they also play strong roles in determining sound volume decisions. Additionally, the consumption space may have ambient sounds that are specific to the consumption experience, and these ambient sounds may interact with the physical properties or geography of that space. The roar of the crowd at a ballpark depends on the interaction of these factors, and it is a key element of the game consumption experience. The complexity of these interactions of ambient and ancillary sounds provides ample rich areas for future work.

References

Areni, C. S., & Kim, D. (1993). The influence of background music on shopping behavior: Classical versus top-forty in a wine store. *Advances in Consumer Research, 20*(1), 336–340.

Dubé, L., Chebat, J., & Morris, S. (1995, July). The effects of background music on consumers' desire to affiliate in buyer-seller interactions. *Psychology and Marketing, 12,* 305–319.

Fisher, N. (2008, February 1). The tune now arriving … *The Times (London)*, Times 2, p. 14.

Harris, R. J., Sturm, R. E., Klassen, M. L., & Bechtold, J. I. (1986). Language in advertising: A psycholinguistic approach. *Current Issues and Research in Advertising, 9*(1), 1–21.

Kunkler-Peck, A. J., & Turvey, M. T. (2000, February). Hearing shape. *Journal of Experimental Psychology: Human Perception and Performance, 26,* 279–294.

Kuwano, S., Fastl, H., Namba, S., Nakamura, S., & Uchida, H. (2006). Quality of door sounds of passenger cars. *Acoustical Science and Technology, 27*(5), 309–312.

Lageat, T., Czellar, S., & Laurent, G. (2003, July). Engineering hedonic attributes to generate perceptions of luxury: Consumer perception of an everyday sound. *Marketing Letters, 14,* 97–109.

Lederman, S. J. (1979). Auditory texture perception. *Perception, 8*(1), 93–103.

Leeds, J. (2008, March 17). Does this latte have a funny mainstream taste to you? *New York Times* [Late Edition], p. C1.

Levine, R. (2008, July 7). It's American brandstand: Marketers underwrite performers. *New York Times*, p. C1.

Ludden, G. D. S., & Schifferstein, H. N. J. (2007). Effects of visual-auditory incongruity on product expression and surprise. *International Journal of Design, 1*(3), 29–39.

McDonnell, J. (2007). Music, scent and time preferences for waiting lines. *International Journal of Bank Marketing, 25*(4), 223–237.

McFadyen, W. (2006, August 16). Manilow a secret weapon. *Sunday Age (Sydney Australia)*, Extra, p. 16.

Milliman, R. E. (1982). Using background music to affect the behavior of supermarket shoppers. *Journal of Marketing, 46*(3), 86–91.

Milliman, R. E. (1986, September). The influence of background music on the behavior of restaurant patrons. *Journal of Consumer Research, 13*, 286–289.

Morris, S. (2005, November 3). Classical deterrent in store for loitering youths. *The Guardian*, p. 14.

North, A. C., Hargreaves, D. J., & McKendrick, J. (1999, April). The influence of in-store music on wine selections. *Journal of Applied Psychology, 84*, 271–276.

Oakes, S. (2007, March). Evaluating empirical research into music in advertising: A congruity perspective. *Journal of Advertising Research, 47*, 38–50.

Pinker, S. (1994). *The language instinct*. New York: William Morrow.

Rocchesso, D., Ottaviani, L., Fontana, F., & Avanzini, F. (2003). Size, shape, and material properties of sound models. In D. Rocchesso & F. Fontana (Eds.), *The sounding object* (pp. 95–110). Firenze, Italy: PHASAR.

Schmitt, B. H., Pan, Y., & Tavassoli, N. T. (1994, December). Language and consumer memory: The impact of linguistic differences between Chinese and English. *Journal of Consumer Research, 21*, 419–431.

Scott, L. M. (1990, September). Understanding jingles and needledrop: A rhetorical approach to music in advertising. *Journal of Consumer Research, 17*, 223–236.

Smith, P. C., & Curnow, R. (1966, June). "Arousal hypothesis" and the effects of music on purchasing behavior. *Journal of Applied Psychology, 50*, 255–266.

Thornton, A. (2007, November 29). *Loud music in some stores bothering you? You're not alone*. Portland, Oregon: KATU.com news. Retrieved May 29, 2009, from http://www.katu.com/news/11926196.html

U.S. Department of Labor: Occupational Safety and Health Administration. (2008). Occupational noise exposure: Standard number 1910.95. In *Occupational Safety and Health Standards: Occupational Health and Environmental Control*. Retrieved May 29, 2009, from http://www.osha.gov/pls/oshaweb/owadisp.show_document?p_table=STANDARDS&p_id=9735

Wallace, W. T. (1991). Jingles in advertisements: Can they improve recall? *Advances in Consumer Research, 18*(1), 239–242.

Yalch, R. F., & Spangenberg, E. (1990, Spring). Effects of store music on shopping behavior. *Journal of Consumer Marketing, 7*, 55–61.

Yorkston, E., & Menon, G. (2004, June). A sound idea: Phonetic effects of brand names on consumer judgments. *Journal of Consumer Research, 31*, 43–51.

Zampini, M., Guest, S., & Spence, C. (2003, November). The role of auditory cues in modulating the perception of electric toothbrushes. *Journal of Dental Research, 82,* 929–932.

Zampini, M., & Spence, C. (2004). The role of auditory clues in modulating the perceived crispness and staleness of potato chips. *Journal of Sensory Studies, 19,* 347–363.

Zampini, M., & Spence, C. (2005). Modifying the multisensory perception of a carbonated beverage using auditory cues. *Food Quality and Preference, 16*(7), 632–641.

12

Understanding the Role of Spokesperson Voice in Broadcast Advertising

Darren W. Dahl

Worldwide, broadcast advertising is a $69 billion industry. Of that total, roughly $21 billion is spent on production and airtime for radio ads, with an additional $48 billion of comparable expenditures in television (Bond, 2008; Radio Advertising Bureau, 2008). When preparing a broadcast advertisement, a key managerial decision involves selection of the voice that will be used to convey the information contained in the advertisement. Whether alone or with sound effects as in radio, or combined with images as in television, the voice in a broadcast advertisement is a key focal point for the audience. It provides the vehicle by which the product claims are conveyed, and thereby plays an important role in seizing the listener's attention in a world of competing messages.

There is considerable evidence to suggest that the meaning of verbal communication is conveyed not only by words, but by the way in which those words are delivered (for examples see Myers, Herndon, & Fryar, 1988; Peterson, Cannito, & Brown, 1995). Apple, Streeter, and Krauss (1979) refer to the linguistic content of a message as the verbal channel and the paralinguistic information conveyed by voice characteristics as the vocal channel. Indeed, under certain circumstances, vocal characteristics appear to have been more important than verbal content in influencing listeners' attitudes and perceptions (e.g., Mehrabian, 1972; Thomas, 1992). As such, it would seem reasonable to conclude that voice plays an important role in the development of attitudes toward the ad and, by extension, toward the brand that the advertisement seeks to promote.

Theories abound regarding the qualities that are desirable in an advertisement spokesperson's voice. Yet most of these are based on the individual manager's intuition or on anecdotal evidence from a small number of very successful advertising campaigns. Although there are some voices and voice types that have been favored by advertisers, little concrete evidence exists to explain (a) whether these voices are truly effective; (b) what characteristics of these voices make them so, and (c) whether there are any boundary conditions that limit the effectiveness of a particular voice type.

Despite the apparently important role of voice in determining the effectiveness of a broadcast advertisement, little research has been done in this area. An examination of the effects of several voice characteristics have been made in a variety of other settings, such as personal selling, telephone interviews, and public speaking. This research suggests that fundamental frequency (voice pitch) and vocal speech rate are two important influencers of listener response to verbal communication and that they affect personal perceptions of the speaker. Using these two voice characteristics to guide this discussion, this chapter provides an overview of voice research in broadcast advertising and outlines opportunities for future research in the area.

Fundamental Frequency

Fundamental frequency refers to the vibration rate of the vocal folds in the throat (larynx), and the perceptual representation of this phenomenon is known as pitch. Extensive research in psychology (Bond, Welkowitz, Goldschmidt, & Wattenberg, 1987) and linguistics (Brown, Strong, & Rencher, 1973) suggests that in general, low-pitched voices are evaluated more favorably than high-pitched voices. A representative study by Apple et al. (1979) reported three experiments in which participants were asked to listen to tape recordings that had been altered such that the fundamental frequency of the speaker's voice was either presented at its normal level or electronically increased or decreased by 20%. Results indicated that speakers with high-pitched voices were judged less truthful, less emphatic, less potent, and more nervous than speakers with low-pitched voices. Indeed, Brown et al. (1973) found that increases in fundamental frequency lead listeners to perceive a speaker as less competent and less benevolent.

Studies of the effects of deception on speech indicate that voice pitch does, in fact, tend to rise when we are lying (Ekman, Friesen, & Scherer, 1976; Streeter, Krauss, Geller, Olson, & Apple, 1977). More generally, a higher-pitched voice has been associated with greater levels of stress, nervousness, and fright. It is argued that low-pitched voices may therefore be a reasonable diagnostic indicator that a person is telling the truth. Evidence suggests that the increased persuasiveness of deeper voices may also result from a second, parallel process. Connections have been found between deep voices and increased message acceptance in low-involvement situations (Gelinas-Chebat & Chebat, 1992). Moreover, it has been found that low-pitched voices are considered more appealing and lead to more favorable evaluations of the personality of the speaker (Zuckerman & Miyake, 1993).

In a marketing context, the limited research that investigates fundamental frequency shows mixed results. Research investigating the effectiveness of telephone market research interviewers shows that interviewers with higher fundamental frequencies (i.e., higher-pitched voices) were more successful and realized lower refusal rates for consumer participation (Oksenberg, Coleman, & Cannell, 1986; Sharf & Lehman, 1984). It is important to note, however, that these two studies use female voices in their testing. In an advertising context, Chattopadhyay, Dahl, Ritchie, and Shahin (2003) directly tested fundamental frequency by digitally varying the vocal pitch of the spokesperson in a radio ad to be either high or low. The results showed a more favorable reaction to the lower-pitched version of the radio advertisement; however, this main effect was qualified by the speech rate of the spokesperson, a vocal characteristic that is examined in the next section.

Vocal Speech Rate

A convincing body of empirical evidence has linked faster speech rates with enhanced persuasive power. Several studies have found that listeners attribute greater competence and credibility to individuals who speak more quickly (for examples see Miller, Maruyama, Beaber, & Valone, 1976; Pearce & Conklin, 1971; Smith, Brown, Strong, & Rencher, 1975; Stewart & Ryan, 1982; Zuckerman & Driver, 1989). Fast speech also seems to encourage listeners to see speakers as more intelligent, knowledgeable, and objective (Miller et al., 1976), as well as more truthful, fluent, emphatic, serious, and persuasive (Apple et al., 1979).

In the marketing context, considerable research attention has been directed toward vocal speech rate in broadcast advertising. The industry practice of time compression in both television and radio broadcast advertisements in the 1970s and 1980s garnered a number of investigations centered on the effects of quickened speech rate on audience's perceptions and attitudes. Notably, James MacLachlan and colleagues in a series of papers (LaBarbera & MacLachlan, 1979; MacLachlan, 1982; MacLachlan

& Siegel, 1980) found that people prefer a vocal speech rate that is moderately faster than normal speed. They suggested that faster speeds are not only preferred, but they cause listeners to devote greater attention in processing advertisement information. Their findings showed that listeners had better recall of advertisements and were more favorable to the ad when time-compression techniques were used. Subsequent work (Lautman & Dean, 1983; Moore, Hausknecht, & Thamodaran, 1986; Schlinger, Alwitt, McCarthy, & Green, 1983; Stephens, 1982; but see Vann, Rogers, & Penrod, 1987 for an alternate outcome) predominately validated the effect of a more positive response to speech-compressed advertisements, but refuted the initial claim that listeners realized improved processing of advertising content. Rather, these papers argue that an increased vocal speech rate in broadcast advertising gives listeners less time to elaborate on the advertisement, reducing their opportunity to process the message. Indeed, listeners may use faster speech as a cue that the processing task will be difficult and effectively "tune out" from the advertisement (Moore et al., 1986). It is suggested that when speech rate is faster than normal, listeners will process the substance of the advertisement less and focus instead on peripheral cues such as likability of the spokesperson's voice in forming their attitudes and judgments. Results from a series of studies, reported by Moore et al. (1986), suggest that when speech rate is high, consumers do in fact process advertisement claims less.

As has been pointed out by several authors in linguistics and psychology (e.g., Cotton, 1936; Kelly & Steer, 1949; Lane & Grosjean, 1973), speech rate is derived by two components: syllable speed and interphrase pausation. *Syllable speed* is the speed at which a syllable is articulated, approximately five per second in normal speech (Grosjean & Lane, 1976). *Interphrase pausation* is the gap between successive phrases, typically 0.5 seconds in normal conversation (Grosjean & Lane, 1976). Although previous research in marketing and speech compression has pointed to this distinction (Schlinger et al., 1983), investigation of these two aspects of speech rate was not conducted independently.

Two more recent papers in the advertising context have sought to disentangle the role that syllable speed and pausation each play in cultivating vocal speech rate effects. Megehee, Dobie, and Grant (2003) used a radio-advertising context to both compress and expand speech rate through either changes to pausation or the speed of syllabic articulation. Their findings indicated that, in general, a faster speech rate resulted in more affective reactions from listeners and a better attitudinal response toward the spokesperson. A slower speech rate enabled greater cognitive elaboration on the message. These results are consistent with assumptions expressed in the Elaboration Likelihood Model (Petty & Cacioppo, 1979) and replicate previous findings in the literature. Interestingly, listeners showed no significant differences in their responses to the two methods of speech manipulation. However, the authors note that pause-compressed speech produced directionally more favorable attitudes toward the message and increased cognitive responses. The authors further contend that the lack of meaningful differences across these forms of speech compression may be an outcome of the narrow range of speech rate used in their study. They speculate that a broader range of speech rates would likely affect listeners.

Chattopadhyay et al. (2003) also sought to tease out differential effects for syllabic speed and interphrase pausation. As noted above, these authors varied vocal pitch and the two aspects of vocal speech rate in a fully crossed experimental design. Utilizing a radio advertising context, findings here indicated no effects for interphrase pausation on ad processing or attitudes. Syllable speed, on the other hand, interacted with the voice pitch of the spokesperson and produced an influence on consumers' responses. When syllabic speed was faster, listeners focused more on the peripheral cue of pitch, exhibiting more favorable responses to a low- versus a high-pitched voice. Specifically, given a faster syllabic speed, more advertisement-directed cognitive responses and more positive ad and brand attitudes emerged in the low- than the high-vocal-pitched condition. As the authors clarified, these results both support and extend the findings of Moore et al. (1986). They show that the effect of increasing speech rate in broadcast advertising is to disrupt, rather than enhance, consumer processing of the advertisement. They also indicate that the peripheral cue of vocal pitch can have substantial effects on listeners. Finally, the authors contend that it is motivation, not ability, to process the advertisement that underlies their findings. This conclusion is derived from the null findings for pausation. Given that both manipulations reduced the advertisement's running time by exactly the same amount, support for a motivational explanation is implicated.

It is interesting to note that very little research attention in marketing has been conducted in spokesperson voice over the past decade. The brief discussion above is seeded in much earlier work and highlights initial findings with respect to two vocal characteristics—fundamental frequency and speech rate—in the broadcast advertising context. This review brings to light inconsistencies in findings and suggests additional questions. For example, in the most recent empirical investigations of interphrase pausation, divergent findings were identified. Megehee et al. (2003) show parallel influence for reduction in speech rate for pausation and syllabic length, whereas Chattopadhyay et al. (2003) show no influence for changes in interphrase pausation. This discrepancy in results and other unanswered questions pertaining to these vocal characteristics indicate opportunities for future research. In the next section, specific opportunities for future investigation are highlighted.

Opportunities

Other Characteristics of Speech

A number of opportunities for additional investigation are found in other defining characteristics of vocal speech. One key characteristic is pitch contour, whether the fundamental frequency is rising or falling over the course of an individual's speech. Previous research indicates that the contour in pitch across a phrase can imbue verbal communication with additional meaning (Ohala, 1981). For example, a phrase ending on a rising pitch is often understood to be a question, whereas the same phrase in a downward pitch may be interpreted as a statement. As such, rising contours might reflect uncertainty and be related to perceptions of low competency and credibility. Future research could systematically vary pitch contour to investigate its impact on the effectiveness of marketing communications. An initial investigation by Peterson et al. (1995) in a sales context examined the role of pitch contour. Their results showed that salespeople made good use of both upward and downward pitch contours, and that use of a falling contour pattern correlated to better sales performance. These exploratory findings provide a good starting point for additional research attention toward this speech variable.

Relatedly, Gelinas-Chebat and Chebat (1992) explored the effects of voice intonation, the level of variation in an individual's fundamental frequency. Working with a sample of 221 participants, the authors assessed attitudes toward two messages that advertised automated teller machines and student loans. A professional male spokesperson was used to produce different voices for the two intonation levels investigated. Their results showed that when the spokesperson used a low level of intonation the message was more effective with the audience than when a high level of intonation was utilized. Importantly, they also showed that this vocal characteristic is a peripheral cue most influential under low involvement situations. Variation in pitch, as a subtle peripheral cue, is a vocal characteristic under the control of the spokesperson and as such enables both theoretical and substantive implications for future research efforts.

Another potentially important characteristic deserving study is voice amplitude (i.e., the loudness or intensity of the voice delivery). Although not typically under the control of the marketing manager in the advertising context, variability on this dimension can play an important role in other marketing contexts such as service encounters. Previous research has shown that dominance, assertiveness, and aggression are characterized by loud voices (Peterson et al., 1995), whereas submission, deference, and uncertainty are conveyed by a quieter vocal delivery (Brown & Bradshaw, 1985). Interestingly, the evidence outlining relationships involving amplitude is less extensive than that for other voice characteristics (Peterson et al., 1995), and this provides a good opportunity for future investigation. Variability in amplitude and interrelationships with other vocal characteristics are additional research prospects in this area.

It is important to note that technological advances over the past few years have created a better experimental environment for the study of voice characteristics. Specifically, the use of digital recordings effectively manipulated through advanced computer software enables researchers to independently alter dimensions of vocal speech while holding all other characteristics constant. Technology provides the ability to manipulate vocal characteristics in almost any manner, facilitates more control in developed manipulations, and allows more precision in realizing exact levels of vocal characteristics targeted by the experimenter. More recent investigations have made use of this type of technology. For example, the Chattopdahyay et al. (2003) paper discussed above uses Pro Tools software (Digidesign, Inc., Daly City, CA) to effectively manipulate fundamental frequency, pausation, and syllabic speed independent of one another. When compared to initial research in this area, which utilized actors or spokespeople attempting to speak with different fundamental frequencies (e.g., Gelinas-Chebat & Chebat, 1992) or multiple spokespeople representing different vocal conditions (e.g., Sharf & Lehman, 1984), the advantages of embracing new methodologies become readily apparent.

Context

A second broad area that demands more research attention is the variation in context in which broadcast advertising voice is studied. The majority of research conducted in this area has been in the context of radio advertising, with very few studies examining the importance of voice in television advertising. Exceptions to this are investigations into time compression in television programming (MacLachlan & Siegel, 1980; Stephens, 1982). This is most likely due to the added complexity of the visual component found in a television advertisement. Additionally, the use of voice in Internet advertising, with its variety of execution formats (e.g., pop-ups, banners, Internet ads, avatars, smart bots), also presents new opportunities for investigation. Differing broadcast media, such as television, radio, and Internet, provide unique advertising contexts where voice may have differing effects.

Beyond the advertising media, the form of the advertisement itself presents interesting research possibilities. For example, the type of product or service being advertised might be an important aspect of an ad that interacts with voice. Or the type of ad appeal (e.g., fear, emotional, informational) may also be a critical factor. Vann et al. (1987) support this research direction by indicating that "There are some, as yet unidentified, aspects of advertisements that interact [with voice]" (p. 18). These authors note that in their study some advertisements showed voice effects and others did not, leading them to conclude that there is no way to currently make an unambiguous prediction of the effects of voice for any particular advertisement. They caution that every advertisement must be tested for voice effects in isolation and conclude that what is needed is the identification and classification of the aspects of advertisements that interact with voice characteristics.

A final opportunity for voice research with respect to the advertisement context is found in the various executional elements within the ad itself. Namely, other audio elements within the broadcast ad, including elements like music and sound effects, could be studied to assess their impact on voice. Initial research in marketing (Zhu & Meyers-Levy, 2005) has identified background music in advertising as an executional element within an ad that can have a significant impact on affective and cognitive responses of the listener. How would voice effects interact with this executional variable? Could music be used to offset or augment previously identified effects for speech rate and fundamental frequency? Studying sound effects is a further opportunity to be explored as little to no research in marketing has been directed toward this area. Environmental sounds, attention-grabbing noises, and product sound logos are all commonly used in advertising in an effort to capture the attention and shape the attitudes of the listening audience. How these stimuli work with voice is an interesting question. Finally, in a television broadcast advertising context, the visual elements inherent in an advertisement could also be investigated for a potential interactive effect with voice. An obvious relationship to examine is the visual image of the spokesperson coupled with voice. However, other visual elements within an advertisement, ranging from the colors utilized to the concreteness of the visual images to the actual images within the ad, could each be investigated for potential relationships with speech effects.

Gender

Whereas the majority of research on voice in linguistics and psychology has been conducted using male voices, there is evidence that female voices differ in systematic ways (Karlsson, 1991, 1992). Indeed, a good deal of the research that has sought to identify desirable voice qualities has either theorized (Apple et al., 1979) or demonstrated (Cox & Cooper, 1981) the existence of gender differences. That is to say, some of the features that are appealing in a man's voice are not necessarily so appealing in a woman's voice. Some studies have concluded that no gender effect exists, but these tend to be the exception rather than the rule.

There is evidence to suggest that a high-pitched voice is desirable for women (Oksenberg et al., 1986; Sharf & Lehman, 1984), while a low-pitched voice is preferable for men (Apple et al., 1979; Oguchi & Kikuchi, 1997). Recall that work in a sales context, discussed previously (Oksenberg et al., 1986; Sharf & Lehman, 1984), indicated a positive response for high-pitched female voices. Characteristics such as breathiness and sex appeal also seem to play a prominent role in determining voice attractiveness in women, but not in men, making analysis of the female voice more complex. In the marketing context, little attention has been devoted to the female voice. Herein lies an excellent opportunity for future study, as the female voice is widely used in advertising and has specific applicability for certain product classes and delivered services. Gender differences do exist in voice effects, and a better understanding of these differences would provide both theoretical and substantive benefits.

Attributions Resulting From Voice

Previous research has established that a spokesperson's voice affects listeners' reactions to radio advertisements (Chattopadhyay et al., 2003;

Megehee et al., 2003). Less clear is whether these effects are due solely to listeners' response to the voice per se or whether they are also reacting to the person who they imagine is speaking. Are the effects of voice mediated by listeners' inferences about characteristics of the spokesperson? How do listeners interpret voice when attributing vocal characteristics to the individual speaking?

Research in psychology and linguistics again provides some guidance in addressing these questions. There is evidence that individuals do in fact make inferences about a spokesperson when exposed to voice. These attributions can be classified into two broad categories of physical attributes (e.g., age, physical attractiveness, weight, and height) and personality characteristics (e.g., honesty, intelligence, friendliness, spontaneity, and masculinity). Seminal work by Allport and Cantril (1934) found that voice conveys correct information concerning outer and inner characteristics of personality. Further, they indicate that more highly organized and deep-seated traits and dispositions are judged more consistently and correctly than the more specific features of physique and appearance. Aronovitch (1976) builds on this work, showing that both male and female voices are stereotyped in personality judgments. In another representative study, Krauss, Freyberg, and Morsella (2002) show that listeners are able to make accurate physical inferences about speakers from the nonlinguistic content of their speech. In one of their experiments they show that after listening to a speaker, participants were able to choose the right photo of the speaker 76.5% of the time. In a second study, participants heard either a test voice or examined a photo of the speaker and then estimated the speaker's age and height. Pooled judgments showed estimates made from photos are not uniformly superior to those made from voices. Finally, Addington (1968) examined specific voice characteristics such as breathiness, nasality, and throatiness and linked these vocal traits to specific personality perceptions. His findings show that specific vocal characteristics raise attributions across gender lines with consistent judgments within gender. For example, a breathy voice for males was rated to be younger and more artistic, whereas females with this quality were seen to be shallow, petite, and prettier. In another example, a voice with orotundity projected males to be more energetic, healthy, and sophisticated, whereas females were perceived more gregarious and lively.

In the marketing literature, there has been specific investigation linking voice to targeted personality characteristics such as knowledge, credibility, and competence (Megehee et al., 2003; Moore et al., 1986; Oksenberg et al., 1986). However, these findings have typically been secondary analyses or personality characteristics specific to the marketing phenomenon investigated (e.g., credibility to salesperson effectiveness). The more general linking of voice characteristics in broadcast advertising to spokesperson personality has been relatively unaddressed. This is surprising given the importance of impression formation and touch point effectiveness in most marketing contexts. A specific area deserving research interest would be the linking of voice and personality attributions to the development of brand image and identity. Given that vocal characteristics such as speech rate and pitch can give rise to personality attributions and stereotypes, what is the effect on the brand represented by the spokesperson in question? How can the brand identity that an organization wishes to foster be facilitated by effective spokesperson voice choices? Linking voice characteristics, audience perceptions, and the formation of brand impressions together provides another excellent opportunity for future investigations.

Conclusions

This chapter has sought to provide an overview of previous research in marketing that has investigated the role of voice characteristics of spokespersons in broadcast advertising. Somewhat surprising, there are very few direct investigations addressing the importance and role of voice characteristics in this context. The limited research that has been centered in this area has focused on the role of vocal speech rate and fundamental frequency in cultivating effective advertisements. The chapter discussion identified some inconsistencies within the reported findings from this work and also pointed to possible extensions in further examination of these vocal characteristics. A second major goal of this chapter was to seed new research directions in this area. Primarily using previous research in psychology and linguistics as a starting point, the discussion identified a number of excellent opportunities. First, broadening our understanding to other aspects of voice, including pitch contour, intonation, and amplitude, in broadcast advertising would be useful. Second, better understanding the role of context, with respect to medium of ad delivery, product advertised, and internal ad elements, in moderating effective voice delivery is critical. Third, shifting attention toward female voice effects and the gender differences that are believed to exist would provide both substantive and theoretical benefits. Finally, future research would also be well targeted to deepen our knowledge on the attributions listeners make when hearing specific voices. How these attributions influence attitudes, purchasing behavior, and the formation of brand impressions is both interesting academically and important to the manager charged with making voice talent decisions.

References

Addington, D. W. (1968). The relationship of selected vocal characteristics to personality perception. *Speech Monographs, 35*, 492–503.

Allport, G., & Cantril, H. (1934). Judging personality from voice. *Journal of Social Psychology, 5*, 37–54.

Apple, W., Streeter, L. A., & Krauss, R. M. (1979). Effects of pitch and speech rate on personal attributions. *Journal of Personality and Social Psychology, 37*, 715–727.

Aronovitch, C. D. (1976). The voice of personality: Stereotyped judgments and their relation to voice quality and sex of speaker. *Journal of Social Psychology, 99*, 207–222.

Bond, P. (2008, August 5). Study: Broadcast beats papers for ad sales. Retrieved June 3, 2009, from http://www.reuters.com/article/televisionNews/idUSN0525769620080805

Bond, R. N., Welkowitz, J., Goldschmidt, H., & Wattenberg, S. (1987). Vocal frequency and person perception: Effects of perceptual salience and nonverbal sensitivity. *Journal of Psycholinguistic Research, 16*, 335–350.

Brown, B. L., & Bradshaw, J. M. (1985). Towards a social psychology of voice variations. In H. Giles & R. N. St. Clair (Eds.), *Recent advances in language, communication, and social psychology* (pp. 144–181). London: Erlbaum.

Brown, B. L., Strong, W. J., & Rencher, A. C. (1973). Perceptions of personality from speech: Effects of manipulations of acoustical parameters. *Journal of the Acoustical Society of America, 54*, 29–35.

Chattopadhyay, A., Dahl, D., Ritchie, R. J. B., & Shahin, K. N. (2003). Hearing voices: The impact of announcer speech characteristics on consumer response to broadcast advertising. *Journal of Consumer Psychology, 13*, 198–204.

Cotton, J. C. (1936). Syllabic rate: A new concept in the study of speech rate variation. *Speech Monographs, 3*, 112–117.

Cox, A. C., & Cooper, M. B. (1981). Selecting a voice for a specified task: The example of telephone announcements. *Language and Speech, 24*, 233–243.

Ekman, P., Friesen, W. V., & Scherer, K. R. (1976). Body movement and voice pitch in deceptive interaction. *Semiotica, 16*, 23–27.

Gelinas-Chebat, C., & Chebat, J. (1992). Effects of two voice characteristics on the attitudes toward advertising messages. *Journal of Social Psychology, 132*, 447–459.

Grosjean, F., & Lane, H. (1976). How the listener integrates the components of speaking rate. *Journal of Experimental Psychology: Human Perception and Performance, 2*, 538–543.

Karlsson, I. (1991). Female voices in speech synthesis. *Journal of Phonetics, 19*, 111–120.

Karlsson, I. (1992). Evaluations of acoustic differences between male and female voices: A pilot study. *Speech Transmission Laboratory Quarterly Progress and Status Report, 1*, 19–31.

Kelly, J. C., & Steer, M. D. (1949). Revised concept of rate. *Journal of Speech and Hearing Disorders, 14*, 222–226.

Krauss, R. M., Freyberg, R., & Morsella, E. (2002). Inferring speakers' physical attributes from their voices. *Journal of Experimental Social Psychology, 38*, 618–625.

LaBarbera, P., & MacLachlan, J. (1979). Time-compressed speech in radio advertising. *Journal of Marketing, 43*, 30–36.

Lane, H., & Grosjean, F. (1973). Perception of reading rate by speakers and listeners. *Journal of Experimental Psychology, 97*, 141–147.

Lautman, M. R., & Dean, K. J. (1983). Time compression of television advertising. In L. Percy & A. G. Woodside (Eds.), *Advertising and consumer psychology* (pp. 219–236). Lexington, MA: Lexington.

MacLachlan, J. (1982). Listener perception of time-compressed spokespersons. *Journal of Advertising Research, 22*, 47–51.

MacLachlan, J., & Siegel, M. H. (1980). Reducing the costs of TV commercials by use of time compressions. *Journal of Marketing Research, 17*, 52–57.

Megehee, C. M., Dobie, K., & Grant, J. (2003). Time versus pause manipulation in communications directed to the young adult population: Does it matter? *Journal of Advertising Research, 43*, 281–292.

Mehrabian, A. (1972). *Nonverbal communication*. Chicago: Aldine-Atherton.

Miller, N., Maruyama, G., Beaber, R. J., & Valone, K. (1976). Speed of speech and persuasion. *Journal of Personality and Social Psychology, 34*, 615–624.

Moore, D. L., Hausknecht, D., & Thamodaran, K. (1986). Time compression, response opportunity, and persuasion. *Journal of Consumer Research, 13*, 85–99.

Myers, V., Herndon, R. T., & Fryar, M. (1988). *Dynamics of speech: Toward effective communication*. Lincolnwood: National Textbook.

Oguchi, T., & Kikuchi, H. (1997). Voice and interpersonal attraction. *Japanese Psychological Research, 39*, 56–61.

Ohala, J. (1981). The nonlinguistic components of speech. In J. K. Darley (Ed.), *Speech evaluation in psychiatry* (pp. 39–49). New York: Grune and Stratton.

Oksenberg, L., Coleman, L., & Cannell, C. F. (1986). Interviewers' voices and refusal rates in telephone surveys. *Public Opinion Quarterly, 50*, 97–111.

Pearce, W. B., & Conklin, F. (1971). Nonverbal vocalic communication and perceptions of a speaker. *Speech Monographs, 38*, 235–241.

Peterson, R. A., Cannito, M. P., & Brown, S. P. (1995). An exploratory investigation of voice characteristics and selling effectiveness. *Journal of Personal Selling and Sales Management, 15*, 1–15.

Petty, R. E., & Cacioppo, J. T. (1979). Issue involvement can increase or decrease persuasion by enhancing message-relevant cognitive responses. *Journal of Personality and Social Psychology, 37*, 1915–1926.

Radio Advertising Bureau. (2008). Radio revenue trends. Retrieved June 3, 2009, from http://www.rab.com/public/pr/yearly.cfm

Schlinger, M. J. R., Alwitt, L. F., McCarthy, K. E., & Green, L. (1983). Effects of time compression on attitudes and information processing. *Journal of Marketing, 47*, 79–85.

Sharf, D. J., & Lehman, M. E. (1984). Relationship between the speech characteristics and effectiveness of telephone interviewers. *Journal of Phonetics, 12*, 219–228.

Smith, B. L., Brown, B. L., Strong, W. J., & Rencher, A. C. (1975). Effects of speech rate on personality perception. *Language and Speech, 18*, 145–152.

Stephens, N. (1982). The effectiveness of time compressed television advertisements with older adults. *Journal of Advertising, 11*, 48–55.

Stewart, M., & Ryan, E. B. (1982). Attitudes toward younger and older adult speakers: Effects of varying speech rates. *Journal of Language and Social Psychology, 1*, 91–109.

Streeter, L. A., Krauss, R. M., Geller, V., Olson, C., & Apple, W. (1977). Pitch changes during attempted deception. *Journal of Personality and Social Psychology, 35*, 345–350.

Thomas, G. P. (1992). The influence of processing conversational information on inference, argument elaboration, and memory. *Journal of Consumer Research, 19*, 83–92.

Vann, J. W., Rogers, R. D., & Penrod, J. P. (1987). The cognitive effects of time-compressed advertising. *Journal of Advertising, 16*, 10–19.

Zhu, R., & Meyers-Levy, J. (2005). Distinguishing between the meanings of music: When background music affects product perceptions. *Journal of Marketing Research, 42*, 333–345.

Zuckerman, M., & Driver, R. (1989). What sounds beautiful is good: The vocal attractiveness stereotype. *Journal of Nonverbal Behavior, 13*, 67–82.

Zuckerman, M., & Miyake, K. (1993). The attractive voice: What makes it so? *Journal of Nonverbal Behavior, 17*, 119–135.

13

Hear Is the Thing
Auditory Processing of Novel Nonword Brand Names

Marina Carnevale, Dawn Lerman, and David Luna

The importance of brand names is well established. Research has shown, for example, that brand names impact recall, recognition, and preference. The particular effect itself depends on the type of name (e.g., word versus nonword; Lerman & Garbarino, 2002), brand name suggestiveness (Keller, Heckler, & Houston, 1998), word frequency (Meyers-Levy, 1989), phonetic symbolism (Lowrey & Shrum, 2007), and the use of a whole range of other linguistic devices (Lowrey, Shrum, & Dubitsky, 2003).

The vast majority of studies on brand naming focus on the visual aspects of the name. In other words, these studies typically examine consumer response to names when consumers are exposed to them visually. Even studies of phonetic symbolism, an area of research concerning sounds and their associated meanings, typically rely on visual exposure. For example, respondents participating in Lowrey and Shrum's (2007) research on phonetic symbolism viewed name pairs on a computer screen. Similarly, the brands names under study in Yorkston and Menon (2004) appeared in a paragraph read by respondents.

The relationship between the written and spoken letter provides the opportunity to investigate the effect of sounds following visual exposure. Given the heavy reliance on visuals in marketing and advertising, exposing respondents visually to brand name stimuli makes both practical and theoretical sense. Consumers see brand names in magazines, on television, on billboards, and on store shelves. They also write them on shopping lists. Yet there are instances when brand name exposure is not visual. In radio advertising, for example, exposure is entirely auditory. Similarly, consumers are regularly exposed to word-of-mouth information, whether brand-sponsored (Walker, 2004) or spontaneous, which requires auditory processing.

Since auditory processing requires the consumer to perform different cognitive tasks than those required for visual processing, our understanding of how brand names are processed is far from complete. For instance, when consumers hear a brand name, they have to encode and store the sound in long-term memory for later use. They could potentially encode only the sound, a visual (e.g., alphabetic) transcription of it, or a combination of both. But even if consumers do not mentally transcribe the brand name as they hear it, eventually they will have to guess, or at least recognize, how the brand name they were initially exposed to auditorily is spelled (visually); otherwise they will not be able to find it in the marketplace.

This chapter seeks to advance our understanding of auditory processing as it relates to brand names. Although auditory processing may be important for all types of brand names, we suggest that understanding auditory processing is particularly critical for nonword names, relative to brands whose names are an existing word in a language understood by the consumer. Nonword brand names (e.g., Pepsi) present a particular challenge because consumers do not have the word in their lexicon, a sort of mental dictionary. Hence, after consumers are exposed to the auditory nonword and recognize it as a brand name, they are likely to have difficulty transcribing it into a visual code; that is, spelling it. This chapter introduces to the marketing literature the notion of mapping sound to spelling, suggesting that ambiguities in word spellings can have significant effects on consumer responses to brand names presented auditorily.

It is important to note that this chapter focuses on brand names in alphabetic-based but not logographic-based languages. In alphabetic-based languages (e.g., English, French, Spanish, etc.), each grapheme (i.e., letter) represents one or more phonemes (i.e., sounds). In other words, there exists a grapheme-to-phoneme and a phoneme-to-grapheme correspondence. In logographic-based languages (e.g., Chinese), characters represent morphemes, the smallest meaningful linguistic elements, and do not necessarily tell the reader how those morphemes should be pronounced. Given both theoretical interest in logographic processing (e.g., Tavassoli, 1999; Tavassoli & Han, 2002) and managerial interest in marketing within the countries where such systems are in place, it would be worth investigating auditory processing of brand names by speakers of logographic-based languages. Although doing so is beyond the scope of this chapter, it is our hope that this review of auditory processing in alphabetic-based languages inspires similar research focused on nonalphabetic-based languages.

Auditory Processing and the Mental Lexicon

It is widely accepted that English speakers, and by extension speakers of other alphabetic-based languages, rely on sound-based coding, whether acoustic or phonological, for auditorily presented information (Salamé & Baddeley, 1982; Tyler & Frauenfelder, 1989). That is, upon exposure to an aurally presented word, listeners search their lexicon for matching sounds. If they identify a matching sound or combination of sounds, then the word is recognized. Such recognition may occur before the listener has heard the word completely, particularly "if the word recognition point corresponds to its uniqueness point, where the word's initial (sound) sequence is common to that word and no other" (Harley, 1995, p. 53).

Relying on such sound-based coding, a hearer can perform a variety of tasks, including word naming and word recognition. In other words, upon hearing a brand name, consumers can repeat the name they just heard and recognize it as one that they have heard before. Because consumers processed the item auditorily initially, they do not need to be literate. So the consumer does not need to know how the sounds correspond to particular letters in the alphabet.

Let us suppose, however, that consumers now want to write this brand name on a shopping list. In this case, they would have to rely on their learned set of phoneme-to-grapheme correspondence rules (i.e., sound–letter associations). Because the acquisition of the sound-to-spelling relationship is one of the fundamental steps when learning a language (Ziegler, Stone, & Jacobs, 1997), this should be a relatively easy task. So, for example, upon hearing an ad for the laundry detergent Dreft, a literate English speaker would know to spell it as d-r-e-f-t.

A large part of the reason why literate English speakers would know how to spell Dreft is that the letters d-r-e-f-t are the only letters that would produce such a sound in English, following the conventions for possible spellings in that language (Ziegler et al., 1997). Suppose, however, that the ad were for a different laundry detergent, Gain. In this case, the name conceivably could be spelled g-a-i-n or as g-a-n-e, as both of these spellings correspond to the same sound. Although both are possible, the consumer might be more likely to spell the brand name g-a-i-n as this spelling matches that of a commonly used word. In other cases, a sound might correspond to more than two letter strings. For example, the phoneme (i.e., sound) /_@f/ corresponds to the graphemes (i.e., spellings) *aff*, *alf*, *aph*, *augh*, as in staff, half, graph, and laugh, respectively. Again, upon hearing one of these words, hearers would rely on their knowledge and experience in an attempt to spell it correctly.

Consistent Versus Inconsistent Mappings

The lack of a one-to-one relationship between phonemes and graphemes is a complexity of English and other so-called *deep* languages. Sound-to-writing correspondence of a word determines that word's level of consistency (Ziegler et al., 1997). Specifically, if a sound can be mapped to one and only one grapheme, then that language is considered to have a consistent mapping; otherwise, it has an inconsistent mapping. Inconsistent mappings appear in 72% of all English monosyllabic words (Ziegler et al., 1997). Conversely, some phonemes (e.g., /_@g/) are represented by only one grapheme, so they have *consistent* mappings for /ag/ used in different words (e.g., tag, rag). As one might imagine, consistency of sound to spelling makes spelling tasks easier and less effortful. In fact, studies have shown that reading and spelling performance is superior for words and nonwords that contain consistent mappings compared to inconsistent mappings (Coltheart & Leahy, 1992; Content, 1991; Ziegler et al., 1997).

Although consistent mapping aids processing for sound to spelling tasks, inconsistency impedes processing, but to varying degrees, as not all inconsistent words (and nonwords) are created equal. The variation is due to the (ir)regularity of the inconsistent word. The frequency of the phoneme-to-grapheme correspondences observed in a given language determines the degree of word (ir)regularity. For example, the phoneme /āk/ can be transcribed into a variety of graphemes (e.g., ake, ache) that differ with respect to their frequency of occurrence; that is, how much more often one spelling of the sound occurs relative to other possible spellings. The word *fake* presents an inconsistent yet regular spelling pattern, since *ake* is the grapheme that most frequently represents the phoneme /āk/ within the English lexical system. The same phoneme, however, is represented by the grapheme *ache* with a very low frequency. Therefore, a word like *ache* is said to have an irregular as well as an inconsistent spelling pattern (see Ziegler et al. [1997] for a list of frequencies of inconsistent mappings). In conclusion, both consistency and regularity (the latter is only relevant to inconsistent phonemes) can make spelling easier. The effect of these factors would presumably be more acute for nonwords, given the lack of consumers' prior knowledge about them.

The number of possible phoneme–grapheme mappings determines the process by which sound may be transcribed (i.e., how auditorily presented words are spelled). Consider, for example, the word *neat*. Hearers may use one of two possible processes for transcribing the word's sound into graphemes. They could retrieve the written form in its entirety from their lexicon, as the lexicon does contain such information, or they could translate the individual phonemes (i.e., /'nēt/) into their corresponding graphemes (i.e., /n/ in n, /ē/ in ea, and /t/ in t). In languages such as Italian, German, and Spanish, where consistent sound-to-writing correspondences tend to be the norm, the second approach would most often lead to the correct output because the individual phonemes are almost always spelled the same way. However, the nature of English, a language with abundant inconsistencies, would prevent this method from leading to the canonical spelling in most cases (Houghton & Zorzi, 2003). In the next section we explore how individuals access the spelling of a word or a nonword, given the consistency and regularity issues discussed above.

A Dual-Route Model to Spelling

Psycholinguistic research has highlighted two main routes to spelling: lexical and sublexical (e.g., Campbell, 1983; Folk, Rapp, & Goldrick, 2002; Houghton & Zorzi, 2003). These routes are found to be distinct yet interactive. The model of these routes is depicted in Figure 13.1.

Lexical Route

Through the lexical (or direct) route, a top–down process occurs as individuals access the spelling of a word by retrieving its lexical representation from long-term memory, the so-called orthographic output lexicon (OOL; Ellis, 1982). These lexical representations may be accessed both phonetically (i.e., from the sound of a familiar word) and semantically (i.e., from its meaning; Barry, 1994; Houghton & Zorzi, 2003). However, while the sound of a familiar word may provide access to its semantic representation automatically, the latter is not considered essential for accurate spelling (Rapcsak, Henry, Teague, Carnahan, & Beeson, 2007). Simply put, individuals access the spelling of the target word by referring to a representation in memory of that word or another word that contains the same pronunciation pattern. Whether the meaning of that word is accessed or

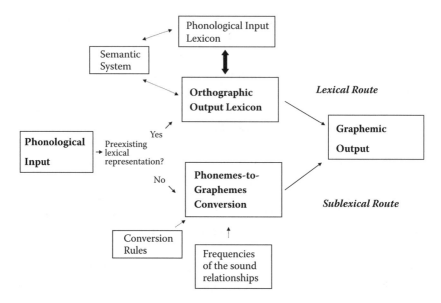

Figure 13.1   Dual Route Model of Spelling (adapted from Houghton and Zorzi [2003]).

not is not crucial to the activation of the lexical route. This route typically applies to frequently encountered words and, in general, to familiar letter strings (Houghton & Zorzi, 2003), regardless of the frequency of the sound-to-writing relationship. Therefore, the spelling of both regular and irregular words is accessed through the direct route, provided individuals have seen the word before and recognize it.

Sublexical Route

When a hearer encounters an unfamiliar word or a nonword, the lexical route will not produce the intended spelling because, by definition, such stimuli lack a lexical representation. In these cases, the sublexical (or indirect) route is used; that is, each phoneme is individually transcribed into its corresponding grapheme in accordance with a bottom–up process. Hence, although units of the orthographic output lexicon activated through the direct route are whole words, in the indirect or sublexical route the units for accessing the spelling are limited to graphemes. It follows then that when the sublexical route is followed, regularities and consistencies of the sound-to-writing relationships, as well as phoneme–grapheme conversion rules of the English language, will all have a role in enhancing (or impeding) the conversion of phonemes to graphemes.

The consistency of the sound-to-spelling mapping may facilitate the spelling task by decreasing the number of possible solutions for the spelling of a new nonword brand name. Given multiple possibilities of translating the phoneme into its corresponding grapheme (i.e., inconsistent mappings), the frequency of the graphemes will influence the choice of the final output, that is, the more frequent the grapheme for an unfamiliar inconsistent word, the higher the probability that it will be chosen. For example, the phoneme /āk/ would have a greater chance of being transcribed into the grapheme *ake* rather than *ache*, as the latter has a lower frequency of occurrence. Similarly, knowledge about contextual and sound-to-spelling prescription rules (e.g., a soft "c" is always followed by "i" or "e") may increase the likelihood of correct transcription.

The indirect route aids sound-to-writing conversions of nonwords as well as novel words that strictly follow language spelling rules and sound-to-spelling regularities. In the case of novel words that violate such rules (i.e., irregular words), however, the indirect route would systematically lead to the regularization, and thus misspelling, of the word. It follows that the lexical route always better supports familiar words. Novel words or nonwords, instead, require the sublexical route. But if the nonword contains an irregular spelling pattern, consumers may attempt to use the lexical route to guess at its spelling (Houghton & Zorzi, 2003), with varying degrees of success.

Processing Motivation and Other Practical Considerations

As discussed, a one-to-one sound-to-spelling correspondence should facilitate the transcription of a novel, nonword brand name. Transcription of inconsistent (one-to-many correspondence) nonword names should be aided by frequently occurring, or regular, mappings. In these cases, we would expect motivation to play a key role in successful spelling. Specifically, we would expect low-motivation individuals in particular to perform transcriptions aided by such mappings. Since low-motivation individuals can be expected to dedicate very few cognitive resources to the spelling task, they should be less likely to explore a variety of potential spellings, consider which of many possible spellings might fit the type of brand at hand, or elaborate on the fit of one particular spelling with similar brands (e.g., froogle vs. frugal) or with the category at large. It follows that low-motivation consumers, when confronted with a challenging spelling (especially inconsistent irregular names), would likely react negatively to the brand name. This should result in poor brand evaluations.

On the other hand, for high-motivation consumers, we might expect that successfully spelling the target nonword should generate a higher level of positively valenced elaboration when a more challenging task is faced (i.e., nonwords containing inconsistent mappings) as opposed to an easier task (i.e., nonwords with consistent mappings). Thus, for individuals under high motivation, brand evaluations could possibly benefit from an inconsistent phoneme–grapheme mapping. Consumers should feel more frustrated when failing to perform a task for which there is only one potential and actual correct solution, rather than one for which there are many potential correct solutions but only one is appropriate. High-motivation consumers might even respond more positively upon successfully spelling inconsistent irregular names than inconsistent regular names.

Moderators

In today's world the opportunity to practice spelling skills is very limited, especially given the fairly recent and widespread use of alternative communication styles. The popularity of text and instant messaging, for example, has grown, as has the use of nonstandard abbreviations, symbols (e.g., emoticons), and numbers that make sense only if read phonetically. "CU2moro" (i.e., see you tomorrow), "URNvited" (i.e., you are invited), and "Wot u up 2" (i.e., what are you up to?) are only a few examples of the way traditional conventions in writing and spelling are being commonly altered for the benefit of some sort of phonetic spelling that little fits with the set structures and styles of the English language. Moreover, spell-checking software products provide a valuable substitute for personal knowledge. As a result, spelling might be a seldom-performed exercise, thus emphasizing the need to help consumers remember, search for, and find the novel (nonword) brand name.

The Interaction of the Two Routes

How can the ability to correctly spell a novel nonword brand name be enhanced? A considerable stream of research has shown that the spelling of a nonword may be enhanced by the spelling of a word heard immediately before that contains the same spelling pattern as the target nonword. For example, in lexical priming a real word that sounds and is spelled like the nonword is presented before the nonword. In this case, individuals can relate the nonword to one for which they already have a phonological representation. In such cases, the direct and indirect route interact to optimize the final choice (Campbell, 1983; Cuetos, 1993; Seymour & Dargie, 1990), as the competition among different graphemes activated at the sublexical level is solved by the graphemes activated at the lexical level (i.e., through the semantic/phonological representation of the priming word).

We mentioned earlier that the lexical (direct) and sublexical (indirect) routes are considered to be two distinct systems. Although this is indeed the case, research suggests that there exist occasions when the two routes may interact (Coltheart, Rastle, Perry, Langdon, & Ziegler, 2001; Houghton & Zorzi, 2003; Rapcsak et al., 2007). Evidence of an interaction is primarily provided by a variety of neuropsychological studies that focus on individuals with spelling deficiencies, such as surface dysgraphia and phonological agraphia (e.g., Folk et al., 2002; Hillis & Caramazza, 1991; Houghton & Zorzi, 2003). Patients affected by surface dysgraphia typically show a damaged lexical route. This results in the ability to spell nonwords in dictation, as well as words with regular phoneme-to-grapheme relationships, but a disproportionate difficulty in spelling irregular words. Generally speaking, these studies suggest that these patients may rely on both lexical and sublexical routes.

To illustrate, consider the Hillis and Caramazza (1991) case study. The patient showed a deficiency at the lexical semantic system such that he was able to read aloud more words than those that he actually comprehended or correctly associated with their visual representation. One would expect to see the same pattern of semantic failures at the spelling task level. However, a similar pattern did not exist. At the same time, the patient made an overwhelming number of phonologically plausible errors (e.g., the spelling of "night" as "n-i-t") but only for those irregular (i.e., low-frequency) words he could not comprehend during the reading task. This suggests that the semantic representation of the word and, therefore, the lexical route actually did play a role in the patient's sound-to-writing processing. That is, if the patient had relied merely on the direct route for spelling, then he would have reproduced the semantic mistakes observed during the reading task. If the sublexical system was the only one activated, then the phonological plausible errors should have been produced for all of the low frequency phoneme-to-grapheme correspondences, independently of their semantic representation (Folk et al., 2002; Hillis & Caramazza, 1991).

While reading, going from visual to sound representations, the interactions between the direct and indirect route result in conflicting outputs for irregular words as reflected in longer pronunciation times. However, in the case of spelling, the interaction between the two routes ultimately reinforces the written representation of the nonword target (Folk et al., 2002). Therefore, the interactions are said to be competitive in the case of reading but cooperative in the case of spelling (Coltheart et al., 2001; Houghton & Zorzi, 2003; Rapcsak et al., 2007). In the latter case, some authors have narrowed the main purposes of the joint lexical/sublexical activation to the reduction of semantic errors (Rapp, Epstein, & Tainturier, 2002). In this scenario, both systems iteratively communicate until one grapheme is selected to represent the phoneme. Specifically, while both the direct and the indirect routes allow for the activation of different potential graphemes, the direct route somehow prevails by narrowing the choice to those graphemes that make more sense at a lexical level (i.e., words that contain them). For example, when attempting to spell the phoneme /'paf/ of a nonword brand name, among possible solutions, such as p-a-l-f, p-a-f-f, p-a-p-h, and p-a-u-g-h activated at a sublexical level, p-a-u-g-h may be the preferred one if a priming word containing the same pronunciation pattern, such as l-a-u-g-h, is aurally introduced immediately before the target nonword is presented. Moreover, some research would suggest that the effect of lexical priming should prevail independently of the frequency of graphemes. In other words, if the most common way of spelling the phoneme /af/ is a-l-f (Ziegler et al., 1997), that would be the preferred spelling. However, it would be overridden if the lexical prime points toward a different direction (i.e., a-u-g-h; Barry & Seymour, 1988; Folk et al., 2002).

When aurally advertising a novel nonword brand name (e.g., via radio), managers could thus consider the opportunity of exploiting slogans, as well as jingles, to phonetically prime, and thus facilitate, the correct spelling of the brand name. For instance, the jingle could include a known word that uses the same intended spelling of the novel brand name; a rhyme, for example. Recall of a brand name and brand evaluations might indeed be affected by the ability of consumers to correctly spell the name because of this rhyming word. This appears applicable to the extent that the nonword is not constrained to be spelled only one way. From this perspective, if the attempt of solving the task stimulates interest and deeper levels of processing, successful spelling performance might result in positive affect that transfers to the brand. Consumer research has uncovered similar patterns in other contexts. For example, studies suggest that the use of rhetorical figures in advertising results in positive elaboration as the ad deviates from expectations and leads to the successful resolution of a puzzle (McQuarrie & Mick, 1996), thus stimulating deeper levels of processing (Morgan & Reichert, 1999) and curiosity about the brand (MacInnis, Moorman, & Jaworski, 1991). In other words, consumers tend to respond with pleasure to rhetorical figures because of the successful elaboration (McQuarrie & Mick, 1996). Similarly, we would expect that successfully solving the challenges of spelling a nonword for which there are multiple possibilities could bring an advantage to the advertiser by leading the consumer to make positive inferences about and create positive associations to the brand. However, we would expect this to be the case only when consumers have the tools (i.e., cognitive capacity) for the successful resolution of the task.

Although lexical priming implemented through rhyming words provides a clear suggestion of the pronunciation pattern to be followed, another interesting way to address the correct spelling of the target nonword may take into account the inclusion of a semantic hint in addition to a phonetic one. In other words, the lexical prime could carry semantic associations (e.g., to the products or services that the brand represents), instead of or in addition to the phonetic prime. By lending meaning to information, semantic associations might enhance capturing individual's interest, facilitating recall as well as recognition, and eliciting positive elaboration. We can conclude, then, that ads for novel, nonword brand names that contain inconsistent sound-to-writing mappings should lexically prime the spelling of the brand name.

Visual Processing and Other Moderators

Lexical priming may also be achieved through visual stimuli. To illustrate, consider some studies that have looked at the relationship between the shape of the brand logo and sound symbolism (e.g., Klink, 2003). Their results indicate that front vowels (for which the tongue is positioned as far forward as possible; e.g., /i/ or /e/) and fricative consonants (produced by the forcing of breath through a constricted passage; e.g., /f/ or /s/) in brand names tend to be associated with lighter colors, as well as smaller and more angular shapes of the logo, relative to back vowels (e.g., /u/ or /o/) and stop consonants (produced by stopping the air flow in the vocal tract; e.g., /p/ or /t/), respectively. Thus, the spelling task of a novel, nonword brand name may be facilitated by providing images that are consistent with the spelling structure of the brand name. Another relatively more immediate and intuitive way to visually prime the spelling of an unfamiliar word might involve the use of images semantically related to the brand name. For example, the logo itself might contain a specific reference to the products or services that the brand represents (Houston, Childers, & Heckler, 1987; Luna, 2005).

Certain elements may moderate the effects discussed thus far. First, individuals who are more knowledgeable about sound-to-spelling correspondence rules may clearly benefit from their ability to check whether the spelling output actually graphically reproduces the sound. The same individuals, however, might have higher expectations about their own ability to successfully solve the spelling task. Consequently, an unsuccessful performance might lead to higher levels of frustration and disappointment than those perceivable by individuals who have lower levels of performance expectations. Conversely, those who are not familiar with spelling rules may be more satisfied by successfully completing a task for which their expectations are relatively low. In other words, the frustration that may derive by misspelling the unfamiliar, nonword brand name on brand evaluations may be moderated by the knowledge that potential consumers have about spelling rules.

Within this scenario, age could make a difference. For example, teenagers, who intentionally use abbreviations and misspellings of English words (e.g., to communicate via text and instant messaging) might be used to making spelling errors or engaging in "creative" spelling and may be less susceptible to the negative influence of spelling mistakes. Additionally, we should take into account that a misspelled search inquiry on the Web is often followed by a spelling suggestion provided by the search engine. Considering a positive scenario, in which spelling suggestions lead the online consumer to the actual brand, the frustration derived by failing the task might be offset by the overall satisfaction of having reached the target. In addition, successive recommendations by the search engine may serve as a sort of rehearsal and thus increase memory for the brand. In a negative scenario, however, in which the suggestions provided by the search engine do not direct the consumer to the correct Web site, the time and energy spent trying to find the brand could negatively impact perceptions about that brand. Then again, teenagers, who are heavy users of the Internet for a variety of purposes (e.g., entertainment), might be more inclined to find their way to the brand using different search criteria or key words, increasing elaboration and memory.

Another element to consider when developing a new nonword brand name from a sound-to-spelling perspective, aside from the nature and extent of spelling knowledge, relates to the underlying processes that might enable the acquisition or use of such knowledge. For instance, need for cognition (Cacioppo, Petty, & Morris, 1983) might motivate individuals in two ways. First, individuals with a higher need for cognition might be more inclined to retrieve phonemes-to-graphemes correspondence rules apt to assist the spelling of the novel nonword brand name. Second, they might enjoy the spelling of ambiguous names (i.e., with inconsistent sound-to-writing mappings) more than easier ones. In a similar vein, the effects of successfully spelling the brand name with the aid of a lexical prime might also vary. Those with a higher need for cognition might prefer to perform the task without the lexical prime. The opposite could be hypothesized to ensue for individuals with a lower need for cognition.

Conclusions

Although ads and various other brand management tactics assist the development of a brand's image, the sound of the brand name in and of itself represents a relevant source of information and differentiation, which is susceptible to consumers' perceptions. Research on phonetic symbolism has shown that the mere sound of a nonword, such as a novel brand name, may affect brand evaluations through the meaning conveyed, for instance, about attribute dimensions of the product. However, even most phonetic symbolism research in marketing has used visual (written) stimuli. Very little research has been done studying auditorily presented brand names as stimuli. This is surprising given that consumers are exposed to novel brand names on a regular basis, through word of mouth, radio ads, and buzz marketing. Building on psycholinguistic research, we explored the way consumers may process and later use these sounds, providing some ideas for marketing practitioners and researchers.

There are two main routes to spelling. Through the lexical route, individuals access the spelling of a word by retrieving its phonological or semantic representation stored in memory. Through the sublexical route, each of the phonemes is individually translated in its written form (i.e., grapheme). Both the regularity and consistency of sound-to-writing correspondences play important roles in the processes individuals employ to access the spelling of a word (or a nonword). Thus, the spelling of familiar words is typically and successfully accessed via the lexical route, regardless of the regularity of the sound-to-writing correspondence. When a non-word or an unfamiliar word is encountered, however, the lexical system does not offer any spelling help. Instead, the sublexical system is invoked and the consistency (vs. inconsistency) of the sound-to-spelling relationship may facilitate the spelling task by decreasing the number of possible solutions. If the sound-to-spelling mapping is inconsistent, regularity of the mapping will also make the task more likely to be successful. Irregular mappings will likely result in failure to spell the brand name as intended.

We propose that successful spelling of a brand name should influence consumer attitudes toward the brand. Thus, if a consumer can find a brand name on the Internet or writes the brand on a shopping list and later finds, at the store, that the brand was correctly spelled, the consumer will be likely to develop a more positive brand attitude. We discuss several factors that could help develop novel nonword brand names and provide some ideas how to present them to consumers (e.g., employing spelling primes). We also describe how this process may be moderated by factors like processing motivation, age of the consumer, or visual elements in the logo.

An important point is that auditorily presented novel brand names are subject to sensory-specific cognitive processes that may not take place for visually presented novel brand names. This notion has significant implications for research methodologies. We suggest utilizing a multisensory presentation of brand names when engaging in brand development research. Specifically, we encourage researchers to use aural presentation of stimuli to explore unique processes that may diverge from visual presentation.

Another area where further research is possible is the comparison across languages of sound-to-spelling processes. English is a "deep" or "opaque" language, in which many graphemes are represented by one phoneme, and vice versa. Spanish, on the other hand, is a "shallow" or "transparent" language, in which one-to-one relationships between graphemes and phonemes are more frequent. Would our discussion of the potential effects of spelling process be mitigated or amplified in such languages? Given consumers' frequent exposure to auditorily presented information, it is surprising how little is known about their responses to brands or advertising that are heard rather than seen.

References

Barry, C. (1994). Spelling routes. In D. A. Brown & N. C. Ellis (Eds.), *Handbook of spelling: Theory, process and intervention* (pp. 27–49). Chichester, UK: Wiley.

Barry, C., & Seymour, P. H. K. (1988). Lexical priming and sound-to-spelling contingency effects in nonword spelling. *Quarterly Journal of Experimental Psychology, 40*, 5–40.

Cacioppo, J. T., Petty, R. E., & Morris, K. J. (1983). Effects of need for cognition on message evaluation, recall, and persuasion. *Journal of Personality and Social Psychology, 45*, 805–818.

Campbell, R. (1983). Writing nonwords to dictation. *Brain and Language, 19*, 153–178.

Coltheart, M., Rastle, C., Perry, C., Langdon, R., & Ziegler, J. (2001). DRC: A dual route cascaded model of visual word recognition and reading aloud. *Psychological Review, 108*, 204–258.

Coltheart, V., & Leahy, J. (1992). Children's and adults' reading of nonwords: Effects of regularity and consistency. *Journal of Experimental Psychology. Learning, Memory, and Cognition, 18*, 718–729.

Content, A. (1991). The effect of spelling-to-sound regularity on naming in French. *Psychological Research, 53*, 3–12.

Cuetos, F. (1993). Writing processes in a shallow orthography. *Reading and Writing: An Interdisciplinary Quarterly, 5*, 17–28.

Ellis, A. W. (1982). Spelling and writing (and reading and speaking). In A. W. Ellis (Ed.), *Normality and pathology in cognitive functions* (pp. 113–146). New York: Academic Press.

Folk, J. R., Rapp, B., & Goldrick, M. (2002). The interaction of lexical and sublexical information in spelling: What's the point? *Cognitive Neuropsychology, 19*, 653–671.

Harley, T. A. (1995). *The psychology of language: From data to theory.* Erlbaum, UK: Taylor and Francis.

Hillis A. E., & Caramazza A. (1991). Mechanisms for accessing lexical representations for output: Evidence from a category-specific semantic deficit. *Brain and Language, 40*, 106–144.

Houghton, G., & Zorzi, M. (2003). Normal and impaired spelling in a connectionist dual-route architecture. *Cognitive Neuropsychology, 20*, 115–162.

Houston, M. J., Childers, T. L., & Heckler, S. E. (1987). Picture-word consistency and the elaborative processing of advertisements. *Journal of Marketing Research, 24*, 359–369.

Keller, K. L., Heckler, S. E., & Houston, M. J. (1998). The effects of brand name suggestiveness on advertising recall. *Journal of Marketing, 62*, 48–57.

Klink, R. R. (2003). Creating meaningful brands: The relationship between brand name and brand mark. *Marketing Letters, 14*, 143–157.

Lerman, D., & Garbarino, E. (2002). Recall and recognition of brand names: A comparison of word and nonword name types. *Psychology and Marketing, 19*, 621–639.

Lowrey, T. M., & Shrum, L. J. (2007). Phonetic symbolism and brand name preference. *Journal of Consumer Research, 34*, 406–414.

Lowrey, T. M., Shrum, L. J., & Dubitsky, T. M. (2003). The relation between brand-name linguistic characteristics and brand-name memory. *Journal of Advertising, 32*, 7–17.

Luna, D. (2005). Integrating ad information: A text processing perspective. *Journal of Consumer Psychology, 15*, 38–51.

MacInnis, D. J., Moorman, C., & Jaworski, B. J. (1991). Enhancing and measuring consumers' motivation, opportunity, and ability to process brand information from ads. *Journal of Marketing, 55*, 32–53.

McQuarrie, E. F., & Mick D. G. (1996). Figures of rhetoric in advertising language. *Journal of Consumer Research, 22*, 424–437.

Meyers-Levy, J. (1989). The influence of a brand name's association set size and word frequency on brand memory. *Journal of Consumer Research, 16*, 197–207.

Morgan, S. E., & Reichert, T. (1999). The message is in the metaphor: Assessing the comprehension of metaphors in advertisements. *Journal of Advertising, 28*, 1–12.

Rapcsak, S., Henry, M. L., Teague, S. L., Carnahan, S. D., & Beeson, P. M. (2007). Do dual-route models accurately predict reading and spelling performance in individuals with acquired alexia and agraphia? *Neuropsychologia, 45*, 2519–2524.

Rapp, B., Epstein, C., & Tainturier, M. J. (2002). The integration of information across lexical and sublexical processes in spelling. *Cognitive Neuropsychology, 19*, 1–29.

Salamé, P., & Baddeley, A. D. (1982). Disruption of short-term memory by unattended speech: Implications for the structure of working memory. *Journal of Verbal Learning and Verbal Behavior, 21*, 150–164.

Seymour, P. H. K., & Dargie, A. (1990). Associative priming and orthographic choice in nonword spelling. *The European Journal of Cognitive Psychology, 2*, 395–480.

Tavassoli, N. T. (1999). Temporal and associative memory in Chinese and English. *Journal of Consumer Research, 26*, 170–181.

Tavassoli, N. T., & Han, J. K (2002). Auditory and visual brand identifiers in Chinese and English. *Journal of International Marketing, 10*, 13–28.

Tyler, L. K., & Frauenfelder, U. H. (1989). The process of spoken word recognition: An introduction. In U. H. Frauenfelder & L. K. Tyler (Eds.), *Spoken word recognition* (pp. 1–20). Cambridge, MA: MIT Press.

Walker, R. (2004, December 5). The hidden (in plain sight) persuaders. *The New York Times Magazine*, pp. 68–75.

Yorkston, E., & Menon, G. (2004). A sound idea: Phonetic effects of brand names on consumer judgments. *Journal of Consumer Research, 31*, 43–51.

Ziegler, J., Stone, G. O., & Jacobs, A. M. (1997). What is the pronunciation for -*ough* and the spelling for /u/? A database for computing feedforward and feedback consistency in English. *Behavior Research Methods, Instruments and Computers, 29*, 600–618.

Section IV

Vision

14

Visual Perception
An Overview

Priya Raghubir

There are oft-quoted clichés that state that "Perception is reality" and "Truth lies in the eye of the beholder." Not surprisingly, therefore, for more than a century researchers in psychology, marketing, art, and aesthetics have examined the manner in which the eye translates visual input into information that it believes to be veridical. In this chapter I briefly summarize some of the classic and contemporary findings in visual perception in as much as they pertain to sensory marketing. The goal of the chapter is not to be comprehensive, but, instead, to provide a simple lens through which to view the literature in visual perception and apply it to study the larger area of sensory marketing.

I start with summarizing a typology of visual cues. The goal of this exercise is to identify areas where relatively little research has been conducted to date, but study of which could lead to rich insights theoretically, as well as for marketing practice, consumer welfare, and public policy.

I focus on the mediating role of attention (the level and focus of attention, imagery, and neural activation) that dictates the type of processing that consumers are engaging in (preconscious, nonconscious, heuristic, systematic, or hardwired).

There are two sets of moderators that can make the link between visual properties and attention contingent. The first set pertains to context (e.g., market norms and regulations, point of view, and task complexity), whereas the second set focuses on individual differences (e.g., in visual ability, beliefs, culture, goals, etc.).

I end with proposing a testable model that predicts when the inputs received from two different sensory systems will be assimilated versus contrasted to make a range of consumer judgments. Thus, the consequences of visual cues include how vision interacts with other sensory stimuli received from the haptic/tactile, olfactory, gustatory, and auditory systems to make judgments pertaining to touch, smell, taste, and sound; and in turn how inputs from the other sensory systems affect visual judgments.

Types of Visual Cues: A Typology

Given the plethora of visual cues, it is necessary to categorize them in a manner that makes their effects easier to understand and allows for a listing of their comprehensive features. I propose a set of seven properties that can be used to categorize visual stimuli: geometric, format, statistical, temporal, goal, structural, and other. Each of these is described below. The proposed typology of visual cues is provided in Figure 14.1.

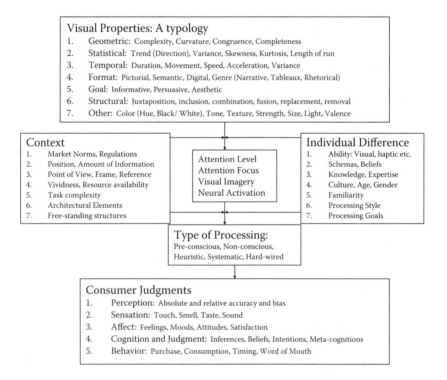

Figure 14.1   A model of visual processing.

Geometric

Greenleaf and Raghubir (2008) categorized geometric properties into four features: their complexity (including their dimensionality, form, regularity, and clutter), curvature (including their circularity, angularity, and convergence), congruence (including their symmetry, stability, and centrality), and completeness (amount of information and the synthesis of this information). One such cue, congruity, encompasses the extent to which a shape is rotationally symmetric (e.g., a square or a circle) versus asymmetric (e.g., rectangles or ovals with a length–width ratio of 1:1.618 or φ), a feature that has been shown to affect consumers' attitudes to two-dimensional products (Greenleaf & Raghubir, 2008; Raghubir & Greenleaf, 2006). The typology proposed by Greenleaf and Raghubir (2008) allows for a listing of a number of visual features of products, their packages, and their promotional materials that have not been systematically examined in the literature in advertising, or product design. For example, whereas the effect of curvature (e.g., squares vs. circles) on area perceptions has been examined in the context of the price people are willing to pay for different products of the same area but of different shapes, the effect of curvature leading to different inferences about products is an open area for future research. Such an inquiry could shed light on whether people associate specific properties with products of different shapes (e.g., balance with a triangular shape, smoothness or gentleness with circular shapes, and sharpness with square shapes) that affect their product evaluations and sensory experience while consuming the product.

Format

Format refers to the modality in which visual information is provided. McQuarrie (2008) provided a typology of varieties of print advertisements. He categorized them into four levels of differentiation. The first level includes the relative picture/word ratio: Ads with a higher word content are called "documentary layout" and have the goal of having consumers read and examine them. On the other hand, ads with a higher pictorial content are those that consumers are likely to view and glance at. Peracchio and Meyers-Levy (2005), for example, examine how changing the stylistic properties of an ad increases its persuasiveness. Beyond McQuarrie's categorization of type of information that is pertinent to a print advertising format, the manner in which numerical information is provided is also relevant. This could be pictorial, semantic, or digital. A graphical illustration of stock prices has been shown to lead to different estimates of their annual return and level of risk than providing the same information as a set of numbers or as text (Raghubir & Das, 2008). Pictorial information, itself, in an advertising context, can be categorized in terms of its genre. McQuarrie (2008) referred to this as the third level of differentiation and categorized the genre of the ad into a tableaux (which presents a point in time), a frozen narrative (which presents a point of time in a story timeline), or a rhetorical figure (which requires inferences to obtain meaning). Examining differences in the format used to provide identical information on judgments could inform the literature on advertising and package design.

Statistical

An understudied area in visual perception is how people encode numerical information presented graphically. Graphs are used to describe or persuade consumers in a wide variety of contexts, ranging from financial information about stocks and indices to health risk information about the odds of death due to different causes. The statistical property of visual numerical information includes information regarding trend (direction), variance, skewness, and kurtosis, the first four moments of a range of numbers. Additionally, run-length, or the number of consecutive upward or downward movements of a set of prices prior to the direction reversing itself, can also affect perceptions of the risk of a stock (Raghubir & Das, forthcoming). Examining the effect of the statistical properties of a set of numbers on judgments related to the risk and return of stocks, or the incidence and risk of a disease, would be of interest to not only marketers, but also have implications for public policy and consumer welfare. This is particularly true if the effects of the different moments of a graph are contingent on the type of graph itself. The types of graphs vary (e.g., line charts, area graphs, bar graphs, pie charts, etc.) as do their features (level of detail of data, length and orientation of X and Y axes, colors, reference indices, labels, etc.). For example, do people estimate the risk of cancer more accurately when the information about the number of deaths by cause is presented using a bar graph versus a pie chart? Do people judge their investment portfolios as having performed better when their mutual fund advisor displays fund prices using a line graph for 2 years versus 20 years, changes the length of the Y axis, or changes the reference indices against which fund performance is assessed (from the Dow to S&P 500 to NASDAQ)? Examining the effect of the statistical properties of a graph is a rich area for future research.

Temporal

Despite the fact that the world is constantly moving, as are all the stimuli in it, most attention has focused on examining static visual cues. However, a variety of stimuli are constantly moving, from progress bars that tell you how long it is before a computer program downloads to real-time graphs and charts in financial markets. The temporal properties of visual stimuli include information regarding their duration, movement, speed, acceleration, and variance. For example, do differences in the speed of a download, given that the overall time is the same, affect perceptions of how long the program took to download? Does acceleration in the speed toward the end of a download reduce perceptions of duration? Does the implied or real movement in a static or dynamic object or person contain cues that affect inferences about the object or person? Temporal aspects of a visual cue present a large canvas for researchers to examine how changes in static visual cues are encoded and judged.

Goal

The goal of a visual cue can also vary. McQuarrie's (2008) second level of differentiation was the goal of the picture in the ad: whether it was meant to infer meaning or whether it was meant to provide aesthetic pleasure. He argued that visual cues that people enjoy looking at are better at providing aesthetic pleasure, whereas visual cues that people look through (e.g., a picture frame) are better suited for domains where the advertiser wants the consumer to infer meaning from the picture. Whereas some visual cues are merely meant to provide information in a modality or form that is easier for some consumers to comprehend, others may be present purely for their aesthetic appeal, and yet others may be present so as to draw attention to the message. Beyond McQuarrie's differentiation of goal into informative and aesthetic, I propose that some visual images are incorporated due to their persuasive power beyond information about the intrinsic properties of the product and are orthogonal with their aesthetic appeal. The goal of the visual element in a stimulus could affect the manner in which it is assimilated or contrasted with other sensory stimuli to make an overall judgment, an issue I discuss later.

Structural

McQuarrie (2008) presented a fourth level of differentiation of visual input that referred to the types of figurative visual structures that are commonly seen in print advertising: juxtaposition (where A is beside B), inclusion (where A is inside B), combination (where A and B combine to form C), fusion (where A and B combine to form AB), replacement (where A is provided in place of B), and removal (where A is provided and not B). The effects of differences in structure on the level and focus of attention, elaboration, and visual imagery, with consequences for recall, inferences, and behavior, are not well known and proposed as areas of future research.

Other

There are a variety of other visual cues including color, hue, placement, tone, texture, strength, size, light, and valence. For example, Chattopadhyay, Gorn, and Darke (see Chapter 15 in this volume) show that people have a universal preference for the hue of blue irrespective of cultural heritage. Greenleaf (see Chapter 16 in this volume) explores whether black and white images have a place in the current color-dominated visual environment and whether the specific effect of black and white images is based on the fact that black and white present two ends of the color continuum (no color and every color), whether they are due to inferences about black and white images referring to classic, retro, and high-status products, or whether they could be effective simply because they stand out in a world of color. Kahn and Deng (see Chapter 17 in this volume) provide a framework to understand the effect of placement of a visual image on a product package. They argue that visual images placed at the bottom right-hand side lead to inferences of greater weight, which is a positively evaluated cue for product categories such as cookies, but a negatively evaluated cue for product categories such as crackers.

In an exploration of the manner in which visual cues are an input to the sensory experience, Hoegg and Alba (2007) show that the effect of the strength of the orange color in an orange juice affects perceptions of the quality of the orange juice: An identical formulation with a deeper color is perceived to taste better, an assimilation effect. The effect of other cues, such as size of visual cues, on perceptions and inferences remains to be investigated.

To summarize, the typology of visual cues includes seven different aspects of visual cues ranging from their geometric properties to their color that could affect a range of consumer judgments from attitudes to size perceptions to taste perceptions. The next section briefly lists the range of consequences of consumer judgments that could be affected by visual cues.

The Process of Visual Perception: Mediating Constructs

The literature on visual perception suggests that the effect of visual cues on judgments is via three distinct, but interrelated, constructs: attention, imagery, and neural activation. Attention is the extent to which the human eye focuses on an aspect of visual information and the specific location of this focus. Thus, it involves both the level as well as the focus of attention. Imagery is the process of visualizing information in the absence of the visual stimulus, akin to visual elaboration of information. Neural activation refers to the extent to which neurons in different areas of the brain light up in the presence of visual and other sensory stimuli, as well as the specific locations where neural activity occurs. With the advent of new technology, specifically eye-tracking as a mechanism to examine level and focus of attention, and functional magnetic resonance imaging (fMRI) brain scans to assess the level and areas of neural activation, direct physiological measures of process are increasingly becoming available to researchers to demonstrate convergent evidence for proposed processes.

There is a wealth of knowledge about how people attend to a variety of visual stimuli in ads and other print media. Based on over three decades of research on the physiology of visual perception, Pieters and Wedel (2008) propose that there are six cornerstones of eye-tracking: eye movements reflect information sampling in time and space, awareness of individual eye movements is limited, the perceptual field during eye fixations is narrow, eye movements are tightly coupled with attention, attention is central to ad processing, and eye movements reflect ad processing. The key aspect of eye movements pertinent to the current discussion is that all the information in a visual field is not attended to, and people are not necessarily aware of the aspects of information they attend to and ignore. Their first fixation gives them the gist of the information contained in an ad and is contingent on the goals of the viewer.

Eye-fixation technology has also been used to examine the effect of in-store visual cues, such as shelf layouts, package design, pricing displays, and placement position (Chandon, Hutchinson, Bradlow, & Young, 2008). Chandon et al. (2008) found that memory-based information regarding brands and stores was used along with information from the visual cues in a store, with marketing tactics aimed at increasing attention (such as price displays) effective at increasing the level of attention, but not always effective at increasing sales.

Individual differences in visual imagery affect the extent to which an individual needs to rely on visual stimulus to make a judgment. Those with a higher ability to visualize need to rely on stimulus-based information less than those with a lower ability to visualize. Using this distinction, Raghubir (2008, Study 1) demonstrated that those with higher visual imagery ability were less prone to the direct distance bias in distance perception (cf. Raghubir & Krishna, 1996). The same pattern was true for those who had a preference for processing visual (vs. verbal) information. Furthermore, people with a visual style of processing were less prone to the direct distance bias than those with a verbal style of processing when the task was stimulus based, with the reverse pattern holding when the task was memory based.

Using this and other empirical evidence on the direct distance bias (Krishna & Raghubir, 1997), Raghubir (2008) proposed the "hardwired" model of visual information processing, where processing outcomes were contingent on awareness of the stimulus, its influence, availability of cognitive resources, processing motivation, and the controllability of the influence of stimuli on judgments. When respondents were unaware of the presence of stimuli, preconscious or preattentive processes, such as subliminal persuasion and priming effects, would occur, where judgments would be assimilated in the direction of the visual stimuli. All other processes invoke attention as a precursor to processing information. These include nonconscious processing, where consumers are unaware of the influence of the stimuli; heuristic processing, where consumers make judgments based on easy-to-use cues available in the context given and do not have the necessary level of motivation or availability of cognitive resources to examine the visual information in detail and incorporate it into their judgments; and systematic processing, where consumers do have levels of motivation, opportunity, and ability to make judgments based on the content of the visual information they are provided. The key difference between the proposed "hardwired" model and the remaining four models is whether the effect of a particular cue on judgments is controllable or not. When it is controllable, then increasing levels of motivation, or availability of cognitive resources, would lead to veridical judgments. But when the influence of a particular cue is not controllable, then increasing levels of attention or motivation would increase the biasing effects of the stimuli on judgments. This is because the additional cognitive resources would be deployed toward the biasing aspect of the stimuli rather than away from it toward alternate debiasing visual information. Such a genre of effects would include optical illusions that are difficult to eliminate. The hardwired model is a simple, unifying framework within which to understand the effects of visual cues on a range of measures, starting with attention.

To summarize, attention to stimuli affects whether processing is preconscious or not, with the awareness of the influence of the stimuli and the ability to control such an influence affecting whether or not effects are nonconscious or hardwired (given that people have the ability and motivation to engage in processing information to make accurate judgments). We now turn to the consequences of the manner of processing of different visual cues on consumer judgments.

Consequences of Visual Perception

The effect of visual cues has been examined for a variety of consumer responses, including perception, sensation, affect, memory, cognition, and behavior (Wedel & Pieters, 2008). These are briefly summarized below.

Perception

The most investigated perception in vision research in marketing has been spatial judgment. In an overview of this area, Krishna (2008) summarized over a century of research of perception of numerosity, length, distance, area, and volume, discussing the key biases documented in each of these spatial judgments, with their implications for consumer actions and managerial decisions. Well-documented biasing effects have been noted for clutter (the amount of visual information in a stimuli), elongation (the ratio of the sides of a two- or three-dimensional space), regression to the mean (whereby smaller quantities are overestimated and larger quantities underestimated, so as to follow a power law psychophysical function with the value of the exponent less than 1), orientation (such that vertical lines appear smaller than horizontal lines of the same length), and categorization (such that points between areas that are grouped together are perceived to be smaller than points between areas that belong to different groups). Such biases can follow through to route, destination, product, and waiting line choices, perception of variety, estimation of calories, and actual levels of consumption. They can also affect perception of the amount consumed that can follow through to postpurchase satisfaction.

The literature in perception has documented two examples of a contrast effect between visual inputs and sensory experience. In one of the first examples of this contrast effect, the size–weight illusion showed that a more voluminous object of the same weight is perceived to be smaller (Cross & Rotkin, 1975). This was presumably because the visual input set up an expectation that was not met by the sensory experience, leading to a backfire effect. In a novel application of this contrast effect to the domain of the interaction between vision and consumption, Raghubir and Krishna (1999) demonstrated that whereas people perceive elongated containers to contain more, their actual experience contradicts this belief, leading them to believe that they have consumed more from the less elongated container: the perceived consumption illusion. This perception during the sensory consumption process leads to them consuming more from the container that they believe they have consumed less from—the more elongated container. Thus, it is the interaction between perceived volume and perceived consumption that leads to an apparent assimilation effect of elongation on actual consumption, with the more elongated container perceived to contain more and thus associated with higher levels of consumption. However, the effect of elongation on actual consumption is brought about by the contrast effect on perceived consumption, a sensory input that contradicts the visual expectation at the time of the consumer experience. Later in this chapter I speculate as to why these two effects are associated with contrast (judgments in the opposite direction), whereas other interactions between the senses have been associated with assimilation (judgments in the same direction).

Beyond spatial perceptions, there is scattered literature in the perception of other visual properties, such as angularity, variance, color, weight, light, strength, assortment, in short, many of the visual properties summarized in the top box of Figure 14.1. Investigations in this area could contribute not only to the growing field of product and package design (see Kahn &

Deng, Chapter 17 in this volume) and obesity (see Chandon, Chapter 20 in this volume), but also to the traditional fields of advertising.

Sensation

Individual chapters in this volume summarize the literature on the sensations of touch (Peck, Chapter 2), smell (Morrin, Chapter 6), taste (Krishna & Elder, Chapter 18), and sound (Meyers-Levy, Bublitz, & Peracchio, Chapter 10), so they will not be addressed in detail here beyond the question as to when the senses interact to produce assimilation versus contrast. For example, the vast majority of the literature in taste perception has shown that people taste what they expect to taste, an assimilation effect, with these expectations based on visual cues (such as color or package design) or memory-based beliefs (such as brand name and country of origin). However, the size–weight illusion and the perceptual-consumption illusion demonstrate robust contrast effects. The question is then what could be the potential points of difference between these two sets of judgments?

A prerequisite for a judgment to change is that it must be tensile, that is, subject to being perceived or sensed in different ways. The literature on sensory experience has demonstrated, without a doubt, that sensory experiences are tensile and contingent on a range of factors, including visual cues, contextual cues, and individual differences. Thus, the flexibility of a judgment is a necessary, but not a sufficient, condition to explain why some judgments lead to assimilation and others lead to contrast.

Based on prior literature on the use of a source of information to make a judgment, I argue that consumers use a cue as a function of its perceived diagnosticity to make a judgment only when it is a controlled and conscious source of information, but use the mere accessibility of the cue as a proxy for its diagnosticity when judgments are automatic (Menon & Raghubir, 2003). Literature has demonstrated that people are typically unaware of the influence of a range of visual and sensory cues on their judgments, and this would suggest that a host of integrative judgments based on multisensory input belong to the nonconscious or hardwired genre. The key question that distinguishes these two judgments is whether the influence of an input is controllable: If it is controllable, then its effect can be mitigated through debiasing or making people aware of its influence; whereas if its influence is not controllable, then those same strategies would lead to the effect being exacerbated (Raghubir, 2008). This leads to three distinct possibilities:

1. *Both cues are nonconscious.* If both cues are nonconscious and people are unaware of the influence of the stimuli, then they are likely to be integrated in an additive manner, leading to assimilation effects that are attenuated as people become increasing aware of the influence of the stimuli on their judgments. This could explain why the tensile aspect of taste perception is contingent on consumers' experience and task difficulty and can be attenuated with debriefing (Raghubir, Tyebjee, & Lin, 2009).

2. *Both cues are hardwired.* If both cues are hardwired, then people will be unable to control their influence, and, therefore, they will have no option but to aggregate the cues in an additive manner, also leading to an assimilation effect. Such a prediction can be tested in future research, as evidence builds to identify the range of cues that are hardwired.

3. *One cue is nonconscious and one is hardwired.* When the influence of a cue that is difficult to control (a hardwired cue) is integrated with the influence of a cue that is easier to control (a nonconscious cue), then it is plausible that the effect of the nonconscious cue will be compared with that of the hardwired cue in such a way as to make the effect of the non-conscious cue consistent with the message (or influence) suggested by the hardwired cue. This recasting of the influence of the nonconscious cue to be consistent with the hardwired cue would lead to assimilation if the two cues are consistent in terms of the implications for a judgment and could lead to contrast when they are inconsistent. That is, if the visual cue points to a larger object being heavier (and is a hardwired cue) and the actual sensation is inconsistent with this (and is a nonconscious cue), then the weight sensation can be recast in a manner to be consistent with the visual cue, and the larger object will feel lighter, producing the size–weight illusion. By the same analogy, if the visual cue suggests that elongated containers contain more (and is a hardwired cue) but the consumption experience (a nonconscious cue) is inconsistent with this expectation, then the consumption experience will be contrasted against the difficulty to change visual perception and will lead to lower perceived consumption from the elongated container, producing the perceptual-consumption illusion (see Krishna, 2008, for a review).

The argument above suggests that the pattern of the interaction of the senses is contingent on (a) their tensile nature, that is, whether the perception or sensation can be recast; (b) their accessibility, that is, their availability to be used as a source of information; (c) their controllability, that is, whether people can change the extent to which they are influenced by the cue; and (d) their cue consistency, that is, whether the information available in the cues points to the same direction or to opposite directions.

This is a testable, falsifiable model that can be examined in future research on the interaction of the senses.

Affect

The effect of visual cues on affect shows that it is a function of whether the cue is consciously selected, ignored, or merely perceived as a function of top–down and stimulus-based characteristics (Tavassoli, 2008). The affect associated with objects that are merely perceived may be processed in an automatic manner and misattributed (Cho, Schwarz, & Song, 2008), whereas the affect associated with objects that are consciously either selected or ignored is directly assimilated into attitude change and affects consumers' behavior. Examples of how visual cues that are merely perceived lead to more favorable attitudes include the research on aesthetic judgments based on an object's geometric properties (Greenleaf & Raghubir, 2008), on attitudes toward an ad based on its goal (McQuarrie, 2008), and attitudes toward an object based on its hue (Chattopadhyay, Gorn, & Darke, Chapter 15 in this volume). However, the effect of other visual cues on affect, feelings, and moods is underinvestigated, with a range of interesting questions that can inform theory and practice. For example, does the level of ambient light in an environment affect moods as would be suggested by conventional wisdom using candlelight and softer hues rather than bright tube lights in a romantic setting? Would this affect store browsing and purchase behavior, and if so, would the effects be contingent on product category or be generalizable? Another example would be to investigate whether the effects of architectural elements, such as ceiling height (Meyers-Levy & Zhu, 2007), windows, wall, and floor composition (Zhu & Meyers-Levy, 2009), contour, and layout, which have been shown to affect product judgments and creativity (Meyers-Levy & Zhu, 2008), also affect consumers' moods and feelings? Beyond the obvious implications for retail, such research can also inform the theory on the antecedents of ambient affective cues and their consequences for other consumer judgments and behavior.

Cognition and Judgment

The effect of visual cues on inferences, beliefs, intentions, and metacognitions is relatively understudied. In a recent examination of the question as to whether visual placement can affect people's judgments, Raghubir and Valenzuela (2006) showed that people believe that those who are placed in the center of a horizontal array are more important, with this belief based on their prior experience and schemas regarding horizontal layout. Such a belief leads to people substituting information about the quality of people in the center for individuating information that could be used as an alternate cue to make a quality judgment when they have minimal cognitive resources to devote to the task. Using data from the television game show *The Weakest Link*, Raghubir and Valenzuela (2006) demonstrated that players who were randomly assigned to the middle two positions in a horizontal semicircular array were likely to play more rounds of the eight-round game, were more likely to make the final dyad, and were more likely to win the quiz show game. Further, this advantage appeared to be due to other players (who had a chance to vote them off the game sequentially over six rounds of elimination) paying less attention to their errors and, therefore, conferring on them the benefit of the doubt; a process that they confirmed using follow-up laboratory experiments. This center advantage was counter-intuitively due to lower levels of attention being paid to those in the center in a context where the goal was to identify poor quality (i.e., attend to errors rather than attend to correct responses), leading to their being referred to as the "centers of inattention."

In follow-up investigations as to whether these effects would also manifest in a product shelf-space context, Valenzuela and Raghubir (2009) demonstrated that shoppers have preexisting schemas for store layouts: popular products are expected to be placed in the center of an array, expensive products on higher shelves, cheaper products and slow-moving products on lower shelves, and promoted products on the horizontal extremes of an array. This led to their inferring that products that were placed in the middle were more popular than those on the extremes of a distribution, which affected their preferences and behavior as a function of whether their goal was to purchase a popular product, a high-quality product, or a less-expensive product.

The intrinsic meaning associated with other visual properties, such as color, shape, light, and so forth, is a fruitful area for further investigation.

Behavior

Studies examining the effect of visual cues on actual behavior have focused on choice, sales, purchase quantity, and consumption (see Krishna, 2008, for a review). However, there is little research on the effect of visual cues on other behavioral measures such as timing (e.g., purchase delay or acceleration), consistency of choices (e.g., brand switching, variety seeking vs. loyalty), and word of mouth. Examining the final consequences of visual cues on actual behavior is of clear relevance to marketing practice, consumer welfare, and public policy.

Conclusions

The goal of this chapter was to summarize the classic and contemporary research on visual information processing to help the theoretician and the practitioner understand the manner in which visual cues interact with one another and the other senses. The model presented a typology of visual cues with their effects on a range of consumer judgments via the mediating constructs of attention, neural activation, and visual imagery. It also proposed two sets of moderators for the effects: context and individual differences. The large question explored in this chapter was when and why two cues were assimilated versus contrasted. I presented a conjectural, speculative model with falsifiable hypotheses that future research investigating the manner of the integration of different senses could test and refine.

Going forward, while there is undoubtedly a large body of research on visual perception, there are a number of unanswered questions ranging from the effect of untested visual cues on consumer judgments, and the effect of moderating factors, to questions regarding how the senses interact and how multisensory experiences are formed (see Krishna [2006] for an example of touch–vision interaction, and Krishna and Morrin [2008] for an example touch–taste interaction). The advent of fMRI technology, which uses as a base the knowledge that different parts of the brain are activated as a function of different sensory systems, will undoubtedly be of great use in providing convergent (or contradictory) evidence that will help us understand how cues from the different senses are integrated.

The next decade is likely to see acceleration in the interest given to visual and sensory cues as ways for marketers to differentiate their products, packages, and promotional materials. Kahn and Deng (see Chapter 17 in this volume) propose that the coming decade will be the "decade of design" in the manner that the 1980s was the decade of the "brand." If this prediction bears out, as is plausible, then the study of visual elements, along with sensory stimuli, will be key to inform this inquiry.

References

Chandon, P., Hutchinson, J. W., Bradlow, E. T., & Young, S. H. (2008). Measuring the value of point-of-purchase marketing with commercial eye-tracking data. In M. Wedel & R. Pieters (Eds.), *Visual marketing: From attention to action* (pp. 225–258). New York: Erlbaum.

Cho, H., Schwarz, N., & Song, H. (2008). Images and preferences: A feelings-as-information analysis. In M. Wedel & R. Pieters (Eds.), *Visual marketing: From attention to action* (pp. 259–276). New York: Erlbaum.

Cross, D. V., & Rotkin, L. (1975). The relation between size and apparent heaviness. *Perception and Psychophysics, 18*(2), 79–87.

Greenleaf, E., & Raghubir, P. (2008). Geometry in the marketplace. In M. Wedel & R. Pieters (Eds.), *Visual marketing: From attention to action* (pp. 113–142). New York: Erlbaum.

Hoegg, J., & Alba, J. W. (2007, March). Taste perception: More (and less) than meets the tongue. *Journal of Consumer Research, 33*, 490–498.

Krishna, A. (2006). The interaction of senses: The effect of vision and touch on the elongation bias. *Journal of Consumer Research, 32*(4), 557–566.

Krishna, A. (2008). Spatial perception research: An integrative review of length, area, volume, and number perception. In M. Wedel & R. Pieters (Eds.), *Visual marketing: From attention to action* (pp. 167–192). New York: Erlbaum.

Krishna, A., & Morrin, M. (2008, April). Does touch affect taste? The perceptual transfer of product container haptic cues. *Journal of Consumer Research, 34*(6), 807–818.

Krishna, A., & Raghubir, P. (1997). The effect of line configuration on perceived numerosity of dotted lines. *Memory and Cognition, 25*(4), 492–507.

McQuarrie, E. F. (2008). Differentiating the pictorial element in advertising: A rhetorical perspective. In M. Wedel & R. Pieters (Eds.), *Visual marketing: From attention to action* (pp. 91–112). New York: Erlbaum.

Menon, G., & Raghubir, P. (2003, September). Ease-of-retrieval as an automatic input in judgments: A mere accessibility framework? *Journal of Consumer Research, 30*(2), 230–243.

Meyers-Levy, J., & Zhu, R. (2007, August). The influence of ceiling height: The effect of priming on the type of processing people use. *Journal of Consumer Research, 34*(2), 174–186.

Meyers-Levy, J., & Zhu, R. (2008). Perhaps the store made you buy it: Toward an understanding of structural aspects of indoor shopping environments. In M. Wedel & R. Pieters (Eds.), *Visual marketing: From attention to action* (pp. 192–224). New York: Erlbaum.

Peracchio, L., & Meyers-Levy, J. (2005, June). Using stylistic properties of ad pictures to communicate with consumers. *Journal of Consumer Research, 32*, 29–40.

Pieters, R., & Wedel, M. (2008). Informativeness of eye movements for visual marketing: Six cornerstones. In M. Wedel & R. Pieters (Eds.), *Visual marketing: From attention to action* (pp. 43–72). New York: Erlbaum.

Raghubir, P. (2008). Are visual perceptual biases hard-wired? In M. Wedel & R. Pieters (Eds.), *Visual marketing: From attention to action* (pp. 143–166). New York: Erlbaum.

Raghubir, P., & Das, S. (forthcoming). The long and short of it: Why are stocks with shorter runs preferred? *Journal of Consumer Research.*

Raghubir, P., & Greenleaf, E. (2006, April). Ratios in proportion: What should be the shape of the package? *Journal of Marketing, 70*(2), 95–107.

Raghubir, P., & Krishna, A. (1996, June). As the crow flies: Bias in consumers' map-based distance judgments. *Journal of Consumer Research, 23*(1), 26–39.

Raghubir, P., & Krishna, A. (1999, August). Vital dimensions: Antecedents and consequences of biases in volume perceptions. *Journal of Marketing Research,* 313–326.

Raghubir, P., Tyzoon, T., and Lin, Y.C. (2009), The sense and nonsense of consumer product testing: How to identify whether consumers are blindly loyal. *Foundations and Trends in Marketing,* Eds, Luce, M., Eliashberg, J., and Ho., T.

Raghubir, P., & Valenzuela, A. (2006, January). Center of inattention: Position biases in decision making. *Organizational Behavior and Human Decision Processes, 99*(1), 66–80.

Tavassoli, N. (2008). The effect of selecting and ignoring on liking. In M. Wedel & R. Pieters (Eds.), *Visual marketing: From attention to action* (pp. 73–90). New York: Erlbaum.

Valenzuela, A., & Raghubir, P. (2009). Position based schemas: The center-stage effect. *Journal of Consumer Psychology, 19*(2), 185–196.

Wedel, M., & Pieters, R. (Eds.). (2008). *Visual marketing: From attention to action.* New York: Erlbaum.

Zhu, R., and Meyers-Levy, J. (2009). The influence of self-view on context effects: How display fixtures can affect product evaluations. *Journal of Marketing Research, 49,* (February), 37–45.

15

Differences and Similarities in Hue Preferences Between Chinese and Caucasians

Amitava Chattopadhyay, Gerald J. Gorn, and Peter Darke

The question of whether color preferences are similar or different across cultures has intrigued color researchers over the years. The literature is mixed in providing an answer, finding both similarities and differences (Adams & Osgood, 1973; Cernovsky, Haggarty, & Kermeen, 1998; Choungourian, 1969; D'Hondt & Vandewiele, 1983; Kastl & Child, 1968; Madden, Hewett, & Roth, 2000; Saito, 1981, 1996; Vandewiele, D'Hondt, Didillon, Iwawaki, & Mwamwenda, 1986; Wiegersma & De Klerck, 1984). We add to this literature by suggesting the conditions under which a similarity in preferences should be obtained and under these conditions examine the color preferences of two distinct cultures: Chinese and Caucasian North American.[1] We also examine the mechanism that should underlie a similarity in preferences across cultures. In addition, we investigate one specific context that could result in differences in color preference or choices, rather than similarities across cultures.

Literature Review

Cross-cultural research on color has investigated a wide variety of responses to colors (e.g., the meaning of colors) (Jacobs, Keown, Worthley, & Ghymn, 1991) and the memory for colors (Tavassoli, 2001). In this research we focus on color preferences and specifically on hue preferences.[2] We next review the cross-cultural research on hue preference. Our goal in this review is to use the literature to explain the confusion that seems to exist regarding the extent to which color preferences are similar or different across cultures.

Similarities and Differences in Color Preference Across Cultures

Eysenck (1941) discussed this confusion and contrasted Guilford's position and findings (cf., Walton, Guilford, & Guilford, 1933), supporting a similarity in hue preferences across cultures with other research (Von Allesch, 1924) that supports cross-cultural differences in preferences. Eysenck's research supported a similarities perspective, which is supported by other research as well, such as research comparing the hue preferences of Vietnamese and American boys and girls (Kastl & Child, 1968) and research comparing Arctic Inuit versus other Canadians (Cernovsky et al., 1998). In marketing, Madden et al. (2000) also found primarily similarities in hue preferences across a number of different cultures.

Much research is in the opposite camp, however, reporting primarily differences in hue preferences across cultures (Choungourian, 1968; Saito, 1996; Vandewiele et al., 1986). For example, the "blue phenomenon" (a strong preference for blue), while found in some cultures, is not found in all cultures (see Wiegersma & Van Der Elst, 1988 for a review). Thus the confusion in the literature Eysenck noted many years ago seems to still be continuing to the present day.

Although it is not clear from a reading of the research studies reviewed as to why some of them found cultural differences and some cultural similarities, it might be expected from looking at the research on the mechanism underlying color preference that the literature should have found greater similarities across cultures. We next outline the mechanism underlying color preference and why that would lead us to expect similarities in color preference across cultures provided certain conditions prevail.

Mechanism Underlying Color Preferences

Hue–Feeling Link

There is considerable evidence to suggest that colors elicit feelings. In early work, Guilford (1934, 1939, as noted in Mehrabian & Russell, 1974) showed that variation in hue systematically influenced feelings of pleasure. More recently, Valdez and Mehrabian (1994) also found that variations in hue led to systematic differences in feelings. They report that short wavelength hues (e.g., blue) will elicit greater feelings of relaxation compared to longer wavelength hues (e.g., red). As well, feelings of excitement will be higher for longer wavelength hues compared to shorter wavelength hues (Antick & Schandler, 1993; Hardin, 2000). Gorn, Chattopadhyay, Yi, and Dahl (1997) built on this research and showed that hues in an ad influenced feelings of relaxation and excitement.

Hue–Feeling Link Across Culture

There are biological reasons why different hues elicit different feelings. Hue is a perceptual element that is associated with specific physiological structures.[3] Research reported by Hardin (2000) suggests that the classification of hues as warm/exciting (e.g., reds) or cool/relaxing (e.g., blues) is linked to the physiological processes involved in color perception. Supporting evidence also comes from the work of Batra, Urvashi, and Muhar (1998), which showed that the hue of the surrounding environment in which a simple experimental task was undertaken affected participants' galvanic skin response (GSR). A red environment was found to elicit GSR levels consistent with higher arousal compared to blue environments. Indeed, based on the physiological evidence linking hue to feelings, Sokolov and Boucsein (2000) have gone so far as to propose a neurophysiological model of emotion based on color space. Together, this evidence suggests a physiological basis for the link between hue and feelings, and therefore we should expect that the effects of hue on feelings would be similar across cultures, since, notwithstanding cultural differences, we share a common physiology.

Feeling–Liking Link

There is also evidence that suggests that feelings are interpreted in the same way across cultures and, thus, hue-induced feelings are likely to lead to hue preferences that are similar across cultures. Evidence for the similarity of interpretation of emotions comes from work on the underlying dimensionality of emotions. In this research, it is widely accepted that feelings can be represented by two dimensions: arousal and valence (Herrmann & Raybeck, 1981; Russell, 2003). This two-dimensional view has been found to capture the variance in emotions across a wide variety of cultures. For example, using both facial expressions to capture emotions as well as words, Russell, Lewicka, and Niit (1989) have shown that, across a set of heterogeneous cultures (Estonian, Greek, Polish, Hong Kong Chinese), the variance in emotions can be captured using the two dimensions of valence and arousal. This finding has been further replicated using data from China, Croatia, India, Japan, Norway, Spain, and Vietnam (Herrmann & Raybeck, 1981; Russell, 1983). Importantly, this research shows that feelings, whether expressed in the form of facial expressions or words, are classified in the same way across cultures. Thus, for example, both excitement and relaxation are judged as being positive in valence across cultures. Furthermore, excitement is judged as high in arousal, while relaxation is judged as low on arousal across cultures (Russell et al., 1989). Since the effects of feelings on attitude judgments are believed to occur through a transfer of the valence associated with the feeling, it would seem that similar feelings should have a similar impact on judgments across cultures. Thus, for example, feelings of relaxation should have a positive effect on attitude judgments, irrespective of culture.

Summary

The research reviewed above suggests that (a) different feelings are likely to be elicited by different hues, (b) the pattern of effects of hues on feelings are likely to be cross-culturally similar (e.g., blue should elicit feelings of relaxation, across cultures), and (c) the effects of feelings on attitude judgments are also likely to be similar across cultures (e.g., feelings of relaxation elicited by blue should lead to it being evaluated favorably, across cultures). This would suggest that hue preferences are likely to be stable across cultures.

Why Then the Mixed Results in the Literature?

Given this research, why do we find mixed results in the literature on hue preferences? As already noted, it is difficult to come to a clear understanding of the reasons for the differences in results from a reading of the published literature. One possibility that might account, at least in part, for the mixed findings relates to the way the various studies were carried out, specifically, regarding the prominence of the hues. For example, in some studies that found differences (Adams & Osgood, 1973; Vandewiele et al., 1986; Wiegersma & Van Der Elst, 1988), no colors were shown while collecting responses, and in Saito's (1981, 1996) work, small color chips were used. It is possible that these conditions were not ideal for elicitation of feelings.

Prominence of Hue

It would appear from the literature, however, that when the colors are more prominent or salient, they do elicit feelings. For example, when the walls of a room are painted a relaxing color people in the room have been found to be less fidgety and less aggressive (Bennett, Hague, & Perkins, 1991; Profusek & Rainey, 1987; Schauss, 1985). Likewise, the effect of hue on feelings and preference in Gorn et al. (1997) was found in a context where the color was the predominant feature of the ad. Gorn, Chattopadhyay, Sengupta, and Tripathi (2004) also report the effects of hues on feelings, and in their studies participants were exposed to computer screens of a particular color.

In the next section we report the results of our study that investigated similarities across cultures when hues were salient. Although previous research has looked at both feelings and preferences, to our knowledge we are the first to examine feelings-based mechanism for preferences by explicitly testing whether the feelings elicited by different hues play a mediating role in hue preference formation. The study also examines whether the underlying mechanism is robust across cultures.

Study 1

Method

To make the hue prominent, Study 1 was conducted by projecting colors onto a screen at the front of the room. Colors on a screen appear more intense than colors in print because of the additional light source coming from the projector.[4] We also projected large patches of the colors rather than small ones, to further increase their prominence.

The design was a 2 × 3 mixed design. Hue (blue vs. red) was the within-subjects factor. We focused on blue and red since they are primary hues and also the most researched hues in the literature, and they elicit the highest levels of relaxation and excitement. Culture was the between-participants factor, with the following three groups: Caucasian Canadians, Chinese Canadians, and Hong Kong Chinese.

152 participants who were enrolled in undergraduate courses participated in this study for course credit. Subjects were randomly assigned to conditions. Of the 88 participants from Canada, 45 were classified as Caucasian Canadians, while 43 were classified as Chinese Canadian. Data from 64 Chinese participants were collected in Hong Kong.

Participants were shown two slides with a large square patch of the specific hue in the middle, with a border of white around it. The specific hues used were Munsell 7.5 PB 4, 24 for blue and Munsell 7.5 R 5, 16 for red. The two different colors were chosen on the basis of data collected by Gorn et al. (1997) that showed that these were the most preferred shades of blue and red. Two different orders of presentation were used. While viewing each hue, participants rated their liking for the hue (three, 9-point rating scales anchored by good [+4]–bad [–4], nice–not nice, and like–dislike), feelings of relaxation (three, 9-point scales for the words relaxed, calm, and soothed on a scale anchored by not at all [1] and very much so [9]), and feelings of excitement (two, 9-point scales for the words excited and active). These scales were adapted from Gorn et al. (1997). Next, participants responded to questions about the language spoken at home, country of birth, and a question asking about the purpose of the study.

Results

Preliminary Analyses
Analyses of the data revealed that the items for each hue preference, feelings of relaxation, and feelings of excitement, loaded on separate single factors when they were subjected to principal components analysis. Further, all the scales were reliable ($\alpha > .79$). Thus, the mean score across the items making up the rating scale measures served as the operational measure in the analyses reported below.

Feelings of Relaxation and Excitement
Our analyses of feelings investigated whether red and blue would elicit, respectively, feelings of relaxation and excitement, not just in the Caucasian group, as has been found in previous research, but also in the two Chinese groups. Two analyses of variance (ANOVAs) were run: one with feelings of relaxation as the dependent variable and the other with feelings of

excitement as the dependent variable. In each case hue served as a within-participant factor with two levels (blue and red), and cultural group served as a between-participants classification variable. Both ANOVAs revealed a similar pattern of results. In each case, the main effect of hue attained statistical significance (relaxed: $F(1,149) = 236.97, p < .01; \eta^2 = .61$; excited: $F(1,149) = 31.43, p <.01; \eta^2 = .17$). Blue elicited greater feelings of relaxation (mean = 5.56) compared to red (mean = 3.18). Red elicited stronger feelings of excitement (mean = 5.68) compared to blue (mean = 4.68). The main effect for culture was significant in each case (relaxation: $F(2,149) = 16.39$, $p < .01, \eta^2 = .18$; excitement: $F(2,149) = 7.87, p < .01, \eta^2 = .10$). The interaction term was statistically significant for feelings of relaxation ($F(2,149) = 52.21, p < .01; \eta^2 = .41$) but not for feelings of excitement ($F(2,149) = 1.49$, $p > .10$). An examination of the means, as a function of hue, and cultural group, for feelings of relaxation, reveals that the difference in feelings of relaxation elicited by blue and red were greatest in the Caucasian group and smallest in the Hong Kong Chinese. Notwithstanding this difference, however, in each of the three cultures, blue elicited higher feelings of relaxation than did red (mean for blue: Caucasian Canadian = 7.01; Chinese Canadian = 5.52; Hong Kong Chinese = 4.14; mean for red: Caucasian Canadians = 2.83; Chinese Canadians = 3.08; and Hong Kong Chinese = 3.64; $p < .05$ for all). The combination of a main effect of hue on relaxation along with the non-crossover interaction between culture and hue for relaxation suggests that there is a strong effect of hue on feelings of relaxation in each culture, although we note some differences in the relative size of the effects, as exemplified by the interaction.

Hue Preferences
The rating scale measure of hue preference was analyzed next. An ANOVA with the preference rating measure as the dependent variable revealed a significant main effect of hue ($F(1,149) = 113.59, p < .01; \eta^2 = .43$). The means revealed that blue was preferred (mean = 2.37) to red (mean = 0.46). We also observed for the feelings measures that the main effect of cultural group was significant ($F(2,149) = 3.98, p < .01; \eta^2 = .05$). The Caucasian Canadians judged all the hues more positively (mean = 1.79) than did the Chinese Canadians (mean = 1.31), who in turn were more favorable than the Hong Kong Chinese (mean = 1.15). The interaction between hue and cultural group was also significant ($F(2,149) = 3.34, p < .05; \eta^2 = .04$). As with the measure of feelings of relaxation reported above, an examination of the cell means revealed that, notwithstanding differences across culture indicated by the interaction, in all three cultural groups examined

here, blue was significantly ($p < .05$) more preferred (means: Caucasian Canadian = 2.96, Chinese Canadian = 2.35, and Hong Kong Chinese = 1.81) over red (means: Caucasian Canadian = .62, Chinese Canadian = .28, and Hong Kong Chinese = .49). Thus, although blue is preferred to red in each of the cultures examined, the size of the preference difference between the two hues differs across the cultures.

Feelings Elicited by Hues Mediate Hue Preference
The results thus far show that hue has systematic effects on both feelings and general hue preferences, and that the patterns are similar across cultures, with some differences, as noted above.

To examine the role of felt relaxation and excitement in mediating the effect of hue on liking, an analysis of covariance (ANCOVA) was conducted with liking as the dependent variable, hue and cultural group as independent factors, and feelings of relaxation and excitement elicited in response to each hue as covariates. We included both the feelings of relaxation and excitement as covariates in a single ANCOVA model, as the two feelings are conceptualized as independent feelings (Apter, 1981, 1982; Thayer, 1986). According to Apter (1981, 1982), there are two dimensions of arousal, one going from boredom to excitement, called feelings of excitement, and the other from relaxation to tension, called feelings of relaxation. Further, Apter argues that it is possible to experience feelings from both these dimensions simultaneously. For example, as elaborated by Gorn et al. (1997), one may feel relaxed but bored on a Sunday afternoon. On the other hand, one could feel bored but tense if there is an important event coming up shortly. One could also be excited but tense, for example, on the first day at a new job. And, when on a vacation while reading an exciting novel, one could be both relaxed and excited.

The analysis revealed that the effect of hue on liking was attenuated by 92% (η^2 reduced from .36 to .03), although it remained statistically significant ($F(1,145) = 4.55$, $p < .05$; $\eta^2 = .03$). As well, all four covariates were significant (red excitement: $F(1,145) = 10.16$, $p < .01$; blue excitement: $F(1,145) = 21.69$, $p < .01$; red relaxation: $F(1,145) = 22.49$, $p < .01$; blue relaxation: $F(1,145) = 4.44$, $p < .05$).

Discussion

The data show that there are differences in the pattern of feelings elicited by red and blue hues. Moreover, notwithstanding the observed interactions between hue and culture, blue was perceived as more relaxing and was more preferred compared to red in each of the cultures examined. Further, feelings of excitement and relaxation mediate the impact of hue on liking. The small but significant residual effect of hue on liking suggests that there is additionally either a direct effect of hue on liking, some other mediating variable(s) not captured in this research, or both. It is also noteworthy that our results are inconsistent with an oft-noted observation that red is the most preferred hue in the Chinese culture (e.g., Copeland & Griggs, 1986; Gunnenrod, 1991; Schmitt & Simonson, 1997).

A question that arises from these results is: Would we observe bigger differences in responses across cultures in situations where cultural norms were important? Moreover, would these cultural norms influence the reporting of underlying preferences toward color or just change situation-specific choices? We examine these questions in the next study. Study 2 also considers all four elementary hues, and not just red and blue, as done in Study 1.

Study 2

Cultural norms sometimes specify particular hues for an occasion or context. For example, green is associated with St. Patrick's Day everywhere it is celebrated. The same is true for black and orange during Halloween. Sometimes there is a hue that is associated with an occasion in one culture but not another. Red, for example, is associated with Chinese New Year, whereas the celebration of the Western New Year has no particular hue associated with it. Whenever a cultural norm specifies a particular hue for an occasion, this norm should drive hue choice for that occasion more than any feelings that might be elicited by the hue for biological reasons. So, if there is a norm specifying a particular hue as appropriate in one culture but not another, and if that hue is not the hue that is preferred for biological reasons, then differences in hue preference for the occasion should emerge between the two cultures. This prediction of differences seems intuitively reasonable even under conditions where the hues are displayed prominently, thereby maximizing their capacity to elicit feelings. When there are no salient norms for an occasion in the two cultures, however, we would expect choice for the occasion to reflect general hue preferences. Consistent with Study 1, they should be similar across cultures, provided that, as in Study 1, the hues are displayed prominently, which they were in Study 2 as well.

In Study 2, we also examined another question: Does making a cultural occasion that is associated with a specific hue salient influence the reporting of general hue preferences? Consider when red is made salient for a Chinese person by asking him or her to make a choice for a New Year's occasion. Will that affect the hues he or she says are preferred in general or will the reporting of underlying preferences remain unaffected?

Method

Study 2 was a 3 × 3 between participants factorial design. Participants were from three cultural groups: Caucasian Canadian, Chinese Canadian, and Hong Kong Chinese. Their task was to choose the color they most preferred as wrapping paper for a gift that was said to be for a friend. The choice occasions were selected based on pretesting (birthday, New Year's, or St. Patrick's Day), such that cultural norms pertaining to color either did or did not exist for one, two, or all three cultural groups. Specifically, there were no cultural color norms for birthdays for any of the three groups. Thus, in this condition, we expected similarity across cultures in terms of the hue of the wrapping paper chosen and a similarity between general hue preference and choice of hue. For New Year's, the color red was the cultural norm for both the Hong Kong Chinese and Chinese Canadians. However, there were no norms for Caucasian Canadians for the celebration of their New Year's. Thus, we expected that the Hong Kong and Canadian Chinese would be influenced by the norm and be more likely to choose red. We expected the Caucasian Canadians to choose colors in consonance with their general hue preference. For St. Patrick's Day, the cultural norm is green among Canadians. This should apply to both Caucasian and Chinese Canadians, as the latter, being a minority community, would have assimilated the values of the dominant cultural group where they did not have a particular norm of their own. Thus, both Caucasian and Chinese Canadians are more likely to choose green in this condition. However, in the absence of norms, we expected the Hong Kong Chinese to choose in consonance with their general color preference.

Participants

Two hundred and forty-five participants who were enrolled in introductory business courses at major universities located in Hong Kong and Canada participated in the study. There were 91 Hong Kong Chinese participants, 69 Chinese Canadians, and 85 Caucasian Canadians. Subjects were randomly assigned to the three choice occasion conditions.

Procedure

Each participant received a questionnaire that began with the instructions for the study. They were told that they had been "invited to dinner by a friend" and they had bought a gift to take with them. The task before them was to choose the color of the gift-wrapping paper for their gift. The instructions indicated that the occasion for the dinner was a birthday, New Year's, or St. Patrick's Day.

A sample of colors was provided on a screen at the front of the room via a standard computer projection system. These included two samples of each of the four elementary hues (i.e., blue, green, red, and yellow),[5] as well as single samples of black and white. The selection of specific elemental hues was based on color preference data collected by Gorn et al. (1997). The two most preferred shades of each of the elemental hues from that data were used (blue: Munsell 7.5 PB 4, 24 and 7.5 PB 5, 18; green: Munsell 7.5 G 7, 10 and 2.5 G 7, 12; red: Munsell 7.5 R 5, 16 and 7.5 R 5, 14; and yellow: Munsell 2.5 Y 8, 12 and 10 Y 9, 12).

The stimulus set appeared as a series of square boxes that contained the target colors, labeled from "A" to "J," for easy reference. Participants were asked to choose the color sample they most preferred as wrapping paper, and then circle the matching letter on their questionnaire.

Participants then reported their general hue preference. There were two measures of preference: participants reported their favorite color from the set of 10 displayed, without reference to any particular purpose or occasion, and rated their liking for the four elemental hues on a 9-point scale (like very much [+4]–dislike very much [−4]), again regardless of any specific purpose. Additionally, subjects responded to a variety of questions pertaining to demographics. Measures of feelings were not included in this study, as our focus was not on the mediating mechanisms, as in Study 1, but on the moderating influence of salient cultural norms on preference and choice.

Results

Hue Choices for Particular Occasions

As might be expected, choice of hue for the gift-wrapping paper made by members of the three cultural groups was influenced by salient cultural norms: when New Year's was specified as the occasion for the gift, the chi-square test, with the three cultural groups as one factor and the choice from the six hue categories as the other factor,[6] was significant (χ-(8) = 22.57, p < .05).[7] In this case, red was chosen in 77% of the cases by the Hong Kong Chinese, compared to only 33% of the cases by Caucasian Canadians. The Chinese Canadians fell in between with 55% choosing red (see Figure 15.1). For St. Patrick's Day, in accordance with the norm, Caucasian Canadians and Chinese Canadians were most likely to choose green (84% and 79%, respectively), while this choice was less likely for the Hong Kong Chinese (21% chose green; χ-(8) = 33.49, p < .01). Interestingly, for birthdays, where no cultural norms existed for any of the cultural groups, the pattern of hue choice was similar across groups (χ-(8) = 6.37, ns). Blue was the most preferred hue for gift-wrapping paper and red the second most preferred hue (blue = 36% vs. red = 26%, yellow = 25%, green = 12%, white = 1%).

General Hue Preferences as a Function of Choice Occasion
A chi-square analysis was conducted for general hue preference as measured by choice of favorite color from the 10 options presented, as a function of the occasion primed (birthday, New Year's, and St. Patrick's). (The choice of favorite color was not context specific.) As in the previous analyses, instead of using all 10 choice options, they were recoded to five levels: red, blue, green, yellow, and white. Black was not a level as no subjects chose black as their favorite color. The analyses revealed no differences in general hue preference as a function of choice occasion primed (χ-(8) = 9.32, ns). Blue was chosen as the most preferred hue (51%).

For the second general hue preference measure, which asked subjects for an evaluation of each of the four elemental hues without reference to a specific instantiation of the hue, an ANOVA was conducted with the four elemental hue evaluations as a within-participant factor and the three choice occasion primes and three cultural groups as between-participants factors. The analyses revealed neither a main effect of occasion ($F(1,236)$ = 1.01, ns) nor an interaction between occasion and general hue preference ($F(6,708)$ = 1.16, ns). The three-way interaction also failed to attain significance (F < 1). Thus, the results do not support salient cultural norms for an occasion having an effect on the reporting of general hue preferences.

To investigate whether hue preferences predict choice when cultural norms are not salient for the 10 displayed colors, we compared subjects' choices for wrapping a birthday gift with the hue they preferred in general. As expected, for a birthday gift, their wrapping paper choice was consistent with their general hue preference (45% chose their favorite color).

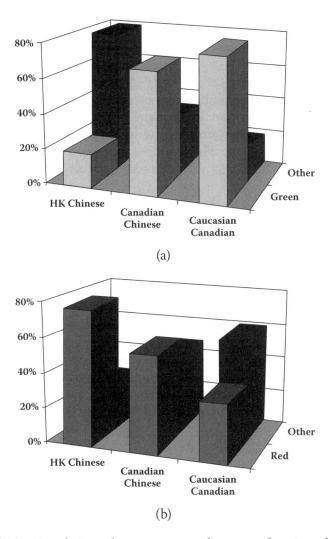

Figure 15.1 Hue choices when norms are salient: as a function of cultural group.

A comparison of the percentage of participants observed as choosing in consonance with their favorite color to the likelihood that the pattern might be observed by chance (chance level = 17%) revealed a significant difference for each of the three cultural groups (binomial test: $p < .001$). Further, participants in the three cultural groups did not differ in their likelihood of choosing wrapping paper for a birthday gift based on their favorite color ($\chi^2(2) = 1.07$, ns). Thus, the data suggest that people choose on the basis of their favorite color when salient cultural norms do not prescribe a particular hue for the choice occasion.[8]

As already reported, hue choice is significantly influenced by the choice occasion, but general hue preference is not. Thus, when asked to choose in contexts where the occasion activates a hue-specific cultural norm, we would not expect general hue preference to predict choices. To test for the likelihood of choosing in line with general preference, we computed a binomial test for participants from the four groups where the primed norm suggested a specific hue choice: Hong Kong Chinese and Chinese Canadians with the New Year's prime and Canadian Caucasians and Chinese Canadians with the St. Patrick's Day prime. The binomial test was not significant ($p > .25$), as only 21% of respondents chose in line with their most preferred hue in general, compared to a chance level of 17%. For the two remaining groups, Caucasian Canadians with a New Year's prime and Hong Kong Chinese with a St. Patrick's Day prime, conditions where the prime did not suggest a specific hue choice, the binomial test revealed that these two groups chose a hue consistent with their general hue preference at a much greater than chance level ($p < .001$; 56% choice consistent with general hue preference, compared to 17% by chance).

General Hue Preferences as a Function of Culture
A chi-square test of consumers' favorite color across the five hue levels (no one chose black as their favorite color) as a function of cultural group revealed an overall similarity in hue preferences between the Hong Kong Chinese, Chinese Canadians, and the Caucasian Canadians ($\chi-(8) = 14.89$, ns). These results support what was found in Study 1. Blue was the most preferred color across the groups, with 51% of respondents reporting it as their favorite color. The dominance of blue as the favorite hue across cultural groups is striking. In all three cultural groups, significantly more participants reported blue to be their favorite color than would be observed by chance (Hong Kong Chinese: 41.2%, binomial test: $p < .001$; Chinese Canadians: 54.4%, binomial test: $p < .001$; Caucasian Canadian:

57.4%, binomial test: $p < .001$). Further, the proportion of participants for whom blue was the favorite color did not vary as a function of cultural group ($\chi^-(2) = .98$, *ns*).

A similar pattern of results was obtained for the rating scale measure of the four elemental hues. The ANOVA reported earlier, with cultural group and choice occasion as between-participants factors and the evaluation of the four elemental hues, red, blue, green, and yellow, as a within-participant factor, revealed that the main effect of cultural group ($F < 1$) and the hue by culture interaction ($F(6,718) = 1.98$, *ns*) were not significant. The effect of hue was the only significant effect in the analyses ($F(3, 236) = 64.09$, $p < .001$, $\eta^2 = .21$). The cell means show that blue was the most liked hue (mean = 3.02), followed by red (mean = 1.99), followed by green and yellow, which were virtually equally liked (mean = 1.34 and 1.31, respectively). Follow-up analyses, using a contrast comparing liking of blue to each of the other three hues, revealed a significant effect in each instance (blue vs. red: $F = 56.23$, $p < .01$; vs. green: $F = 165.03$, $p < .01$; vs. yellow: $F = 166.36$, $p < .01$). These results are consistent with the results obtained for the choice of favorite color reported above. Taken together, they provide strong evidence that while general preference for hues varies significantly across hues, this pattern of general preference for hues (i.e., blue is most preferred, and so on, as above) does not vary across cultures.

Discussion

As might be expected, the findings suggest that hue choice is determined by relevant and salient cultural norms. Cross-cultural differences in situation-specific color choices emerge when these norms are salient in one culture but not another, as was the case with New Year's for the Chinese versus the Caucasian participants. When no norms exist, as is the case for birthdays or St. Patrick's Day for the Hong Kong Chinese and New Year's for Caucasian Canadians, the specific choices for wrapping paper reflect people's general hue preferences. This study thus supports the thesis that where the choice occasion does not have a specific hue prescribed by the culture, consumer choices are influenced by their general hue preference.

Our findings also suggested that while choice is affected when the choice occasion has a culturally prescribed hue, general hue preferences are not affected by making these norms salient. Red is both lucky and important in Chinese cultures. Despite this and despite our exposing Chinese participants to the New Year's scenario, the general hue preferences of the

Chinese participants were not affected and were similar to those of the Caucasian participants.

General Discussion

We began this chapter by pointing to the mixed findings in the literature on hue preferences across cultures. We noted that some of the studies that found differences did not use actual colors in their studies. In those that did, it was typically difficult to tell how prominent the hues were from the description of how the studies were done (Vandewiele et al., 1986; Wiegersma & De Klerck, 1984; Wiegersma & Van Der Elst, 1988). Focusing on the mechanism underlying color preferences, we suggested that similarities in hue preferences should be expected provided that the hues are displayed prominently. They should be expected because feelings elicited by a hue are likely to be maximized when such is the case, feelings that are likely biological in origin and therefore similar across cultures.

Although previous research suggests that feelings and preferences are different for different hues (Mehrabian & Russell, 1974), to our knowledge the role feelings play in hue preferences has not been explicitly tested in previous research. We proposed that under the conditions we ran our studies, conditions where the hues were made very salient by both using a large patch of the color and by projecting the color onto a screen, the hues will elicit feelings and these in turn will have a strong influence on preferences. The results of Study 1 supported our perspective and found an overall similarity in the hue preferences of the three cultures examined. There was a general preference for blue across all three cultures. This was true in Study 2 as well. Although it is always difficult to know why previous cross-cultural research has sometimes supported the "blue phenomenon" and other times not, our results do seem to suggest that if the hues are made salient, preferences are likely to be similar. Salient hues are more likely to elicit strong feelings, and if strong feelings are elicited, they should in turn influence preferences. Future research might test this idea by examining experimentally the role of feelings in hue preferences as a function of hue salience.

Study 2 examined more hues and, as might be expected, found that even when hues were displayed prominently, salient cultural norms regarding an appropriate hue for an occasion dominated hue choice for the occasion. When there were no such norms, then general hue preferences influenced hue choices for the occasion. For the norm-free occasions, consistent with Study 1, hue preferences were similar across cultures.

Although norms affected situation-specific choices, general hue preferences were not affected. Thus, there was no evidence of any biasing effect of situation-specific choices on the reporting of general hue preferences, even though the two measures were used back to back. Perhaps the bluntness of the priming of the hue associated with a particular occasion in a culture accentuated the distinction in a participant's mind between his or her preference for that occasion as well as general hue preference, lessening the likelihood of any biasing effects. Consistent with this possibility, previous mood research suggests that if a mood state is primed, it will not affect subsequent attitude judgments when participants are made aware of the prime before they are asked for their attitude judgments by, for example, asking them about their mood state first (Schwarz & Clore, 1983).

Despite the overall similarity in responses between cultures in our research, we recognize that there are differences as shown by the significant interactions we observed. For example, we observed an interaction between hue and culture for feelings of relaxation and preference. However, these effects do not influence either the ordering of preferences or the propensity of one hue to elicit greater feelings of excitement compared to relaxation as a function of culture. Moreover, we only studied two cultures, even though the cultures compared are very different from each other (Nisbett, 2003). Thus, we recognize that we should offer our perspective with caution, emphasizing similarities when hues are displayed prominently. Future research on other cultures would be needed to determine the generalizability of our results. In addition, we focused on the hue dimension in this research. Future research might examine cultural differences in preferences related to the two other dimensions of color, chroma, and value.

The results of Study 2 suggest that consumers are likely to choose socially prescribed hues when norms exist, even if they are not their preferred hues. Although we only studied norms for particular occasions, other norms are also likely to have similar effects; for instance, color norms for product categories. To the degree this is true, making appropriate color choices requires understanding the underlying general hue preference of consumers as well as norms that may apply to the specific category, choice occasion, and the like. Future research could explore whether a broader set of norms has similar effects. Future research could also examine whether the effects of norms on the expression of general hue preferences depend on the level of subtlety with which the norms are made salient. For example, if before being asked for their general preferences, Chinese people were subtlety primed with the concept of New Year's by being asked to read a story about

Chinese New Year or by subliminally priming the concept, would that increase the likelihood of them reporting a general hue preference for red?

Notes

1. This research was supported by a grant from the Hong Kong government (HKUST 6149/02H). We use the terms Caucasian North American to refer to North Americans of European descent. We realize that the term Caucasian includes non-Europeans, such as Indians, but preferred this term to White North Americans.
2. Hue (e.g., red, blue) is the color dimension that has been the subject of the majority of the research and the dimension that has been of most concern to managers as well. The other two dimensions of color are chroma (saturation) and value (the lightness-darkness of a color).
3. Human color vision is dependent on three types of cones in the retina (L, M, and S). Each cone type responds most strongly to light at a specific wavelength. The maximum excitation is reached for the cones at wavelengths that correspond to light perceived as blue, red, yellow, and green. Information from the retinal response travels along the optic nerve to the part of the brain called the lateral geniculate nucleus (LGN), which contains four specialized cells that are responsible for color vision. They respond to retinal excitation corresponding to red, blue, green, and yellow light (e.g., Abramov, 1997; Ratliff, 1976).
4. This is true for computer screens as well. Golding and White (1997) suggest that the additional light source from a monitor intensifies contrasts on a computer screen.
5. These are called elementary hues as there are specialized cells in the lateral geniculate nucleus (LGN; the part of the brain connected to the optic nerve) that detect these four hues. All other hues are detected through the simultaneous firing of combinations of the four cell types at different intensities. Thus, these four hues are distinct in that one cannot see any other hues in them, as they are perceived through the unique activation of a single cell type in the LGN (e.g., Abramov, 1997; Ratliff, 1976).
6. We collapsed across each of the two shades of a specific elementary hue, thus the levels for the analysis we report could have had six levels: red, blue, green, yellow, black, and white. However, since none of the respondents chose black, we ended up with five levels of this factor in the analysis.
7. The chi square has eight degrees of freedom: four coming from the five levels of hue and two from the three levels of culture.
8. The rating scale measure of general hue preference was not appropriate for this analysis, as this measure was concerned with the four elemental hues and did not map directly on to the choice from the 10 hues presented.

References

Abramov, I. (1997). Physiological mechanisms of color vision. In C. L. Hardin & L. Maffi (Eds.), *Color categories in thought and language* (pp. 89–117). Cambridge: Cambridge University Press.

Adams, F. M., & Osgood C. E. (1973). A cross-cultural study of the affective meanings of color. *Journal of Cross-Cultural Psychology, 4,* 135–157.

Antick, J. R., & Schandler, S. L. (1993). An exploration of the interaction between variation in wavelength and time perception. *Perceptual and Motor Skills, 76,* 987–994.

Apter, M. J. (1981). On the concept of bistability. *International Journal of General Systems, 6,* 225–232.

Apter, M. J. (1982). *The experience of motivation: The theory of psychological reversals.* New York: Academic Press.

Batra, P., Urvashi, & Muhar, I. S. (1998). Hue and variation in CFF. *Journal of the Indian Academy of Applied Psychology, 24,* 83–86.

Bennett, C. P., Hague, A., & Perkins, C. (1991). The use of Baker-Miller pink in police operational and university experimental situations in Britain. *International Journal of Biosocial and Medical Research, 13*(1), 118–127.

Cernovsky, Z. Z., Haggarty, J., & Kermeen P. (1998). Lüscher color preferences of Arctic Inuit and of Southern Canadians. *Perceptual and Motor Skills, 86,* 1171–1176.

Choungourian, A. (1968). Color preference and cultural variation. *Perceptual and Motor Skills, 26,* 1203–1206.

Choungourian, A. (1969). Color preferences: A cross-cultural and cross-sectional study. *Perceptual and Motor Skills, 28,* 801–802.

Copeland, L., & Griggs, L. (1986). *Going international.* New York: Plume Books/ New American Library.

D'Hondt, W., & Vandewiele, M. (1983). Colors and figures in Senegal. *Perceptual and Motor Skills, 56,* 971–978.

Eysenck, H. J. (1941). A critical and experimental study of color-preferences. *American Journal of Psychology, 54,* 385–394.

Golding, M., & White, D. (1997). *Web designer's guide to color.* Indianapolis: Hayden Books.

Gorn, G. J., Chattopadhyay, A., Sengupta, J., & Tripathi, S. (2004). Waiting for the Web: How screen color affects time perception. *Journal of Marketing Research, 41,* 215–225.

Gorn, G. J., Chattopadhyay, A., Yi, T., & Dahl, D. (1997). Effects of color as an execution cue in advertising. *Management Science, 43,* 1387–1400.

Guilford, J. P. (1934). The affective value of color as a function of hue, tint, and chroma. *Journal of Experimental Psychology, 17,* 342–370.

Guilford, J. P. (1939). A study in psychodynamics. *Psychometricka, 4,* 1023.

Gunnenrod, P. K. (1991). Marketing cut flowers in Japan and Hong Kong. *International Trade Forum, 27,* 28–29.

Hardin, C. L. (2000). Red and yellow, green and blue, warm and cool: Explaining color appearance. *Journal of Consciousness Studies, 7,* 113–122.

Herrmann, D. J., & Raybeck, D. (1981). Similarities and differences in meaning in six cultures. *Journal of Cross-Cultural Psychology, 12,* 194–206.

Jacobs, L., Keown, C., Worthley, R., & Ghymn, K. (1991). Cross-cultural colour comparisons: Global marketers beware! *International Marketing Review, 8,* 21–30.

Kastl, A. J., & Child, I. L. (1968). Comparison of color preferences in Vietnam and the United States. *Proceedings of the 76th Annual Convention of the APA, 3,* 437–438. (ERIC Document Reproduction Service No. ED038003)

Madden, T., J., Hewett, K., & Roth, M. S. (2000). Managing images in different cultures: A cross-national study of color meanings and preferences. *Journal of International Marketing, 8,* 90–107.

Mehrabian, A., & Russell, J. A. (1974). *An approach to environmental psychology.* Cambridge, MA: MIT Press.

Nisbett, R. E. (2003). *The geography of thought: How Asians and Westerners think differently … and why.* New York: Free Press.

Profusek, P. J., & Rainey, D.W. (1987). Effects of Baker-Miller pink and red on state anxiety, grip strength, and motor precision. *Perceptual and Motor Skills, 65,* 941–942.

Ratliff, F. (1976). On the psychophysiological bases of universal color terms. *Proceedings of the American Philosophical Society, 120,* 311–329.

Russell, J. A. (1983). Pancultural aspects of the human conceptual organization of emotions. *Journal of Personality and Social Psychology, 45,* 1281–1288.

Russell, J. A. (2003). Core affect and the psychological construction of emotion. *Psychological Review, 110,* 145–172.

Russell, J. A., Lewicka, M., & Niit, T. (1989). A cross-cultural study of a circumplex model of affect. *Journal of Personality and Social Psychology, 57,* 848–856.

Saito, M. (1981). A cross-cultural research on color preference. *Bulletin of the Graduate Division of Literature of Waseda University, 27,* 211–216.

Saito, M. (1996). A comparative study of color preferences in Japan, China and Indonesia, with emphasis on the preference for white. *Perceptual and Motor Skills, 83,* 115–128.

Schauss, A. G. (1985). The physiological effect of color on the suppression of human aggression: Research on Baker-Miller pink. *International Journal of Biosocial Research, 7*(2), 55–64.

Schmitt, B., & Simonson A. (1997). *Marketing aesthetics: The strategic management of brands, identity, and image.* New York: Free Press.

Schwarz, N., & Clore, G. L. (1983). Mood, misattribution, and judgments of well-being: Informative and directive functions of affective states. *Journal of Personality and Social Psychology, 45,* 513–523.

Sokolov, E. N., & Boucsein, W. A. (2000). Psychophysiological model of emotion space. *Integrative Physiological and Behavioral Science, 35,* 81–119.

Tavassoli, N. T. (2001). Color memory and evaluations for alphabetic and logographic brand names. *Journal of Experimental Psychology: Applied, 7,* 104–111.

Thayer, R. E. (1986). Activation and deactivation: Current overview and structural analysis, *Psychological Reports, 58,* 607–614.

Valdez, P., & Mehrabian, J. (1994). Effect of color on emotions. *Journal of Experimental Psychology: General, 123,* 394–409.

Vandewiele, M., D'Hondt, W., Didillon, H., Iwawaki, S., & Mwamwenda, T. (1986). Number and color preference in four countries. *Perceptual and Motor Skills, 63,* 945–946.

Von Allesch, G. J. (1924). Die aesthetische Erscheinungsweise der Farben. *Psychologische Forschung, 6,* 1–91.

Walton, J., Guilford, R. B., & Guilford, J. P. (1933). Color preferences of 1279 university students. *American Journal of Psychology, 45,* 322–328.

Wiegersma, S., & De Klerck, I. (1984). The "blue phenomenon" is red in the Netherlands. *Perceptual and Motor Skills, 59,* 790.

Wiegersma, S., & Van Der Elst, G. (1988). "Blue phenomenon": Spontaneity or preference? *Perceptual and Motor Skills, 66,* 308–310.

16

Does Everything Look Worse in Black and White? The Role of Monochrome Images in Consumer Behavior

Eric A. Greenleaf

Is there still a place for black-and-white images in consumer communication? Black and white images are becoming scarce for consumers. Media that once relied on monochrome images have switched partly or completely to color images. Black-and-white television, the childhood mainstay of baby boomers, is virtually extinct. Most newspapers include color ads and photographs, a trend pioneered by *USA Today*'s heavy use of color photographs and charts. New types of media, such as iPods, the Internet, and cell phones, have always used color images since the time that consumers widely adopted them. Even the photographic images that consumers create themselves are almost entirely in color, the black-and-white film photographs taken to commemorate special occasions having given way to far cheaper digital images taken by the hundreds for every purpose, casual and serious. While older consumers may recall a time when many marketing communications were black and white, younger consumers are familiar with a world of inexpensive and plentiful color images.

Is there still a place for black-and-white images in today's consumer world, or are monochrome images destined to become a narrow niche, appealing only to a small group of nostalgic cinema and photography enthusiasts? In a marketing world where color dominates, can black and white ever more be effective than color for consumer communications? Will black-and-white images survive even in a world dominated by color images, ranging from the tiny 1-inch screen of an iPod Nano to a 10-foot flat-screen LCD television? Was black and white only a technological artifact that deserves to be discarded now that advances in image reproduction make color cheap and plentiful, or do monochrome images serve a purpose for consumers and marketers that color cannot supplant?

These questions matter to marketers who are looking for ways to create images that are distinctive from their competitors and can motivate consumers to attend to, and process, information and eventually purchase. These image decisions could include an ad for a restaurant, a Web site for a new car launch, the image on a wine label, and even the manual included with a pair of golf clubs. In each instance, the decision to make an image black and white or color can affect consumer responses.

The refusal of black-and-white images to yield completely to color gives consumer behavior researchers good reason to investigate why, and under what conditions, black-and-white images differ from color in their impact on consumer behavior. This behavior includes product perceptions, ability to store and retrieve product information presented through images, and comparisons with competitors who use the same versus different kinds of images.

Most consumer research that examines chromatic characteristics of products and images has focused exclusively on color. This research includes how color values affect reactions to ads (Gorn, Chattopadhyay, Yi, & Dahl, 1997; Lichtle, 2007), affect toward different colors (Adams & Osgood, 1973), and cross-cultural differences in color preferences for malls (Chebat & Morrin, 2007) and in product logos (Madden, Hewett, & Roth, 2000). There has been relatively less work that compares color and black-and-white images, or that has focused on black and white in particular. Meyers-Levy and Peracchio (1995) compare the cognitive demands of processing color versus black-and-white ads and examine the impact of these ads on attitudes toward the advertised products. Gilchrist (2006) examines a number of issues in visual perception of black-and-white images, but does not focus on the consumer behavior domain.

One aspect of black-and-white images that has been examined extensively in the social sciences is the use of monochrome as a vehicle for nostalgia, particularly in movies, ads, and magazine covers. For example, in studies that use movies to examine the impact of nostalgia on consumption preferences and differences in nostalgia preferences among consumers, Holbrook (1993) finds that the age of a movie plays a role in consumers' perceptual spaces and discusses how this can affect preferences for an original of a movie versus a colorized version.

In an in-depth treatment of the connection between nostalgia and monochrome images, Grainge (2002) proposes that a revival in the use of monochrome in 1990s America was caused not by a "nostalgia mood," conveying a sense of loss for a simpler era that used these images or a yearning to return to those times, but rather that monochrome was a method used by media and marketers to create a "nostalgia mode" that consumers could indulge in without a sense of loss, adopting nostalgia as a cultural style rather than a longing for the past. He advances this theory first with a discussion of these different kinds of nostalgia and then using specific examples of movies, ads, and magazine covers, along with a discussion of the controversy over "colorizing" movies. For Grainge, the nostalgia motivated by commercial interests in the 1990s who capitalized on monochrome is very different from the nostalgia of earlier eras, which were primarily motivated by a sense of loss.

Here I propose that there are many reasons why marketers may use monochrome images in a world dominated by color. These motivations include a variety of factors with physiological as well as cultural motivations, which extend beyond nostalgia. I also propose a research agenda to examine these issues, generally based on a positivist, scientific approach.

I propose that black-and-white images are likely to have distinctive characteristics that color cannot easily copy. I also argue that these characteristics, which may lead to distinctive uses, stem from two differences between black-and-white and color images. First, the human eye and brain process black-and-white images differently from color images. As a result, the impact of black-and-white images on consumer reactions such as attention, perception, cognition, recall, emotions, affect, and purchase intention may differ from the impact of color. We expect that a difference between black-and-white and color that is rooted in physiological differences will be relatively durable across consumers and cultures. Furthermore, we expect that even if several firms use an effect with primarily physiological origins, making the effect relatively common in the marketplace, consumers will still be influenced.

Second, black and white also has a particular cultural meaning to consumers that sets it apart from color. Most consumers have different expectations and preconceptions of when and why black-and-white images are used, compared to color. Since these differences depend on a person's cultural context, they must be expected to vary across individuals according to culture, age, and perhaps educational background. Marketers need to be more cautious in capitalizing on these differences, since using black-and-white images more frequently, or changing the kinds of products and communications that use them, can change these cultural meanings for monochrome. For example, if black-and-white ads are culturally associated with more sophisticated, understated products, and marketers decide to use monochrome ads for cheaper products, the cultural meaning of these ads might change. Furthermore, if a marketer uses a black-and-white ad for a product category where monochrome is rarely used, such as a restaurant, and other restaurants follow suit, the distinctiveness of the monochrome ads may disappear, due to a "contrast effect" with color ads. It is possible that some of the culturally based differences between black and white and color may be inconsistent with physiologically based differences. As I discuss later, for example, film noir movies, which usually had a disturbing emotional backdrop, were filmed in black and white, but I also speculate that black-and-white images may be more relaxing than color ones.

In what follows, I describe some potential differences between black and white and color and discuss their importance for marketers and consumer behavior researchers. For each difference, I propose a research agenda to investigate both general and particular issues on the role that black-and-white images can play in consumer culture today. My purpose is to encourage research in this area, which has been generally overlooked by consumer behavior researchers.

This chapter is not meant as a comprehensive discussion of the relative characteristics of black-and-white versus color images and how consumers process them. I focus on a few issues that I feel highlight important potential differences between the two kinds of images that are most relevant to consumer behavior and marketing practice. I do not claim that all of these differences have, or will be, supported by positivist research, but rather that they deserve investigation and have the potential to affect consumer behavior in important ways.

Lastly, I am not interested in examining a world where images are entirely black and white or advocating that marketers should attempt to create one. There is an extremely rare visual disorder, termed monochromacy, that results in total color blindness. The visual reactions of people with this disorder have been studied (Hurvich, 1981), but caution is advised against generalizing the impact of this condition to a larger population with easy access to both color and black-and-white images. The interest here is on examining the role of monochrome images for people who have a normally functioning visual system, living in a world where they are surrounded by color images, both natural and artificial.

I also do not consider images where some parts are black and white and others are color, but do want to note that this combination creates intriguing possibilities for marketers that are worth exploring. Although such images have not been used often in consumer communications because they are difficult to produce (but see Meyers-Levy and Peracchio [1995] for an interesting experimental use), digital manipulation has made it easier to produce marketing communications that combine black and white and monochrome. Combining the two image types might allow marketers to create interesting effects. For example, when a monochrome area is surrounded by a colored one, the monochrome area is perceived in the opposite color, an effect known as chromatic induction. The strength of chromatic induction can depend on both the colors used and their relative brightness compared to the monochromatic areas (Gordon & Shapley, 2006). Consumers might find chromatic induction effects novel and pleasing, creating a possible method to increase an ad's efficacy.

How Does Black and White Affect the Cognitive Demands of Processing Consumer Images?

Consumer behavior researchers and marketers are both interested in the cognitive demands of processing consumer-oriented stimuli, such as marketing communications. When stimuli are more difficult to process, consumers may have fewer cognitive resources left for higher-order processing or comparisons. Furthermore, consumers may be less willing to engage in processing tasks that are more demanding and where they have less fluency. For monochrome images in marketing, there are arguments worth considering that these images may be more demanding, or less demanding, to process compared to color.

Black-and-white images may be less demanding to process because they require fewer physiological resources. Since there is no color, the cones in the retina, which are primarily responsible for processing color information, will be less active and send less information to the brain. Color images contain more information on temperature, color, texture, and location compared to black-and-white images (Shafer & Maxwell, 2000), and the design of visual imaging systems for robots has relied on this information. From this perspective, color may use more cognitive resources than black and white. Research examining the impact on attitudes when consumers process ad claims from ads in color, black and white, and both color and black and white also suggests that color consumes greater cognitive resources than black and white for assessing ad claims (Meyers-Levy & Peracchio, 1995).

However, in some circumstances, black and white may be more difficult to process than color. First, since people are used to seeing in color and not black and white, the latter presents a more novel and challenging experience that may require greater cognitive resources to identify and decode the scene being viewed and its characteristics. An example is the plant photographs taken by the English photographer Charles Jones (ca. 1895–1910; Sexton & Johnson, 1998). Familiar vegetables such as peas, beans, leeks, turnips, onions, celery, cucumber, broccoli, cabbages, and radishes are transformed in these images into strange and unfamiliar objects.[1] Taken out of their garden context and photographed in monochrome against plain, light-colored studio paper, these subjects take on a metallic sheen that makes them difficult to identify quickly and sets them apart from our usual preconception of vegetables.

Another example of how monochrome can make images more difficult to comprehend is the photographs of Ansel Adams. In an image such as *Aspens* of 1958, showing a sunlit aspen grove, the lack of color reverses the usual relationship between leaves and bark. The green leaves are now lighter and luminous, while the white bark is darker and at times disappears into the distant forest. Although beautiful, the scene is also unusual and more difficult to process cognitively than a color view would be. It is worth noting that color did play an important indirect role in many of Adams's monochrome images. For example, he credits a dense red filter for darkening the sky and emphasizing the shadows in his famous image *Monolith: Face of Half Dome* of 1927 (Adams & Alinder, 1996).

Research Opportunities

It is likely that the relative cognitive demands of processing monochrome as opposed to color images depend on a variety of factors that marketers can identify, and perhaps even manipulate. For example, it is possible that objects that are popularly associated with a particular color, such as yellow corn, red tomatoes, green grass, or oranges, become more difficult to process when presented in monochrome. Objects whose color varies in most consumers' experience, such as clothes and buildings, may be relatively easy to process in monochrome. Since many natural objects are associated with a particular color, but fewer man-made objects are, this dichotomy might also be useful to investigate. In addition to measuring how monochrome images affect the cognitive demands of image processing, it is also worth examining how monochrome affects willingness to attend to these images in the first place, the ability to retrieve the images from memory, and the consequences of this willingness for product affect.

Research should also try to identify instances where the higher mental processing demands of monochrome images can be used to increase the effectiveness of marketing images. Although increased processing demands can lead to lower fluency and greater cognitive load, more demanding tasks can also increase stimulation levels (Steenkamp & Baumgartner, 1992) and novelty, which can lead to more positive consumer responses and serve as a point of differentiation from competition. Thus, a monochrome ad for vegetables, using photographic images similar to those Charles Jones created a century ago, might prompt a higher level of stimulation and involvement from consumers compared to a conventional color ad.

To the extent that color is considered "missing information" by consumers, they may enjoy tasks that require them to fill in the missing information. Although the kinds of completions needed for tasks involving shapes has been studied, such as "local" versus "global" completions (Van Lier & Wagemans, 1999), more work is needed on the kinds of completions, involving not only color, but perhaps texture and temperature, people make when viewing a monochrome image. Furthermore, if a particular product is rarely presented in monochrome, then a monochrome image may create a novel situation for the consumer, which can translate into higher liking. Thus, monochrome images have the potential to let marketers create images that consumers not only enjoy more, but also process more deeply, leading to higher affect for a product and greater purchase likelihood.

Can Black and White Influence Emotion and Mood?

Mood and emotion are important influences on consumer behavior. It is widely accepted that colors can influence emotions and mood. Artists have, for centuries, used color in attempts to convey certain emotions and moods in their work. The connection between color and emotion has been a hallmark of many "modern" art movements of the late 19th and 20th centuries, including Post-Impressionism, Fauvism, German Expressionism, Abstract Expressionism, and Color Field painting. The impact of color on consumer moods and emotions has also been studied (Gorn et al., 1997). Although less attention has been given to the impact of black-and-white imagery on emotions and mood, there is evidence that this impact differs from that of color.

One possibility worth considering is that black-and-white imagery makes people feel more relaxed. People see very little color under low light conditions, when we see primarily using the rods in the retina, which are sensitive to light but do not process color, whereas under higher light conditions we also use our retinal cones, which are sensitive to color, and exist in three types, favoring each of the primary colors, but are less sensitive to light. From this perspective, color may be associated with daylight, and thus a heightened mental state, whereas monochrome may be associated with night and a more relaxed state. Thus, a monochrome image may, from a physiological perspective, be more likely to put a consumer in a relaxed mood than a color one.

There is also evidence that the release and suppression in the brain of melatonin, a chemical that is important in regulating daily circadian rhythms of sleep and wakefulness, depend not only on the intensity, but also on the color of light. In particular, light with a 460-nanometer wavelength, which is relatively blue, suppresses melatonin production (thus promoting wakefulness) more strongly than does a relatively more violet, 420-nanometer light (Brainard et al., 2008). Thus, when color is absent, it is possible that the production or suppression of melatonin may differ compared to when color is present. Melatonin production and suppression are relatively slow processes compared to the amount of time that most consumers spend viewing an ad, but the effect could be significant while watching a television show or movie that is completely in black and white versus color.

Black and white has also acquired a particular meaning for emotion and mood in certain cultural contexts. For example, many of the films noir made in the early 1940s to the late 1950s were filmed in black and white. Most of these films, such as *Fallen Angel*, *The Maltese Falcon*, and *The Postman Always Rings Twice*, shared a common focus on tense situations involving considerable ambiguity, characters down on their luck or on the way down, betrayal, and sometimes crime mystery, creating an atmosphere often described as simply "creepy." These movies were certainly not intended to induce a mood of relaxation and were the opposite of the feel-good technicolor musicals being filmed during the same period. Although many of these films were probably filmed in black and white for budgetary reasons, this consistent choice has given black-and-white movies a particular cultural value that still persists. As the generations that remember film noir are replaced by younger people unfamiliar with these movies, this cultural significance may disappear.

Research Opportunities

To examine the impact of monochrome images on mood, consumers could be shown ads that are identical except for their color content, and self-reported or observational measures of moods and emotions could be collected, along with measures of consequences of these moods, such as product attitudes and purchase intentions. The impact of more extended exposures, such as to monochrome movies or television shows, should also be investigated, since here the impact of monochrome is likely to be larger.

It is also possible that reactions to monochrome images could vary across the day. If consumers prefer that the qualities of the images they view match the status of their circadian clock, then there may be a preference for color images during the day and monochrome ones at night. This prediction does run opposite to the ubiquitous habits of the 2000s of watching color television and browsing the full color Web in the evening, but at present consumers do not have many opportunities for monochrome images in their evening entertainment.

Researchers might also examine whether ads and images are more effective if there is a confluence between the emotional meaning of the product and the emotion and mood created by the ad. For example, do monochrome ads work better for products intended to induce calm and restfulness, such as meditation lessons or yoga?

When Is Black and White "Highbrow" Versus "Lowbrow"?

One aspect of black and white that is largely, if not entirely, cultural in nature is whether consumers perceive that monochrome images are inexpensive and transient or represent sophisticated reticence. Although these perceptions can be expected to vary across cultures and time, they are likely to be well entrenched in consumers' minds and so are worth studying.

Black-and-white print ads are less expensive than color and are more typically associated with ephemeral media such as daily newspapers, which still contain many monochrome ads, despite their recent addition of color capabilities. Furthermore, many budget movies, up until the 1970s, were made in black and white. Thus, consumers may perceive monochrome images as a sign that a firm is financially weak or makes shoddy, transient products. Older consumers, who remember when most television and all newspapers were black and white, may also associate monochrome with a low-tech, cheap image.

However, black and white is sometimes associated with artistic refinement and elegance. The so-called golden age of television was filmed almost entirely in black and white. Many highly respected movie directors, such as Ingmar Bergman and Woody Allen, made movies in black and white long after color became the norm, and did so for reasons apparently unrelated to cost. In the recent past, major studio releases such as *Good Night and Good Luck* and *Schindler's List* were made exclusively or mostly in black and white.

In the 1980s, many older monochrome movies were "colorized," a process where human judgment is used to establish the basic color of objects in each frame, and then a computer program varies that color in keeping with the density of the gray tones in the original monochrome image. Perhaps the most enthusiastic user of colorizing was Ted Turner, who had the process applied to a large library of old movies for which he owned broadcasting rights. Colorizing quickly prompted a great backlash from film enthusiasts and arts groups, who felt that the process destroyed the artistic intent of a film's creators. Eventually colorizing lost favor and is no longer popular (see Grainge [2002] for an extensive discussion of the colorizing controversy). The failure of colorization, political issues aside, suggests that images that are conceived in black and white may not always translate successfully to color. Although novel, the colorized images often were not very naturalistic or convincing.

Black and white can also convey a sense of exclusivity and refinement, that of a scarce medium enjoyed by a relatively few informed consumers and not appreciated by the general public. The marketer using a black-and-white image may want to convey an implicit message that monochrome was chosen over an alternate color image that, while more appealing to the masses, would be gaudy and tacky. Thus, the use of monochrome can be an advantage when a marketer wants to convey a psychographic positioning that it is not intended for a large mass market, but rather for a smaller set of consumers, perhaps those who are more intellectual or simply willing to pay a higher price. As such, monochrome ads may invoke nontarget market reactions from the segment that the ad is clearly not intended for as well as target market effects from the intended target segment (Aaker, Brumbaugh, & Grier, 2000).

In 2008 Sprint Wireless introduced a black-and-white television ad featuring Dan Hesse, the CEO of Sprint Nextel, inviting consumers to drop by a Sprint store to learn more about how to use all the features of Sprint wireless phones. Here, Sprint may be using monochrome to give its phones a more sophisticated image and differentiate it from other cell phone providers.

Another use of monochrome to convey a sophisticated image is the Web site Blackle (www.blackle.com), a Google-based search engine that appears in black and white. Its motivation is that when a computer monitor shows a monochrome image, particularly one with a black background, it saves power compared to a monitor showing a full-color image. The middle of the Blackle home screen contains a counter, reporting how many watt-hours of electricity have been saved by Blackle users. In this instance, Blackle appears to be using monochrome to portray an image of energy saving, in contrast to the energy wasting excesses of color.

Research Opportunities

Consumer researchers may wish to examine how the particular context in which an image appears, and the product category it represents, determines whether it is perceived as relatively highbrow or lowbrow. For example, use of a black-and-white image on network television, which is rare these days, might be perceived as highbrow, while using these same images in a newspaper might appear lowbrow, since the image would have little distinctiveness in that setting.

Consumer researchers might also examine how preexisting attitudes about the elevated versus lowly status of monochrome are related to consumer characteristics. For example, positive attitudes toward black and white might increase with education or income levels. As discussed earlier, researchers should also investigate whether consumers who are not drawn to black and white are particularly put off by these images, as compared to other approaches used to make target segments distinct from nontarget segments, such as implied price levels or targeting toward particular cultural groups.

Monochrome might also be useful for repositioning products and services to make them more highbrow. For example, a novel marketed using black-and-white ads might be perceived as more serious in its literary intent than one using a color ad. At a more comprehensive level, an apartment pictured in monochrome in a real estate ad might be perceived as more sophisticated than in a color ad.

Lastly, at a time when consumers are becoming more concerned with conserving energy and reducing their carbon footprint, it would be interesting to know whether monochrome, as in the Blackle example, conveys a more ascetic image of energy savings and concern for the environment.

How Does Black and White Affect Perceptions of Form?

Form is an important part of product design. Products are often praised for using basic forms rather than excessive ornamentation and expressing those forms succinctly. The Apple iMac computer, consisting of a white half-sphere with a rectangular monitor protruding from it, was praised for its use of basic forms. The Eero Saarinen Womb Chair, considered one of the classics of 20th-century furniture design, has also been cited as a sophisticated use of basic, undulating forms. More recently, the Dirt Devil Kone hand-held vacuum uses a conical form, while each Tea Forté brand tea bag is contained in its own freestanding pyramidal box. Although marketers are not always interested in emphasizing basic form in their marketing communications, many marketers do want to know what kind of images are most effective at conveying form. In this respect, there is some contradictory evidence of whether use of black and white or color is more effective.

A classical regimen of artistic instruction, such as that taught in many art academies since the Renaissance, begins with young artists learning to draw in monochrome media such as charcoal, ink, silverpoint, and pencil, and only advancing to creating colored images once they have mastered expressing themselves in monochrome. Even highly skilled, mature artists often prefer to work out the basic forms of a composition using monochrome drawing, or oil painting in monochrome, known as grisaille, a method favored by Rubens.

This practice raises the question of whether, from a cultural perspective, monochrome is regarded as superior to color for expressing basic forms. For example, the drawings of Rembrandt, which are virtually all monochrome, have been praised for their powerful expression of form and emotion. The artist David Hockney has singled out in particular a Rembrandt image of women teaching a young child to walk as "the single greatest drawing ever made" (Wullschlager, 2005). The figures, laid out with only a few strokes, have a weight and balance that might easily be missing from a colored version. It is also interesting to note that, while Rembrandt used a variety of methods to make his prints, including etching, drypoint, and engraving, and often varied the inking of plates to create highly individual impressions, he always kept to monochrome images for works on paper, with the exception of a single colored drawing.

Many 20th-century photographers have also chosen monochrome over color images for expressing basic form, even after color photography became more technically accessible and less expensive. The twisting anthropomorphic form of Edward Weston's *Pepper* (1930) is difficult to imagine if the pepper were presented in its natural green or red. Weston also felt that each medium had its own special uses for capturing form: "As in black-and-white one learns to forget color, so in color one must learn to forget the black-and-white forms. ... You find a few subjects that can be expressed in either color or black-and-white. But you find more that can be said only through one of them" (Weston, 1953, p. 54). The blocky forms in Ansel Adams's *Saint Francis Church, Ranchos de Taos, New Mexico* (ca. 1929) owe much of their appeal to the black-and-white medium. Color photographs of the same structure, showing the pastel tones of the stucco, lack the same weight of Adams's image.

There are also physiological reasons to believe that black and white may have advantages over color for perceiving basic forms. Although infants do have the ability to perceive color, their perception of color is not as advanced as that of adults (Teller, 1998). This dominance of monochrome in early life raises the possibility that, early on, we become used to using monochromatic information to judge the basic shapes and forms understood by an infant. If these early experiences also shape adult tendencies, then black and white might have an advantage over color for conveying form.

However, there is also evidence that color may aid in the perception of form. Studies of visual processing in macaque monkeys (Johnson, Hawken, & Shapley, 2001) show that in the primary visual cortex (V1), some neurons tend to favor color processing while others favor black-and-white (luminance) processing, while other neurons do both kinds of processing. The neurons that favor color processing also are used to analyze form, such as by identifying boundaries between different areas that compose the form.

Furthermore, color differences can act as a cue to perceptions of form. Areas of form that are lit more directly, in reference to the viewer, tend to have warmer colors, such as reds and yellows. Areas that are lit less directly, from the side or by reflection, tend to have cooler colors, such as blues or purples. Monochrome images lack this information.

Research Opportunities

Although the above discussion does not yield a clear answer to how monochrome affects perceptions of form, it does suggest that color and monochrome are likely to create different perceptions of form, and that these differences may be due to both cultural and physiological factors. As a start, it is worth examining how consumers react to basic forms, such as spheres, cubes, and pyramids, depending on whether they are presented in monochrome or color. These studies could also include classic product designs that have been praised for their strong forms, such as a Perrier bottle, the Eero Saarinen Womb Chair, the iMac, and even the Dirt Devil Kone vacuum cleaner, as well as artificial products that could be produced using these basic forms, to control for perceptions and affect of existing products.

Since many basic forms, such as pyramids or cubes, are often associated with solidity and stability, it is possible that consumers may perceive products that use these forms and are imaged in monochrome to be more stable and solid compared to a product imaged in color. Basic forms are also often perceived as more immutable than complicated forms, in that they seem more difficult to alter. Here, too, it is possible that products reproduced in monochrome might seem more durable compared to products reproduced in color, if the products use a basic form, while the reverse might apply for complicated forms.

Are There Individual Difference in Preferences for Monochrome?

Just as consumer behavior researchers have found that people vary in their preferences for visual versus verbal stimuli (Holbrook, Chestnut, Oliva, & Greenleaf, 1984), there is ample evidence that people differ in their preferences for monochrome versus color images. Many Renaissance artists put most of their efforts into the colorful medium of oil paint or stained glass, while others, such as Albrecht Durer, produced a considerable output of monochromatic prints, such as etchings, engravings, drypoints, and woodcuts. Although these prints had the additional advantage that they could be produced in multiples from a single plate, and thus bring in a steady source of income (a point not lost on the thrifty Durer), it is likely that some artists also enjoyed monochromatic media more than others. Furthermore, while some consumers of these prints were happy to leave them be, other collectors wanted hand-colored versions, and a cottage industry grew in response. Even in the 20th century, when color printing is much cheaper and more sophisticated, some artists, such as David Hockney, have produced many colored prints, while others, such as Lucian Freud, have produced very few or none (in Freud's case, the sole exception being *Lord Goodman in His Yellow Pyjamas* of 1987).

This relative appeal of color versus black and white has involved the greatest artists of the 20th century. Picasso and Matisse admired each other's work and were very influenced by the other, but were also very competitive. In this respect, Picasso is said to have commented to Matisse "I have mastered drawing and am looking for color, you have mastered color and are looking for drawing" (on each artist's use of color versus mono-chrome, see also Gilot [1990]). Art collectors also often gravitate toward color or monochrome. This is particularly so in photography collecting, where many collectors tend to specialize in one or the other kind of image. Other collectors specialize in old-master prints, most of which are mono-chrome (though colored woodcuts are an exception).

Marketers themselves have also segmented consumers based on using monochrome or color. For example, print ads in the United States for Patek Phillipe, a Swiss brand of fine watches, use color for women's watches but black and white for men's. Studies of business-to-business print advertis-ing have found that these ads in France and Venezuela use color more frequently than those in the United States (Clarke & Honeycutt, 2000).

We should use caution, however, in inferring a preference for black and white simply because the images or objects from a particular time are not available in color. For example, since color photography did not become common until the first decade of the 20th century, there is a tendency to look at the monochromatic photographs taken before this time and pic-ture a color-deprived world, even though we know from paintings, prints, and visual descriptions that these times were as colorful as our own.

Ancient Greek and Roman sculpture is an even more extreme instance where modern observers have inferred a preference for monochrome where none existed. For centuries, many art critics, and popular beliefs, advocated that the unpainted carved stone of these sculptures and build-ings reflected a preference in these ancient cultures for pure forms and a bias against color. However, it has been known for some time that build-ings such as the Parthenon were painted in color. More recently, faint traces of paint found on many of these sculptures, revealed using ultra-violet photography and microphotography, show that they were originally polychromed, often with patterned paint schemes that are not closely related to the forms underneath, which depict the intricate color patterns found in ancient Greek and Roman dress (Brinkmann et al., 2007). Only time and internment have robbed them of their color. When these sculp-tures are shown with the original colors restored using virtual computer images, the results can be very surprising to the modern eye.

Research Opportunities

Marketers may find it helpful to segment consumers based on their reaction to color versus black-and-white images by examining several questions.

First, to what extent do these consumer reactions vary, and are these differences large enough to warrant creating different communications for different segments? Second, are there useful segmentation variables that help predict these consumer reactions, such as a consumer's age, gender, education level, or psychographic profile? Third, since, as discussed earlier, some differences may be based on culture and others on differences in the physiology of the visual system, researchers may wish to examine how durable these differences are and whether they change with different cultural contexts and perhaps different product categories. Lastly, can marketers intentionally change consumer preferences for black and white versus color images? For example, could a firm that has decided to position its advertising by using only monochrome take steps to increase preferences for monochrome over color in its target segment?

Conclusions

Black-and-white images will never return to the dominant role they once played in consumer images before color became inexpensive and reliable. This chapter has proposed several reasons why monochrome images retain an appeal that color cannot easily copy. Some of these reasons are rooted in the human vision system and its different reactions to black and white versus color, while others depend on cultural norms. Given that the former are likely to be more stable and ubiquitous than the latter, it may be difficult to create a cohesive theory for the role of color in consumer images that applies to all situations. Some of the reasons underlying monochrome's distinctiveness, such as its impact on moods and emotions, are likely to depend on both physiological and cultural reasons, making them even more difficult to examine precisely in a global manner.

However, given that black-and-white consumer images continue to appear to be used in media when there is no longer any technological reason for using them instead of color, marketers do need to examine reasons for this durability. In the end, it is felt that there is a lasting place for monochrome images in consumer culture, due in part to the special characteristics discussed here. The place of monochrome in consumer culture is much like that given it by the great photographer Edward Weston, who used both monochrome and color, when he wrote in 1953: "But those who say that color will eventually replace black-and-white are talking nonsense. The two do not compete with each other. They are different means to different ends" (Weston, 1953, p. 54).

Notes

1. Web links to images referred to in this article, current as of the time of writing, are posted on the author's home page (http://pages.stern.nyu.edu/~egreenle/).

References

Aaker, J. L., Brumbaugh, A. M., & Grier, S. A. (2000). Nontarget markets and viewer distinctiveness: The impact of target marketing on advertising attitudes. *Journal of Consumer Psychology, 9*(3), 127–140.

Adams, A., & Alinder, M. S. (1996). *Ansel Adams: An autobiography*. Boston: Little, Brown.

Adams, F. M., & Osgood, C. E. (1973). A cross-cultural study of the affective meanings of color. *Journal of Cross-Cultural Psychology, 4*(2), 135.

Brainard, G. C., Sliney, D., Hanifin, J. P., Glickman, G., Byrne, B., Greeson, J. M. et al. (2008). Sensitivity of the human circadian system to short-wavelength (420-nm) light. *Journal of Biological Rhythms, 23*(5), 379–386.

Brinkmann, V., Wünsche, R., Koch-Brinkmann, U., Kellner, S., Köttl, J., Herzog, O. et al. (2007). *Gods in color: Painted sculpture of classical antiquity*. Munich: Stiftung Archäologie Glyptothek.

Chebat, J. C., & Morrin, M. (2007). Colors and cultures: Exploring the effects of mall décor on consumer perceptions. *Journal of Business Research, 60*(3), 189–196.

Clarke, I., & Honeycutt, E. D. (2000). Color usage in international business-to-business print advertising. *Industrial Marketing Management, 29*(3), 255–261.

Gilchrist, A. (2006). *Seeing black and white*. New York: Oxford University Press.

Gilot, F. (1990). *Matisse and Picasso: A friendship in art*. New York: Doubleday.

Gordon, J., & Shapley, R. (2006). Brightness contrast inhibits color induction: Evidence for a new kind of color theory. *Spatial Vision, 19*(2), 133–146.

Gorn, G. J., Chattopadhyay, A., Yi, T., & Dahl, D. (1997). The role of color as an executional cue: They're in the shade. *Management Science, 43*(10), 1387–1400.

Grainge, P. (2002). *Monochrome memories: Nostalgia and style in retro America*. Westport, CT: Praeger.

Holbrook, M. B. (1993). Nostalgia and consumption preferences: Some emerging patterns of consumer tastes., *Journal of Consumer Research, 20*(2), 245.

Holbrook, M. B., Chestnut, R. W., Oliva, T. A., & Greenleaf, E. A. (1984). Play as a consumption experience: The roles of emotions, performance, and personality in the enjoyment of games. *Journal of Consumer Research, 11*(2), 728.

Hurvich, L. M. (1981). *Color vision*. Sunderland, MA: Sinauer Associates.

Johnson, E. N., Hawken, M. J., & Shapley, R. (2001). The spatial transformation of color in the primary visual cortex of the macaque monkey. *Nature Neuroscience, 4*, 409–416.

Lichtle, M. C. (2007). The effect of an advertisement's colour on emotions evoked by an ad and attitude towards the ad. *International Journal of Advertising, 26*(1), 37.

Madden, T. J., Hewett, K., & Roth, M. S. (2000). Managing images in different cultures: A cross-national study of color meanings and preferences. *Journal of International Marketing, 8*(4), 90–107.

Meyers-Levy, J., & Peracchio, L. A. (1995). Understanding the effects of color: How the correspondence between available and required resources affects attitudes. *Journal of Consumer Research, 22*(2), 121.

Sexton, S., & Johnson, R. F. (1998). *Plant kingdoms: The photographs of Charles Jones*. London: Thames and Hudson.

Shafer, S. A., & Maxwell, B. A. (2000). Color as a carrier of physical information. In S. Davis (Ed.), *Color perception: Philosophical, psychological, artistic and computation perspectives* (pp. 52–71). New York: Oxford University Press.

Steenkamp, J. E. M., & Baumgartner, H. (1992). The role of optimum stimulation level in exploratory consumer behavior. *Journal of Consumer Research, 19*(3), 434.

Teller, D. Y. (1998). Spatial and temporal aspects of infant color vision. *Vision Research, 38*(21), 3275–3282.

Van Lier, R., & Wagemans, J. (1999). From images to objects: Global and local completions of self-occluded parts. *Journal of Experimental Psychology. Human Perception and Performance, 25*(6), 1721–1741.

Weston, E. (1953, December). Color as form. *Modern Photography, 17*, 54.

Wullschlager, J. (2005, December 30). Rembrandt at 400: Master of the inner life. *Financial Times*.

17

Effects on Visual Weight Perceptions of Product Image Locations on Packaging

Barbara E. Kahn and Xiaoyan Deng

Marketers have known for a long time that a majority of consumer purchase decisions are made in the store where product packaging is the primarily means of marketing communications (Point of Purchase Advertising Institute, 1995), yet historically, surprisingly little academic research has focused on consumer inferences constructed as a function of packaging features. On the other hand, there is significant research examining how consumer inferences are formed through advertising and pricing (Underwood & Klein, 2002). Packaging differs from advertising not only because it is the communication medium at the point of sale, but also because it physically surrounds the product. As such, extrinsic features of the package are likely to directly affect consumers' inferences about intrinsic aspects of the product. The primary research on the influence of packaging that has existed in the past has focused on the role packaging plays in attracting attention (Underwood, Klein, & Burke, 2001), in the literal communication of product (Underwood & Ozanne, 1998), or on nutritional information (Moorman, 1996; Russo, Staelin, Nolan, Russell, & Metcalf, 1986).

This has recently changed as more researchers are beginning to study the role of packaging in the formation of consumer inferences and how these inferences can affect consumption behavior and judgment. Some of this new research has focused on how the shape of the package influences judgment about the volume of the product (Folkes & Matta, 2004; Krishna, 2006; Raghubir & Greenleaf, 2006; Raghubir & Krishna, 1999; Wansink & Van Ittersum, 2003; Yang & Raghubir, 2005). Other research has studied how the size of the package or container can influence subsequent consumption behavior (Coelho Do Vale, Pieters, & Zeelenberg, 2008; Scott, Nowlis, Mandel, & Morales 2008; Wansink, 1996). Underwood and Klein (2002) have studied how product imagery can affect brand evaluations, again showing that an extrinsic package cue can be used by consumers to infer intrinsic product attributes.

In this chapter we build on this recent research to study the role of visual package imagery, specifically layout decisions regarding the use of a product image on the package. Visual imagery dominates other modalities (e.g., touch; Krishna, 2006) when consumers process packaging cues (Posner, Nissen, & Klein, 1976). Further, consumers often shop with "their eyes" (Folkes & Matta, 2004) and ignore package label information (Dickson & Sawyer, 1990). The presence of a product image has been shown to increase the likelihood that a consumer will use it as an extrinsic cue (Olsen & Jacoby, 1972) and as a surrogate indicator of product quality (Richardson, 1994). Thus we predict that the presence of a product picture can encourage the consumer to imagine how a product looks, tastes, feels, smells, or sounds (Pavio, 1986; Underwood et al., 2001).

We are specifically interested in consumers' inferences about tactile features of the product. We discuss how layout decisions, such as the location of the product picture on the package, can influence a salient attribute about how a product feels—its perceived visual heaviness. Perceived visual heaviness is likely to be a cue for product preference, although whether heaviness or lightness is preferred will depend on the product category (Deng & Kahn, forthcoming). Consumer goals may also impact whether heaviness or lightness is preferred (Deng & Kahn, 2009).

We organize our discussion as follows. We begin with a brief review as to how graphic design on packaging in general can be used to attract attention, communicate product information, and build attitudes. We then review the visual design literature to suggest design factors that have been used to influence perceived visual weight. We present our spatial/location framework that suggests how the location and suggested location of the product image on the package can influence visual perceived heaviness. We then discuss how other theories of visual perceptual biases can lead to testable hypotheses regarding perceived visual heaviness. We conclude with a general discussion.

Use of Packaging Graphic Design to Influence Product Attitudes

Visual graphic information on a package, such as layout, color combination, typography, and product photography, is more vivid than informational text and therefore should be noticed earlier (Underwood et al., 2001) and attract more attention (McGill & Anand, 1989). The increased attention to the product through the graphic information may help break through competitive clutter and increase the likelihood that a brand is brought into the consumer's consideration set. The more attention consumers pay to the graphic elements, the more the likelihood that they will think about features of the product increases, and that can facilitate the formation of attitudinal judgments (Kisielius & Sternthal, 1986).

In particular, previous research specifically focusing on the inclusion of a product image on the package (Underwood & Klein, 2002; Underwood et al., 2001) has shown that product pictures can elicit imagery processing (Pavio, 1986) and may serve as a central cue to communicate information about intrinsic product characteristics and its sensory features. As such, the visual picture of the product can set expectations and serve as an "advance organizer" for the other graphic, verbal, or tactile packaging information that might be available (Houston, Childers, & Heckler, 1987). The product picture may also be able to enhance incidental learning about the product (MacInnis & Price, 1987). Therefore, following Feldman and Lynch's (1988) accessibility-diagnosticity framework, since a picture of the product on a package is accessible (because it attracts the consumer's attention) and is diagnostic (because it aids in the expression of sensory features), it should contribute to the formation of product attitudes.

The predicted effect of these graphic visual elements on attention and product inferences, though, should be moderated by the familiarity that the consumer has with the brand (Underwood et al., 2001), the likelihood the consumer can judge the product based on the intrinsic aspects of the product itself (Ziethaml, 1988), and whether or not the consumers are under time pressure (Pieters & Warlop, 1999). If consumers are familiar with the brand, able to judge quality based on the intrinsic aspects of the product, or have enough time to evaluate, then visual packaging cues are less likely to impact product inferences.

Most of the previous research has empirically verified that graphic package design features can increase attention, increase the likelihood that the brand is included in a consideration set, and affect aesthetic responses (see Underwood et al., 2001 for a review). Underwood and Klein (2002) have shown that product imagery on packages affects consumers' beliefs about the brand and their global evaluations of both the brand and the package. However, no research that we know of has studied the specific ways that graphic design packaging elements can directly influence specific perceived product features. To begin this more focused inquiry, we identify visual package elements that can play a role in creating consumers' perceptions of the heaviness of the product. Although this has not been studied in marketing, the art and visual design literatures have devoted considerable attention to the study of "visual heaviness."

A Spatial/Location Framework for Visual Weight Perceptions

The literature of art and visual perception has studied the role of visual design features in communicating visual heaviness, as this is an important dimension in artistic and structural renderings. In particular, two authors who have studied this issue in depth are Puffer (1903) and Arnheim (1974). Puffer (1903) identified several factors that can affect visual weight: size, depth, movement, and interest. Arnheim (1974) identified the following properties of visual objects that affect visual weight: location, spatial depth, size, intrinsic interest, isolation, and shape. We build on both theories to develop a framework that provides predictions as to how the layout of a product image on a package can influence consumers' inferences about the visual heaviness of a product.

The central premise of our framework is that the location of the product image on the package facade directly determines its visual weight. Although there are potentially infinite locations a product image can be placed, we focus on four dimensions that can characterize the package facade.

Principle One: (Two-Dimensional Space)

The first two dimensions are characterized by the two-dimensional area of the package: the height and the width. We identify four critical locations in this two-dimensional space: top versus bottom and left versus right. We hypothesize based both on the design literature and empirical support found by Deng and Kahn (forthcoming) that the bottom side and the right side of the package facade are the heavy locations, and when product images are placed in those places the product appears visually heavier. The top and the left side of the package facade are the light locations, and when product images are placed in those areas, the product appears visually lighter.

Principle Two: (Three-Dimensional Space)

The third dimension conceptualizes the package facade as a three-dimensional cube, and we identify two more critical locations: front versus back along a third dimension (depth). Although we have yet to show this empirically, we hypothesize that a product image located in the foreground makes the product looks lighter than the same product (controlling for other aspects including the size of the product image on the package) with a product image located in the background of a rendering on a package. Also we hypothesize that a package that shows a vista in its graphics, whether the product image is depicted in the vista or not, thus allows for the perception of three dimensions and looks heavier than the same package with no vista.

Principle Three: (Fourth Dimension: Time)

Finally, using time as a fourth dimension we allow for change in direction in location or movement of the product image along any of the three physical dimensions (height, width, and depth). If we hypothesize that, as above, the right and bottom sides of the package are visually heaviest, then suggested movement of the product image going right will make the product look heavier than the same product depicted as moving left, and suggested movement of the product image to the bottom will make the product look heavier than the same product moving up; and theories of perspective would predict that suggested movement of a product toward the front of a vista will make it look lighter than the same product depicted as moving toward the back.

As we describe in more detail below, the above hypotheses for suggested movement depend on "reading" the visual field or package from left to right, which orients the visual fulcrum on the left. In some cases, the design literature suggests the orientation of the fulcrum of a visual frame to be in the center. If this is the case, the design literature would suggest that if the direction of the image is pointed away from the central fulcrum, it will appear visually heavier; if the direction is pointed inward toward the center, then the image will appear visually lighter. Similarly, an image depicted as moving along a "curve in" (concave curve) will look lighter than the same image depicted as moving along a "curve out" (convex curve).

Further Discussion and Theoretical Support for Our Predictions

Location of Product Image in a Two-Dimensional Package Facade

Arnheim (1974) identifies the heavy locations of a two-dimensional visual field as the bottom and right sides, and the light locations as the top and left sides. Bottom heaviness occurs because the laws of gravity in the physical world are applied to the visual space. Since we live in a world dominated by gravity, we constantly observe that heavy things (e.g., rock, house) are on the ground, while light things (e.g., cloud, balloon) are in the air, and we generalize from this observation that items on the bottom of a visual space are heavy and items on the top are light. Arnheim speculated about the right-heaviness principle based on two observations: (a) the principle of the lever and (b) the left-to-right reading orientation. The principle of the lever states that the greater the distance from the fulcrum position that an object is placed on a lever, the heavier the weight that is needed on the other side to balance the object. The left-to-right reading orientation suggests that just like we read left to right, we also "read" a picture (or any visual field) from left to right. This is why the diagonal that runs from bottom left to top right is seen as ascending and the one from top right to bottom left is seen as descending (i.e., if "read" from right to left, these two diagonals will then be seen as descending and ascending, respectively; Wölfflin, 1950). Combining both observations suggests that since we read a visual field from left to right, we anchor on the left, which becomes the "visual fulcrum." Thus, the farther an object is placed away from the left side (or the fulcrum), the heavier the perceived weight. Arnheim labels this the "visual lever effect."

Deng and Kahn (forthcoming) test both of these principles (bottom heavy and right heavy) of visual weight in the context of product packaging and find support for both (Figure 17.1). Specifically, they show that the bottom and right sides of a package facade are the heavier sides, and when product images are placed in those locations, the visual weight of the product is perceived to be heavier. They also find that how these perceptions of heaviness relate to package preference depends on product category and consumer goals. For products for which heaviness is considered a positive attribute (e.g., hedonic food categories), packages with the product image placed at the heavy locations (the bottom, right, and bottom right of the package facade) are preferred; whereas for products for which heaviness is negative (e.g., when portability is an asset), packages with the product image in the light locations (top, left, top left) are preferred. Further, in the hedonic food category (snacks), a salient health goal, as opposed to a neutral goal, weakens the preferences for packaging where the product image is placed in a heavy location, although this moderating effect of goal is weaker for healthy snacks compared to regular snacks.

Store shelf context is found to be a boundary condition such that the effects of location on perceived product heaviness and package evaluation appear in a contrasting context but disappear in an assimilating context.

Heavy Locations: Bottom and Right	Light Locations: Top and Left

Figure 17.1   (See color insert.) Two-dimensional space.

Moreover, perceived product heaviness mediates (a) the effect of location on package evaluation and (b) the moderating role of store shelf context (i.e., mediated moderation).

In testing Arnheim's (1974) principles of visual weight, Deng and Kahn (forthcoming) also identify another explanation for the principle of "right heaviness": ocular dominance. Ocular dominance is the preference for the use of one eye over the other (similar to handedness, only with the use of eyes). Research shows that 65% of the population are right-eye domi-nant, 32% left-eye dominant, and 3% ambiocular (Bourassa, McManus, & Bryden, 1996; Porac & Coren, 1976). Ocular dominance suggests that visual input from the dominant eye is accentuated and that affects the pro-cessing of visual information. For example, right-eyed people perceive an object on the right side of a frame to be larger (Coren & Porac, 1976) and closer (Scott & Sumner, 1949). When asked to assign a visual balance point anywhere along the straight line anchored by two objects, people who are right eyed tend to set the balance point to the right side of the physically expected balance point, suggesting that the object on the right seems to weigh more (Mefferd & Wieland, 1969).

Deng and Kahn (forthcoming) propose that, based on ocular domi-nance, right-eyed people should perceive an object located at the right visual field to be heavier than the object located at the left visual field.

Because right-eyed people comprise the majority of the population, there should be a general right-heavy effect. Therefore, they propose and show that ocular dominance moderates the right-heavy effect. They find that for right-eyed participants, there is a strong right-heavy effect, but for left-eyed participants, the effect disappears. Their empirical evidence suggests that both explanations of right heaviness, visual lever effect and ocular dominance, play a role. If ocular dominance were the only reason for right heaviness, then for left-eyed participants, there should be a left-heavy effect. The lack of such an effect suggests that for this group of people, the visual lever effect, which leads to a right-heavy effect, and their ocular dominance, which leads to a left-heavy effect, wash each other out, and we observe a null effect.

Location of Product Image on the Third Dimension of a Package Facade: Spatial Depth

There are several ways to add depth to a package's facade. One way is to add dimensionality by moving the product image off the flat two-dimensional grid and drawing in the third dimension, using the graphic tools of perspective. Another way is to layer graphic items on the package so the product image is in front of or behind text or other graphic elements. Finally, the third way is to add a vista to the package. Examples of all of these are presented in Figure 17.2.

Puffer (1903) concluded, based on a series of experiments, that allowing for spatial depth in a visual frame inherently carried more weight as compared to a flat two-dimensional space. Puffer used the following experimental paradigm to test his visual weight hypotheses. Along the horizontal axis of a rectangular board he fixed stimulus A and asked his subjects to assign a location for stimulus B. The subjects moved stimulus B to different places before they decided on a final position that they found most aesthetically pleasing. If the distance between B (whose location was assigned by the subjects) and the center or fulcrum was shorter than the distance between A (whose location was fixed by the experimenter) and the center or fulcrum, then an inference was made that B was perceived to be visually heavier than A, and vice versa. These inferential conclusions were based on the principle of mechanical balance, or lever principle, wherein a heavy object near the center balances a light object farther from the center.

For example, using this experimental paradigm, Puffer compared two visual objects differing only with respect to the degree to which they

Product image (cereal bar) is brought to the foreground by moving out of the flat 2-dimensional plane and adding cartoon figures to the background.

The product image (cereal) is in the foreground and the cartoons are in the background.

The product image (large tomato) is closer to the foreground on the left and more to the background on the right through the use of layered graphic elements.

These milk cartons create spatial depth by adding a vista.

Figure 17.2   (See color insert.) Examples of spatial depth on packages.

expressed the third dimension of depth. He found that when spatial depth is present in a visual graphic, that image is perceived to be heavier. Specifically he used two pictures of a railway tunnel. In one picture the mouth of the tunnel was closed tightly by a massive door (i.e., shallow vista). In the other picture, the opening to the tunnel was left open and trains were shown winding their way to the farther end of the tunnel (i.e., deep vista). He fixed the location of one picture on a board and asked the study participants to assign a location to the other picture to create an aesthetically pleasing balance. He found that when the shallow vista was fixed, subjects located the deep vista closer to the fulcrum, suggesting it was heavier than the shallow vista. Similarly, when the deep vista was put in a fixed position, subjects located the shallow vista farther from the fulcrum, suggesting it was lighter.

Based on this finding, we hypothesize that a package that allows for the third dimension, depth, to be depicted looks heavier than the same package that only depicts the graphic elements in two dimensions. We further theorize that if a product image is shown at different locations along this third dimension, its visual weight also varies. Since items that are far away appear smaller than items that are close, if size is held constant, we hypothesize that the product image in the background will appear larger and therefore heavier than the same product image in the foreground of a package facade.

As mentioned before, graphic layering can also express spatial depth because it also creates foreground and background. Similarly, here we also hypothesize that the product image in the background should look heavier than the same-sized product image in the foreground.

Movement or Change of Direction in the Location of the Product Image

When we talk about movement on a package facade, we mean suggested movement, or motion that is indicated by a visual object's form or direction. Specific movement patterns suggest different changed locations, which have implications for visual weight (see Figure 17.3 for examples of movement and direction in package design). In the same way that allowing for depth in a visual image in and of itself creates weight, we suggest that presence of motion or movement in a visual frame may in and of itself create weight. In other words, we believe that this suggestion of movement, or the idea that there is more than one location for the specific graphic element, should convey a kind of weightiness as opposed to the light, ethereal impression of a static element. Although this hypothesis was not specifically tested in the visual design literature, Deng and Kahn (forthcoming) have conducted some preliminary experiments that find support for this conjecture.

Again, although not specifically tested, Puffer's (1903) beliefs about movement in visual space support the conjecture that the suggestion of movement in and of itself conveys weight. He believed that suggested movement has essentially the same effect as if the movement has been already carried out. He suggested that this was consistent with the notion of "perceptual causality" where people perceive a causal relationship even in the absence of evidence of physical causality (Michotte, 1963). Thus the suggestion of movement of an object would cause the perceived visual

Product image (cereal) moves out of the facade.

Left: Direction product image (chili) is to the front and left.
Right: Direction product image (sliced meat) is to the back and to the right.

Product image (cereal) moves up and to the right.

Product image (cereal) moves up.

Movement of Product image (pancakes) in and of itself can add visual weight.

Movement of Product image (cereal) in and of itself can add visual weight.

Figure 17.3 (See color insert.) Examples of movement and direction on packaging.

heaviness of that object to be a function of its initial starting position and the suggested end position. He further proposed that suggested movement implies that the empty space would be filled with the energy of the suggested movement and is hence not empty anymore, again suggesting increased visual weight.

Puffer also believed that the direction of the movement was important in the final estimation of the perceived heaviness of the object. If the end position was at a "heavier" location, the net result should be that the item that has movement is visually heavier than the static item at the same starting position. Similarly, if the end position is at a "lighter" location, the net result should be that the item that has movement is visually lighter than a similarly initially placed static item. However, Puffer started with the assumption that the fulcrum of a visual frame was at its center, whereas we are assuming that the fulcrum of a package facade is at the left. This leads to different conclusions as to where the heavy locations would be. We first describe Puffer's experiments and then hypothesize our conclusions with regard to package facades.

Puffer (1903) conducted a series of experiments using the same experimental paradigm described above to test the weight properties of the influences of end locations. In particular, he examined the direction of a straight line as a whole and the expression of internal energy conveyed by a curve or part of a line. He found that a straight line pointing inward was perceived by subjects to be lighter than a line pointing outward. He speculated that this result was because an inward-pointed line suggests that the line is moving toward the center, whereas an outward-pointed line suggests that the line is moving out from the center. According to the theory of mechanical balance or the principle of the lever, the movement that is farther from the center "weighs more" than movement toward the center. Therefore, the former movement would arrive at a position where the object's weigh "counts" more according to the mechanical balance. Further, a line pointing inward would only fill up space in the inner circle of the visual field, whereas a line pointing outward would fill up space at the outskirt of the visual field. Again the line pointing outward would be perceived to weigh more because "filling up" the outer space would give the perception of weigh more than filling up the inner space.

In another experiment, Puffer fixed a straight line and asked the study participants to assign a location for a "curve out," a line convex to the origin of the perpendicular axes. He then fixed the curve and treated the straight line as the "variable." It was found that when the location of the straight line was fixed, participants assigned a location to the curve that was nearer to the center. This suggests that the curve out is "heavier" than the straight line. Furthermore, the greater curvature of the curve, the "heavier" it is. When Puffer compared a straight line to a "curve in," a line concave to the origin, he found that when the location of the straight line was fixed, subjects assigned a location to the curve that was farther from the center, suggesting that the curve was "lighter" than the straight line. Similarly, the greater curvature of the curve, the "lighter" it was.

Puffer's experiments related to direction of lines and assumed that the fulcrum was the center of the visual field. We are interested in the suggested movement of a product image and are assuming that the visual fulcrum on a package facade is on the left. Using these assumptions, we hypothesize that if the suggested movement of the product image is to the lighter locations of the package facade (i.e., the top, left or front), then the perceived heaviness of that product image would be lighter than a static image that starts in the same initial position. Similarly, if the movement is to the heavier locations (i.e., bottom, right or back), then the perceived heaviness of that product image would be heavier than a static product image that starts in the same position.

Predictions Based on Previous Visual Perception Research

Our spatial/location framework specifically looks at the effects on perceived visual heaviness of location and suggested location of a product image on a package facade. However, we also believe that implications for perceptual visual heaviness principles can be found by building on other recent research on visual perceptual biases. Recent work has provided interesting conclusions on (a) perceived area and volume judgments (see Krishna, 2007 for a review), (b) biases about complex versus simple shapes (see Krishna, 2007 for a review), and (c) the role of attention in assessing perceived volume judgments (Folkes & Matta, 2004). We believe that those previous findings could be extended to form hypotheses about the visual heaviness of product images on package facades.

Predictions Building on Research in Perceived Area and Volume Judgment Biases

Both Arnheim (1974) and Puffer (1903) believed that larger images were perceived to be visually heavier than smaller images. This seems obviously true. Perhaps more interesting, we would hypothesize that the previous research findings that showed biases in perceptual volume judgment (e.g., Raghubir & Krishna, 1999) would also hold for estimations of perceived heaviness, although they would be operating through perceived area judgments rather than through volume judgments. Specifically, we would hypothesize that if the area of a product image was perceived to be larger than the area of another product image (even if the actual areas were the same), the image that was perceived to be larger would also be perceived to be visually heavier. For example, the elongation effect that Raghubir and Krishna (1999) identified in volume perceptions, but have also been found in area perceptions (Anderson & Cuneo, 1978), would suggest that rectangular product images would be visually heavier than square images, and oval images would be visually heavier than circle images, holding actual areas constant in all cases. We would also predict that the moderators found in the previous literature (e.g., the relative salience effect; Krider, Raghuhibr, & Krishna, 2001) would also hold here.

Complex and Novel Shapes Should Be Visually Heavier

Although used in a different context, Krishna (2007) proposed several models that might be adaptable to explaining why complex or novel images might seem to be visually heavier. Adapting her analysis we would suggest that in the context of a package facade, an *information storage model* (Sadalla & Staplin, 1980) would predict that people judge complex or novel images to be bigger than simple or common images because people have to scan and store more information about the complex or novel images. Further, the *analog timing* model (Thorndyke, 1981) that Krishna identifies suggests that when a person visually scans an image, an internal clock is activated that is stopped at the end of the scan. If the scan takes longer for a complex or novel image than for a simple, common image, then the suggestion would be that the complex image was visually heavier.

This proposal is supported by experiments that Puffer (1903) performed on objects that had intrinsic interest, which he defined as novel or changed. Specifically, he ran an experiment using black-and-white reproductions of postage stamps from various countries. During the experiment, one stamp on the board remained unchanged, while the other stamp was changed for each trial, using the change in stamps to manipulate intrinsic interest. Using the experimental paradigm described earlier to measure visual weight, Puffer fixed the location of the unchanged stamp and asked subjects to assign a location to the changed stamp (and vice versa). He found that subjects assigned a location that was closer to the center to the changed stamp as opposed to the unchanged stamp, suggesting that novelty in and of itself is perceived to be weightier.

Role of Attention as a Mental Contaminant

Folkes and Matta (2004) argue that visual attention is directed toward objects as a whole rather than to specific areas of interest in a visual field, following a gestalt theory of attention (e.g., Bloch, 1995). Further, Folkes and Matta argue that because larger-sized objects command more attention in general, subjects are "mentally contaminated" to assume that the reverse is also true: if more attention is given to an object then it is larger. Through experimental evidence, they show that packages that are perceived as attracting more attention are also perceived to be of greater volume than packages that attract less attention.

Extending this theory to perceived visual heaviness of product images, we would propose that product images on a package facade that attract more attention would be perceived to be visually heavier. Package images could attract more attention through size (larger is more attention getting than smaller), color (bright colors attract more attention than dull colors), whether the product image is shown in isolation or not (isolated objects command more attention than those surrounded), complexity of shape (complex shapes command more attention), or objects that have intrinsic interest or novelty (novel, complex objects command more attention than routine, simple objects). The concept that the more attention paid to an object the visually heavier it is, is consistent with Arnheim's (1974) and Puffer's (1903) theories. They argue that attention can be thought of as a type of psychological force that can be measured similarly to the way physical force is measured, gauging the magnitude of psychological force engendered by the consumer's attention.

Conclusions

The influence of packaging features on consumer inferences about product features has received surprisingly little attention in the marketing literature. We offset this void by studying how the location or suggested location of a product picture on its package facade can affect consumers' inferences about the perceived visual weight of the product. Depending on whether product weight is perceived to be a benefit (i.e., the heavier the product the better) or a liability (i.e., the lighter the product the better), perceived visual heaviness is likely to be a cue for product preference. Our central hypothesis is that the location of the product image on the package facade determines its visual weight. In two-dimensional space, we identify the "heavy" locations of a package facade as the bottom or right side, and the "light" locations as the top or left side. When product images are placed in the heavy locations, the products are perceived to be visually heavier. Empirical support for these two-dimensional proposals is found in Deng and Kahn (forthcoming), who also found that the effects are moderated by product category and consumer goals.

If we allow the package facade to have three dimensions, either through the use of graphic perspective, layering of graphic elements, or the addition of a vista to the package, then we propose that if the product image is in the foreground of the space, its visual heaviness is less than if the product image is in the background of the space (controlling for other aspects including the size of the product image on the package). Finally, if we allow for movement or direction in location, we hypothesize that "moving" product images are inherently visually heavier than static images, and further, product images that move to heavier locations (e.g., bottom, right, or back) are visually heavier than product images that move to light locations (e.g., top, left, or front). Although these proposals are based on sound design theory (Arnheim, 1974; Puffer, 1903), they have not been tested empirically in the realm of package design.

These suggested location effects of product imagery on packaging are likely to be moderated by several factors. As mentioned above, all of our hypothesized location effects should be moderated by product category and consumer goals (Deng & Kahn, forthcoming). Further, as found in other research on the influence of graphic package design features on consumer decision making, we would expect these locations effects to be stronger when the consumer is less familiar with the product category (Underwood et al., 2001), under time pressure (Pieters & Warlop, 1999), and less able to judge product quality from intrinsic features of the product (Ziethaml, 1988). The location effects should also be attenuated by how unique the package design is relative to other packages on the shelf. If all product images on competing packages are in the same locations, then the specific effects on perceived visual heaviness will be attenuated. If the product image locations are in contrast with those on competing pack-

Heavy Locations: Bottom and Right	Light Locations: Top and Left

Figure 17.1 Two-dimensional space.

Product image (cereal bar) is brought to the foreground by moving out of the flat 2-dimensional plane and adding cartoon figures to the background.

The product image (cereal) is in the foreground and the cartoons are in the background.

The product image (large tomato) is closer to the foreground on the left and more to the background on the right through the use of layered graphic elements.

These milk cartons create spatial depth by adding a vista.

Figure 17.2   Examples of spatial depth on packages.

Product image (cereal) moves out of the facade.

Left: Direction product image (chili) is to the front and left.
Right: Direction product image (sliced meat) is to the back and to the right.

Product image (cereal) moves up and to the right.

Product image (cereal) moves up.

Movement of Product image (pancakes) in and of itself can add visual weight.

Movement of Product image (cereal) in and of itself can add visual weight.

Figure 17.3 Examples of movement and direction on packaging.

ages, the location effects on visual heaviness will be magnified (Deng & Kahn, forthcoming).

We also hypothesize that previous marketing research on visual perceptual biases will have a natural extension into visual heaviness perceptions. Specifically, volume and area biases, such as the elongation effect (Raghubir & Krishna, 1999), should operate similarly in visual heaviness perception. For example, we would predict that rectangular product images would be visually heavier than square images, and oval images would be visually heavier than circle images. We would also predict that complexity in product images, either through unusual shapes, intrinsic interest or novelty, or complex photographic or graphic design, would also increase visual weight, similar to the findings on perceived volume and size (Krishna, 2007).

Finally, we predict that consumer attention is likely to serve an interesting role with regard to perceived visual weight. Similar to the mental contamination argument suggested by Folkes and Matta (2004), we hypothesize that the more attention a consumer pays to a product image, the visually heavier that image will appear to be. This suggests that larger, more brightly colored, more novel or interesting product images should be seen as visually heavier than smaller, duller, more routine images. Further, if the product image is isolated on the package, it should seem visually heavier than if it is surrounded by many other visual elements that would detract from the attention paid to the product image itself.

Although these latter proposals seem to follow naturally from previous research and would be support by design theory (e.g., Arnheim, 1974; Puffer, 1903), they have not been empirically tested. Wc believe our framework and subsequent observations based on previous research provides a compelling agenda for future research to empirically test these conjectures.

References

Anderson, N. H., & Cuneo, D. O. (1978, December). The height + width rule in children's judgments of quantity. *Journal of Experimental Psychology: General, 107*(4), 335–378.

Arnheim, R. (1974). *Art and visual perception: A psychology of the creative eye.* Berkeley: University of California Press.

Bloch, P. (1995, July). Seeking the ideal form: Product design and consumer response. *Journal of Marketing, 59*, 16–29.

Bourassa, D. C., McManus, I. C., & Bryden, M. P. (1996). Handedness and eye-dominance: A meta-analysis of their relationship. *Laterality, 1*, 5–34.

Coelho Do Vale, R., Pieters, R., & Zeelenberg, M. (2008). Flying under the radar: Perverse package size effects on consumption self-regulation. *Journal of Consumer Research, 35,* 380–390.

Coren, S., & Porac, C. (1976). Size accentuation in the dominant eye. *Nature, 260,* 527–528.

Deng, X., & Kahn, B. E. (work in progress). When less is more: An examination of the effects of location, movement, and color on consumers' visual weight perception.

Deng, X., & Kahn, B. E. (2009). Is your product on the right side? The "location effect" on perceived product heaviness and package evaluation. *Journal of Marketing Research.*

Dickson, P. R., & Sawyer, A. G. (1990). The price knowledge and search of supermarket shoppers. *Journal of Marketing, 54,* 42–53.

Feldman, J., & Lynch, J. Jr. (1988). Self-generated validity and other effects of measurement on belief, attitude, intention, and behavior. *Journal of Applied Psychology, 73,* 421–435.

Folkes, V., & Matta, S. (2004). The effect of package shape on consumers' judgments of product volume: Attention as a mental contaminant. *Journal of Consumer Research, 31,* 390–401.

Houston, M. J., Childers, T. L., & Heckler, S. E. (1987). Picture-word consistency and the elaborative processing of advertisements. *Journal of Marketing Research, 24,* 359–369.

Kisielius, J., & Sternthal, B. (1986). Examining the vividness controversy: An availability-valence interpretation. *Journal of Consumer Research, 12,* 418–431.

Krider, R., Raghubir, P., & Krishna, A. (2001). Pizza—pi or squared?: The effect of perceived area on price perceptions. *Marketing Science, 20*(4), 405–425.

Krishna, A. (2006). Interaction of senses: The effect of vision versus touch on the elongation bias. *Journal of Consumer Research, 32,* 557–566.

Krishna, A. (2007). *Spatial perception research: An integrative review of length, area, volume and number perception.* University of Michigan, Working Paper.

MacInnis, D. J., & Price, L. L. (1987). The role of imagery in information processing: Review and extensions. *Journal of Consumer Research, 13,* 473–491.

McGill, A. L., & Anand, P. (1989). The effect of imagery on information processing strategy in a multiattribute choice task. *Marketing Letters, 1,* 7–16.

Mefferd, R. B., Jr., & Wieland, B. A. (1969). Influence of eye dominance on the apparent centers of simple horizontal lines. *Perceptual and Motor Skills, 28,* 847–850.

Michotte, A. (1963). *The perception of causality* (T. R. Miles & E. Miles, Trans.). London: Methun. (English translation of original 1954 edition).

Moorman, C. (1996). A quasi-experiment to assess the consumer and informational determinants of nutrition information processing activities: The case of the nutrition labeling and education act. *Journal of Public Policy and Marketing, 15,* 28–44.

Olsen, J. C., & Jacoby, J. (1972). Cue utilization in the quality perception process. In M. Venkatesan (Ed.), *Proceedings of the third annual conference of the Association of Consumer Research* (pp. 167–179). Iowa City, IA: Association of Consumer Research.

Pavio, A. (1986). *Mental representations. A dual coding approach.* New York: Oxford University Press.

Pieters, R., & Warlop, L. (1999). Visual attention during brand choice: The impact of time pressure and task motivation. *International Journal of Research in Marketing, 16,* 1–16.

Point of Purchase Advertising Institute. (1995). *The 1995 POPAI consumer buying habits study.* Englewood, NJ: Author.

Porac, C., & Coren, S. (1976). The dominant eye. *Psychological Bulletin, 83,* 880–897.

Posner, M. I., Nissen, M. J, & Klein, R. M. (1976). Visual dominance: An information-processing account of its origins and significant. *Psychological Review, 83,* 157–171.

Puffer, E. D. (1903). Studies in symmetry. *Psychological Monograph, 4,* 467–539.

Raghubir, P., & Greenleaf, E. A. (2006). Ratios in proportion: What should the shape of the package be? *Journal of Marketing, 70,* 95–107.

Raghubir, P., & Krishna, A. (1999). Vital dimensions in volume perception: Can the eye fool the stomach? *Journal of Marketing Research, 36,* 313–326.

Richardson, P. S. (1994). Cue effects on evaluations of national and private-label brands. In C. W. Park & D. C. Smith (Eds.), *Marketing theory and applications* (Vol. 5, pp. 165–171). Chicago: American Marketing Association.

Russo, J. E., Staelin, R., Nolan, C. A., Russell, G. J., & Metcalf, B. L. (1986). Nutrition information in the supermarket. *Journal of Consumer Research, 13,* 48–70.

Sadalla, E. K., & Staplin, L. J. (1980). The perception of traversed distance: Intersections. *Environment and Behavior, 12*(2), 167–182.

Scott, M. L., Nowlis, S. M., Mandel, N., & Morales, A. C. (2008). The effects of reduced food size and package size on the consumption behavior of restrained and unrestrained eaters. *Journal of Consumer Research, 35,* 391–405.

Scott, R. B., & Sumner, F. C. (1949). Eyedness as affecting results obtained with the Howard and Dolman depth perception apparatus. *Journal of Psychology, 27,* 479–482.

Thorndyke, P. W. (1981), Distance estimation from cognitive maps. *Cognitive Psychology, 13,* 526–550.

Underwood, R. L., & Klein, N. M. (2002). Packages as brand communication: Effects of product pictures on consumer responses to the package and brand. *Journal of Marketing Theory and Practice, 10,* 58–68.

Underwood, R. L., Klein, N. M., & Burke, R. R. (2001). Packaging communication: Attentional effects of product imagery. *Journal of Product and Brand Management, 10,* 403–422.

Underwood, R. L., & Ozanne, J. L. (1998). Is your package an effective communicator? A normative framework for increasing the communicative competence of packaging. *Journal of Marketing Communication, 4*, 207–220.

Wansink, B. (1996). Can package size accelerate usage volume? *Journal of Marketing, 60*, 1–14.

Wansink, B., & Van Ittersum, K. (2003). Bottom up! The influence of elongation on pouring and consumption volume. *Journal of Consumer Research, 30*, 455–463.

Wolfflin, H. (1950). *Principles of art history: The problem of the development of style in later art* (M. D. Hottinger, Trans.). New York: Dover.

Yang, S., & Raghubir, P. (2005). Can bottles speak volumes? The effect of package shape on how much to buy. *Journal of Retailing, 81*, 269–281.

Zeithaml, V. (1988). Consumer perceptions of price, quality, and value: A means-end model and synthesis of evidence. *Journal of Marketing, 52*, 2–22.

Section V

Taste

18

The Gist of Gustation
An Exploration of Taste, Food, and Consumption

Aradhna Krishna and Ryan S. Elder

Consider in detail your last vacation, not the business trip you went on or the conference you attended, but your last therapeutic, relaxing break from the world. If you were to recount your trip to a colleague, what would you begin with? Assuming you didn't lose your luggage or experience a 4-hour delay at Chicago's O'Hare Airport, but rather had a generally positive experience, you might begin with the weather but then quickly move to the food. Of all the multiple sensory pleasures you experienced throughout the duration of your trip, the ones that gave you the most joy and excitement, likely involved food. Indeed, even when planning the trip our solicitations from friends on what to do primarily revolve around where to eat and when.

Food, including the taste sensations food gives us, plays a vital role in our lives, both from a physical, survival perspective as well from a social and emotional one. Given the importance of food in our lives, it is not surprising that billions of dollars are spent annually on food marketing. However, it is quite perplexing that research within consumer behavior and psychology has largely overlooked this arena. This chapter will lay the foundation for future research and hopefully spark scholarly interest in this valuable and fruitful domain.

The gustatory journey we take within this chapter begins with a basic and physiological perspective of taste. Citing literature in biology, neuroscience, psychology, and consumer behavior, we show the underpinnings of how taste perceptions are generated, as well as the impact marketers can have in the process. We next present timely research on actual and perceived consumption, highlighting the effects of perceptual biases, product packaging, as well as labels on what we eat as consumers. Finally, we introduce novel ideas for future research, such as the social impact on taste perceptions and consumption, the ritualized and mythical powers of food, and the cross-modal interaction of taste with the other senses, including the unique case of lexical-gustatory synesthesia. Exploring the impact of marketing on taste perceptions and consumption experiences presents a promising future for both academics and practitioners alike.

Taste

When we think of taste, most initially localize the sensation to the mouth. Specifically, we think of the tongue, with its numerous taste receptors (taste buds) and the variety of taste perceptions these afford. The taste buds themselves are onion-shaped structures on the tongue and in other parts of the mouth with 50 to 100 taste cells in each bud. These cells provide information to the brain (primarily in the insula and operculum) based on the chemical qualities of the food in the mouth that form the basic sense of taste.

It is popularly believed that certain areas of the tongue pick up the different tastes of sweet, salty, sour, bitter (and umami, discussed later in this chapter). In fact, many illustrations have been made of the tongue with these areas demarcated. However, recent evidence from neuroscientific studies suggests that this is indeed not true; areas of the tongue are *not* specific to certain tastes, but rather the distribution of tastes across the tongue is rather uniform. This is because the sensory nerve fibers contained in the taste buds capture all of the different tastes (Lindemann, 2001). Thus, the different taste sensations are found in all areas of the tongue (Huang et al., 2006).

Despite the initial thought of taste stemming from sensations based solely in the mouth, our intuition and experience tell us that taste is considerably more complex. We next highlight research explicating the factors that contribute to a full composition of taste perceptions.

Taste Is All Five Senses

This section is based on research done by Elder and Krishna (2010). We begin with a stimulus used in one of their many experiments:

> Emerald Aisle popcorn delivers the smell of a movie theater in your own home. You'll see the perfect amount of butter and salt in every handful. With its

delicious, buttery texture and a crunch that's music to your ears, Emerald Aisle popcorn is the perfect choice for all your snacking.

This food ad tries to involve all our senses. Why? As discussed earlier, humans can merely distinguish between five pure tastes, that is, there are basically five disparate biochemical and cellular interactions in our bodies related to taste: sweet, salty, sour, bitter, and umami. The last, umami, has recently been discovered by Japanese researchers and its approximate meaning is "deliciousness" or "savory." It refers to the taste from monosodium glutamate (MSG), the taste of pure protein. Every single taste from milk to chocolate to wine to prosciutto is a combination of these five taste sensations. However, we can distinguish tastes with great sophistication. How does that come about? All other tastes that humans perceive besides the basic five are a result of the input from the other senses: from smell (how the food smells), touch (temperature, fattiness, and other textures of food, painfulness such as from hot spices), vision (how the food looks, aesthetic appeal including color), and also audition (e.g., the sound of the potato chip cracking when you bite it).

Even though we eat regularly, we are not very good at discerning one taste from another when using only our sense of taste. Thus, when we cannot smell or see the food, it is difficult to tell a potato apart from an apple, or red wine apart from coffee (Herz, 2007, p. 187). One reason for this limited capability is the few distinct tastes that we can detect, only five as mentioned earlier. As such, what we find "tasty" may have little to do with the "taste" sense, but may be largely dependent on the other senses and even other cognitive inputs.

How Do Other Outside Influences Affect Taste Perception?

Research on sensory perception within marketing has largely focused on the study of vision (see Krishna, 2007 for a review), with the other senses receiving scattered attention; however, this attention is intensifying (see Peck & Childers, 2008 for a review). Peck and Childers (2008) claim that of the 81 sensory studies in consumer behavior focusing on the other four senses (aside from vision), 28 are from the past 5 years. Clearly, sensory perception and sensory marketing are growing fields, and there is much research yet to be done. One factor that makes the research difficult, but also presents many opportunities for research, is the potential impact of outside influences on sensory perception. Since sensory perception by its very nature is ambiguous or subjective, it is more susceptible to such out-side influences (Hoch & Ha, 1986). Consistent with this, there is a fair body of research that examines the effect of various factors on taste perception. We organize this review by the factors that affect taste.

Taste and Smell

Smell is considered to be one of the most important drivers of taste perception (Small & Prescott, 2005). The combination of smell and taste generates the concept of flavor. Smell has such an important role in taste largely because of the nose's close proximity to the mouth. We smell the food when it is outside our mouth (orthonasal) and once again when we are actively chewing on the food (retronasal; Rozin, 1982). This is the reason why eating something unthinkable, like raisin pie, is suddenly tolerable when blocking the air passageway by pinching your nose.

Taste and Color

Much of the research on the interaction of vision and taste has looked at the impact of product color. DuBose, Cardello, and Maller (1980) show that participants blind to the color of a fruit-flavored drink can accurately identify only 20% of the flavors compared to 100% when they can see the color of the drink. Additionally, when the color is deliberately manipulated so that a cherry drink is colored orange, 40% of the participants identify the flavor as orange. Although receiving mixed support, the general consensus is that increasing color intensity also has a strong impact on increasing taste intensity (DuBose et al., 1980; Johnson & Clydesdale, 1982).

Recently, Hoegg and Alba (2007a) show the impact of several extrinsic cues for orange juice, including brand name, price, and region of origin, on taste discrimination and taste preference. Interestingly, the authors find that color is used by subjects as the dominant input in taste discrimination, whereas brand name is used as the determinant of preferences. They also find that brand names have an effect on taste preference only after a learning phase (when the range of tastes has been learned by the subjects).

Taste and Sound

Visualize yourself biting into a bright green, refreshingly cold stalk of celery. What if one important element was missing—the audible crunch? Undoubtedly this would affect your perceptions of the celery, both in perceived freshness and in actual perceived taste. Zampini and Spence (2004) provide empirical support for this process. The authors show that changing the loudness and the frequency of the sound a potato chip makes when bitten impacts how fresh the chip is perceived to be. Participants in the experiment were in a soundproof booth eating in front of a microphone. The participants also wore headphones so that the sound of biting the chips was relayed to their headphones, bypassing their natural perceptions. This allowed the experimenters to alter the sound frequency and volume. Interestingly, the louder the sound of the bite, the fresher the participants thought the chips were.

Taste and Haptics

Krishna and Morrin (2008) explore the effect of an extrinsic cue, product haptics, on taste perception. In a series of experiments, they show that the haptic quality of glasses from which water and other drinks are consumed can affect taste perception, such that water from a firm disposable glass tastes better than water from a flimsy disposable glass. Interestingly, haptics affect taste for consumers who are high in "autotelic need for touch" (a need to touch for the sake of touch alone and not for any functional purpose; see Peck & Childers, 2003) and not people who are low in need for touch. The authors explain this by suggesting that people who are high in need for touch, over time, have formed connections in memory between haptic and other properties of objects, so that they know instinctively when haptics are diagnostic for a decision or not. In the case of the taste of water, the haptic properties of the glass or bottle in which the water is given are clearly not diagnostic and are not taken much into account.

Taste and Brand Name

Researchers have examined the impact of brand name on perceived beer characteristics (Allison & Uhl, 1964) and taste preferences and discrimination for orange juice (Hoegg & Alba 2007a, 2007b). Allison and Uhl (1964) explore the impact of brand name on subsequent taste preferences. The authors administer a blind taste test of beers (by removing identifying labels) to experienced beer drinkers and find that participants cannot correctly discriminate between the beers. However, when the beers are labeled, the participants rate their favorite beer higher than the others.

Hoegg and Alba (2007b) build on the premise that people minimize differences between stimuli within the same category and exaggerate differences between stimuli in different categories, thus proposing that "labels might influence perception at the boundaries but not necessarily within a category" (p. 9). They show experimentally that when subjects do not learn the taste range of a stimulus (orange juice), taste trumps brand in discrimination tasks (i.e., subjects can accurately discriminate between taste of the juices). However, when there is no learning phase, brand trumps taste (juice pairs of the same brand but different taste are perceived more similar than juice pairs of different brands but similar taste).

Ads and Taste

In a series of three experiments, Elder and Krishna (2010) show how ads can also affect taste perception. They demonstrate that ads for food do not merely affect awareness and intention to purchase, but can also affect perceived taste. In particular, they show that ads incorporating multiple versus a single sense can lead to heightened taste perceptions. They suggest that this occurs through the ad's effect on generating positive sensory thoughts and consequent sensory perception. They also show that the effect is moderated by cognitive load; when there is a cognitive load, multiple sense ads have a weaker positive effect. In a typical experiment, they show consumers either a single sense or a multiple sense ad, balanced on the number of pieces of information subjects get and also the appeal of the ad itself. Then subjects taste the food product that the ad was for and provide taste ratings and other thoughts about the food. They show the effect to be robust across chewing gum, popcorn, and potato chips.

Ingredients and Taste

Prior studies have also examined the effect of nutritional information on perceived taste (Raghunathan, Naylor, & Hoyer, 2006; Wansink, Park, Sonka, & Morganosky, 2000), of fat amount in meat or perceived leanness and taste of the meat (Levin & Gaeth, 1988), and of beer ingredients on choice of beer (Lee, Frederick, & Ariely, 2006).

To elaborate on some of these studies, Raghunathan et al. (2006) examined the effect of labeling a food item as either healthy or unhealthy. The authors show that consumers implicitly hold an assumption that food categorized as unhealthy is better tasting than healthy food. Similarly, when participants are left to infer that the product is healthy due to its ingredients (i.e., soy), taste perceptions are lowered (Wansink et al., 2000).

Other researchers have examined the impact of nutritional value on perceived taste. When identical samples of ground beef are labeled 75% lean versus 25% fat, the former is rated as being leaner and higher quality than the latter (Levin & Gaeth, 1988).

Addressing a similar issue of "ingredients," Lee et al. (2006) convincingly show that such extrinsic cues not only alter taste preferences, but actually change one's taste experience. In a series of three experiments, consumers at local pubs were asked to participate in short taste tests of beer. One of the beers was a standard, unaltered beer, while the other contained an additional ingredient: a small amount of balsamic vinegar, which makes the beer superficially less appealing but actually enhances the flavor. By carefully utilizing three experimental conditions—a blind taste test, where the additional ingredient was not given; a before condition, where the subject was told the ingredient before the taste test; and finally, an after condition, where the subject was told the ingredient following the sampling—the authors show that the information of the additional ingredient does not merely alter preferences, but actually changes the consumption experience. The results show that the after condition reports similar preferences as the blind condition, but differed significantly from the before condition. Having the additional knowledge of the balsamic vinegar additive altered the taste experience.

Several researchers have shown the impact of both intrinsic (primarily sensory) and extrinsic cues on taste perceptions. Others researchers have focused on the effects at the individual level characteristics such as obesity (Steinberg & Yalch, 1978), and cognitive states (e.g., level of distraction, Nowlis & Shiv, 2005; Shiv & Nowlis, 2004). Given taste's documented susceptibility to external influences, the study of marketing and taste perceptions warrants further attention.

In addition to focusing on the construction of taste perceptions and the impact that marketing can ultimately have on theses perceptions, we next choose to focus on consumption. Specifically, we discuss relevant research addressing perceived versus actual consumption. The results of this research hold many implications for marketing, public policy, and general consumer well-being.

Consumption and Perceived Consumption

Standard portions, as defined by the federal government for the Food Guide Pyramid and the Dietary Guidelines for Americans, are considerably smaller than portions typically consumed by the public (Young & Nestle, 2003). Moreover, there is limited consistency in the range of portion sizes offered across different food and drink providers. Both the discrepancy between the standard portion and the typically consumed portion and the inconsistency in portions sizes across providers contribute to people's uncertainty about the appropriate amount to eat (Young & Nestle, 1998).

Pierre Chandon, in his chapter in this book, highlights many factors affecting consumption. Here, we focus on some aspects of consumption not covered in detail in Chandon's chapter. We also present findings that show that what we actually consume and what we think we have consumed can be quite different.

Visual Biases and Consumption

Over 50 years ago, Piaget studied children's perceptions of volume. In a typical Piagetian experiment, colored liquid was poured from a tall cylinder into a shorter and wider cylinder. The height of the liquid in the latter cylinder was lower. Children were then asked whether the volume of the liquid had remained the same or had reduced. In a series of studies, Piaget found that primary schoolchildren appeared to only use the height of the container while making volume judgments; they believed that the volume had reduced when the liquid was poured into a wider glass (Piaget, 1967, 1968; Piaget, Inhelder, & Szeminska, 1960). The predominant use of a single dimension—height—to make three-dimensional judgments was termed the *centration hypothesis*.

This simple experiment has been replicated many times and the effect is found to be very robust even among adults and with frequently purchased packaged goods (Raghubir & Krishna, 1999). Many other visual biases have also been shown over the years, and a summary of the ones applying to three-dimensional objects is presented in Table 18.1. An overview of visual biases as a whole may be found in Krishna's (2007) work. As Table 18.1 shows, there is research on volume estimation biases within a form class (e.g., within cylinders) and volume estimation biases across form class (e.g., cylinders vs. cuboids of equal volume). Researchers have further studied how volume perception changes as the size of an object changes and proposed theories of volume estimation biases. Table 18.1 also provides a summary of some factors that have been shown to affect actual and perceived consumption. Thus, quite a few researchers have shown that people consume more if they have larger package sizes (Folkes, Martin, & Gupta, 1993; Wansink, 1996; Wansink & Park, 2001) and also if products are more salient, visible, conveniently packaged, hedonic, or conveniently located (Chandon & Wansink, 2002; Painter, Wansink, & Hieggelke, 2002; Wansink & Ray, 1996).

TABLE 18.1 Volume Perceptions, Choice, Consumption, Satisfaction

Perceived Volume Across Different Shapes Within Form-Class

Centration hypothesis: Use of height to make volume judgments	Piaget et al., 1960
Elongation hypothesis: Use of height/width ratio to make volume judgment	Frayman & Dawson, 1981; Holmberg, 1975

Perceived Volume Due to Different Shapes Across Form-Class

Mixed results:

Cylinders < cuboids (even though taller)	Holmberg, 1975
Cylinders and tetrahedrons > spheres and cubes; Cubes < spheres	Frayman & Dawson, 1981
Elongation hypothesis: Use of height/width ratio to make volume judgment	Frayman & Dawson, 1981; Holmberg, 1975

Perceived Volume Due to Increasing Size of the Same Shape

Perceived Size Is an Underestimate

The degree of underestimation increases as the object grows larger and is not contingent on the shape of the figure, Perceived size = Actual Size^e, where e < 1	Techtsoonian, 1965
The exponent range of 0.50–1.00 appears fairly robust across 3D figures:	Baird, Romer, & Stein, 1970; Frayman & Dawson, 1981; Moyer et. al., 1978

Theories Proposed for Perceived Volume Shape and Size Biases

Information Selection—people underutilize one or more dimensions in their judgments of size	Verge & Bogartz, 1978
Information Integration—different rules have been suggested for integrating information, but all dimensions are assumed to be appropriately utilized	Anderson & Cuneo, 1978
Psychophysical model of area judgment—dimensions are used per their salience in a multiplicative information integration model	Krider, Raghubir, & Krishna, 2001

Perceived and Actual Consumption

Perceived-size consumption illusion:

A reversal in perceptions of volume pre- versus post-consumption. More elongated containers lead to greater (smaller) pre-consumption (post-consumption) perceived volume, and to greater actual consumption.	Raghubir & Krishna, 1999; Wansink & van Ittersum, 2003
People consume more if they have larger package sizes	Folkes et al., 1993; Wansink, 1996; Wansink & Park, 2001

Continued

TABLE 18.1   Volume Perceptions, Choice, Consumption, Satisfaction (*Continued*)

If products are more salient, visible, conveniently packaged, hedonic, or conveniently located, then they will be consumed more	Chandon & Wansink, 2002; Painter, et al., 1994; Wansink & Ray, 1996
Reversal of perceived-size consumption illusion when sight versus touch is used for input	Krishna, 2006

Perceived Size, Actual Consumption, and Perceived Consumption

There is a rich literature on expectancy disconfirmation (see Stangor & McMillan, 1992 for a review). While the expectancy disconfirmation literature in social psychology focuses on traits and behaviors of others as inputs, some expectancy disconfirmation literature in cognitive psychology focuses on self-experienced sensory inputs. A highly researched effect of this genre is the size–weight illusion (SWI). Charpentier (1891) first demonstrated the SWI, where bigger objects of the same weight were perceived to be lighter. For example, a pound of cotton wool felt lighter than a pound of lead. A number of explanations have been proposed for the SWI illusion. The most accepted explanations are based on expectancy theory. People expect the smaller object to be lighter. However, when they actually lift the small object, their experience contradicts their expectation, leading to a contrast effect. The opposite is true of the large object. This results in the smaller object being perceived to be heavier than the larger object. Across seven experiments, Raghubir and Krishna (1999) show that subjects expect taller containers to contain more than an equivolume short, fat container when they see them. However, after subjects drink from the container, the effect reverses, such that people think they have drunk more from a short, fat versus from a tall, thin container. The same expectancy argument applies: People think that the tall (short) container will contain more (less) but are surprised when they drink from it. They more than compensate when they judge perceived volume. Based on the perceived volume results, Raghubir and Krishna (1999) propose and show that actual volume consumed will be larger from the taller container. Building off Raghubir and Krishna's work, Wansink and van Ittersum (2003) show that children, adults, and even bartenders will pour more into short, fat glasses versus tall, thin ones, and also consume more from the short, fat glasses.

Krishna (2006) then shows that when only touch is used to judge volume (and not vision), the short, fat container is perceived to be larger than the equivolume tall, thin one. This is because information on diameter is haptically obtained by the enclosure exploratory procedure (see the chapter by Roberta Klatzky in this book), which is a natural procedure, whereas information on height is obtained by contour following along the outside of the glass, which is less natural.

Labels and Consumption

In the current context of large portion sizes and consumer uncertainty about appropriate food intake, Aydinoglu and Krishna (2009) propose that the size labels chosen by vendors can have a major impact on consumers' purchase and consumption behavior. Additionally, the same portion size can be called small or medium across vendors, as can be seen with soft drinks and French fries sold at fast food establishments (e.g., compare McDonald's with Wendy's for soft drinks). They propose that the mental representation of the size of a product may be construed from a combination of the actual size of the product and the semantic cue (the size label and other verbal descriptors) associated with it. Consumers are faced with the task of integrating these two pieces of information in order to make their size estimations. Aydinoglu and Krishna then demonstrate that size labels affect size judgments and also affect actual and perceived consumption. In a series of laboratory studies and one field study, they show that consumers rely to a large extent on size labels to provide them direction in estimating the size of food and drink items, such that the same portion of food labeled small versus medium will result in a perception of smaller size, greater consumption, but less perceived consumption. Interestingly, the effect is asymmetric in that larger items labeled smaller are credible, but the reverse is not true. Aydinoglu and Krishna explain this by consumers' natural skepticism for marketer intentions: Marketers would want a small item to appear larger, but not the other way around. Another reason for the asymmetry is that large items being labeled small allow consumers to indulge in guiltless gluttony. An implication of their results is that consumers can continue to consume large sizes that are labeled as small and feel that they have not consumed too much. This can clearly have dire consequences for health reasons. They also show that the impact of size labels is moderated by people's nutrition consciousness. Consumers who are concerned about being accurate about nutrition intake are less prone to the size label effect. Hence, making consumers more nutrition conscious may reduce the effect of size labels that marketers adopt.

Krishna (2005) explores the existence of a multitude of size labels that exist today (e.g., petite, small, short, medium, tall, large, super-quencher, extra-large, jumbo) for soft drinks. She tests whether these newly coined words have somehow managed to get a common understanding across consumers and finds that they have, leading to consequences in both actual and perceived consumption.

Package Sizes, Self-Control, and Consumption

Do Vale, Pieters, and Zeelenberg (2008) show that the belief that small package sizes lead to greater self-control and less consumption may be misfounded. They demonstrate that activating self-regulatory concerns has no impact on consumption when tempting products (e.g., potato chips) come in small sizes. However, it does when they come in large sizes. They argue that when chips are in small packages, consumers will not think they need to exert self-control, whereas when chips come in large packages they will have to. Small packages may be perceived as an external self-control device and thus are all right to consume fully. As such, small package sizes will "fly under the radar" of consumer vigilance. Scott, Nowlis, Mandel, and Morales (2008) similarly show that restrained eaters consume more calories from small food in small packages versus unrestrained eaters who consume more calories from large food in large packages. They found that subjects who cared most about counting calories (especially chronic dieters) were the ones who consumed the most calories when packages were smaller. The small packages seem to undermine the good intentions of dieters, who took the small packaging and bite-sized sweets to be like diet food.

In contrast to this, Wansink, Geier, and Rozin (2009) show that putting consumption interrupters in boxes will decrease both actual and perceived consumption. In their experiment, they had 59 subjects eat from a tube of 82 potato chips while watching television. In the experimental chip boxes, they put red chips after every 7 or 14 chips in the box. They show that consumers eat more chips without interrupters than with: They eat 45 chips with no interrupters, 24 with interrupters after 14 chips, and 20 with interrupters after 7 chips. In their paper they seem to claim that small package sizes will also act as consumption interrupters. But, clearly this was not the case for all consumers, as seen above. Thus, it may be a good idea to examine the work of Wansink et al. (2009) in conjunction with the work of Do Vale et al. (2008) and Scott et al. (2008), which also account for self-control on the part of consumers.

Emotional Calibration and Consumption

Kidwell, Hardesty, and Childers (2008) point to a completely new direction for research on consumption, namely, the effect of mood and emotions on consumption. They show that consumers' emotional ability (the ability to interpret their own emotions, realize how they make them feel, and regulate their emotions; using emotional information to obtain a desired outcome) and emotional confidence (confidence in their emotional ability) also affects their food choices in terms of their impulsive eating and caloric intake; there is immense room for research here. For instance, one could study the interaction effects of mood and gender, age, or marital status on consumption, why some people eat more when they are happy and others when they are depressed, and if specific foods are eaten more in certain moods.

Food as a Social Activity

Emotions and consumption, as well as emotions and taste perception, provide intriguing opportunities for future research. One such opportunity is to explore the impact of a social consumption setting on both the amount of consumption and the sensory pleasure derived from eating. Relevant research has shown that the actual amount of consumption can both increase or decrease with the presence of others (for a thorough review see Herman, Roth, & Pulivy, 2003). Eating with others increases the duration of the meal, leading to more consumption; however, if the others we are eating with are strangers, then we tend to follow normative consumption rules and eat only as much as or less than the others eat.

Perhaps more interesting than the amount of consumption is the pleasure derived from consumption within social settings. To the best of our knowledge, researchers have not examined the impact of the presence of others on taste perceptions. Presumably, eating socially would generate positive mood effects that would then be transferred to the meal. Therefore, the very act of eating with others would lead to heightened taste perceptions. Over time, this relationship could become so well learned that merely portraying a food item as a social product could enhance its taste. For example, advertisements for food items could show a product typically consumed in isolation (e.g., frozen foods) in social situations (e.g., a party). If this image were to remain with the consumer, taste perceptions on a subsequent consumption occasion may be altered versus if the product was advertised in an individualized manner.

Across cultures food is consumed socially, oftentimes in a celebratory manner or as a reward. Most of our defining events and accomplishments in life are celebrated with food. Religious and secular holiday traditions center around meals (e.g., Thanksgiving, Ramadan, Diwali, Christmas, Fourth of July, Labor Day, and even Valentine's Day), where family and friends gather to feast. Yet the reason why food plays such a substantial role in our celebrations and social events needs further explication. As such, the social nature of food deserves more scholarly attention from psychology and consumer behavior researchers.

Mythical Powers of Foods

In addition to playing a role in social celebration, certain foods have long been posited to hold somewhat mythical powers that promote consumption, creating in essence, "yes" foods, while others (primarily animals) are strictly forbidden, creating taboo or "no" foods. These allowances and restrictions in diet stem largely from religion but are also derived from folk legend and popular culture.

Foods are not merely eaten for their taste or nutritional value but are also consumed to bestow upon the eater certain powers or desired states. For example, a considerable amount of research has explored the aphrodisiacal powers of certain foods. Foods such as oysters, bananas, vanilla, and chocolate have historically been used to increase sexual potency, both because of perceived active ingredients and phallic representativeness. Among the listed aphrodisiacs, chocolate has received the most scholarly attention, although conclusive evidence of its role as an aphrodisiac has proved somewhat illusive. Still, chocolate can cause the release of serotonin, which is a neurotransmitter contributing to feelings of happiness (Salonia et al., 2006). Regardless of any actual biological effects from the food on subsequent physical or cognitive state, the desired state may be actualized due to a placebo effect (Irmak, Block, Fitzsimons, 2005; Shiv, Carmon, & Ariely, 2005). This placebo effect possibility, occurring largely below consciousness, introduces many realms for consumer behavior researchers to explore.

Other "yes" foods and drinks fulfill normative, ritualized roles with their consumption. Champagne accompanies nearly every major celebration, chicken soup is prescribed for practically all the infirm, and hedonically rich cakes conclude most parties. In fact, in the United States, some foods are so inextricably linked to events and locations that one's experience is unfulfilled without their consumption. It is practically a sin to attend a professional baseball game and not eat a hot dog, your trip to Chicago lacks completion until a deep-dish pizza is consumed, and all the rides at the fair will not satisfy you until you have had a funnel cake. Creating such a strong attachment between an attraction and a food product or brand is a goal pursued by many marketers. In the examples above, marketers would ideally mandate that the champagne has to be Korbel, the chicken soup Campbell's, and the cakes from Baskin-Robbins in order to satisfy normative demands.

Within the current discussion, taboos or "no" foods come largely from restrictions placed within religion. The vast majority of these restrictions are in relation to animals, as meat is historically more likely to become unclean and carry diseases than vegetation (Fessler & Navarrete, 2003). Fessler and Navarrete (2003) find that meat was nearly five times more likely to be a tabooed item than all other sources of food combined. This is very interesting to note, as meat is also one of the most sought after sources of food in nearly every culture. In addition to meat, tabooed foods items include those that are sacred as well as those that are perceived harmful. Further, some items are prohibited due to their symbolic nature, particularly in respect to sexuality and procreation. For example, the Wik-mungkan, an Australian Aboriginal tribe, has numerous restrictions on who can eat what and from whom (McKnight, 1973). Children and the aged are allowed to eat practically anything, as health and strength are of primary concern; however, adult males are not allowed to receive yams, turtle eggs, or animals killed by the spear from other males, especially from their son or brother-in-law, due to their sexual symbolism. Hence, there are numerous reasons that foods are labeled as "no" foods, most of them not directly linked to the actual taste of the food. However, discovering the cognitive inhibitions that lead individuals to avoid certain nontaboo foods presents a promising avenue for future research. In particular, finding ways to increase consumption of healthy "no" foods (e.g., broccoli, brussels sprouts) would have several consequential implications for public health.

Taste as a Stimulator for Other Senses

As mentioned in the beginning of this chapter, the sense of taste heavily relies on the other four senses in generating full perceptions. It would be interesting to determine to what extent the other senses are affected by taste. For example, would describing a smell with taste components lead to a different, more pleasant, olfactory experience? Current advertising seems to be exploring this possibility. A recent introduction of a men's fragrance is intriguingly named "Chocolate." In the television commercial for the fragrance, the lead character is a life-sized chocolate man. Throughout the advertisement, women grab off chunks of the chocolate man and then eat the chunks. What remains to be seen, however, is how this naming with a taste perception impacts the sense of smell. Additional exploration of cross-modal interactions of taste on vision, haptics, and even sound may also prove valuable.

The interaction of senses is perhaps most perplexing within the concept of synesthesia. Although most of us distinguish clearly among our five senses, for some people this distinction gets muddled so that two or more senses get intermingled. For example, some individuals can see colors when hearing sounds (light colors for high-pitched and dark for low-pitched) and others can actually "taste" words. The latter is called lexical-gustatory synesthesia. Until recently, the belief was that sounds of words trigger tastes so that, for instance, the sounds "eh" and "mmmm" tasted of mint and "aye" tasted of bacon. However, recent findings (Simner & Ward, 2006) indicate that the connection is not phonetically based but lexically (i.e., meaning) based. Simner and Ward (2006) showed individuals pictures of uncommon items so that the sound and form of the word were merely on the tip of the tongue (TOT) but not completely processed, whereas the meaning was fully present. These gustatory synesthetes actually tasted the concept of the word and were accurate with the retest of the taste over a year later, showing that the tastes were not merely constructed on the spot. The concept of synesthesia will continue to receive attention, hopefully furthering our understanding of the multisensory interactions among the senses and better explicating the neural structure of sensation.

Conclusions

In this chapter we have identified some exciting new research on taste perception and also on consumption. Taste research is still relatively new to marketing. On the other hand, with brands no longer having the cache they once had, food marketers are looking for ways to increase consumer preference for their products. One way to do this may be to make the purchase or consumption experience of food more exciting for the consumer. Although research has focused on the latter, there is little work on the former.

While food marketers are trying to make their products more appealing, public policy officials are trying to reduce obesity among consumers and restrain consumption. Consumption interrupters like smaller package sizes and different colored chips in cylinders of chips have been shown to affect consumption. These are all "physical" interrupters. But what about verbal interrupters, like "individual serving size"? Perhaps increasing the salience of the nutritional information would also change consumption by creating verbal interrupters in memory.

Undoubtedly individuals differ in taste perceptions and consumption across cultures; however, such cross-cultural differences have not received much attention. While self-construal theory has typically been applied for social judgment, recently, Krishna, Zhou, and Zhang (2008) applied self-construal theory to spatial perception. They showed that individualist versus collectivist cultures vary greatly in the visual biases they are prone to, with individualists being more prone to biases that require the context to be considered, and collectivists being more prone to biases that require the context to be ignored. It is worth looking into similar work for other types of sensory perception.

By utilizing cross-disciplinary knowledge and expertise, research on taste perception and consumption will continue to be an exciting arena with direct applications to consumer behavior.

References

Allison, R. I., & Uhl, K. P. (1964, August). Influence of beer brand identification on taste perception. *Journal of Marketing Research, 1*, 36–39.

Anderson, N. H. & Cuneo, D. O. (1978, December). The height + width rule in children's judgments of quantity. *Journal of Experimental Psychology: General, 107*(4), 335–378.

Aydinoglu, N., & Krishna, A. (2009). *Guiltless gluttony: The asymmetric effect of size labels on size perceptions and consumption.* Working paper.

Baird, J. C., Romer, D., & Stein, T. (1970). Test of a cognitive theory of psychophysics: Size discrimination. *Perceptual and Motor Skills, 30*(2), 495–501.

Chandon, P., & Wansink, B. (2002). When are stockpiled products consumed faster? A convenience-salience framework of postpurchase consumption incidence and quantity. *Journal of Marketing Research, 39*(3), 321–335.

Charpentier, A. (1891). Analyze experimentale de quelques elements de la sensation de poids [Experimental study of some aspects of weight perception]. *Archives de Physiologie Normales et Pathologiques, 1*(3), 122–135.

Do Vale, R. C., Pieters, R., & Zeelenberg, M. (2008). Flying under the radar: Perverse package size effects on consumption self-regulation. *Journal of Consumer Research, 35*(3), 380–390.

DuBose, C. N., Cardello, A. V., & Maller, O. (1980). Effects of colorants and flavorants on identification, perceived flavor intensity, and hedonic quality of fruit-flavored beverages and cake. *Journal of Food Science, 45*(5), 1393–1399.

Elder, R. S. & Krishna A. (2010). The effects of advertising copy on sensory thoughts and perceived taste. *Journal of Consumer Research, 36.*

Fessler, D. M. T., & Navarrete, C. D. (2003). Meat is good to taboo: Dietary proscriptions as a product of the interaction of psychological mechanisms and social processes. *Journal of Cognition and Culture, 3*(1), 1–40.

Folkes, V. S., Martin, I. M., & Gupta, K. (1993, December). When to say when: Effects of supply on usage. *Journal of Consumer Research, 20,* 467–477.

Frayman, B. J., & Dawson, W. E. (1981). The effect of object shape and mode of presentation on judgments of apparent volume. *Perception and Psychophysics, 29*(1), 56–62.

Herman, C. P., Roth, D. A., & Pulivy, J. (2003). Effects of the presence of others on food intake: A normative interpretation. *Psychological Bulletin, 129*(6), 873–886.

Herz, R. (2007). *The scent of desire: Discovering our enigmatic sense of smell.* New York: William Morrow.

Hoch, S. J., & Ha, Y. W. (1986, September). Consumer learning: Advertising and the ambiguity of product experience. *Journal of Consumer Research, 13,* 221–233.

Hoegg, J., & Alba, J. W. (2007a, March). Taste perception: More than meets the tongue. *Journal of Consumer Research, 33,* 490–498.

Hoegg, J., & Alba, J. W. (2007b). Linguistic framing of sensory experience: There is some accounting for taste. In T. M. Lowrey (Ed.), *Psycholinguistic phenomena in marketing communications* (pp. 3–21). Mahwah, NJ: Erlbaum.

Holmberg, L. (1975). The influence of elongation on the perception of volume of geometrically simple objects. *Psychological Research Bulletin, Lund University, 15*(2), 1–18.

Huang, A. L., Chen, X., Hoon, M. A., Chandrashekar, J., Guo, W., Trankner, D., et al. (2006). The cells and logic for mammalian sour taste detection. *Nature, 442*(7105), 934.

Irmak, C., Block, L. G., & Fitzsimons, G. J. (2005). The placebo effect in marketing: Sometimes you just have to want it to work. *Journal of Marketing Research, 42*(4), 406–409.

Johnson, J. L., & Clydesdale, F. M. (1982). Perceived sweetness and redness in colored sucrose solutions. *Journal of Food Science, 47*(3), 747–752.

Kidwell, B., Hardesty, D. M., & Childers, T. L. (2008). Emotional calibration effects on consumer choice. *Journal of Consumer Research, 35*(4), 611–621.

Krider R., Raghubir, P., & Krishna, A. (2001). Pizza—pi or squared?: The effect of perceived area on price perceptions. *Marketing Science, 20*(4), 405–425.

Krishna, A. (2005). How big is "tall"? *Harvard Business Review, 83*(4), 18–20.

Krishna, A. (2006). Interaction of the senses: The effect of vision versus touch on the elongation bias. *Journal of Consumer Research, 32*(4), 557–566.

Krishna, A. (2007). Spatial perception research: An integrative review of length, area, volume, and number perception. In M. Wedel & R. Peters (Eds.), *Visual marketing: From attention to action* (pp. 167–192). Marketing and Consumer Psychology Series. New York: Erlbaum.

Krishna, A., & Morrin, M. (2008, April). Does touch affect taste? The perceptual transfer of product container haptic cues. *Journal of Consumer Research, 34*, 807–818.

Krishna, A., Zhou, R., & Zhang, S. (2008). The effect of self-construal on spatial judgments. *Journal of Consumer Research, 35*(2), 337–348.

Lee, L., Frederick, S., & Ariely, D. (2006). Try it, you'll like it: The influence of expectation, consumption, and revelation on preferences for beer. *Psychological Science, 17*(12), 1054–1058.

Levin, I. P., & Gaeth, G. J. (1988, December). How consumers are affected by the framing of attribute information before and after consuming the product. *Journal of Consumer Research, 15*, 374–378.

Lindemann, B. (2001). Receptors and transduction in taste. *Nature, 413*(6852), 219.

McKnight, D. (1973). Sexual symbolism of food among the Wik-Mungkan. *Man, 8*, 194–209.

Moyer, R. S., Bradley, D. R., Sorenson, M. H., Whiting, J. C., & Mansfield D. P. (1978, April). Psychophysical functions for perceived and remembered size. *Science, 200*(4339), 330–332.

Nowlis, S. M., & Shiv, B. (2005, May). The influence of consumer distractions on the effectiveness of food-sampling programs. *Journal of Marketing Research, 42*, 157–168.

Painter, J. F., Wansink, B., & Hieggelke, J. B. (2002). How visibility and convenience influence candy consumption. *Appetite, 38*(3), 237–238.

Peck, J., & Childers, T. L. (2003). Individual differences in haptic information processing: The "need for touch" scale. *Journal of Consumer Research, 30*(3), 430–442.

Peck, J., & Childers, T. L. (2008). If it tastes, smells, sounds, and feels like a duck, then it must be a …: Effects of sensory factors on consumer behaviors. In C. P. Haugtvedt, P. M. Herr, & F. R. Kardes (Eds.), *Handbook of consumer psychology* (pp. 193–219). New York: Psychology Press.

Piaget, J. (1967). Cognitions and conservations: Two views. *Contemporary Psychology, 12*, 532–533.

Piaget, J. (1968). Quantification, conservation and nativism. *Science, 162*, 976–979.

Piaget, J., Inhelder, B., & Szeminska, A. (1960). *The child's conception of geometry*. New York: Basic Books.

Raghubir, P., & Krishna, A. (1999, August). Vital dimensions in volume perception: Can the eye fool the stomach? *Journal of Marketing Research, 36*, 313–326.

Raghunathan, R., Naylor, R. W., & Hoyer, W. D. (2006, October). The unhealthy = tasty intuition and its effects on taste inferences, enjoyment, and choice of food products. *Journal of Marketing, 70*, 170–184.

Rozin, P. (1982, April). Taste-smell confusions and the duality of the olfactory sense. *Perception and Psychophysics, 31*, 397–401.

Salonia, A., Fabbri, F., Zanni, G., Scavini, M., Fantini, G. V., Briganti, A., et al. (2006). Chocolate and women's sexual health: An intriguing correlation. *Journal of Sexual Medicine, 3*(3), 476–482.

Scott, M. L., Nowlis, S. M., Mandel, N., & Morales, A. C. (2008). The effects of reduced food size and package size on the consumption behavior of restrained and unrestrained eaters. *Journal of Consumer Research, 35*(3), 391–405.

Shiv, B., Carmon, Z., & Ariely, D. (2005). Placebo effects of marketing actions: Consumers may get what they pay for. *Journal of Marketing Research, 42*(4), 383–393.

Shiv, B., & Nowlis, S. M. (2004, December). The effect of distractions while tasting a food sample: The interplay of informational and affective components in subsequent choice. *Journal of Consumer Research, 31*, 599–608.

Simner, J., & Ward, J. (2006, November 23). The taste of words on the tip of the tongue. *Nature, 44*, 438.

Small, D. M., & Prescott, J. (2005, October). Odor/taste integration and the perception of flavor. *Experimental Brain Research, 166*, 345–357.

Stangor, C., & McMillan, D. (1992). Memory for expectancy-congruent and expectancy-incongruent information: A review of the social and social development literatures. *Psychological Bulletin, 111*(1), 42–61.

Steinberg, S., & Yalch, R. F. (1978). When eating begets buying: The effects of food samples on obese and nonobese shoppers. *Journal of Consumer Research, 4*(4), 243.

Techtsoonian, M. (1965). The judgment of size. *American Journal of Psychology, 78*, 392–402.

Verge, C. G., & Bogartz. R. S. (1978, April). A functional measurement analysis of the development of dimensional coordination in children. *Journal of Experimental Child Psychology, 25*(2), 337–353.

Wansink, B. (1996, July). Can package size accelerate usage volume? *Journal of Marketing, 60*, 1–14.

Wansink, B., Geier, A. B., & Rozin, P. (2009). Packaging cues that frame portion size: the case of the red potato chip. In McGill, A. L. & Shavitt, S. (Eds.), *Advances in Consumer Research* (36), 195–197. Duluth, MN.

Wansink, B., & Park, S. (2001). At the movies: How external cues and perceived taste impact consumption volume. *Food Quality and Preference Journal, 12*(1), 69–74.

Wansink, B., Park, S. B., Sonka, S., & Morganosky, M. (2000). How soy labeling influences preference and taste. *International Food and Agribusiness Management Review, 3*, 85–94.

Wansink, B., & Ray, M. L. (1996, January). Advertising strategies to increase usage frequency. *Journal of Marketing, 60*(1), 31–46.

Wansink, B., & van Ittersum, K. (2003, December). Bottoms up! The influence of elongation on pouring and consumption volume. *Journal of Consumer Research, 30*(3), 455–463.

Young, L. R., & Nestle, M. (1998, April). Variation in perceptions of a "medium" food portion: Implications for dietary guidance. *Journal of the American Dietetic Association, 98*, 458–459.

Young, L. R., & Nestle, M. (2003, February). Expanding portion sizes in the US marketplace: Implications for nutrition counseling. *Journal of the American Dietetic Association, 103*, 231–234.

Zampini, M., & Spence, C. (2004). The role of auditory cues in modulating the perceived crispiness and staleness of potato chips. *Journal of Sensory Studies, 19*(5), 347–363.

19

Psychology and Sensory Marketing, With a Focus on Food

Paul Rozin and Julia M. Hormes

The Power of Sensation and the Perception of "Mouth Objects"

One of the hardest reservations to get in the world is for dinner at El Bulli, in northeast Spain, the world's most creative restaurant and by many considered to be the best. The chef, Ferran Adria, essentially the founder of molecular gastronomy, has added new dimensions to the experience of food. Largely by changing the physical form of food with high technology, using foams, gels, and the like, coupled with an exquisite aesthetic sense of what works for the human palate, Adria has created a panoply of new food experiences. There were 34 of them in a 6-hour meal one of us (PR) had the pleasure of consuming a few years ago. This extraordinary sensory experience does not need to be marketed, since reservations are essentially unattainable. (It is *not* true that El Bulli is so popular that nobody goes there anymore!) This new wave in cooking, spreading around the Western world, gives us an integrated multisensory experience, with a special focus on the texture of foods and textural contrasts. The smells, tastes, flavors, feels, sights, and sounds of food provide an enveloping experience. One example from El Bulli: a glass containing at the bottom a steaming hot, aromatic extract of pine nuts. The hot liquid sits at the bottom of a glass, the top of which is coated in a layer of ice. When you sip it, you get all the aroma that comes from a hot aromatic substance paired with the cold temperature that normally suppresses aroma: a new and unexpected experience. Molecular gastronomy sets the stage for a discussion of sensory marketing.

When it comes to senses, much of psychology has been focused on exploring vision and hearing. Vision and hearing can legitimately be thought to be our most important senses, as indicated by the devastation

TABLE 19.1   The Human Senses

Sense	Distance/ Surface/Internal	Valence	Comment
Vision	Distance	Neutral	
Hearing	Distance	Neutral	
Haptic*	Surface	Negative/neutral/positive	Incorporative
Smell	Distance/internal	Negative/positive	Dual/incorporative
Taste	Internal	Negative/positive	Incorporative
Visceral	Internal	Negative	
Muscle	Internal	Negative/neutral	
Equilibrium	Internal	Neutral	

*Including touch, irritation, temperature sense, and pain.

caused by blindness and deafness. The eyes and ears—both distance receptors—constitute our principal way of finding out about the world around us. It is quite easy to generate stimuli in vision and hearing, and the very fast response time of the system allows for exquisite temporal control of stimuli, such as flashes of light. In their reasonably "raw" forms, excluding that very small subset of all visual and auditory experiences that we might call art and music, light and sound are affectively neutral. They serve principally to inform about what is going on in the outside world. The other senses are often characterized as the "minor" senses (Table 19.1). Three—taste, smell, and contact/haptic—sensations constitute the core of the food experience. Since eating is a major activity of humans, the third most time consuming (including preparation of food), and the single most economically important activity of humans, the senses that contribute most to the appeal of food are perhaps not so minor after all, and certainly worthy of study. Unlike sights and sounds, most tastes, smells, and feels (skin sensations) are positive or negative in valence. Although there is important participation from sight and sound, the major aspect of eating is mouth sensations, which are a combination of taste, smell, and a number of haptic modalities, including irritation or pain, contact, and hot or cold. The mouth is a highly innervated organ, and along with the hands, the only sense organ that actually manipulates the stimulus. What we perceive is food objects, a blend of taste, smell, and haptic inputs. Indeed, flavor is a seamless combination of taste and smell. The distinctive qualities of most foods are conveyed by odor carried from the mouth to the nose, via the retronasal route, but the sensation is experienced as coming from the mouth. Hence, the surprise when people discover that when they have a head cold that blocks the sense of smell, food loses much of its taste. When we eat, we do not experience modalities, we experience "mouth objects." These objects change their properties—textures, temperatures, flavors—as we chew them, and they produce a dynamic range of sensations in the period of a few to many seconds that we might describe as a bite, a unit of eating.

The experience of a bite of chocolate may last for minutes: In the first stages, the sight of the wrapped chocolate, the smell as it is unwrapped, the feel of the chocolate in the hand; then, the bite itself. The initial firm impact, the growing aroma as the chocolate warms in the mouth and coats the inner surfaces, the change in texture from firm to a thick, silky liquid, the slide down the throat, and the enduring after-flavor. A bite of chocolate is a minisymphony of experiences.

Individuals differ in their acuity with respect to the various senses involved in eating, as they do in audition and vision. In particular, there are many different bitter receptors in the mouth, and at least a few are known to be absent in some individuals based on the presence or absence of specific genes. Olfactory acuity varies widely, and the olfactory sense deteriorates more with age than many other systems, such as the taste system.

Although it is sort of absurd to ask individuals how important vision or hearing is for them, it is quite reasonable to ask about the importance of smell, and we have done this (Wrzesniewski, McCauley, & Rozin, 1999). For example, inquiring of both Belgian and American college students, we asked what was the worst thing to lose: the sense of smell, hearing in one ear, or the big toe on one foot. About half of respondents thought losing the sense of smell was most threatening. Of course, many did not realize that food would lose most of its "taste" without a sense of smell. We developed a measure of the importance of odor to individuals and found wide variation. Most of it was not attributable to olfactory acuity (also assessed by self-report), but rather to the value placed on olfactory sensations: food aromas, perfumes, the smells of the natural world, and so forth.

Gestalt psychology was a major movement in psychology in the middle of the 20th century. Originating in studies of perception, it emphasized the importance of context. The role of context cannot be exaggerated, but it is still often ignored in research in psychology, perhaps because context makes things complicated. It requires expanding the universe of concern beyond what laboratory experimenters want to do. It means considering a sensory experience in terms of its immediate precursors and successors. The chocolate bite is not captured in a momentary flash of sensation. The melt-in-the-mouth process is critical. Part of the experience of a bite of an egg roll is the change in sensation as one bites into different components, of different crispness and different flavors, each producing a momentary burst of mouth experience. Classic taste research using water solutions of glucose or sodium chloride bypasses these critical contexts, the contexts that make eating food such a pleasant, often aesthetic experience. Studies on the sensory side of eating rarely consider the dynamic unfolding of mouth experiences over short periods of time (see Hyde and Witherly [1993] for an extended discussion of this perspective and the papers of Pangborn et al. [Larson-Powers & Pangborn, 2006; Pangborn, 1980]).

For the case of eating, and by the way also the appreciation of most other products, such as clothing, the important context extends well beyond the seconds of actual exposure. This makes it all the more important to expand the universe of concern, and all the more difficult to do rigorous experimentation.

A piece of chocolate may taste delicious until one discovers that it was harvested with child labor or contained detectable insect residues. A subtly flavored fish paté may be perceived as exquisite at a fine restaurant but tasteless at a local diner. Wansink, Payne, and North (2007) report that the same wine is judged to be lower in sensory quality if it has a label that indicates that it comes from North Dakota as opposed to California. Some people who claim to love Coke and hate Pepsi cannot tell them apart in taste tests. Chicken in a sauce flavored with chocolate (one variety of Mexican mole) may be found distasteful because of the known mixture of chocolate with a savory food, rather than because of a detached judgment of the orosensory experience. Many people think bottled water tastes superior to tap water, when they in fact cannot tell them apart. But it is important to realize that to the Coke-lover, Pepsi-hater, who cannot tell them apart, Coca-Cola drunk from a properly labeled bottle does taste better than Pepsi (if Coca-Cola had realized this, they would not have produced the new Coke). The taste experience of a food, the liking for the food, includes the broad context in which it is consumed. It includes the immediate social context; the reactions of those one is eating with influence the experience a person has.

Just as it is unreasonable to think that Picasso's great artistic output is a result of extraordinary visual acuity he appreciation of food is only weakly based on matters of acuity. Like all perception, evaluating food (or clothing, movies, cars or any other product, for that matter) involves a blend of bottom–up and top–down processes. So far as we know, people who like the burn of chili pepper and people who do not are getting the same irritation signal from their mouth. It is their interpretation that changes. Furthermore, most chili likers do not enjoy the disembodied burn of chili, but want that burn in association with the flavor of the peppers and the other associated foods.

The context expands further (see Kass [1994] and Rozin [2007a] for discussions of eating in a cultural context). Food is a basic source of nutrition. That is its fundamental function. But in human cultural history, by a process we describe as cultural preadaptation, the initial purpose of food has been expanded so that it serves many other functions. The aesthetic function is obvious. But it also serves a variety of social functions, as with chocolate gifts in a romantic context, as with meeting a new person over a meal, as in discussing family issues over the dinner table. Meals are occasions, sometimes the principal occasions, for social interaction. The much longer than 1-hour duration of a French dinner is significantly more than the time it takes to consume the food. It involves savoring the food, discussing it, and general conviviality. For some minority in Western developed cultures eating is like refueling, but for most it is an anticipated pleasure. Of course, for many women in developed Western cultures, it is an ambivalent experience: enjoying the sensations but feeling bad about taking in calories.

Food also enters into the moral domain, as has clearly happened with alcohol and tobacco in American culture, and more subtly now with stigmatization of obesity and high-fat foods. In other cultural contexts, food in general has moral implications. Within the Hindu caste system, particular foods, and the social status of the preparers of the food, have strong moral implications. Appadurai (1981) describes food as a "biomoral" substance in Hindu India.

The specific powerful influence of culture on the appreciation of food and the evaluation of its sensory properties can be described under the generic term "cuisine." Elisabeth Rozin (1982, 1983) analyzes cuisine, focusing on the actual dishes, in three components: staple foods, preparation techniques, and flavor principles. Thus, Chinese cuisine focuses on rice as a principal staple, the stir-fry technique, and a flavor principle made up of soy sauce, ginger root, and rice wine. The flavor principles, a quintessentially sensory component, more than any other feature of the food, bestow the ethnic quality on the food. Potatoes made with Chinese flavor principles taste Chinese (even though potatoes are rarely used in Chinese cuisine), and potatoes made with Mexican flavor principles (e.g., chili and tomato) taste Mexican. In addition to the characteristic sensory combinations, derived from staples, techniques, and flavor principles that characterize a cuisine, there are a whole set of additional contexts that are part of the cultural frame of food consumption. These include table manners, the utensils used, the social organization of eating, and the order of courses. Howard Schutz

(1989) describes many of these traditions with the term "appropriateness." Thus, in the United States and many other countries, there are foods particularly appropriate for breakfast and others for special holidays. There are combinations of food that are discouraged, such as many mixtures of sweet and savory substances in most Euro-American cuisines. Whipped cream and meat are each typically desired foods, but not appropriate (or liked) in combination. For similar appropriateness reasons, carbonated milk was a failure on the American market, as was carbonated coffee (coffee soda). So far as we can tell, many of these rules are the arbitrary results of culinary history, although some can be argued to be nutritionally adaptive or enhancing of certain generally appealing aspects of food flavors.

In any particular cuisine, certain foods and flavors find very restricted uses, and others are widely employed. In Italy, garlic is appropriate on almost any savory food, as is soy sauce on almost any savory food in China. Coffee, on the other hand, in almost all cultures that consume it, is narrowly restricted to a hot beverage context; it is rarely used as a flavoring and virtually never in savory foods.

Sensory Pleasure as a Particular Type of Pleasure

Most of what we do, and buy, is motivated by either necessity or increasing pleasure. As wealth increases, the importance of maximizing pleasure grows with respect to meeting basic biological needs. Thus, while food constitutes about 50% of total expenses in developing world countries, it falls to below 20% in the developed world. Of course, there is no complementarity between pleasure and necessity. Food is perhaps the major domain in which the two motivations interact. At least in the developed Western world, where it has been assessed, flavor (read pleasure) is the major determinant of food choice (assuming availability and affordability). Depending on the individual and the culture, other prominent reasons are tradition, convenience, and perceived healthiness. Given the central role of maximizing pleasure in choice, in food and elsewhere, it is very appropriate to discuss pleasure in the context of sensory marketing. Many of the pleasures of food, that is, of eating food, are rather elemental and raw, and hence can be called sensory pleasures.

According to some frameworks (Rozin, 1999), one can partition pleasures into three types: sensory, aesthetic, and mastery. Sensory pleasures are relatively unadorned, such as the taste of sweet, the aroma of chocolate, the feel of massage, the sensations associated with sexual arousal and orgasm. These pleasures are context sensitive, but in the usual experience, where the context is positive and appropriate, they produce a rather simple enjoyment. Although they show adaptation over short periods, they can be experienced hundreds or thousands of times over a period of months to years without declining. A good piece of chocolate is a sensory pleasure today, tomorrow, and every day of the week for a year. Aesthetic pleasures typically have a sensory root, but are more cognitively elaborated, and more likely to be acquired over a period of time (note that Krishna and Elder's chapter in this volume suggests that sensory pleasures are also cognitively elaborated on; thus the distinction between sensory and aesthetic is a matter of degree and type of elaboration). They are often modality specific, as with the enjoyment of Picasso or Mozart, but the representations in the mind/brain that give rise to these pleasures must be many synapses away from primary sensory cortical representations. In the domain of food, the appreciation of fine wines and other elaborated foods constitute sensory derived but yet aesthetic pleasures. A third source of pleasure comes from the sense of mastery, for example, the accomplishment of being able to perform something challenging (from walking, to riding a bicycle, to playing the piano). But just as aesthetic and sensory pleasures are linked, so too are mastery and aesthetic pleasures. Some types of mastery are not instantiated by skills, but rather by appreciation. As one learns to identify different grapes and vintages in the process of becoming a wine connoisseur, there is a sense of aesthetic mastery.

Sensory marketing relates most directly to sensory pleasure. However, since sensations are at the root of most aesthetic and many mastery pleasures, all three types of pleasure have a place in sensory marketing. A sweet taste may be quite simple and sensory; the experience of chocolate has strong basic sensory roots, but it can move into the aesthetic domain as one become sensitive to the subtleties of chocolate aroma and the qualities of the mouth-melting experience and informed about the sources and nature of processing of particular chocolates. The pleasures of Mozart are almost incidentally auditory; it is in large part the internal structure, cognitively appreciated, that provides the pleasure. We will focus principally on sensory pleasures, primarily in the domain of food, as we adopt a temporal perspective.

The Temporal Domains of Sensory Pleasure

An experience can last for a moment, a few moments, or an hour or more, for the case of a meal or an opera. A meal is a natural unit of eating

(Meiselman, 2000; Pliner & Rozin, 2000). In the food domain, it is probably at the "basic" unit level, so that we say, for example, "that was a great meal." On the other hand, we are unlikely to lump yesterday's lunch and dinner into a unit, and hence will rarely assign an affective value to such a combination. Of course, there are important smaller units in the food domain, most particularly the bite, the dish, and the course. Any of these smaller units can and often are given evaluative labels, especially dishes ("the omelette was delicious").

Daniel Kahneman, often in collaboration with Barbara Fredrickson (Fredrickson, 2000; Fredrickson & Kahneman, 1993; Kahneman, Fredrickson, Schreiber, & Redelmeier, 1993) has provided a powerful framework for understanding pleasure in its temporal domains (Kahneman, Wakker, & Sarin, 1997). They refer to experienced (E), remembered (R), and anticipated (A) pleasure. The meanings of these terms are obvious, once this classification is expressed. Of course, this ERA framework is contingent on the selection of the reference unit, that is, the definition of the present. For example, for eating, is it the bite or is it the meal?

Kahneman et al. (1997) have made important claims about the relations between present and prospect and between present and past. The most critical claim about present and prospect is that people are quite poor at anticipating future experienced pleasures. That is, on the basis of the present, they often make poor predictions about how they will enjoy a particular experience. In the initial study by Kahneman and Snell (1992), individuals sampled a flavored yogurt and rated their liking for it and agreed to eat the same yogurt every day for a week. At the onset, they were asked to estimate how much they would like the yogurt after 1 week. Then after 1 week of experience, they rated it again. The predicted and actual ratings were essentially uncorrelated. A subsequent study (Rozin, Hanko, & Durlach, 2006) exposed individuals to four new products (two unfamiliar East Asian food snacks and an unfamiliar toothpaste and shower gel). Again, according to the procedure of Kahneman and Snell (1992), individuals tried and rated their liking for each product, agreed to use each daily, and estimated what their ratings would be after a week of use. Again, as with the Kahneman results, people were poor at anticipating the changes in their preferences. They often were incorrect in even predicting the direction of change. Two other findings of interest emerged from this study. First, relative accuracy at predicting the change for any one product did not predict accuracy for predicting changes for other products. Second, the participants in this study were 20 college students and 20 parents (one parent from each of the students). We hypothesized that with age people would have a great deal of experience with their hedonic trajectories and become better at anticipating hedonic changes. In fact, there was no improvement at all consequent on more than 20 additional years of experience with oneself.

The inability to predict the effect of exposure on one's future sensory and other preferences is important for marketing, especially since people are typically unaware of how poorly they perform in this domain. Much of the inaccuracy comes from overconfidence that the present reaction to a new entity will be like the future reaction once it has become familiar. People typically both underestimate adaptation (Loewenstein & Frederick, 1997) and underestimate the positive effects of mere exposure on increasing liking. This causes them, for example, to make long-term commitments to products (such as annual subscriptions to an initially engaging magazine) on the assumption that present responses will be sustained, or to fail to give a new product a second chance if the initial response is mildly negative or neutral.

The study of the relations between experienced and remembered pleasure by Kahneman and others (Frederickson, 2000; Fredrickson & Kahneman, 1993; Kahneman et al., 1993) has been a particularly fertile area. This research, based almost entirely on hedonically negative experiences, has led to three principles that represent major distortions of experience that occur when the experience is remembered. The hedonic peak (i.e., the most highly valenced point in the experience) and the hedonic state at the end point of the experience have a predominant influence on the memory for the experience (the "peak-end" rule). The peak rule is often apparent, as when a few seconds of discomfort in the dentist chair completely dominate the hedonic memory of a half hour of more or less painless experience. The third rule is described as duration neglect: our memory does not seem to track duration well and tends to remember events and not their duration. As a result, a continuous or repetitive experience is typically remembered as a single event. Two or eight sips of an excellent wine tend to be remembered as the same sipping of the wine and the associated flavor experience. We have extended this work on remembered pleasure into the positive domains of enjoyment of meals (Rode, Rozin, & Durlach, 2007), music (Rozin, Guillot, & Rozin, in preparation; Rozin, Rozin, & Goldberg, 2004), and art exhibits (Rozin & Taylor, in preparation). We find powerful support for duration neglect; for example, doubling the size of the portion of the favorite food in a meal, which clearly increases experienced pleasure, has no effect on remembered pleasure. On the other hand, we have not found reliable evidence for a peak effect (a particularly strong effect in an overall evaluation from the favorite paintings in an art exhibit, a favorite musical selection in a "concert," or a favorite dish in a meal). Our own experience suggests a strong peak effect, but we have been unable to find it in controlled laboratory situations. In these studies, we have found about as much evidence for a primacy as an end effect. We still do not know the conditions under which peak, end, and onset come to dominate an experience. We also do not know the conditions that blunt duration neglect, although it is likely that division of an event into distinct segments may be one factor that reduces it (Ariely & Zauberman, 2000).

The disparity between experienced and remembered pleasure has major implications for marketing. At the point of purchase, say in a food store or restaurant, we consult our *memory* of the food or dish in question, since we do not have direct access to our past experience with it. Hence, the representation of past experiences in memory is the critical base for understanding most current choices. (Obviously, this is not true in cases where a person is actually sampling the choice of foods available or directly comparing items of clothing or pictures.)

Individual and Cultural Differences in ERA Profiles

Individuals vary in the amount of time and importance they devote to experiencing in the moment, rehearsing memories, and anticipating the future (Rozin & Hanko, in preparation). A great meal may last 2 hours, but its memory may be activated for dozens of hours over the following years. And the second visit to the source of the great meal may engage many hours of anticipation. When a person chooses to schedule an anticipated positive event in the near or distant future, he or she is making a choice about whether to increase anticipation, at the cost of having less time to "consume" the memory, or reducing anticipation in order to have more time to remember. People differ in the decisions they make in choices of this sort. So far as our still unpublished data indicate, their pattern of favoring anticipation or memory tends not to be general but rather specific to particular domains (Rozin, Hanko, & Gohar, 2009; Rozin, Remick & Fischler, 2008). Some people, faced with a platter of three foods (say the standard meat, potatoes, and vegetable), consistently eat their favorite food first, others eat their favorite food last, and many do neither. But the people who eat their favorite food first are not more likely to listen to their favorite music first than those who eat their favorite food last (Rozin, Hanko, & Gohar, in preparation).

It is probably true that cultures differ in the importance they bestow on memories versus anticipation (perhaps translatable into the past vs. the future), and it is also likely that the remembered or anticipated balance shifts with age. Older people have the same potential experience anticipating a positive event that will occur in the near future, but will have less opportunity to consume the memory because of a shorter lifespan ahead. The utility of building memories declines with age, even assuming the acuity of memory remains intact! The psychology of savoring and reminiscing, and their tradeoffs, and the parallel psychology of dreading and remembering negative events have many implications for marketing and for optimizing the pleasure of life.

Comforts and Joys

Tibor Scitovsky (1992) draws a distinction between what he calls comforts and pleasures. (We think joy is a better word to describe his important contrast, because it implies a shorter time interval, and we use joy to substitute for pleasure.) In his view, comforts make life easier, they are like good mattresses and air conditioning, and ice dispensers on refrigerators. Joys are unique events, such as a meal, a concert, a meeting with friends. He holds, we think with good reason, that comforts are subject to major adaptation effects and are almost invisible as part of remembered pleasure. Joys, because they are unique events, are well remembered. When we reflect on whether last year was good or not, we do not cite our air conditioning, mattress, or automatic garage door opener. We think of the personal family events, the trips, the plays, movies, concerts, sport events, and so forth. Americans spend disproportionately on comforts compared to the French (Rozin et al., 2009) and presumably do not harvest as much remembered pleasure. This important point relates to duration neglect and adaptation and the idea that what we remember is events, preferably events woven into a narrative.

We have instantiated the comfort–joy distinction with its relationship to remembered pleasure in a simple choice paradigm. We ask people whether, when they go to their favorite restaurant, they order their favorite dish or something new (Rozin et al., 2009). We ask the same question about hearing their favorite musical group or traveling. If you opt for your favorite, you will probably have higher anticipation and a better experience, but you will add little to your memory, since the memory is already in place. The memory of eating the same foie gras recipe twice is about the same as that of eating it once. But if they opt for the new dish, although the anticipation will be less certainly positive and the experience will probably be less positive (thinking in terms of regression to the mean), a new positive memory will have been created (Rozin, Hanko, & Gohar, in preparation; Rozin et al., 2009).

The Origin of Preferences

Often, when a person prefers object X to Y (e.g., a food or music), it is the sensory properties that determine the choice. They *like* X more than they like Y. Likings about food in particular are mostly about sensory matters. Where do these sensory-based likings come from? We are remarkably ignorant in this area, about food, music, sports, sport teams, clothing, or anything else. Psychologists have not been that interested in this area of life, which is of fundamental daily importance and a core issue for marketers and economists (for general reviews on the origin of food and other preferences, see Birch, Fisher, and Grimm-Thomas [1996], Booth [1994], and Rozin [2006a, 2007a]).

In the food domain, as omnivorous animals, humans have a very open-ended attitude toward foods and principally acquire most of their food likes and dislikes under the heavy guidance of culture. There appear to be no innately negative or positive odors (Bartoshuk, 1990), but there is an innate aversion to irritant or extreme oral temperature sensations, bitter, and reasonably strong sour or salty tastes. Sweetness is positive, for some, at any level, and for others up to a high level, at which point it declines as sweetness continues to rise (Pangborn, 1980). People rarely come to dislike sweets through experience, but they frequently come to like innately negative oral properties, such as ice cold beverages, bitter foods or beverages (e.g., coffee), or irritant foods (e.g., foods seasoned with chili pepper). Everything we know suggests that this is a hedonic reversal, that is, the sensory input is unchanged, but its valence inverts from negative to positive. We do not know how this happens, but it is very common (Rozin, 1990).

Three processes have been identified that can change the reaction to a sensory experience. One is mere exposure, which at modest frequencies, tends to enhance liking (Zajonc, 1968). A second is evaluative conditioning, the pairing of a relatively neutral sensory experience (say a mild odor) with an already positive (e.g., sweet) or negative (e.g., bitter) experience. The common phenomenon of acquired taste aversions, in animals and humans, is a result of evaluative conditioning and is easily demonstrated in the laboratory as well as by questionnaire (Pelchat & Rozin, 1982). This Pavlovian process has been studied extensively in the laboratory in animals and clearly produces a change in liking for a taste or flavor stimulus. For humans, evaluative conditioning has been demonstrated many times in the laboratory, usually in the framework of increased liking by continued pairing of a neutral taste or situation with an already positive situation (De Houwer, Thomas, & Baeyens, 2001; Rozin, Wrzesnieswski, & Byrnes, 1998). Although evaluative conditioning is surely important in real world situations, it appears to be a rather fragile phenomenon in the laboratory (Rozin et al., 1998). We do not know why. The third and probably most powerful force for creating likes and dislikes masquerades under the general name of "social influence." We do not fully understand how it works, but it is clear that under some conditions, the reactions of respected others to a food, piece of music, or clothing can change our liking for it (Birch et al., 1996). Advertisers use all three of these pathways to induce liking for their products. But like psychologists, they do not know how to create likings reliably. All three methods can backfire.

There are two special mechanisms that may be involved in the common conversion of aversions into preferences by humans. These reversals (referred to above) include, on the sensory side, coming to like very cold beverages, bitter or very sour or salty tastes, and oral irritants. Going past the sensory level, these include coming to like the experience of fear (e.g., in roller coasters), disgust (e.g., in disgust humor), and sadness (e.g., with sad music or movies). Since this seems to be a unique human experience, the explanation might be expected to invoke uniquely human processes. Mere exposure and evaluative conditioning are clearly present in animals. Social influence has been demonstrated in animals, but is much more powerful in humans. So one possibility, for sensory or other reversals, is the generally powerful effects of elders and peers during development and in adulthood. Pleasure experienced by others in consumption of something may, perhaps by a link with evaluative conditioning, induce preferences, and there are a few demonstrations of this (Baeyens, Kaes, Eelen, & Silverans, 1996).

The second mechanism, which we have called benign masochism, results from a unique human enjoyment of a negative experience that our mind knows is not threatening. It is a matter of mind over body; we enjoy irritant tastes or disgusting experiences *because* they are negative, our body responds as if they are, but we know better than our body, and this mastery produces pleasure. It is interesting in this regard that we find that for many chili pepper likers, their favorite level of burn is just below the level they consider too painful (Rozin, 1990, 2007a; Rozin & Schiller, 1980). Humans seem to enjoy pushing the envelope of bearability and getting pleasure out of it.

One can examine sensory likings, as for food, from a developmental perspective. Here the question is what are the relative roles of parents, peers, the media, and particular influential people in establishing likes and dislikes? Common sense looks primarily to parents who contribute genes, predominant control over the environment for the first 5 years of life, and substantial influence for the rest of childhood. It is thus sobering to realize that within cultures, the correlation between the food or music likes of parents and those of their adult children are very low, usually in the range of .15 to .30 (Rozin, 1991). Values, such as attitudes to abortion, show higher parent–child correlations. If the parents aren't the shaping force, what is? Peers are the most likely principal source, although one study that directly tested this for food and music preferences found a surprisingly small role for peers, either in elementary school or college (Rozin, Riklis, & Margolis, 2004). We can describe the current situation as the family and the peer paradox.

There is one important finding in this area that comes out of the marketing literature and is not widely known in psychology. Holbrook and Schindler (1989) have shown, particularly for music, that exposure to music styles (presumably peer related) during the ages of 15 and 30 is most influential in creating lifetime preferences. We have gathered supporting data for this point, for music and to some degree for food. It is notable that 15 to 30 years of age is a period of peak peer influence. Somewhere in our 20s or 30s, most Americans settle down and have families and withdraw from the intense peer activity and those strong social influences that characterized their adolescence and young adult years. This is a very promising hint about taste formation.

Some Reflections on Sensory Marketing from the Psychological Perspective

So far as we can tell, to a considerable degree, marketing is a branch of psychology, built principally on prior research in social psychology and the psychology of judgments and decision making. Sensory marketing brings in another branch of psychology, namely the study of sensation and perception. The psychology of sensation and perception is probably the most advanced and "scientific" part of psychology. Historically, it has been based primarily on the description of basic phenomena and functional relations, such as the dark adaptation curve and the laws of color mixing, followed by sophisticated theory and experimentation. Social psychology, in contrast, has accomplished much less than sensation and perception, at least partly because what it is studying is much more complex and multidetermined than the subject of sensation and perception. By its nature, it involves more than one person and often requires the consideration of context, which, as we have discussed already, can be extremely difficult.

Perhaps because social psychology stands at the less accomplished edge of psychology, it has the most potential. There is more to find out. But it is also the most insecure about its natural scientific status and has responded to this by the development of incredible sophistication in the design of experiments and the use of sophisticated statistics to analyze the results. It is focused on the hypothesis-experiment model of science. The art of sophisticated experiment, including proper controls, careful exploration and elimination of alternative explanations, and manipulation checks, has reached a new high in the field. But this has come at a price. Unlike physics, chemistry, biology, and the psychology of sensation and perception, social psychology has paid little attention, and assigns little prestige, to the first stages of science: accurate description of the social world, the identification of fundamental invariances (either within or between cultures), and the description of the fundamental functional relations in the social world (the equivalent of the dark adaptation function, or Boyle's law in physics). It has focused on the sophisticated testing of hypotheses without first identifying the fundamental things that are to be explained. Erving Goffman, among others, did this, just as Darwin did it for some branches of biology (Haig, 2005; Rozin, 2001, 2006b, 2007b).

This critique of modern social psychology is not original to us: it was stated clearly in 1952 by the great social psychologist of the 20th century Solomon Asch:

> Before we inquire into origins and functional relations, it is necessary to know the thing we are trying to explain. (Asch, 1952, p. 65)

> If there must be principles of scientific method, then surely the first to claim our attention is that one should describe phenomena faithfully and allow them to guide the choice of problems and procedures. If social psychology is to make a contribution to human knowledge, if it is to do more than add footnotes to ideas developed in other fields, it must look freely at its phenomena and examine its foundations. (Asch, 1952, p. xv)

The result of this focus on hypothesis testing has been great sophistication in studying the mechanisms of laboratory findings. The findings may or may not have generality within the laboratory (that is, they may be fragile and dependent on a limited selection of parameters), and they may or may not map onto the real world. The result is that the great majority of experiments are done on American college students. No doubt their visual systems work in the same basic way as that of adults around the world. But their social world, as they enter this peculiar period of life that is a transition between home and independent life, particularly in the United States, is very different from most social worlds of other humans (Arnett, 2008; Rozin, 2001, 2006b). The American college undergraduate is not as good a model for *Homo sapiens* as the fruit fly or *Escherichia coli* is for genetics.

The result is that the premier journal in the field, the *Journal of Personality and Social Psychology* (JPSP), is difficult to read and is about narrowly defined laboratory phenomena and the mechanisms or causes of them. It is not about the phenomena of the social world, and it is not about the domains of life (Rozin, 2007b).

Sadly, in our view, marketing, at least the part that is built on psychology, has adopted the JPSP model, and this can be evidenced in its premier journals. We are hopeful that by integrating the psychology of sensation and perception into marketing, sensory marketing will also turn our attention more to describing the basic phenomena in the world of marketing, as was true in the history of sensation and perception. Description, generality, replicability, and documentation of functional relations should be central in the field. Showing that color matters in food selection is more than doing an experiment on the fact that color (often represented by two different colors) influences food choice in college students. We have to be very careful not to make the mistake of finding a repeatable laboratory paradigm, dependent on the selection of a particular set of parameters from a wide range of possibilities, and analyzing it to death.

From this perspective, it seems most auspicious that sensory marketing brings to bear a great fund of knowledge in sensation and perception and a set of methodologies that are at once highly sophisticated, often quantitative, but soundly based on basic empirical relationships. In its history, sensation and perception went through a period when the Gestalt model, which privileges context, played a central role. It was out of that tradition that Solomon Asch wrote what we consider the great book of the field, *Social Psychology* (1952), which is still very much worth reading. Our challenge in marketing and in social psychology is to be as rigorous as we can be, while at the same time keeping an eye on the real world. We must carefully consider whether what we are modeling in the laboratory is something that is out there. Simplifying is a powerful tool and the heart of experimentation. But too simple borders on the meaningless. Studying human responses to sugar in water has limited value, and studying frozen moments of human facial expressions, while very important and productive, leaves out much of what goes on in the world.

References

Appadurai, A. (1981). Gastro-politics in Hindu South Asia. *American Ethnologist, 8*(3), 494–511.

Ariely, D., & Zauberman, G. (2000). On the making of an experience: The effects of breaking and combining experiences in their overall evaluation. *Journal of Behavioral Decision Making, 13*(2), 219–232.

Arnett, J. J. (2008). The neglected 95%: Why American psychology needs to become less American. *American Psychologist, 63,* 602–614.

Asch, S. (1952). *Social psychology.* New York: Prentice Hall.

Baeyens, F., Kaes, B., Eelen, P., & Silverans, P. (1996). Observational evaluative conditioning of an embedded stimulus element. *European Journal of Social Psychology, 26,* 15–28.

Bartoshuk, L. M. (1990). Distinctions between taste and smell relevant to the role of experience. In E. D. Capaldi & T. L. Powley (Eds.), *Taste, experience and feeding* (pp. 62–72). Washington, DC: American Psychological Association.

Birch, L. L., Fisher, J. O., & Grimm-Thomas, K. (1996). The development of children's eating habits. In H. L. Meiselman & H. J. H. MacFie (Eds.), *Food choice, acceptance and consumption* (pp. 161–206). London: Blackie Academic and Professional.

Booth, D. A. (1994). *Psychology of nutrition.* London: Taylor and Francis.

De Houwer, J., Thomas, S., & Baeyens, F. (2001). Association learning of likes and dislikes: A review of 25 years of research on human evaluative conditioning. *Psychological Bulletin, 127*(6), 853–869.

Fredrickson, B. (2000). Extracting meaning from past affective experiences: The importance of peaks, ends, and specific emotions. *Cognition and Emotion, 14,* 577–606.

Fredrickson, B. L., & Kahneman, D. (1993). Duration neglect in retrospective evaluations of affective episodes. *Journal of Personality and Social Psychology, 65,* 44–55.

Haig, B. D. (2005). An abductive theory of scientific method. *Psychological Methods, 10,* 371–388.

Holbrook, M. B., & Schindler, R. M. (1989). Some exploratory findings on the development of musical tastes. *Journal of Consumer Research, 16,* 119–124.

Hyde, R. J., & Witherly, S. A. (1993). Dynamic contrast: A sensory contribution to palatability. *Appetite, 21,* 1–16.

Kahneman, D., Fredrickson, B. L., Schreiber, C. A., & Redelmeier, D. A. (1993). When more pain is preferred to less: Adding a better end. *Psychological Science, 4,* 401–405.

Kahneman, D., & Snell, J. (1992). Predicting a changing taste: Do people know what they will like? *Journal of Behavioral Decision Making, 5,* 187–200.

Kahneman, D., Wakker, P. P., & Sarin, R. (1997). Back to Bentham? Explorations of experienced utility. *Quarterly Journal of Economics, 112,* 375–405.

Kass, L. (1994). *The hungry soul: Eating and the perfecting of our nature.* Chicago: University of Chicago Press.

Larson-Powers, N., & Pangborn, R. M. (2006). Paired comparison and time-intensity measurements of the sensory properties of beverages and gelatins containing sucrose or synthetic sweeteners. *Journal of Food Science, 43*(1), 41–46.

Loewenstein, G., & Frederick, S. (1997). Predicting reactions to environmental change. In M. H. Bazerman (Ed.), *Environment, ethics, and behavior* (pp. 52–72). Lanham, MD: Lexington Books.

Meiselman, H. (Ed.). (2000). *Dimensions of the meal: The science, culture, business, and art of eating.* Gaithersburg, MD: Aspen Publishers.

Pangborn, R. M. (1980). A critical analysis of sensory responses to sweetness. In P. Koivistoinen & L. Hyvonen (Eds.), *Carbohydrate sweeteners in foods and nutrition* (pp. 87–110). London: Academic Press.

Pelchat, M. L., & Rozin, P. (1982). The special role of nausea in the acquisition of food dislikes by humans. *Appetite, 3,* 341–351.

Pliner, P., & Rozin, P. (2000). The psychology of the meal. In H. Meiselman (Ed.), *Dimensions of the meal: The science, culture, business, and art of eating* (pp. 19–46). Gaithersburg, MD: Aspen Publishers.

Rode, E., Rozin, P., & Durlach, P. (2007). Experienced and remembered pleasure for meals: Duration neglect but minimal peak-end effects. *Appetite, 49,* 18–29.

Rozin, E. (1982). The structure of cuisine. In L. M. Barker (Ed.), *The psychobiology of human food selection* (pp. 189–203). Westport, CT: AVI.

Rozin, E. (1983). *Ethnic cuisine: The flavor principle cookbook.* New York: Hawthorn Books.

Rozin, P. (1990). Getting to like the burn of chili pepper: Biological, psychological and cultural perspectives. In B. G. Green, J. R. Mason, & M. R. Kare (Eds.), *Chemical senses,* Vol. 2: *Irritation* (pp. 231–269). New York: Marcel Dekker.

Rozin, P. (1991). Family resemblance in food and other domains: The family paradox and the role of parental congruence. *Appetite, 16,* 93–102.

Rozin, P. (1999). Preadaptation and the puzzles and properties of pleasure. In D. Kahneman, E. Diener, & N. Schwarz (Eds.), *Well being: The foundations of hedonic psychology* (pp. 109–133). New York: Russell Sage.

Rozin, P. (2001). Social psychology and science: Some lessons from Solomon Asch. *Personality and Social Psychology Review, 5,* 2–14.

Rozin, P. (2006a). Food choice: An introduction. In L. J. Frewer & H. van Trijp (Eds.). *Understanding consumers of food products* (pp. 3–29). Cambridge, UK: Woodhead.

Rozin, P. (2006b). Domain denigration and process preference in academic psychology. *Perspectives on Psychological Science, 1*, 365–376.

Rozin, P. (2007a). Food and eating. In S. Kitayama & D. Cohen (Eds.), *Handbook of cultural psychology* (pp. 391–416). New York: Guilford.

Rozin, P. (2007b). Exploring the landscape of modern academic psychology: Finding and filling the holes. *American Psychologist, 62*, 754–766.

Rozin, A., Guillot, L., & Rozin, P. (2007). *Memory for the attributes (liking, happy, sad) for three-piece concerts: Distortions and accuracies.* Manuscript in preparation.

Rozin, P., Hanko, K., & Gohar, D. (2009). *Individual differences in the importance of experienced, remembered and anticipated pleasure across different domains of life.* Manuscript in preparation.

Rozin, P., Hanko, K., & Durlach, P. (2006). Self-prediction of hedonic trajectories for repeated use of body products and foods: Poor performance, not improved by a full generation of experience. *Appetite, 46*, 297–303.

Rozin, P., Remick, A. R., & Fischler, C. (2009). *Broad themes of difference between French and Americans in attitudes to food and pleasure: Individualized vs collective values, abundance vs moderation, quantity vs quality, and comforts vs joys.* Submitted manuscript.

Rozin, P., Riklis, J., & Margolis, L. (2004). Mutual exposure or close peer relationships do not seem to foster increased similarity in food, music or television program preferences. *Appetite, 42*, 41–48.

Rozin, A., Rozin, P., & Goldberg, E. (2004). The feeling of music past: How listeners remember musical affect. *Music Perception, 22*, 15–39.

Rozin, P., & Schiller, D. (1980). The nature and acquisition of a preference for chili pepper by humans. *Motivation and Emotion, 4*, 77–101.

Rozin, P., & Taylor, S. (2006). *Determinants of remembered pleasure after experiencing an art exhibit with rooms devoted to three different artists.* Manuscript in preparation.

Rozin, P., Wrzesniewski, A., & Byrnes, D. (1998). The elusiveness of evaluative conditioning. *Learning & Motivation, 29*, 397–415.

Schutz, H. G. (1989). Beyond preference: Appropriateness as a measure of contextual acceptance of food. In D. M. H. Thomson (Ed.), *Food acceptability* (pp. 115–134). Essex, Eng.: Elsevier Applied Science Publishers.

Scitovsky, T. (1992). *The joyless economy.* Oxford, UK: Oxford University Press.

Wansink, B., Payne, C. R., & North, J. (2007). Fine as North Dakota wine: Sensory expectations and the intake of companion foods. *Physiology and Behavior, 90*, 712–716.

Wrzesniewski, A., McCauley, C. R., & Rozin, P. (1999). Odor and affect: Individual differences in the impact of odor on liking for places, things and people. *Chemical Senses, 24*, 713–721.

Zajonc, R. B. (1968). Attitudinal effects of mere exposure. *Journal of Personality and Social Psychology, 9*, 1–27.

20

Estimating Food Quantity
Biases and Remedies

Pierre Chandon

When thinking about food, consumers focus on qualitative decisions about what to eat rather than quantitative decisions about how much to eat (Rozin, Ashmore, & Markwith, 1996). For example, a majority of Americans say that they finish all the food on their plates, no matter how much food they find there; and even more think that to lose weight, the kind of food they eat matters more than how much they eat (Collins, 2006). Thinking of foods as either good or bad regardless of quantity is also common in the dieting industry and among policy makers who tend to promote qualitative remedies of the "eat this, not that" sort. For example, the USDA Dietary Guidelines for Americans (Thompson & Veneman, 2005) contain dozens of recommendations on which food groups to encourage and which ones to avoid, but no guidance on how to better estimate portion or meal sizes.

The prevailing focus on consumer's qualitative decisions about food has obscured the importance of their quantitative judgments regarding how much food they should buy, store, and consume. Understanding how people estimate food quantity—especially changes in food quantity—is particularly important given the current twin trends of supersizing and bulk buying, two of the primary drivers of the obesity epidemic (Ledikwe, Ello-Martin, & Rolls, 2005). Yet we have no overarching understanding of how people estimate food quantity, or of the potential sources of bias in these estimations, or of the interventions that can improve the accuracy of food quantity estimations.

In this chapter I develop a framework of how people estimate food quantity, particularly changes in food quantity. Following Arkes (1991), the framework distinguishes among quantity-based, salience-based, and association-based biases, and it allows us to make predictions about the effectiveness of three common remedies: education and motivation, increased salience, and piecemeal estimation. I then review empirical and experimental research that tests the predictions of the framework.

A Framework of How People Estimate Food Quantity

In out-of-home consumption contexts, quantity information is either not available or hard to obtain, so people have no choice but to estimate food quantity visually. For packaged food, people can obtain information about quantity from the label. However, surveys of shoppers have shown that many people do not read labels and rely instead on memory or visual estimates. In some cases, this is because they think that the size of the package itself is a valid proxy for the quantity of food it contains (Lennard, Mitchell, McGoldrick, & Betts, 2001). In others, it is because quantity information is difficult to process, especially with nonmetric units (Viswanathan, Rosa, & Harris, 2005). Computing quantity information is even more difficult when people have to aggregate across different unit sizes, for example, when estimating the quantity of food in a home pantry or refrigerator. For all these reasons, food quantity is more often estimated visually than computed, and food quantity estimations are influenced by three potential sources of bias: (a) the quantity of the food itself, (b) its visual salience, and (c) its association with health primes and numeric anchors.

Quantity-Based Bias

Research in psychophysics (Stevens, 1986) and in marketing (Krider, Raghubir, & Krishna, 2001) has shown that quantity estimates follow an inelastic power function of actual quantity. This relationship, known as the power law of sensation, can be expressed mathematically as:

$$ESTQ = a \times (ACTQ)^b \qquad (19.1)$$

where ESTQ is the estimated quantity, ACTQ is the actual quantity, a is an intercept, and b is the power exponent that captures the elasticity of the estimation.

In her review of psychophysics research on quantity perception, Krishna (2007) showed that power exponents b tend to fall between .5 and 1.0, and thus that estimations are inelastic to the actual change in quantity. This inelasticity means that people underestimate the magnitude of quantity changes. If the actual quantity is multiplied by a factor of r, the perceived quantity is multiplied by a factor of $(r)^{\wedge}b$, which is a smaller number since $b < 1$. It also means that quantity estimations are nonlinear and exhibit marginally decreasing sensitivity. In other words, the subjective impact of increasing food quantity diminishes as the quantity of food increases. As a result, underestimation becomes more likely and increases in magnitude as food quantity increases, even when the magnitude of the underestimation is measured as the percentage deviation from actual quantity (for mathematical proof, see Chandon & Wansink, 2007b). Equation (1) implies that small quantities (below $ACTQ^* = a^{\wedge}[1/(1 - b)]$) are likely to be overestimated, whereas large quantities (above $ACTQ^*$) are likely to be underestimated.

Salience-Based Bias

Studies have shown that the power exponent measuring the elasticity of estimations is influenced by the perceptual salience of the different spatial dimensions of the stimulus. For example, Krider et al. (2001) found that the power exponent of area estimations for two-dimensional objects is greater when the salience of secondary dimensions (those which are not used as anchors) is increased. Building on this idea, I predict that visual salience will also be influenced by the number of spatial dimensions that change when food quantity changes. Food marketers can supersize a package by increasing only one dimension (e.g., its height) or by increasing all three spatial dimensions (height, width, and length). This hypothesis is supported by prior research that showed that three-dimensional objects (e.g., spheres) appear to grow more slowly than one-dimensional objects (e.g., segments), partly because it is visually easier to notice quantity changes when only one dimension changes (see Krishna, 2007 for a review).

Generalizing these findings, I also predict that the elasticity of quantity estimation will increase with the perceptual salience of the food quantity itself (e.g., its visibility at the time of the estimation). For example, estimation should be more sensitive to a change in quantity when food quantity is highly visible than when it is not.

Association-Based Bias

When estimating food quantity, associations with numeric reference points or semantic primes can bias estimations through a variety of mechanisms such as selective accessibility, anchoring and adjustment, or conversational norms (Krishna & Raghubir, 1997; Mussweiler, 2003; Wansink, Kent, & Hoch, 1998). Association-based bias can therefore have a major effect on quantity estimation. However, there is no indication that it interacts with quantity-based bias to influence people's sensitivity to changes in quantity.

In the context of food quantity estimation, numeric reference points can be provided externally. For example, people may have information about the quantity of other food available at the time of the estimation (such as the number of calories of other dishes on the menu). Even completely irrelevant contextual information, such as the quantity of packages per shipping box, can influence quantity judgments (Wansink et al., 1998). In the absence of an external reference point, people may generate a reference point internally, for example, by using the average or usual quantity of food. Semantic primes can occur in the form of the health positioning adopted by food and restaurant brands, by the type of food available on the menu or in the store, or by specific nutritional claims made (e.g., "low-fat"), which are often erroneously extrapolated (Andrews, Netemeyer, & Burton, 1998).

Summary

Figure 20.1 summarizes the key predictions of the framework. In all conditions, estimated food quantity follows an inelastic power function of actual food quantity (ESTQ = $a \times$ (ACTQ)^b where $a > 0$ and $b < 1$). Increasing the salience of food quantity makes estimation less inelastic (i.e., increases b). In contrast, association bias has a main effect (i.e., the intercept a changes) but does not interact with the effects of the actual quantity (b remains constant).

Improving the Accuracy of Food Quantity Estimations

This framework allows us to make predictions about the effectiveness of three common interventions designed to improve the accuracy of food quantity estimation: (a) consumer education and motivation, (b) increasing the salience of the food quantity, and (c) encouraging people to use a piecemeal estimation.

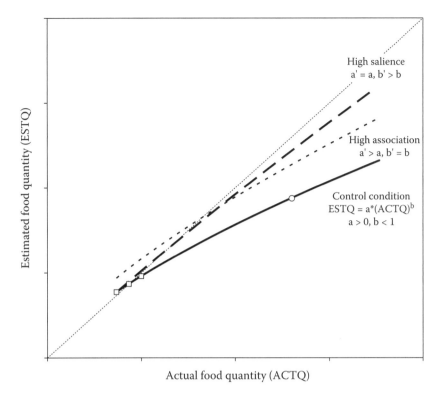

Figure 20.1 Predicted effects of size-, salience-, and association-based biases on food quantity estimations.

Education and Motivation

Disclosing information about biases and motivating consumers to be more accurate can help reduce the association-based bias caused by numeric anchors or by semantic primes. To be really effective, however, the intervention has to do more than alert people to the existence of the bias; it needs to specifically prompt them to question the validity of the biasing association. For example, Mussweiler, Strack, and Pfeiffer (2000) show that asking people to give reasons why an anchor is inappropriate reduces association-based bias.

Education and motivation, however, cannot reduce psychophysical biases because the automatic low-level perceptual processes drive the shape of the psychophysical function (Arkes, 1991; Raghubir, 2007). Education and motivation can only influence the intercept of the power function, and hence shift the curve up or down in Figure 20.1, but cannot improve the accuracy with which people notice a change in actual food quantity.

Salience

A straightforward way to improve the accuracy of food estimation is to increase the visual salience of the food quantity itself. In contrast to the educational and motivational strategy, increasing the salience of food quantity can improve how accurately people perceive changes in food quantity because it increases the elasticity of quantity estimation. By influencing both the intercept and exponent of the psychophysical functions, an enhanced salience can improve both the mean food quantity estimate and people's responses to changes in food quantity.

To improve the salience of food in pantries or refrigerators, the visual area or volume taken up by the food must be a good indicator of its actual quantity. This can be done by storing food visibly, by reducing clutter, and by avoiding stacking packages at different depths in the pantry shelves. This can also be done at the single pack level by increasing the correlation between package size and the actual quantity of the contents. For example, multiple packages of food can be spread and put in a visible place in the center of the pantry. The shape of the package itself can also be simplified so that it does not imply more food than it actually contains (Folkes & Matta, 2004). Finally, when packages or portions are supersized or downsized, marketers can increase the salience of the quantity change by changing only one of the dimensions of the package (e.g., its height) rather than by changing all of its dimensions.

Piecemeal Estimation

Compared to the first two remedies, the piecemeal estimation procedure does not attempt to correct the level or the shape of the psychophysical functions but follows Arkes' recommendation to exploit the level or the shape of the existing psychophysical function by changing the location of the options or the location of one's reference point on the curve. The basic notion is to avoid significantly underestimating a large quantity by dividing it into multiple smaller portions and by asking people to estimate each of these smaller portions. The piecemeal estimation therefore replaces a single estimation of a large quantity located on the flatter portion of the psychophysical curve (e.g., the white circle in Figure 20.1), which is likely to be significantly underestimated with multiple estimations of smaller quantities located on the steeper portion of the curve where the slope is closer to 1 and the curve is close to the 45° line (e.g., the black squares in Figure 20.1).

Note that, in addition to increasing the sensitivity to changes in meal size, the piecemeal decomposition strategy also leads to an overall increase in food quantity estimation because it reduces the likelihood of forgetting a component of the meal (Srivastava & Raghubir, 2002). It is unclear, however, whether piecemeal estimation can reduce association-based bias. In addition, this procedure is only appropriate for the estimation of large quantities, which tends to be underestimated. Conversely, with very small quantities it is possible that the estimation will exceed the actual amount; using the piecemeal estimation procedure would compound the overestimation error. In this case, people should be encouraged to estimate the amount of food contained in a larger quantity than the one that they are first estimating (e.g., estimate for two packages and divide the estimate by 2).

In practice, to estimate a total amount of product inventory, people can first estimate the amount of food contained in one single package and then multiply it by the total number of packages. To estimate the amount of food contained in one meal, people can estimate the quantity of food in the main dish and the side dish and then add them. To estimate the size of a single food portion (e.g., the number of calories in a sandwich), people can mentally cut the sandwich in four portions and then multiply their estimate by 4.

Summary

At least three strategies are available to help people estimate food quantity more accurately. Educating consumers and motivating them to be more accurate is the standard strategy and can help reduce association-based bias by prompting people to question the validity of the associations. However, education and motivation alone cannot improve the elasticity of quantity estimation. In contrast, increasing the visual salience of food quantity can help reduce all types of bias. Adopting a piecemeal estimation procedure can also help reduce quantity-based bias and the underestimation of large quantities. Compared to the salience-based approach, it does not involve actually changing the way the food is packaged or displayed.

Unlike the educational approach, it does not require a lot of explaining and can be easily implemented. However, it needs to be reversed for very small quantities and may not reduce association-based bias.

Experimental and Empirical Evidence

In this section I review empirical and experimental research (conducted primarily with Brian Wansink) that tests parts of the framework in three different contexts: (a) when estimating the amount of calories contained in restaurant meals, (b) when estimating the amount of food available in household pantries, and (c) when estimating the size of food portions.

There is a large body of research on how people estimate consumption intake (Livingstone & Black, 2003). Although some of their findings, such as the overreporting of small intakes and the significant underreporting of large intakes, are consistent with the predictions of the framework, they are not reviewed here because these studies were not designed to test the predictions of the framework. For that same reason, I do not review the studies examining the consequences of food quantity estimation biases (for a recent review, see Krishna, 2007).[1]

Restaurant Meal Estimation

Brian Wansink and I (Chandon & Wansink, 2007a, 2007b) examined how people estimate the quantity of calories or food contained in fast-food meals in a series of field and laboratory studies. In the field studies, we asked people who had just finished eating a meal at either Subway (which claims to serve healthy meals) or McDonald's (which does not make that claim) to estimate the total number of calories in the meal. We recorded and confirmed the type and size of the food and drinks from the wrappings left on the tray and obtained information about the actual number of calories in the food and beverage from the restaurant's Web site. To increase the comparability of McDonald's and Subway meals, we restricted the analysis to meals consisting of a sandwich, a soft drink, and a side order.

The first panel of Figure 20.2 shows the mean estimated and actual number of calories for each quartile of the meals ordered at Subway and McDonald's. The predicted power curves fitted the quantity estimations very well for both restaurants, indicating that quantity estimations followed an inelastic power function of actual quantity, as expected. The

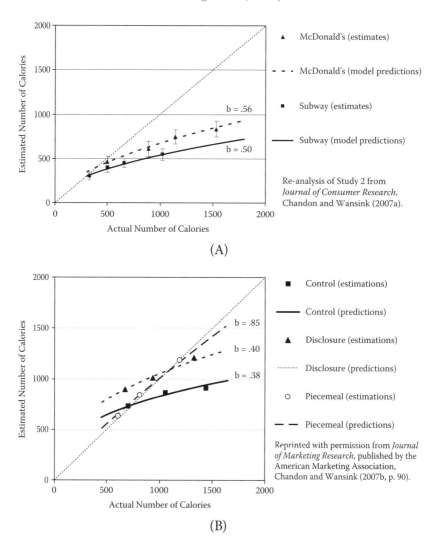

Figure 20.2 Restaurant meal estimations: effects of health claims (A) and of two remedies (B).

power exponent was approximately .5 for both restaurants, which meant that meals twice as large only appeared about 41% bigger (2^.5) and hence that perceived quantity grew a lot more slowly than actual quantity. As a result, people were roughly accurate for small meals but significantly underestimated the number of calories in the large meals ordered from both Subway and McDonald's. More importantly, although Subway meals tended to be smaller (the median meal contained 504 calories at Subway vs.

891 at McDonald's), calorie estimations were higher for McDonald's meals than for Subway meals of the same size. For example, the mean predicted calorie estimation for a 1,000-calorie meal was 744 calories for McDonald's but only 585 calories for Subway. In summary, the stronger association of Subway with healthy meals led people to believe that Subway meals contained fewer calories than same-calorie McDonald's meals but did not influence how accurately people responded to changes in meal size.

In a laboratory study, Brian Wansink and I (Chandon & Wansink, 2007b) examined the ability of two remedies to improve the accuracy of fast-food meal size estimation: increased information and motivation, and the piecemeal estimation procedure. Participants were first asked to order the amount of chicken nuggets, fries, and beverage that they wanted. Participants in the control condition were simply asked to estimate the total number of calories of the meal that they had ordered. Participants in the bias disclosure condition were informed about the direction and magnitude of quantity-based biases and given an incentive to provide accurate estimates. Participants in the piecemeal estimation condition were asked to estimate the number of calories of the nuggets, fries, and beverage separately.

As the bottom panel of Figure 20.2 shows, the lab study replicated the findings of the field study even in a controlled setting in which the type of food was held constant and only its quantity varied. More importantly, Figure 20.2B shows that increasing information and motivation led to a general increase in calorie estimation but did not improve people's sensitivity to changes in quantity (the exponent remained unchanged). In contrast, the piecemeal estimation procedure raised the exponent to a value that was not statistically different from 1, thereby effectively removing quantity biases. These results were also replicated in a study of certified dieticians who, although generally more accurate than the average consumer, provided more elastic, and hence more accurate, estimations when asked to evaluate each component of a meal separately (for details on this study, see Chandon & Wansink, 2007b).

Pantry Inventory Estimation

Brian Wansink and I (Chandon & Wansink, 2006) also examined people's estimations of the quantity of remaining product inventory by conducting four studies, two in the lab and two in the field. In one study we asked people to examine a picture of a pantry containing eight target products.

We manipulated food quantity (one, three, seven, or nine units) and the salience (high or low) of these products. Salient products were located on the top or middle shelf of the pantry (as opposed to the bottom shelf), separate from other products (rather than being crowded together with them), and were given multiple facings when available in more than one unit (rather than being stacked together in an overlapping fashion). After evaluating some nontarget brands, the pantry picture was removed and participants were asked to estimate the number of units of the eight target products and their home inventory for these products.

Figure 20.3 shows that, as expected, pantry inventory estimations followed an inelastic power function of the actual product quantity (average power exponent $b = .42$). Second, estimations of low quantity levels were slightly above the truth, whereas estimations of large quantity levels were significantly below the truth. The first panel of Figure 20.3 also shows that the elasticity was lower when salience was low ($b = .32$) than when it was high ($b = .49$). As a result, estimations were more accurate when product quantity was salient than when it was not. These findings were replicated in two field studies in which we asked supermarket shoppers to estimate the home inventory of 23 food products, to rate the visibility of these products in their pantries, and to then check the actual home inventory levels. These studies also showed that the least elastic—and thus least accurate— estimations were those of product categories often bought on impulse and difficult to stockpile.

To test the biasing effects of anchors, we categorized participants into a low and high internal anchor groups based on their average home inventory level for each product. The second panel of Figure 20.3 shows that quantity estimations were higher among participants with a high (vs. low) home inventory, but that the power exponent remained unchanged. This shows that, as predicted by the framework, association-based bias has a main effect on quantity estimations but does not interact with quantity effects. Similar reference effects were found in another study that showed that providing high and low external anchors, by asking people whether the quantity was above or below nine or one, shifted quantity estimations but did not change the power exponent.

Food Portion Estimations

Nailya Ordabayeva and I (Chandon & Ordabayeva, forthcoming) studied people's estimations of the quantity of product contained in packages

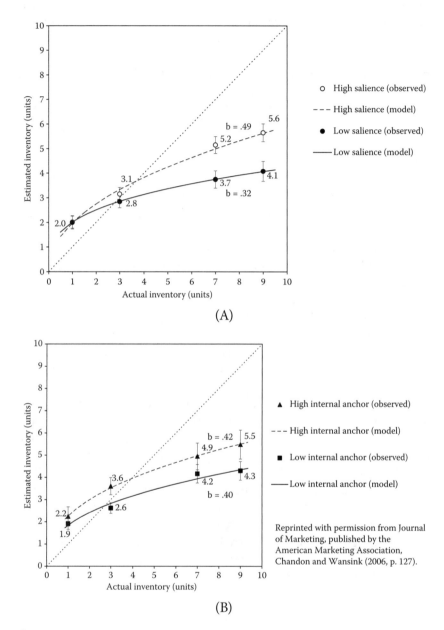

(A)

(B)

Reprinted with permission from Journal of Marketing, published by the American Marketing Association, Chandon and Wansink (2006, p. 127).

Figure 20.3   Pantry inventory estimations: effects of quantity and salience (A) and of internal anchors (B).

or portions that either increased in all three spatial dimensions (height, weight, length) or in only one dimension (height only). In the first two studies we asked people to estimate the weight of six sizes of the same product that either grew along one spatial dimension (e.g., strands of wool with increasing length) or along three spatial dimensions (e.g., spherical balls of wool of increasing diameter). Participants were given the weight of the smallest size and were supposed to realize that each increasing size contained twice as much product. Although we did not use food products in these studies, three other studies show that the effects of dimensionality apply equally well to food and nonfood products.

As Figure 20.4 shows, quantity estimations were highly inelastic in the three-dimensional condition (b = .68) and almost perfectly elastic in the one-dimensional condition (b = .93). For example, an eightfold increase in product quantity gave the appearance of being a fourfold increase in the three-dimensional condition and a sevenfold increase in the one-dimensional condition. This study therefore provided additional evidence of the quantity-based bias predicted by the framework. It also showed that, as expected, increasing the salience of the product quantity change (by increasing the physical size of the product along one dimension only) improved the accuracy of people's estimations. These findings

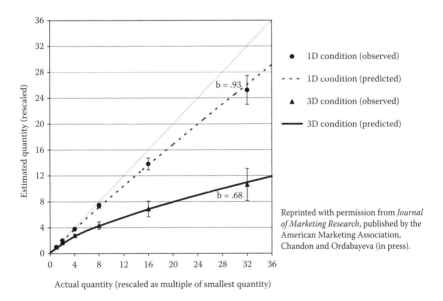

Reprinted with permission from *Journal of Marketing Research*, published by the American Marketing Association, Chandon and Ordabayeva (in press).

Figure 20.4 Portion and package estimations: effects of the spatial dimensionality of product size change.

were replicated in a quantity production task (as opposed to a quantity estimation task) in which participants had to pour predetermined quantities of product into or out of cylindrical glasses (in which volume changes in one dimension) or conical glasses (e.g., martini cocktail glasses, in which volume changes in three dimensions). Again, changes in quantity appeared smaller in the three-dimensional condition. When participants were asked to triple an existing volume of alcohol, they poured roughly the right amount into cylindrical glasses, but almost four times the amount into the conical glasses.

In two papers, Brian Wansink and I studied the effect of association-based bias on portion size estimation by examining the effects of specific nutritional claims such as "low-fat" (Wansink & Chandon, 2006) and the health claims of the food brand (Chandon & Wansink, 2007a). In one study, we showed a ham sandwich and manipulated the health claim by changing the name of the restaurant ("Good Karma Healthy Foods" vs. "Jim's Hearty Sandwiches") and the other items on the menu. In the control condition, we asked participants to estimate the number of calories of the target food. To test the effectiveness of providing debiasing instructions, participants in the "consider the opposite" condition were first asked to find arguments supporting the idea that the ham sandwich was a generic meal that was not typical of the restaurant that served it. Figure 20.5A shows that in the control condition calorie estimations were significantly lower for the healthy menu than for the unhealthy menu. Conversely, in the "consider the opposite" condition calorie estimations were essentially the same regardless of the health associations. Prompting people to question the validity of health primes therefore eliminated association-based bias.

In Wansink and Chandon (2006), we examined the effects of association-based bias on food quantity estimation and also on actual food consumption. We gave people who were going to watch a movie a bag of granola that was either labeled "regular" or "low-fat." In order to test the debiasing effect of providing information about the actual quantity of product, half the bags were labeled "Contains one serving," whereas the other half did not have any serving size information. At the end of the movie, we asked people to estimate how much granola they had eaten, and we weighed what was left in their bags to measure how much they had actually eaten. As Figure 20.5B shows, "low-fat" labels led to underestimation in all conditions. When serving size information was absent, calorie estimations were similar in both conditions, even though calorie intake was higher by 51% in the "low-fat" condition. When serving size information was present,

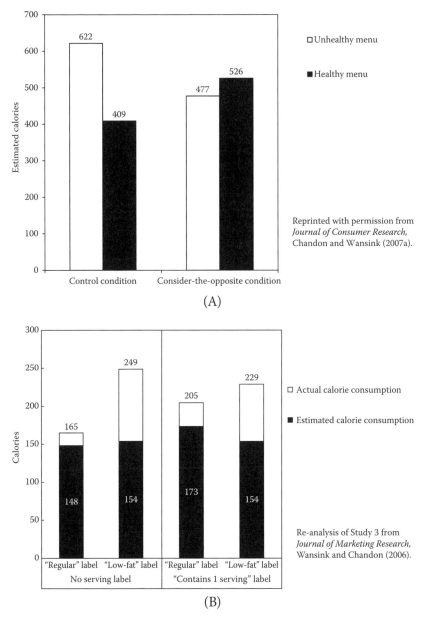

Reprinted with permission from
Journal of Consumer Research,
Chandon and Wansink (2007a).

Re-analysis of Study 3 from
Journal of Marketing Research,
Wansink and Chandon (2006).

Figure 20.5 Portions estimations: effects of health claims and remedies on estimations (A) and on estimations and actual consumption (B).

"low-fat" labels actually reduced calorie estimation despite increasing calorie intake by 12%. Overall, these studies provide additional evidence that health associations bias quantity estimation, and that encouraging people to question their validity can reduce this type of associative bias, but simply providing serving size information is not enough.

Conclusions

In the battle against overeating, the current emphasis on what to eat has obscured the importance of quantitative decisions about how much to eat. This chapter builds a framework of how people estimate food quantity, what should be done to improve their accuracy, and what we know about how people estimate the quantity of food in restaurant meals, pantry inventory, and portion sizes. Table 20.1 summarizes the key findings.

There still are, of course, a number of important unresolved issues about the process through which people estimate food quantities. With the exception of those studies in which quantity was estimated postintake, all the studies reviewed here focused on visual estimation. Future research should examine how people integrate different sensory modalities. For example, Krishna (2006) showed that sensory modality (touch vs. vision) influences judgments of the size of cylindrical glasses. It would also be interesting to examine individual differences. For example, Krishna, Zhou, and Zhang (2008) found that individuals with independent (vs. interdependent) self-construals are more prone to spatial judgment biases.

Finally, it would be interesting to conduct a systematic analysis of the differences between experienced, remembered, and predicted quantity estimations. This would allow us to study the dynamics of quantity estimation and hence to examine why so little learning seems to occur over time.

TABLE 20.1   Key Findings on Food Quantity Estimation Biases and Remedies

Findings	References
Biases in How People Estimate Food Quantities	
Food quantity estimations are inelastic to actual quantity changes (i.e., they change more slowly than they should). As a result, people accurately estimate small food quantities but strongly underestimate large quantities.	(Chandon & Ordabayeva, in press; Chandon & Wansink, 2006; Chandon & Wansink, 2007b; Krider et al., 2001)
Estimations are more elastic when a) the secondary spatial dimension of the product is perceptually salient, b) the visual area in the pantry is correlated with actual quantity, or c) packages or portions increase along only one spatial dimension.	(Chandon & Ordabayeva, in press; Chandon & Wansink, 2006; Krider et al., 2001)
Health associations created by a) branding, b) nutrition labels or c) reference points bias quantity estimations but do not influence people's sensitivity to changes in quantity.	(Chandon & Wansink, 2007a; Chandon & Wansink, 2006; Wansink & Chandon, 2006)
How to Improve the Accuracy of Food Quantity Estimations	
Providing information about the existence of biases and incentives can shift estimations but does not reduce association-based bias unless consumers are specifically asked to question the validity of the health claim	(Chandon & Wansink, 2007a; Chandon & Wansink, 2007b).
Increasing the salience of food quantity by making it more visible in the pantry, or by only supersizing packages and portions along one dimension, improves both the mean accuracy of estimation and sensitivity to quantity changes.	(Chandon & Ordabayeva, in press; Chandon & Wansink, 2006; Krider et al., 2001)
Piecemeal estimation procedure improves sensitivity to quantity changes and reduces the underestimation of large quantities, but is only appropriate for large quantities and does not reduce association-based bias.	(Chandon & Wansink, 2006; Chandon & Wansink, 2007b).

Note

1. Prior research has shown that quantity biases influence consumption incidence and quantity (Folkes & Matta, 2004; Raghubir & Krishna, 1999; Wansink, 1996, 2004; Wansink & Chandon, 2006; Wansink et al., 1998), repurchase timing (Chandon & Wansink, 2006), side-dish consumption (Chandon & Wansink, 2007a), food waste (Chandon & Wansink, 2006), and the stereotyping of obese people (Chandon & Wansink, 2007b).

References

Andrews, J. C., Netemeyer, R. G., & Burton, S. (1998). Consumer generalization of nutrient content claims in advertising. *Journal of Marketing, 62*(4), 62–75.

Arkes, H. R. (1991). Costs and benefits of judgment errors: Implications for debiasing. *Psychological Bulletin, 110*(3), 486–498.

Chandon, P., & Ordabayeva, N. (forthcoming). Supersize in 1D, downsize in 3D: Effects of spatial dimensionality on size perceptions and preferences. *Journal of Marketing Research*.

Chandon, P., & Wansink, B. (2006). How biased household inventory estimates distort shopping and storage decisions. *Journal of Marketing, 70*(4), 118–135.

Chandon, P., & Wansink, B. (2007a, October). The biasing health halos of fast food restaurant health claims: Lower calorie estimates and higher side-dish consumption intentions. *Journal of Consumer Research, 34,* 301–314.

Chandon, P., & Wansink, B. (2007b). Is obesity caused by calorie underestimation? A psychophysical model of meal size estimation. *Journal of Marketing Research, 44*(1), 84–99.

Collins, K. (2006). *New survey on portion size: Americans still cleaning plates.* Washington, DC: American Institute for Cancer Research.

Folkes, V., & Matta, S. (2004). The effect of package shape on consumers' judgments of product volume: Attention as a mental contaminant. *Journal of Consumer Research, 31*(2), 390–401.

Krider, R. E., Raghubir, P., & Krishna, A. (2001). Pizzas: Pi or square? Psychophysical biases in area comparisons. *Marketing Science, 20*(4), 405–425.

Krishna, A. (2006). Interaction of senses: The effect of vision versus touch on the elongation bias. *Journal of Consumer Research, 32*(4), 557–566.

Krishna, A. (2007). Spatial perception research: An integrative review of length, area, volume and number perception. In M. Wedel & R. Pieters (Eds.), *Visual marketing: From attention to action* (pp. 167–192). New York: Erlbaum.

Krishna, A., & Raghubir, P. (1997). The effect of line configuration on perceived numerosity of dotted lines. *Memory and Cognition, 25*(4), 492–507.

Krishna, A., Zhou, R., & Zhang, S. (2008). The effect of self-construal on spatial judgments. *Journal of Consumer Research, 35*(2), 337–348.

Ledikwe, J. H., Ello-Martin, J. A., & Rolls, B. J. (2005). Portion sizes and the obesity epidemic. *Journal of Nutrition, 135*(4), 905–909.

Lennard, D., Mitchell, V.-W., McGoldrick, P., & Betts, E. (2001). Why consumers under-use food quantity indicators. *International Review of Retail, Distribution and Consumer Research, 11*(2), 177–199.

Livingstone, M. B. E., & Black, A. E. (2003). Markers of the validity of reported energy intake. *Journal of Nutrition, 133*(3), 895S–920S.

Mussweiler, T. (2003). Comparison processes in social judgment: Mechanisms and consequences. *Psychological Review, 110*(3), 472–489.

Mussweiler, T., Strack, F., & Pfeiffer, T. (2000). Overcoming the inevitable anchoring effect: Considering the opposite compensates for selective accessibility. *Personality and Social Psychology Bulletin, 26*(9), 1142–1150.

Raghubir, P. (2007). Are visual perceptual biases hard-wired? In M. Wedel & R. Pieters (Eds.), *Visual marketing: From attention to action* (pp. 143–166). New York: Erlbaum.

Raghubir, P., & Krishna, A. (1999). Vital dimensions in volume perception: Can the eye fool the stomach? *Journal of Marketing Research, 36*(3), 313–326.

Rozin, P., Ashmore, M., & Markwith, M. (1996). Lay American conceptions of nutrition: Dose insensitivity, categorical thinking, contagion, and the monotonic mind. *Health Psychology, 15*(6), 438–447.

Srivastava, J., & Raghubir, P. (2002). Debiasing using decomposition: The case of memory-based credit card expense estimates. *Journal of Consumer Psychology, 12*(3), 253–264.

Stevens, S. S. (1986). *Psychophysics: Introduction to its perceptual, neural, and social prospects*. Oxford, UK: Transaction Books.

Thompson, T. G., & Veneman, A. M. (2005). *Dietary guidelines for Americans* (6th ed.). Washington DC: U.S. Government Printing Office.

Viswanathan, M., Rosa, J. A., & Harris, J. E. (2005, January). Decision making and coping of functionally illiterate consumers and some implications for marketing management. *Journal of Marketing, 69*, 15–31.

Wansink, B. (1996). Can package size accelerate usage volume? *Journal of Marketing, 60*(3), 1–14.

Wansink, B. (2004). Environmental factors that increase the food intake and consumption volume of unknowing consumers. *Annual Review of Nutrition, 24*, 455–479.

Wansink, B., & Chandon, P. (2006). Can "low-fat" nutrition labels lead to obesity? *Journal of Marketing Research, 43*(4), 605–617.

Wansink, B., Kent, R. J., & Hoch, S. J. (1998, February). An anchoring and adjustment model of purchase quantity decisions. *Journal of Marketing Research, 35*, 71–81.

21

Do Size Labels Have a Common Meaning Among Consumers?

Nilufer Z. Aydinoglu, Aradhna Krishna,
and Brian Wansink

The influence of language on perception and cognition has been observed for a long time. A number of studies have shown that labels influence visual perception (Lewis, 1963; O'Hare, 1987), sound recognition (Bartlett, 1977), music perception (Meyer, 1956), tactile simulation (Hoshikawa, 1991), color perception (Roberson, Davies, & Davidoff, 2000), and olfactory perception (Herz, 2003). However, the effects of labels on perception are relatively untouched within the domain of consumer behavior. In this chapter, we explore the effects of labeling on size perceptions of consumers.

SuperSize, Value-Size, Double-Gulp

In the past three decades, package sizes and portions have increased two to five times across a wide range of food and drink categories in the United States, with the greatest increases occurring for food consumed at fast food establishments (Goode, 2003; Young & Nestle, 2002). At the same time, there has been a great proliferation of size labels used by vendors in these categories in an effort to differentiate themselves. In order to stand out as having better size value or to discourage size comparisons with other brands, many firms came up with new size labels. Consider the Whopper (Burger King), the Big Gulp (7-11), the Super-Quencher (Jack in the Box), and even the ill-fated Super-Size (McDonald's). As part of their image-building activities and to downplay size as a feature, some firms have also devised their own size labels, such as Venti (Starbucks), Sixteen, Original, and Power (Jamba Juice), which are even more difficult to compare with products of other firms in terms of size.

The question then arises, when there are so many different size labels, how can they get absorbed into the everyday vocabulary of consumers, and do they have a common meaning? Thus, is a Super-Quencher drink considered bigger than a large or a jumbo drink and does this hold for the majority of the population? Is a big-kid-size food portion considered bigger or smaller than a small portion? Is a king-size portion larger than a family-size portion? What connotations do these labels have; what linguistic characteristics have they come to acquire if any? When there are a large number of sizes for an item (e.g., soft drinks, food portions), is there a common ranking of sizes perceived across customers? A second and related question is whether the perception of a size label is affected by who is offering it—that is, if McDonald's versus California Pizza Kitchen offers a large drink, do people have the same perception of what the size of this large drink is, or is the size perception affected by the source?

The impact of commercial practices on American literature and language has been partly explored by Friedman (1985), where he finds support for the usage of brand names and generic names as part of everyday language through his analysis of American literature. Furthermore, with commercialization, brand names are taking the place of actual product categories in everyday language, some examples being FedEx, Kleenex, or Jeep. We examine whether the commercial practice of labeling actually introduces *new words* into the common language of the consumer. In other words, our major objective is to demonstrate whether many of the commercially invented size labels have come to share common meaning across customers.

Size Labels as Discriminating Attributes

Judgments are suggestible. Information processing theories assume that recent and frequently employed knowledge structures are more accessible in memory and are weighed more heavily in judgment than the information that originally generated them (Feldman & Lynch, 1988; Menon, Raghubir, & Schwarz, 1995). Thus, judgments may be influenced both by the stimulus itself and by the label given to the stimulus, the latter may be weighed more heavily in the judgment of the target even though the former generated the latter.

At the start of the chapter we mentioned that various studies demonstrate the influence of verbal context on different modes of sensory perception. In these studies, verbal context is seen as a mediator for different dimensions of cognitive processes such as perceptions of similarity and the mental organization of objects. For instance, with sound perception, Bartlett (1977) showed that if a sound is labeled as either *cat meow* or *baby crying*, it will subsequently be recognized in accord with its label. Similar effects have been found with olfactory perception, where, for example, the same stimulus was perceived in entirely different ways when it was labeled *Parmesan cheese* or *vomit* (Herz, 2003). Likewise, with taste perception, labels suggesting food as *tasty* have been shown to influence perceptions of taste and also the past recall of taste more than the food itself (Wansink, Painter, & Van Ittersum, 2001).

These effects draw a close parallel to the categorization literature, which may help us better understand the potential impact of size labels on consumer perception. Categorization refers to phenomena whereby perceivers' interpretations, evaluations, or judgments of different targets depend on the groups to which the individual targets belong (Jussim, Manis, Nelson, & Soffin, 1995). Once an object is categorized, category knowledge is utilized in the evaluations of the target (Bagozzi, Gurhan-Canli, & Priester, 2002). Within consumer research, categorization has been shown to influence information search, memory, inference, and choice (Alba & Hutchinson, 1987; Cohen & Basu, 1987; Loken & Ward, 1990; Schmitt & Zhang, 1998). Murphy and Medin (1985) show that the construction and retrieval processes in categorization are constrained by internal structures in people's minds. One important internal structure is language structure, where linguistic labels exercise a top–down influence on categorization and related behavior (Hunt & Agnoli, 1991). Through their effect on perceived similarity, labels act as classifiers and affect judgment and choice. Once individuals have classified objects into categories based on perceived similarities, they expect certain attributes to be present and as a result draw schema-consistent inferences. Thus, categorization can influence consumer expectations.

Under the categorization perspective, size labels can be seen as representing categories such that two products, which have the same specific size label attached to them, will be categorized under the same unique size class. Thus, if consumers perceive a product to belong to a certain size category through inferences from its size label, this categorization may facilitate information processing, evaluations, and decisions (Hollis & Valentine, 2001). Accordingly, as new labels are learned and become part of a common understanding, they will be influential as discriminating attributes. Gelman and Markman (1987) and Yamauchi and Markman (2000) found that *people should derive inductive perceptions of size relating to different size labels based primarily on that category (i.e., the size label itself), and these judgments should be invariant across different product sources.*

This chapter examines two studies that we conducted to determine if size labels have a common meaning across customers and if this holds across different product sources. The results are presented in the next sections.

Study 1: Do Size Labels Have a Common Meaning Across Consumers?

Study 1 tests whether size labels have a common meaning across consumers. For purposes of robustness, we chose two categories with different connotations of size: soft drinks (size of a glass) and package sizes of potato chips (size of a plastic bag).

Study 1 Stimuli and Method

Pretest
In a pretest with 42 undergraduate students, we generated size labels for the two categories mentioned above. For each category, 12 common labels were provided to participants, and they were asked to add to this list. We chose the most commonly appearing labels from the participants' lists, so that we ended up with 14 labels in each category. The list of labels used for each category can be found in Figures 21.1 and 21.2. Some of these are traditionally used size labels (petite, small, medium, large, extra-large), while others are commercially introduced labels, whose dictionary meanings are nonexistent or which are used differently from their lexical (dictionary) meanings (e.g., super-quencher, big-kids size).

Design
A 2 (category) × 14 (size label) within-subject design was used to assess people's understanding of size labels. Given our objective of obtaining relative size perceptions, we needed estimates for different size labels from the same person. Thus, "size label" needed to be a manipulated within-subject factor. Product category was also a manipulated within-subject

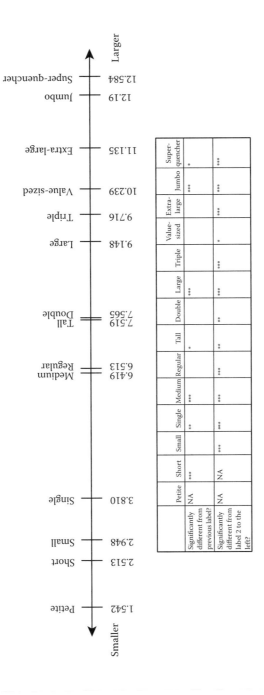

Figure 21.1   A relative comparison of perceived size differences of soft drinks (Study 1). NA, not available; *, $p < .1$; **, $p < .05$; ***, $p < .01$.

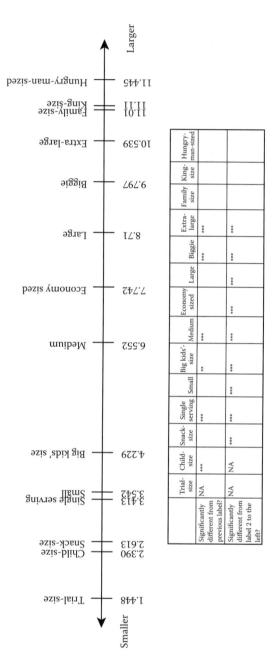

Figure 21.2 A relative comparison of perceived size differences of potato chips (Study 1). NA, not available; *, $p < .1$; **, $p < .05$; ***, $p < .01$.

factor for greater sample size. Thirty-seven respondents participated in the experiment for course credit.

Procedure

For each category, participants were given a thermometer scale and were asked to place the 14 randomly ordered labels on this scale in terms of their size. They did this by writing the respective number for each label on the line in a way that indicated their relative size to each other. For soft drinks, for instance, participants were given the following scenario and instructions:

> What follow are 14 different sizes of fountain drinks that you can get at fast food restaurants, sit down restaurants, and at convenience stores.
>
> What we would like you to do is to write each of these numbers on the line below according to their relative size. For each size, simply write the number on the line. If you think two numbers are the same size you can put the two numbers at the same point on the line.

← -- →
Smaller   Larger

  1. Petite
  2. Medium
  3. Jumbo

This procedure was repeated for potato chips. Consistent with other work on magnitude estimation (Choplin & Hummel, 2002), the primary dependent variable was the relative length (perceived size) of each size label on the thermometer scale. More specifically, it was the number of centimeters from the left arrowhead that a size label was placed by the subject. We did not anchor the scale with the actual number of ounces of soft drinks or potato chips. If consumers are prone to underestimating actual sizes, as they often do (Raghubir & Krishna, 1996), they may feel that the smaller sizes lay to the left of the leftmost point on the scale. Further, we were interested in relative perceived sizes and not absolute perceived sizes; so having ounces to anchor the scale was less important.

Seven cases were deleted from each category because of missing data (perceived size of at least one of the 14 size labels was missing); for analyses across the two categories, 11 cases were deleted (at least one of the 28 size labels was missing). We do not compare perceived size to actual size since that is not the focus of this research.

Study 1 Results and Discussion

We used a repeated measures analysis of variance to analyze results. Perceived size was the dependent variable, and product category and size label were the two independent variables, both repeated factors. Product category ($F(1,26) = 7.56, p < .05$) and size label ($F(13,338) = 228.84, p < .01$) were both significant. Simple effect tests show that size label was significant within each of the two product categories, soft drinks ($F(13,338) = 119.21, p < .01$) and potato chips ($F(13,338) = 122.39, p < .01$). Figures 21.1 and 21.2 show the positions of the size labels on each of the two thermometer scales based on mean perceived size (across subjects for that product category).

Significant size label effects for each category imply that the variance of perceived size estimates (for different size labels) among consumers is not large enough to render them nonsignificant. In other words, consumers think of size labels similarly enough that mean perceived sizes of different labels across consumers are significantly different. What is not clear is the extent to which the actual magnitude-related perceptions of labels differ from the more conventional magnitudes of small, medium, and large and from one another. That is, where do the various size labels find a place on the size continuum? To investigate this, we lined up the size labels per mean size (see Figures 21.1 and 21.2) and conducted contrast tests. The first set of contrasts compares adjacent (in mean size) size labels; the second set of contrasts compares pairs of size labels that are two labels apart. In addition, we also compare some other pairs of specific interest. Tests use the complete data for that product category (i.e., using all 14 size labels for that product category). Thus, the tests are univariate F tests with $(1, 30)$ degrees of freedom. The p values reported are for two-sided tests. Because contrasts for adjacent pairs (and also pairs of size labels two labels apart) are nonorthogonal, we perform appropriate linear transformations of the dependent variables in order to do these contrasts.

Comprehensive contrast results are reported in Figures 21.1 and 21.2. The figures show, for instance, that for soft drinks, "small" was perceived as being smaller than a "single" ($F(1,30) = 4.47, p < .05$). The pairs "large"-"triple," "triple"-"value-sized," and "value-sized"-"extra-large" were considered to be about equal in size ($p > .1$). However, "extra-large" was seen as being smaller than "jumbo" ($F(1,30) = 44.08, p < .01$), and "super-quencher" (as offered by Jack in the Box) was perceived as being the biggest of them all, even (marginally) larger than "jumbo" ($F(1,30) = 3.49, p < .1$).

For potato chips, we find that "trial-size" was considered smaller than "child-size" ($F(1,30) = 9.51$, $p < .01$), whereas the latter was considered about the same size as the "snack-size" ($p > .4$). A notable finding is that "single-serving" was similar to a "small" ($p > .6$), but a "big-kid" serving was perceived to be larger than a "single-serving" or a "small" ($F(1,30) = 4.56$, $p < .05$); this finding calls into question how much food quantity (and that includes junk food too) we feel is appropriate for our kids. On the larger end, "biggie" has an established place that is bigger than plain old "large" ($F(1,30) = 20.53$, $p < .01$). Similarly, "family-size" and "hungry-man" size have established a place in the conventional size continuum so that "family-size" is considered larger than "biggie" (which is considered bigger than large), and "hungry-man" size is considered to be larger than "extra-large" ($p < .01$ for all).

The results of Study 1 indicate that consumers have a similar understanding of new or commercially generated size labels: a "single," for example, is considered larger than "small" but smaller than "medium." "Single" is also considered larger than another commercially generated label, "petite." Our method for showing this rests on the fact that a "common meaning" for two size labels implies that there are significant differences between the perceived sizes for these two size labels. This can only happen if the variance across people in the interpretation of these size labels is not too large, that is, they have similar perceptions of these size labels. If the variance was too large, then the differences between perceived sizes associated with size labels would not be statistically significant. In devising a method to test where a company's relatively new size label fits on the size spectrum and seeing whether it has a common meaning, we offer companies an approach to test whether their own perceptions of size are consistent with reality and whether the size label is achieving what it was intended to achieve.

Thus, Study 1 findings suggest that size labels may connote unique size "categories"; consumers have a certain knowledge of these size categories and this knowledge is commonly shared across consumers. They, then, use this knowledge to draw inferences about the amount of product associated with a specific size category.

The next question of interest is whether these common meaning perceptions hold across different product sources. In other words, does the same label have the same meaning irrespective of who is offering the product? In this next study, we demonstrate that the effects are not due to the source, and that label effects are valid over and above source effects.

Study 2: Is the Perceived Size of a Size Label
Related to the Source of the Product?

One could argue that a consumer needs to know how a specific manufacturer or retailer, such as Café Kopi, labels the different sizes of its coffees before one can be reasonably certain of how large the sizes are. If this is the case, perceptions of size labels may vary by the source offering the product. In contrast, if size labels are well accepted as connoting a specific size category, then per Menon and colleagues (1995) and Yamauchi and Markman (2000), people's inductive perceptions of size should be invariant across different product sources. In Study 2, using names of real coffee houses, we investigate whether perceptions of size for different size labels (of coffee cups) vary by the offering source (the coffee house).

Study 2 Stimuli and Method

Design

A 7 (size labels) × 7 (café names) randomized complete block design was used for Study 2. Seven different size labels were selected on the basis of being commonly used in practice: medium, petite, tall, large, short, regular, and small. Similarly, seven different café names were used: Aroma Café, Espresso Royale, Café Kopi, Green Street Coffee, Coffee Jitters and Rush, Columbia Street Roastery, and Gloria Jean's Gourmet. The seven cafés did not exist in the town where the experiment was conducted but are in fact the names of actual coffee houses in a distant college town. A pretest revealed that each of these coffee houses varied on perceived quality; this is what we wanted, since higher quality stores may conceivably be perceived to have smaller servings for the same size label.

Consistent with the randomized complete block design, seven different questionnaires (referred to as seven between-subject conditions) were created so that for each subject, each of the seven size labels was linked to one of the seven cafés only once. However, across subjects, each of the cafés was linked to each size label. Thirty-seven respondents participated in the experiment for partial course credit.

Procedure

Participants were given a list of coffees from seven different coffee shops (e.g., *medium coffee from Aroma Café*). They were then asked to state how big they thought the coffee was in ounces. The principal dependent variable of interest was perceived size. A pretest indicated that domestic college students were familiar with estimating the size of liquids—principally soda and coffee. In this context, we reasonably believed participants would have no difficulties with such estimation, and manipulation debriefings confirmed this.

Study 2 Results and Discussion

We used a repeated-measures analysis of variance to analyze results. When investigating "perceived size for a size label," the size label was used as a within-subject factor and condition was used as a between-subject factor. We found a significant effect for size label ($F(6,162) = 30.62$, $p < .01$), but not for condition ($p > .5$) or for the size label by condition interaction ($p > .7$). Thus, "perceived size for a specific size label" varied significantly by size label but not by café name (café name for each size label varied by condition). The mean perceived sizes are presented in Table 21.1.[1]

Study 2 supports the same basic finding as in Study 1: people have a common understanding of size labels. It additionally shows that product source and implied product quality do not affect these size perceptions. These results support Yamauchi and Markman's (2000) proposition that inductive inference is a fundamental use of categories, that is, when an object is likely to belong to a category, people tend to derive inductive judgments about the object based primarily on that category.

Conclusions

The two studies reported in this chapter demonstrate that the many varied size labels being used today in the marketplace have indeed come to acquire unique meanings and can be distinguished from one another by consumers. The studies further show that this effect holds across different product categories and also is valid over and above the effect of product source. This emphasizes the influence of commercial practices on the English language by showing how commercially induced size labels have acquired a common understanding across consumers.

Having established that the many size labels used in food and drink categories today have a shared understanding, the next step should be to explore their effect on consumer behavior. Additional questions arise that have

TABLE 21.1   Within-Subject Magnitude Comparisons of Means Across Contexts (Study 2)

	Average Size Label Means	Aroma Café	Expresso Royale	Café Kopi	Green Street Coffee	Coffee Jitters and Rush	Columbia Street Roastery	Gloria Jean's Gourmet
Petite	6.71	5.25	8.00	7.33	6.88	6.80	6.20	7.00
Small	7.74	8.67	7.25	7.80	7.60	8.20	6.75	8.00
Short	8.02	7.60	7.80	7.50	7.00	8.00	8.67	8.75
Regular	11.06	12.00	9.20	10.40	12.20	9.75	10.00	12.00
Medium	11.09	10.00	12.33	12.00	9.60	10.40	11.40	10.00
Tall	13.29	14.40	10.75	14.00	14.00	15.25	11.40	12.00
Large	14.44	14.00	13.60	13.25	12.00	19.00	14.25	12.00
Store Means	**10.33**	**10.56**	**9.89**	**9.87**	**9.59**	**12.06**	**10.24**	**10.15**

important legislative and liability-related implications. For instance, can size labels create misperceptions about the quantities of food and beverages involved and lead to unintended overeating? It has been argued in the media that the use of these labels is an image-building activity and is divorced from any description of reality (Crossen, 1996). Policy officials have started to direct legislative attention toward food companies they believe are exploiting labeling laws to make their products more appealing (Day, 2003).

Furthermore, research from psychology on the influence of language on perception and cognition indicates the pressing need to make further inquiry into the effect of labels on various sensory processes within the domain of consumer behavior. The demonstrated impact of labels on visual (Lewis, 1963; O'Hare, 1987), olfactory (Herz, 2003), tactile (Hoshikawa, 1991), auditory (Bartlett, 1977), and taste (Wansink et al., 2001) perception suggests that there should be further implications of the commercial use of labels on consumer perception, product evaluations, and actual consumption.

Note

1. Note that the results for size perceptions of specific size labels for this study are similar to those for Study 1. Differences in Study 1 versus Study 2 in the mean size order appear only where the mean sizes were not significantly different from one another (small vs. short and medium vs. regular).

References

Alba, J. W., & Hutchinson, J. W. (1987, March). Dimensions of consumer expertise. *Journal of Consumer Research, 13*, 411–454.

Bagozzi, R. P., Gurhan-Canli, Z., & Priester, J. R. (2002). *The social psychology of consumer behavior.* Buckingham: Open University Press.

Bartlett, J. C. (1977). Remembering environmental sounds: The role of verbalization in input. *Memory and Cognition, 5*, 404–414.

Choplin, J. M., & Hummel, J. E. (2002). Magnitude comparisons distort mental representations of magnitude. *Journal of Experimental Psychology: General, 131*(2), 270–286.

Cohen, J. B., & Basu, K. (1987, March). Alternative models of categorization: Toward a contingent processing framework. *Journal of Consumer Research, 13*, 455–472.

Crossen, C. (1996, February 26). Case of the vanishing medium. *Wall Street Journal*, p. B1.

Day, S. (2003, November 15). The smoke and mirrors of food labeling. *New York Times*, p. B1.

Feldman, J. M., & Lynch, J. G. (1988, August). Self-generated validity and other effects of measurement on belief, attitude, intention, and behavior. *Journal of Applied Psychology, 73*, 421–345.

Friedman, M. (1985, March). The changing language of a consumer society: Brand name usage in popular American novels in the postwar era. *Journal of Consumer Research, 11*, 927–938.

Gelman, S. A., & Markman, E. M. (1987, December). Young children's inductions from natural kinds: The role of categories and appearances. *Child Development, 58*, 65–71.

Goode, E. (2003, July 22). The gorge-yourself environment. *New York Times*, p. F1.

Herz, R. S. (2003). The effect of verbal context on olfactory perception. *Journal of Experimental Psychology: General, 132*(4), 595–606.

Hollis, J., & Valentine, T. (2001, January). Proper-name processing: Are proper names pure referencing expressions? *Journal of Experimental Psychology, 27*, 99–116.

Hoshikawa, T. (1991). Effects of attention and expectation on tickle sensation. *Perceptual and Motor Skills, 72*, 27–33.

Hunt, E., & Agnoli, F. (1991, July). The Whorfian hypothesis: A cognitive psychology perspective. *Psychological Review, 98*, 377–389.

Jussim, L., Manis, M., Nelson, T. E., & Soffin, S. (1995, February). Prejudice, stereotypes, and labeling effects: Sources of bias in person perception. *Journal of Personality and Social Psychology, 68*, 228–246.

Lewis, M. M. (1963). *Language, thought, and personality in infancy and childhood.* New York: Basic Books.

Loken, B., & Ward, J. (1990, September). Alternative approaches to understanding the determinants of typicality. *Journal of Consumer Research, 17*, 111–126.

Menon, G., Raghubir, P., & Schwarz, N. (1995). Behavioral frequency judgments: An accessibility-diagnosticity framework. *Journal of Consumer Research, 22*(2), 212–228.

Meyer, L. B. (1956). *Emotion and meaning in music.* Chicago: University of Chicago Press.

Murphy, G. L., & Medin, D. L. (1985, July). The role of theories in conceptual coherence. *Psychological Review, 92*, 289–316.

O'Hare, C. B. (1987, November). The effect of verbal labeling on tasks of visual perception: An experimental investigation. *Educational Research, 29*, 213–219.

Raghubir, P., & Krishna, A. (1996, June). As the crow flies: Bias in consumers' map-based distance judgments. *Journal of Consumer Research, 23*, 26–40.

Roberson, D., Davies, I., & Davidoff, J. (2000, September). Color categories are not universal: Replications and new evidence from a stone-age culture. *Journal of Experimental Psychology: General, 129*, 369–398.

Schmitt, B. H., & Zhang, S. (1998, September). Language structure and categorization: A study of classifiers in consumer cognition, judgment, and choice. *Journal of Consumer Research, 25*, 108–122.

Wansink, B., Painter, J., &Van Ittersum, K. (2001, December). Descriptive menu labels' effect on sales. *Cornell Hotel and Restaurant Administration Quarterly, 42,* 168–173.

Yamauchi, T., & Markman, A. B. (2000, May). Inference using categories. *Journal of Experimental Psychology: Learning, Memory, and Cognition, 26,* 776–795.

Young, L. R., & Nestle, M. (2002, February). The contribution of expanding portion sizes to the US obesity epidemic. *American Journal of Public Health, 92,* 246–250.

Section VI

The Future

22

A Sense of Things to Come
Future Research Directions in Sensory Marketing

Ryan S. Elder, Nilufer Z. Aydinoglu, Victor Barger,
Cindy Caldara, HaeEun Chun, Chan Jean Lee,
Gina S. Mohr, and Antonios Stamatogiannakis

The exciting exploration on sensory marketing presented in this book is just the foundation upon which to build future research. There are myriad unexplored questions and innumerable directions in which to take this research. Our goal in this chapter is not to provide an exhaustive array of these future directions, but rather to stimulate the reader into exploring new ideas. We present possible future directions for each sense individually (vision, audition, smell, touch, taste), and conclude with ideas for future research addressing the interplay among multiple senses within consumer behavior.

Vision

Although vision to date is the most studied sensory domain within consumer research, there are still numerous future directions to explore. We present a few directions here, including the impact of vision on sensory imagery, the impact of color on consumer behavior, as well as the consequences of visual salience.

Imagery is defined as a process by which sensory information is represented in working memory (MacInnis & Price, 1987). In the consumer behavior literature, visual imagery has been shown to assist in processing product information and in facilitating memory and persuasion (e.g., Alesandrini & Sheikh, 1983; Bone & Ellen, 1992; McGill & Anand, 1989). Conversely, a lack of imagery-facilitating visual input may have negative effects on persuasion (Kisielius & Sternthal, 1984; Petrova & Cialdini,

2005). For example, when a product or ad is not presented in a visually vivid way, this impairs the fluency of consumption imagery, or the ease with which consumers can generate imagery of the consumption experience, leading to a negative effect of imagery appeals.

Research on imagery in consumer behavior and psychology has predominantly focused on vision. Prior literature neglects to address how the different modalities interact to create a more complete image beyond visual. Supplementing visual cues with other sensory cues may enhance the influence of consumer imagery on perceptions, attitudes, and behaviors. That is, even under conditions where the visual information presented to consumers is insufficient in generating visual imagery, other sensory input may enhance the generation of visual imagery. For example, even when the visual information in a print ad is not vivid enough, coupling the ad with a touch, smell, or sound element may transfer the richness of one modality to another (i.e., vision), thereby enhancing one's imagined visual experience. Conversely, it is likely that a visual input will contribute to the ease of generating imagery of other sensory modalities or enhancing the intensity of experiencing them. The consequences of visual imagery may be greatly enhanced by the addition of other sensory inputs.

Another underexplored aspect of vision is color. Studies on color have provided evidence as to how certain colors in ads are more likely to lead to positive attitudes (e.g., Gorn, Chattopadhyay, Yi, & Dahl, 1997). However, the explication of the process that leads to such attitudinal changes has been left largely unexplored. We need to establish boundary conditions as to when certain colors are more preferred and why. We also need to investigate how consumers react to combination of colors (e.g., red and white) and combination of colors and shapes (e.g., red and round vs. red and rectangle), as the visual cues consumers encounter in the market are mixtures of multiple aspects. Another interesting question is how visual cues interact with consumer emotions. Would color or shape preference change depending on how consumers feel? For example, would some colors or shapes be more preferred when consumers are happy (vs. sad)? More broadly, examining emotion as it relates to sensory processing may serve to explain the vast individual heterogeneity in response to visual and other sensory cues.

Finally, the role of salience of visual cues has produced exciting results such as biases in perception of volume (Raghubir & Krishna, 1999; Wansink & Van Ittersum, 2003), distances (Raghubir & Krishna, 1996), taste (Hoegg & Alba, 2007), and consequently product evaluations and choices. We expect selective attention to salient visual cues to be a continuously rich source of research. One aspect of consumer behavior we expect to be particularly affected is information search. As practitioners recognize the importance of quick conveyance of information, we see a shift from verbal to visual displays of information. The consequences of such a strategy should be more fully explored; some recent research has begun to address these issues. For example, online product ratings, such as 5-star customer ratings on Amazon. com, are visual cues through which companies and consumers communicate. If a particular star rating (e.g., 5-star) is more salient than other ratings (e.g., 1-star), the higher attention to the salient rating could bias how consumers process other star ratings and how consumers make decisions based on online ratings (Lee & Raghubir, 2008). Understanding how these visual biases are formed and the confidence with which they are held will allow us to improve the information search process for consumers.

Audition

Audition (like smell, but unlike vision, touch, and taste) is a sense that requires no effort to operate. People have no control over the auditory stimuli they perceive, although they have some control over which stimulus they are attending to. This nonvoluntary perception of sounds can make the fit (congruence) of an auditory stimulus (e.g., music) with either the environment (e.g., a store) or other auditory stimuli (e.g., the next music track) problematic. In large department stores, supermarkets, bars, restaurants, and other locations, sound incongruence cannot be avoided. If the same music is played everywhere in the store, there will be some parts of the store where the music will not fit. If different music is played in different parts, then the different music themes are very likely to not fit with one another. Considering that in general, music congruence has been found to have positive effects for product and ad evaluations (see Peck & Childers, 2008), this raises three important questions. First, the marketing literature has not yet addressed the effects (if any) of incongruence between sequential or simultaneous auditory stimuli. Second, in cases where incongruence is unavoidable, should a store opt for one or the other form of incongruence? Third, the marketing literature should identify boundary conditions for the positive effects of sound congruence in the same way it has identified boundary conditions for desirable properties of visual stimuli, such as symmetry and unity (Stamatogiannakis, Chattopadhyay, & Gorn, forthcoming).

Another issue that research so far has not resolved is a possible confound of music familiarity and pleasantness. The effects of the two have been found to be very similar: Perceived time duration is longest for positively valenced music (Kellaris & Kent, 1992), but the same holds for more familiar music (Yalch & Spangenberg, 2000). Furthermore, the effects of music on mood and on product evaluation (Gorn, Goldberg, & Basu, 1993) might be partially explained by music familiarity. We are not aware of any study that orthogonally manipulates music familiarity and music valence, although researchers have identified them as two separate moderators of music effects (Bruner, 1990). Such studies are necessary in order to understand whether well-grounded effects of music valence on mood can be attributed to valence alone or whether music familiarity can explain part of the effects. An additional point regarding auditory effects on the perception of time arises from recent research. When resources required match resources available, people perceived that more time has passed than when available and required resources do not match (Mantel & Kellaris, 2003). Assuming that familiar and pleasant music requires less resources to be processed, then the results of the studies showing that pleasant and familiar music leads to longer time estimates might not hold in situations when one has plenty available resources (e.g., in a relaxing dinner).

Another field of research in audition is the sounds that are inseparable from product usage, for example, the sound a car door makes when it shuts, the sound a DVD player makes when it opens, or even the sound an electronic device (e.g., an air conditioner or a car alarm) makes when switched on. It is possible that through phonetic symbolism people infer product attributes from these sounds, in the same way they do from the sound of a brand name (Yorkston & Menon, 2004).

A final point that merits attention is if and how speech can create inferences for a product. Chattopadhyay, Dahl, Ritchie, and Shahin (2003) have shown that when a male speaks, then low pitch and a little fast syllable speed produce the best responses to the speech. However, more qualitative insights might be useful: Can the accent (or the pitch or the speed) of the speaker in an ad (or the origin and the tempo of the music) imply the product's possession of certain characteristics or act as a quality signal? Additionally, are consumers cognizant of the sources of these inferences?

Smell

In the early 1990s, Bone and Jantrania (1992) proposed that "the sense of smell has for the most part been overlooked by market researchers" (p. 289). However, in the past two decades, researchers across several disciplines have shown a profound interest in the topic of olfaction and have produced foundational research in the area. We propose here additional directions to explore in order to more fully understand the role smell plays in consumer behavior. Specifically, we direct further attention to the role of scent congruence, the generation of semantic meanings of scents, the impact of attention, as well as highlight the emergence of new methodologies to study smell.

The presence of a scent is generally acknowledged as having a positive impact on consumer attitudes, in both ambient form, such as in stores and other environments, or in a more direct form, such as those infused in products. Among the cognitive moderators potentially involved in these effects, perceived congruence is the most frequently reviewed one. In general it is defined as a contextual fit between the scent and the product category (Bosmans, 2006; Mitchell, Kahn, & Knasko, 1995; Morrin & Ratneshwar, 2003; Spangenberg, Sprott, Grohmann, & Tracy, 2006). The effects of congruence are directionally shared among the studies claiming congruence has a more positive impact on memory and evaluation than incongruence. However, research should focus on specifying the types of positive impacts that scents have. For example, do scents result in greater attachment to the product as more sensory modalities are stimulated, and how does congruence affect these consequences?

Congruence, as mentioned, plays a significant role in determining the impact of scent on consumer perceptions and attitudes. However, the reasons why a scent is perceived as congruent are not always clear. It may be posited that scents hold shared semantic meanings that lead to a perception of congruence between a smell and an object. Brand and Millot (2001) argue that the explanation of gender differences in olfaction may be related to the fact that olfactory stimuli can have a greater meaning for one gender than for the other. The types and relative importance of scent meanings and the way in which individuals learn them should receive more attention. Cultural or social meanings attributed to scents may be derived largely from experience, in some form of a conditioning framework. It would be useful to identify the sources of such conditioning, establish typologies for them, pay attention to the way they are processed by individuals, and determine whether there is a way to replicate this learning process in a consumer context.

Another variable that should be more actively considered is the impact of attention in processing scents. Recently, Zelano and colleagues (2005) highlighted the role of different levels of attention on scent perception at a neural level. One of the main characteristics of a scent is that it can be processed preattentively (Davies, Kooijman, & Ward, 2003). As such, it would be useful to determine whether the presence of scents has to be consciously perceived by consumers to positively affect the target variable (e.g., store environment perceptions or product evaluation). Indeed, if the process occurs largely below consciousness, then a large responsibility of the marketer is to create the aforementioned semantic associations between the product and scent in order for the associations to be operative.

The study of individual differences should also constitute a further step in smell research. Anatomic and physiologic differences (gender, age, genetics) have been documented (Brand & Millot, 2001), and it is likely that other individual differences exist that affect scent perceptions. For example, do individuals differ in their need for smell (similar to the need for touch; Peck & Childers, 2003a), the centrality of smells in their lives, or in their emotional reaction to smells? Wrzesniewski, McCauley, and Rozin (1999) have developed a scale measuring individual differences in the affective impact of odors on places, objects, and persons, demonstrating that differences other than biologic ones influence scent perception. Among others, one promising direction for future research would be to develop a general scale measuring the susceptibility of an individual to using scent as an input for decisions and evaluations.

Finally, recent advances in physiological instrumentation provide an opportunity to capture process beyond self-report measures. Brain imaging (e.g., functional magnetic resonance imaging; Zelano et al., 2005) and other psychophysiological measures such as galvanic skin response, heart rate, and blood pressure all provide levels of sensory stimulation and activation that should prove useful in more fully understanding the mysteries of scents within marketing.

Touch

Touch research in marketing is, in many respects, still in its infancy. Although advances have been made in recent years (see Chapter 2), there are still numerous avenues for future research. In this section, we outline three such avenues that hold great promise. First, focus should be given to ways of motivating consumers to touch. Second, researchers should examine how consumers interpret stimuli. Finally, researchers can explore alternatives to direct physical contact that result in similar consequences.

Touch is rarely ambient, meaning that consumers must make an effort to experience haptic stimuli. As such, marketers need to understand the motivation for touch before they can reap the benefits, benefits that are, as revealed in Chapter 2 of this book, significant: touch enhances the purchase experience (Peck & Childers, 2003a), leads to greater confidence in product judgments (Peck & Childers, 2003a), and increases the amount consumers are willing to pay for products (Peck & Shu, 2009).

Three aspects of the purchase experience determine motivation to touch: the product, the consumer, and the environment. We know from prior research (Klatzky & Lederman, 1992, 1993) that objects differ on material properties, such as texture, softness, and weight, and that touch enables us to sense these differences more effectively than other senses. More recently, Peck and Wiggins (2006) showed that material properties of objects influence whether haptic stimuli are perceived as pleasant or unpleasant. This link between material properties and hedonic touch remains relatively unexplored, however. What causes a material property to be perceived as pleasant? Are there particular textures or shapes that are universally pleasing? How can marketers leverage the material properties of products to induce touch?

Of course, material properties alone cannot explain why some consumers touch when others do not. To investigate this, Peck and Childers (2003a) designed a scale that measures individual preference for touch information. The availability of this scale has opened numerous opportunities for further research on touch. For example, do individuals differ in motivation to touch by demographics such as gender and age? What impact does culture have on motivation to touch? How does the ability to differentiate haptic attributes vary across individuals? We do know that sensitivity to touch declines with age (Stevens & Patterson, 1995; Thornbury & Mistretta, 1981), but what are the implications for marketing?

Beyond the level of the product and the individual, situational factors also influence motivation to touch. Changes in the retail environment, for example, can have a substantial impact on the willingness of consumers to touch products, as shown by Peck and Childers (2006). Social influence may also play a role in motivating touch. For example, if a consumer sees someone touch an object, he or she may view that as a sign that touching is acceptable. Moreover, the observation may engender curiosity and encourage firsthand experience. Of course, he or she may also fear product contagion (Morales & Fitzsimons, 2007); whether observing another individual touch a product has a positive or negative effect on consumer affect and attitudes is open to investigation.

Once a consumer is induced to touch, consideration turns to how he or she interprets the haptic stimuli. This is likely a complex function of product attributes, individual characteristics, and situational factors. Consider, for example, the interaction between the material properties of an object and ambient temperature. First, the diagnosticity of touch changes with temperature; that is, the same material feels different at different temperatures. Second, the temperature of the object is subject to interpretation. For instance, warmth in an item of clothing may indicate that the item had just been tried on, raising concerns of product contagion. Finally, there are individual differences in ability to differentiate haptic stimuli. The ramifications extend to all aspects of marketing, from product design to retail display.

Unfortunately, touch is not feasible in all consumption contexts. The most notable is online shopping, where consumers must rely entirely on visual stimuli. It is not surprising, then, that consumers who prefer tactile input are less likely to purchase online (Citrin, Stem, Spangenberg, & Clark, 2003). The problem is exacerbated in product categories where touch is particularly diagnostic, such as clothing and bedding. Alternatives to physical touch are thus of great practical interest. Although verbal descriptions may help (e.g., inferring softness from thread count), such descriptions do not satisfy the need for autotelic touch (Peck & Childers, 2003b). One promising alternative is haptic imagery (Peck & Barger, 2008), which may act as a surrogate for touch; further research in this area is needed, however.

Taste

As noted in Chapter 18 in this volume, the sense of taste has received sparse attention within the consumer behavior literature. However, extant literature addressing taste does provide a solid foundation from which to build future research. Attention to three specific areas in taste and consumer behavior may result in substantial progress of this exciting domain. First, we recommend devoting further attention to the interplay of affect and cognition in taste experiences. Second, we propose that future research focus more deeply on the conscious and unconscious determinants of taste perception, including the perceptual effects of extrinsic and intrinsic cues. Finally, research should address individual differences in taste perceptions, such as food expertise and an individual's ability to generate sensory imagery.

Food is an essential component of human existence, with much of our daily efforts devoted to ensuring that we have sufficient amounts for our needs. However, beyond this subsistence perspective, food, and more specifically the sense of taste, provides us with some of our greatest pleasures.

Prior literature on the topic of affect and cognition, as it relates to taste, suggests that many taste experiences are primarily affective, with cognitive or informational components muting enjoyment during consumption (Nowlis & Shiv, 2005; Shiv & Fedorikhin, 1999; Shiv & Nowlis, 2004). For example, Nowlis and Shiv (2005) show that reducing attention to informational components enhances taste perceptions and consumption enjoyment of chocolate and also leads to greater selection of the more affective option within a choice set.

In general, taste perceptions tend to be affectively driven, with more attention to sensory cues leading to heightened affective responses. However, with the current health-conscious focus, particularly within the United States, the enjoyment of food may have several negative consequences, leading many to believe that "eating is almost as dangerous as not eating" (Rozin, Fischler, Imada, Sarubin, & Wrzesniewski, 1999, p. 164). Therefore, an underlying question is to what extent marketers and other professionals can balance this interplay between affect and cognition to increase subsequent enjoyment of healthy food items. A similar question to be addressed is what attributes of the taste experience make the focus primarily cognitive rather than affective. Finally, as prior literature suggests that affective components function more automatically and cognitive inputs function in a more deliberative manner (Compeau, Grewal, & Monroe, 1998; Shiv & Fedorikhin, 1999), is there a way to enable cognitive components to be processed more automatically, thereby reducing the detrimental impact of negative cues?

Within cognitive psychology, several researchers have posited that most of our lives are driven by automatic processes, outside of our own consciousness (Bargh, 2002; Bargh & Chartrand, 1999). The environment and other extrinsic cues outside of consciousness influence perceptions and even behaviors. Understanding the unconscious and conscious determinants of taste perceptions, including the aforementioned affective and cognitive inputs as well as intrinsic and extrinsic cues, is a second fruitful domain to explore.

Intrinsic cues such as appearance, tactile properties, smell, and other sensory characteristics of the food item may be operative at both the conscious and unconscious levels. Therefore, manipulating the level of consciousness devoted to these intrinsic cues may affect subsequent taste perceptions. Researchers have addressed the impact of additional intrinsic cues on taste perceptions such as product color (DuBose, Cardello, & Maller, 1980; Hoegg & Alba, 2007), product smell (Prescott, Johnstone, & Francis, 2004), and product texture (Christensen, 1980); however, future research should determine to what extent these intrinsic cues act automatically and below consciousness or whether they require cognitive elaboration and consciousness. For instance, does the congruity of the intrinsic cues with expectations determine whether or not further cognitive resources are expended and consequently affect how sensory characteristics are attended to? Determining when intrinsic product cues have the most prominent impact on taste perceptions will aid in understanding the role of extrinsic cues.

Extrinsic cues, such as advertising (Elder & Krishna, 2010), brand name (Allison & Uhl, 1964; Hoegg & Alba, 2007), product ingredients (Lee, Frederick, & Ariely, 2006; Raghunathan, Naylor, & Hoyer, 2006), and even product packaging (Krishna & Morrin, 2008), also operate at conscious and unconscious levels on taste perceptions. The underlying process with which these extrinsic cues are operative remains to be fully addressed. One future area of research could determine to what extent, and at what level of consciousness, expectations influence perceptions. Lee et al. (2006) introduce a negatively valenced ingredient for beer (balsamic vinegar) both before and after consumption and show that the introduction of the ingredient before consumption altered the perceptual experience, whereas the introduction of the ingredient after consumption had little effect on taste perceptions. This research shows the power of expectations in affecting the experience itself, not merely perceptions of the experience, but fails to address the consciousness of such an effect. The general field of sensory marketing, and in particular taste marketing, will largely benefit from a focus on the conscious and subconscious effects of intrinsic and extrinsic cues.

The third and final recommendation for future research within taste marketing is to focus on individual differences. What characteristics of individuals make their taste experiences susceptible to marketing actions? One obvious area for exploration is the individual's level of expertise within the food domain. Such differences in expertise have been shown to have a discernible impact on taste perceptions, particularly in respect to an individual's focus during a consumption experience. Specifically, experts are more likely to focus on automatic, affective components of the consumption experience rather than the more deliberate, cognitive components (Nowlis & Shiv, 2005). Therefore, experts may not pay as much attention to the marketing communications, but rather focus on the sensory experience of eating. Other individual differences, such as the ability to imagine taste experiences, could potentially moderate the effect of marketing on taste perceptions. These individual-level moderators, as well as many more, can provide insight into when and how marketing affects taste.

Multisensory

Much of the literature on consumer sensory processing examines sensory modalities singularly. Yet, consumers rarely process information in this way. Rather, we know that information is perceived and processed in multiple sensory modalities. For example, somebody who is choosing among sweaters may use both visual (color) and haptic (texture) cues to arrive at a preference. Moreover, marketers make appeals to consumers in many sensory modalities in order to attract attention, to give information, or to accentuate product features (e.g., a visual cue of a lemon to instantiate the fragrance in a cleaning product). Recognizing the significance of the multisensory nature of perception and information processing, some marketing scholars have begun to direct attention toward the interplay between the senses. For example, intersensory effects and synergies between vision and taste (Hoegg & Alba, 2007), vision and touch (Raghubir & Krishna, 1999), touch and taste (Krishna & Morrin, 2008), and sound and taste (Zampini & Spence, 2004) have begun to be explored. However, considering the complex nature of such multisensory processing and its significant effect on consumer perception and behavior, we believe that more systematic inquiry is needed to expand our understanding of this complex, yet natural, way in which consumers interact with their surroundings.

It is important to understand multiple-sensory interactions because cross-modal cues may facilitate or interfere with one another in how they affect consumers' perceptions, attitudes, and preferences. For example, does the preference for a fragranced product change as a function of the additional sensory cues that are provided? In studying such joint effects, attention should be directed toward the different roles played by the different modalities of cues and the processes by which they affect outcomes of interest. Zampini and Spence (2004), for instance, study how the auditory cues produced during the biting action of potato chips affect the perception of crispness and staleness of the chips, which is a very important attribute for the product category. Hoegg and Alba (2007) investigate how color differences in orange juice samples affect taste discrimination. Even in these instances, where such cues might initially be thought of as secondary (i.e., auditory for potato chips and visual for orange juice), we see their significant role in affecting consumer judgment and consequently preference. Identification of such specific roles and relationships would shed light on the processes leading to the desired response from consumers.

Another reason that further investigation into multiple-sensory interactions is important is that cross-modal cues may affect consumer memories differently. The interactive effects of modality on memory can be investigated at both encoding and retrieval. For example, a consumer watching an advertisement may encode a brand name with an auditory cue (song) and a visual cue (logo). However, each cue may differentially facilitate (or inhibit) the encoding and retrieval of the brand name or brand concept. This effect may be further moderated by congruity among the cues or the familiarity of these cues. Existing literature on congruity effects in other domains of consumer behavior research suggest that incongruent cues can enhance memory for a product (Lee & Mason, 1999; Unnava, Agarwal, & Haugtvedt, 1996). However, to our knowledge there has been little research that examines how these congruity effects extend into multisensory interactions.

Moreover, studying the interplay between sensory cues should not be blind to contextual and individual contingencies. There might be important differences among consumers in their inclination to use a certain modality in their perceptions and judgments. Krishna and Morrin (2008), for example, show that different levels of "need for touch" (Peck & Childers, 2003a) result in different effects within the context of the interplay of vision and touch. As mentioned earlier, the development of such respondent-level scales is another promising venue for research, as it will enhance our understanding of consumers, giving more weight to certain modalities while neglecting others, when there is opportunity to use different sensory cues. The same is true for the moderating effects of different contextual variables; Grohmann, Spangenberg, and Sprott (2007), for instance, show that touch matters more for high-quality products. Studying these moderating effects would provide more information to the marketer about the relative importance of different modalities of cues in designing an offer or in formulating communication.

Conclusions

Although not representing an exhaustive list of possible future directions, it is our intention that the preceding discussion on sensory marketing research areas would excite and inspire the reader. This nascent field has much promise, particularly while garnering the scholarly attention of top researchers. Hopefully this chapter has given the reader a sense of things to come.

References

Alesandrini, K., & Sheikh, A. (1983). Research on imagery: Applications to advertising. In A. Sheikh (Ed.), *Imagery: Current theory, research and application* (pp. 535–556). New York: John Wiley.

Allison, R. I., & Uhl, K. P. (1964). Influence of beer brand identification on taste perception. *Journal of Marketing Research, 1*(3), 36–39.

Bargh, J. A. (2002). Losing consciousness: Automatic influences on consumer judgment, behavior, and motivation. *Journal of Consumer Research, 29*(2), 280–285.

Bargh, J. A., & Chartrand, T. L. (1999). The unbearable automaticity of being. *American Psychologist, 54*(7), 462–479.

Bone, P. F., & Ellen, P. S. (1992). The generation and consequences of communication-evoked imagery. *Journal of Consumer Research, 19*(1), 93–104.

Bone, P. F., & Jantrania, S. (1992). Olfaction as a cue for product quality. *Marketing Letters, 3*(3), 289–296.

Bosmans, A. (2006). Scents and sensibility: When do (in)congruent ambient scents influence product evaluations? *Journal of Marketing, 70*(3), 32–43.

Brand, G., & Millot, J. L. (2001). Sex differences in human olfaction: Between evidence and enigma. *Quarterly Journal of Experimental Psychology, 54*(3), 259–270.

Bruner II, G. C. (1990). Music, mood, and marketing. *Journal of Marketing, 54*(4), 94–104.

Chattopadhyay, A., Dahl, D. W., Ritchie, R. J. B., & Shahin, K. N. (2003). Hearing voices: The impact of announcer speech characteristics on consumer response to broadcast advertising. *Journal of Consumer Psychology, 13*(3), 198–204.

Christensen, C. M. (1980). Effects of solution viscosity on perceived saltiness and sweetness. *Perception and Psychophysics, 28*(4), 347–353.

Citrin, A. V., Stem, D. E., Spangenberg, E. R., & Clark, M. J. (2003). Consumer need for tactile input: An Internet retailing challenge. *Journal of Business Research, 56*(11), 915–922.

Compeau, L.D., Grewal, D., & Monroe, K. (1998). Role of prior affect and sensory cues on consumers' affective and cognitive responses and overall perceptions of quality. *Journal of Business Research, 42*(3), 295–308.

Davies, B. J., Kooijman, D., & Ward, P. (2003). The sweet smell of success: Olfaction in retailing. *Journal of Marketing Management, 19*(5–6), 611–627.

DuBose, C. N., Cardello, A. V., & Maller, O. (1980). Effects of colorants and flavorants on identification, perceived flavor intensity, and hedonic quality of fruit-flavored beverages and cake. *Journal of Food Science, 45*(5), 1393–1399.

Elder, R. S. & Krishna A. (2010). The effects of advertising copy on sensory thoughts and perceived taste. *Journal of Consumer Research, 36*.

Gorn, G. J., Chattopadhyay, A., Yi, T., & Dahl, D.W. (1997). Effects of color as an executional cue in advertising: They're in the shade. *Management Science*, 43(10), 1387–1400.

Gorn, G. J., Goldberg, M. E., & Basu, K. (1993). Mood, awareness, and product evaluation. *Journal of Consumer Psychology*, 2(3), 237–256.

Grohmann, B., Spangenberg, E. R., & Sprott, D. E. (2007). The influence of tactile input on the evaluation of retail product offerings. *Journal of Retailing*, 83(2), 237–245.

Hoegg, J., & Alba, J. W. (2007). Taste perception: More than meets the tongue. *Journal of Consumer Research*, 33(4), 490–498.

Kellaris, J. J., & Kent, R. J. (1992). The influence of music on consumer's temporal perceptions: Does time fly when you're having fun? *Journal of Consumer Psychology*, 1(4), 365–376.

Kisielius, J., & Sternthal, B. (1984). Detecting and explaining vividness effects in attitudinal judgments. *Journal of Marketing Research*, 21(1), 54–64.

Klatzky, R. L., & Lederman, S. J. (1992). Stages of manual exploration in haptic object identification. *Perception and Psychophysics*, 52(6), 661–670.

Klatzky, R. L., & Lederman, S. J. (1993). Toward a computational model of constraint-driven exploration and haptic object identification. *Perception*, 22(5), 597–621.

Krishna, A., & Morrin, M. (2008). Does touch affect taste? The perceptual transfer of product container haptic cues. *Journal of Consumer Research*, 34(6), 807–818.

Lee, C. J. & Raghubir, P. (2008). *Psychological values of ratings*. Working paper.

Lee, L., Frederick, S., & Ariely, D. (2006). Try it, you'll like it: The influence of expectation, consumption, and revelation on preferences for beer. *Psychological Science*, 17(12), 1054–1058.

Lee, Y. H., & Mason, C. (1999). Responses to information incongruency in advertising: The role of expectancy, relevancy, and humor. *Journal of Consumer Research*, 26(2), 156–169.

MacInnis, D. J., & Price, L. (1987). The role of imagery in information processing: Review and extensions. *Journal of Consumer Research*, 13(4), 473–491.

Mantel, S. P., & Kellaris, J. J. (2003). Cognitive determinants of consumers' time perceptions: The impact of resources required and available. *Journal of Consumer Research*, 29(4), 531–538.

McGill, A. L., & Anand, P. (1989). The effect of vivid attributes on the evaluation of alternatives: The role of differential attention and cognitive elaboration. *Journal of Consumer Research*, 16(2), 188–196.

Mitchell, D. J., Kahn, B. E., & Knasko, S. C. (1995). There's something in the air: Effects of congruent or incongruent ambient odor on consumer decision making. *Journal of Consumer Research*, 22(2), 229–238.

Morales, A. C., & Fitzsimons, G. J. (2007). Product contagion: Changing consumer evaluations through physical contact with "disgusting" products. *Journal of Marketing Research*, 44(2), 272–283.

Morrin, M., & Ratneshwar, S. (2003). Does it make sense to use scents to enhance brand memory? *Journal of Marketing Research, 40*(1), 10–25.

Nowlis, S. M., & Shiv, B. (2005). The influence of consumer distractions on the effectiveness of food-sampling programs. *Journal of Marketing Research, 42*(2), 157–168.

Peck, J., & Barger, V. A. (2008). *In search of a surrogate for touch: The effect of haptic imagery on psychological ownership and object valuation.* Working paper.

Peck, J., & Childers, T. L. (2003a). Individual differences in haptic information processing: The 'Need for Touch' scale. *Journal of Consumer Research, 30*(3), 430–442.

Peck, J., & Childers, T. L. (2003b). To have and to hold: The influence of haptic information on product judgments. *Journal of Marketing, 67*(2), 35–48.

Peck, J., & Childers, T. L. (2006). If I touch it I have to have it: Individual and environmental influences on impulse purchasing. *Journal of Business Research, 59*(6), 765–769.

Peck, J., & Childers, T. L. (2008). If it tastes, smells, sounds, and feels like a duck, then it must be a …: Effects of sensory factors on consumer behaviors. In C. P. Haugtvedt, P. M. Herr, & F. R. Kardes (Eds.), *Handbook of consumer psychology* (pp. 193–219). New York: Psychology Press.

Peck, J., & Shu S. (2009). The effect of mere touch on perceived ownership. *Journal of Consumer Research,* (36).

Peck, J., & Wiggins, J. J. (2006). It just feels good: Consumers' affective response to touch and its influence on attitudes and behavior. *Journal of Marketing, 70*(4), 56–69.

Petrova, P. K., & Cialdini, R. B. (2005). Fluency of consumption imagery and the backfire effects of imagery appeals. *Journal of Consumer Research, 32*(3), 442–452.

Prescott, J., Johnstone, V., & Francis, J. (2004). Odor-taste interactions: Effects of attentional strategies during exposure. *Chemical Senses, 29*(4), 331–340.

Raghubir, P., & Krishna, A. (1996). As the crow flies: Bias in consumers' map-based distance judgments. *Journal of Consumer Research, 23*(1), 26–39.

Raghubir, P., & Krishna, A. (1999). Vital dimensions in volume perception: Can the eye fool the stomach? *Journal of Marketing Research, 36*(6), 313–326.

Raghunathan, R., Naylor, R. W., & Hoyer, W. D. (2006). The unhealthy = tasty intuition and its effects on taste inferences, enjoyment, and choice of food products. *Journal of Marketing, 70*(4), 170–184.

Rozin, P., Fischler, C., Imada, S., Sarubin, A., & Wrzesniewski, A. (1999). Attitudes to food and the role of food in life in the U.S.A., Japan, Flemish Belgium and France: Possible implications for the diet-health debate. *Appetite, 33*(2), 163–180.

Shiv, B., & Fedorikhin, A. (1999). Heart and mind in conflict: The interplay of affect and cognition in consumer decision making. *Journal of Consumer Research, 26*(3), 278–292.

Shiv, B., & Nowlis, S. M. (2004). The effect of distractions while tasting a food sample: The interplay of informational and affective components in subsequent choice. *Journal of Consumer Research, 31*(3), 599–608.

Spangenberg, E. R., Sprott, D. E., Grohmann, B., & Tracy, D. L. (2006). Gender-congruent ambient scent influences on approach and avoidance behaviors in a retail store. *Journal of Business Research, 59*(12), 1281–1287.

Stamatogiannakis, A., Chattopadhyay, A., & Gorn, G. J. (Forthcoming). Can you fix it?: Effects of visual processing capacity on visual aesthetic response. *Advances in Consumer Research.*

Stevens, J. C., & Patterson, M. Q. (1995). Dimensions of spatial acuity in the touch sense: Changes over the life span. *Somatosensory and Motor Research, 12*(1), 29–47.

Thornbury, J. M., & Mistretta, C. M. (1981). Tactile sensitivity as a function of age. *Journal of Gerontology, 36*(1), 34–39.

Unnava, H. R., Agarwal, S., & Haugtvedt, C. P. (1996). Interactive effects of presentation modality and message-generated imagery on recall of advertising information. *Journal of Consumer Research, 23*(1), 81–88.

Wansink, B., & Van Ittersum, K. (2003). Bottoms up! The influence of elongation on pouring and consumption volume. *Journal of Consumer Research, 30*(3), 455–463.

Wrzesniewski, A., McCauley, C., & Rozin, P. (1999). Odor and affect: Individual differences in the impact of odor on liking for places, things and people. *Chemical Senses, 24*(6), 713–721.

Yalch, R. F., & Spangenberg, E. R. (2000). The effects of music in a retail setting on real and perceived shopping times. *Journal of Business Research, 49*(2), 139–147.

Yorkston, E., & Menon, G. (2004). A sound idea: Phonetic effects of brand names on consumer judgments. *Journal of Consumer Research, 31*(1), 43–51.

Zampini, M., & Spence, C. (2004). The role of auditory cues in modulating the perceived crispness and staleness of potato chips. *Journal of Sensory Studies, 19*(5), 347–363.

Zelano, C., Bensafi, M., Porter, J., Mainland, J., Johnson, B., Bremner, E. et al. (2005). Attentional modulation in human primary olfactory cortex. *Nature Neuroscience, 8*(1), 114–120.

Author Index

Subject Index

A

Adams, Ansel, 253
Advertising. *See also* Sensory marketing
    format of, 203–204
    geometric shapes used in, 203
    monochromatic images in. *See*
        Monochrome images in advertising
    music in. *See* Music in advertising
    perception biases, 209–210
    presentation of statistics in, 204–205
    spokespersons' voice. *See* Voice, human
    taste, impact on perceived, 286
    worldwide broadcast expenditures, 169
Ambient sounds, 160. *See also* Music,
        background
Analog timing model, 272
Ancillary sounds
    consumption context, 164–165
    incongruence, 159
    inseparable from product usage, 364
    pitch, 159
    predictions made regarding, 158–159
Anosmia, 75
Arousal, sensory, 6
Auditory sense
    mental lexicon, relationship between,
        185–186
    multisensory experience, as part of,
        150–151, 160
    processing, 8, 151, 184, 185
    purchase process, during consumer, 21. *See*
        also Music, background
Auxiliary sounds, 164

B

Benign masochism, 315–315
Bilingual marketing, 143–144
Brand names
    alphabetic-based, 184
    auditory exposure to, 183–184
    global marketing factors, 143
    language used in, 141–142, 145
    logographic processing, 184, 196
    mental lexicon, role of in auditory
        processing, 185–186
    music, influence of, 146
    nonword names, 192–193, 195
    sound of, 195
    spelling issues, 185–186, 187, 189–190,
        190–193
    taste, impact on perceived, 285–286
    visual element, 183
Branding, sensory signature of, 4–5. *See also*
        Brand names

C

Code switching, 144–145
Color
    advertising, use in, 206–207
    art movements, associated with, 247
    case study, hue preferences, 223–226,
        227–230, 232–234
    cross-cultural preferences, 206–207,
        223–226
    excitation, colors linked to, 224–225
    feelings, link to liking, 221–222
    hue, link to feelings, 220–221
    hue, prominence of, 223
    neurophysiological model of emotional
        response to, 220
    occasion-linked by culture, 227, 229, 230,
        232
    relaxation, colors linked to, 224–225
    similarities in color preferences, 220, 221,
        222, 235
    taste, relationship between, 284
    versus monochrome use in advertising. *See*
        Monochrome images in advertising
Comfort-joy distinction, 313–314
Consumer behavior
    atmospheric elements, relationship
        between, 132
    food-related. *See* Food
    haptic sense, influence of, 366–367
    incidental touch, 59–60
    language, influence of, 142–143
    monochrome images in advertising as a
        preference type, 254–255
    packaging, influence of, 259
    scent marketing, effect of, 79, 80, 123
    smell, impact of, 21, 78–82, 365
    visual perception, influence of, 21–22, 213,
        362
Consumer contamination, theory of, 52–53. *See*
    also Contagion, law of